In Praise of the Whip

Translated by Graham Harman

In Praise of the Whip

A Cultural History of Arousal

Niklaus Largier

ZONE BOOKS · NEW YORK

2007

© 2007 Urzone, Inc.
ZONE BOOKS
1226 Prospect Ave.
Brooklyn, NY 11218

Printed in the United States of America.

Distributed by The MIT Press,
Cambridge, Massachusetts, and London, England

© Verlag C.H. Beck OHG, Munich, 2001.

Library of Congress Cataloging-in-Publication Data

Largier, Niklaus, 1957–
    [Lob der Peitsche. English]
    In praise of the whip / by Niklaus Largier; translated by
Graham Harman.
        p. cm.
    Translation of: Lob der Peitsche.
    Includes bibliographical references and index.
    ISBN 978-1-890951-65-8
    1. Flagellation–History. 2. Sadomasochism–History.
I. Title.
    HQ79.L3513 2006
    306.77'5–DC22

                                    2005044705

For Karen

Who can imagine ... the red-hot desire with which Saint
Francis was filled as he grasped the image of Christ with
the boundless power of his imagination?

— Johannes Eck, *De non tollendis Christi et
sanctorum Imaginibus*, 1522

I would ... find boundless pleasure in leading the life of a
monk.... I would live through ten hours in a single hour,
and lose all concept of time ... eat whenever I was hungry,
sleep without any determinate schedule, whenever I was
finished with something.... And when the exhausted
body rebelled against its burdens with burning desire, the
discipline would strike it like a whip and subject it to pain.
Or in the mountains, where with steps of giants the path
leads up rocky slopes to the very edge of the snow, until
my body, breathless and exhausted, would scream out,
vanquished by grace. Or even in deep snow, I would roll
about like a deluded animal, and with this icy feeling
I would sense an extraordinary shuddering.

— André Gide, *Journal*, February 24, 1889.

I have invented a new genre of verse.... This evening
I have recited ... the first examples of it.... In doing so I
noticed that my voice, to which no other option remained,
assumed the primeval cadence of priestly lamentation, the
style of songs in the Mass, which wails throughout the
Catholic churches of East and West.... I began to sing my
series of invocations in the style of a recitative, in the
churchly style.... For a moment it seemed to me as if, in
my Cubist mask, there arose the pale, distraught young
face — that half-terrified, half-curious face of a ten-year-
old boy, who in the Requiems and High Masses of his
home parish hangs on every word of the priest, trembling
and filled with craving. Then, as I had ordered, the electric
light was put out, and, covered with sweat, I was lowered
through the trap door as a magic bishop.

— Hugo Ball, *The Flight From Time*, June 23, 1916

Contents

Acknowledgments

I am grateful to Ramona Naddaff and Michel Feher at Zone Books for their interest in this project and for making the publication possible. Thanks also to Graham Harman, who found the right tone in his translation, and to Vincent Bynack, who did exemplary copyediting. Heather and Madar and Chris Lakey took care of the illustrations. And finally, Meighan Gale helped — with great patience — at every stage of the production and made this book what it is now.

Berkeley, September 2006

Introduction

When the whip is raised, when leather, scourge, and cane strike against covered or naked flesh, we stand before a stage — a stage on which a ritual unfolds. This happens not only with the thief or adulteress whipped as examples before the crowd, and not only in the erotic displays that amuse the jaded libertine, but equally so for the solitary hermit in the desert who beats his limbs raw before the eyes of God. Wherever the flogger and his victim appear, they inhabit a space that becomes the site of a drama by way of this ritual inflicted on the body: a drama in which punishment and penance, carnality and shame, torment and desire, as well as ascesis, ecstasy, and pain all coalesce in specific fashion and are exposed to our gaze in an exemplary way.

In this respect, flogging and the use of the whip can be distinguished from brawls and other outbursts of rage. In these cases, too, blows are landed, but without any measured dosage and still less with any precise sense of theatrical staging. The eighteenth-century English noblewoman, the French libertine, the monk in his cell, the flogger in the late medieval marketplace, the interrogated prisoner and his torturer, the slave standing before the master, the English governess and her pupils, the customers of a dominatrix — all of these figures take shape in a real space that is both exemplary and fantastic, a space determined through simple gestural action as the site of some sort of staging that on closer examination proves to be quite obscure. Flogging is not merely a type of beating or a manner of generating pain. Instead, it evokes a complex, multilayered, imaginary horizon that encompasses religious, erotic, and legal frames of reference no less than the emotions already mentioned. The dormitory, schoolroom, monastic cell, church, parade ground, marketplace, prison, and brothel are strictly delimited and privileged sites where we encounter flogging in the course of human history. All of these scenarios, so different at first glance, are united in a single praxis of flagellation: as sites where flogging takes place, they gain definition through the rhythms of ritual, much like late medieval cities with their processions of flagellants. Sites of this kind thereby become a stage that holds spectators under a spell or drives them away in revulsion from the spectacle of bloodied torsos.

I have spoken of flogging in all its spiritual, punitive, and erotic contexts as a sort of ritual because here an action is performed in a formalized manner that assumes a public character — even if it be the action of just one person. This formalization is directly recognized by the spectators and allows them to participate in what is happening. In the performance of a ritual, even one that is notably theatrical or self-conscious, there is a clear contrast with actual drama, since in ritual, the participants themselves are no less transfixed than the spectators. Moreover, the ritual of flogging aims at a very specific effect whose significance cannot entirely be grasped or represented by concepts. The physical blows of punitive ritual signify more than the making public of a judgment; erotic and spiritual tortures signify more than the words of a prayer or a declaration of love. In all of these cases, the boundary of what is utterable becomes the basis for a deed that consists of actualizing through performance something that words cannot reach — something on which words run aground. What is practiced upon the body, what stirs the senses, the emotions, and imagination, finds its basis and its full significance in the actuality of the performance and the gaze of the spectator — and nowhere else.

Much like a picture, which can never be fully translated into words and which shows a fundamental resistance to language, flogging is a tableau vivant, a living image or act never fully resolvable into words. Its "meaning" withdraws from view as soon as it is named, for the action itself does not aim at any sort of meaning, but rather at what *might* be said, yet *cannot* be said, insofar as its significance is never fulfillable in a word. Hence, even today, declarations of guilt in the church are accompanied by the beating of one's breast — signaling that it is neither words nor the representational aspect of our actions that are able to express what is at stake. Instead, ritual gesture and pictorial drama deploy a physicality or emphatic sense of performance that undermines both words and the order of representation more generally.

Conceived as ritual and reduced to the gestural, the self-castigation of the female mystic is comparable (if not identical) to the agitation of the jaded libertine; the exemplary disciplining of a slave matches all the frenzied rituals of the Roman fertility cults. What is at stake here is not just an invocation, enacted in the body, of power, discipline, penance, atonement, shame, lust, pain, and ecstasy. More than this, it is a question of theater or of a game — a transfiguration that stages the scenario of the body and elicits something from its surface, rather than from its depth. It is a matter of something that otherwise cannot be found in the performance of ritual: trembling, groans, screams, someone being stripped entirely naked, confessions coerced by torture, the unveiling of conscience, or simple erotic laughing and giggling. In each of these forms of exclamation, all of them provoked by flagellation and staged in its particular theatrical space, it is flagellation that gives the event its rhythm and specific character and that allows the bodies and souls of victims and observers alike to become engrossed in fascinating, gripping, or outright revolting events. Against all expectations, there is no concealed truth at work here — no spiritual, animal, or legal depth of the body. Instead, there is an extroversion that stages the ungraspability of anything inward while also awakening anxiety, desire, or horror.

This becomes especially clear when we consider voluntary flagellation, as the present book will do. Naturally, whoever speaks of whips and rods thinks above all of the French and English libertines of the eighteenth and nineteenth centuries: certainly of the Marquis de Sade, and perhaps of Leopold von Sacher-Masoch or Guillaume Apollinaire, whose works depict flogging rituals either as precise geometrical exercises and erotic arrangements or as the abysmal passions of perverse monks, decadent aristocrats, corrupted young maidens, and grisly dominant madams. Yet in the following chapters, we will actually speak of these figures only in passing. For the whip also finds a role in other sites and other traditions where it serves a staging of the body. These traditions will be addressed in all their multiform character, without flagellation being described as a univocal phenomenon or as a single event with a unitary morphogenetic or historical basis. Moreover, I will not be concerned with the psychological or psychopathological aspects of the theme. Ever since the middle of the nineteenth century, the psychological standpoint has been concerned with "sadistic" and "masochistic" desires and dismisses voluntary flagellation to an enlightened audience as pathological, sick, perverse — in a word, as "hysterical." This historically conditioned and hopelessly biased judgment is still encountered in historical works of the late twentieth century. Despite the numerous breakthroughs of Freud and Lacan, such books adopt the stance of a dubious normality, describing as "pathological fits" the methods by which female mystics of the late Middle Ages reached states of ecstasy through flagellation, thereby attaining a special form of grace.

We are interested neither in psychohistorical explanations nor in the psychological motives that feed the desire for the whip. The point is to give an account that avoids describing flagellation as a pathological state, one that asks not about the inner or outer causes of voluntary flagellation, but rather about the parameters of staging, the forms of ritualization, and the actual function of the whip in the contexts where it is employed.

For this reason, we will avoid the viewpoint already adopted by the Renaissance philosopher Giovanni Pico della Mirandola, who attempted to understand the reasons why one of his personal acquaintances felt such a passion for the whip. Partially anticipating Freud, Pico pointed to the role of childhood upbringing in generating his friend's strange passion. This sort of explanation, which he used as an argument against the supposed explanatory power of astrology, is the one still dominant in the work of Richard von Krafft-Ebing and the modern psychology of sadistic and masochistic passions. Childhood factors were also widely discussed in the seventeenth and eighteenth centuries, when it was still a matter of explaining the desire for the whip without viewing this desire as something genuinely perverse. In the sources from that period, flagellation is viewed as an ascetic religious ritual or as a medical means for stimulating the circulatory system and perhaps even for enlivening the libido or curing impotence. Yet while the link between flagellation and the stimulation of the libido came to the fore during the seventeenth century, it really has been the moderns (especially in the nineteenth and twentieth centuries) who have viewed the desire for flagellation as "sexual deviance" and therefore as a phenomenon that, like masturbation, belongs to the realm of medical symptoms.

For Jacques Boileau, the harshest critic of religious flagellation, things were different. What he criticized around 1700 was not a "sexual" but a religious perversion, one that expressed a deep ambivalence between religious observance and erotic stimulation. In the nineteenth century, this was no longer the case. With the introduction of "sexuality" as a concept, the desire to be whipped came to be seen as a pathology, and even religious flagellation was viewed as a secret or concealed perversion. Beginning in the nineteenth century, authors not only submitted erotic flagellation to psychopathological explanation, but even treated ascetic-ecstatic practices in the same way, without the least scruple. In this view of flagellation, the religious practices of ascetics, so dubious to the modern enlightened mind, count only as a perverse translation from the realm of "abnormal sexuality" and as products of "overheated fantasy." With the establishment of this discourse of sexual pathology in the eighteenth and nineteenth centuries, tales of flagellants naturally began to be treated as a privileged object of psychopathology and also, one might add, of a historical voyeurism that has often adopted the mantle of medical history to gain legitimacy.

In the following chapters, our interest lies not in the typical late modern maneuver of finding profuse psychological explanations for the desire to whip or be whipped. Instead, what interests us is the voluntary practice and praise of the whip, the ritual of flagellation, the staging of the body, and the corresponding affirmative or critical, literary or scientific discourses in which flagellation has been discussed. Sexual psychopathology, developed in the nineteenth century and firmly established by psychoanalysis in the twentieth, describes for us only *one* of these forms of discourse and only *one* historically determined type of text that treats of the praxis of flagellation.

Long before all the tableaux of flagellation came to be viewed "as histories of human mental illness, as monuments to madness, as nocturnes of fantasy, as an anatomical gallery of moral skeletons and abnormalities," as Giovanni Frusta put it in 1843 in the foreword to his *Der Flagellantismus und die Jesuitenbeichte* (Flagellantism and the Jesuit confession), they were given a thorough treatment by spiritual and medical writers from the Middle Ages onward. For a long time thereafter, whipping played an important role in modern libertinage, as well as in the soft and hard S and M cultures of the twentieth century. The very multitude of themes is precisely what interests us. What is at stake are the metamorphoses of a practice exercised on the body — a practice that shines forth from the texts as a peculiar behavior of enthusiastic souls, as spiritual discipline, as punishment, or as *ars erotica*. Like other practices, such as the visionary experiences of medieval nuns and the radical forms of ecstatic spirituality in the nineteenth and twentieth centuries, it finally became the object of a modern *scientia sexualis*, of psychopathology and psychoanalysis.

This book more closely resembles a literary-historical broadsheet of flagellation than any sort of systematic historical or psychohistorical analysis. It is not an investigation of grounds and causes, but rather a phenomenological and genealogical typology of the praxis of flagellation, dispersed across historical time and space. The goal is neither a positivistic historiography nor a comprehensive genealogy of the type familiar since Nietzsche, but

18

rather a procedure we might describe as "historical topology." It brings together numerous forms of archivization, description, textual paraphrase, archaeological cross sections, and genealogical links. A historical topology is simply a history of fascination. It follows the rhetoric and logic of texts that speak of flagellation, discursively interweaves them, and links them with other practices. Only in this way can it constitute our object for us as a "historical site."

For our purposes, the most interesting topic is the staging of the body in its connection with the arousal of fantasy. Flagellation is a manifold cultural phenomenon that we encounter as a specific gesture, whether it takes the form of a burning eroticism, disconcerting self-mortification, or actions widely regarded as perverse and repulsive. What could be simpler than the strokes of a whip? How could punishment and penance be enacted more purely or univocally or staged more publicly than in this very immediacy of pain, submissiveness, and domination? What could be easier for any narrator or didactic observer to explain than this absolute assault upon oneself or upon another person? Yet this simple practice is encountered not just as a traditional, rustic, or barbaric means of punishment, but also as a genuine ritual — whether in pornographic texts aiming at erotic arousal or in medical texts on dietary and therapeutic practice. Flagellation is well positioned to serve as the interface for various discourses that illuminate it and that are always closely interlinked. In the domains of ascesis/spirituality, science/medicine, enlightenment/libertinage, historiography/ethnography, and erotism/pornography, it is visible in the sources and even pictorially described, and it is also justified or rejected in theoretical terms. By reading these texts, we not only gain a sense of medieval flagellant practices, but can also follow the growth since early modern times of a literature of flagellation — one nourished by a fund of anecdotes that was always voyeuristic and hence always indebted to drama and emotional excitement. In the nineteenth century, this stock of anecdotes was systematically compiled by an anonymous author in a *History of Flagellation Among Different Nations: A Narrative of the Strange Customs and*

Cruelties of the Romans, Greeks, Egyptians, etc. with an Account of Its Practice among the Early Christians as a Religious Stimulant and Corrector of Morals; Also Anecdotes of Remarkable Cases of Flogging, and of Celebrated Flagellants, with numerous illustrations, and it lived on in this book and in the hearts of its readers.

The ritual of voluntary flagellation employs participants and instruments. Like other tools, the whip is an extension of the hand. At first one might think it makes little difference in the practice of beating whether the devices used are whips, switches, rods, chains, or cords. But the names and forms of these implements already evoke the entire imaginary horizon across which flagellation roams free. When one speaks of the cat-o'-nine-tails or the lash, of a riding crop or a cane, of a buggywhip or a bullwhip, each of these implements (like every other form of whip) summons up an entire imaginary context belonging to it. In this way we are confronted with the use of a multitude of instruments that prod our bodies and fantasies to arousal.

Since most of these devices are no longer well known, we should briefly discuss the basic concepts underlying them. The first essential distinction is that between the whip and the rod. The former type has two parts, one fixed and the other movable. Bullwhips and lashes belong to this category, as do all handles furnished with cords, leather straps, and simple ropes. Riding crops, by contrast, belong to the class of rods. The same holds for switches and other flexible utensils, which for all their suppleness work with a more rigid immediacy than whips. Even stiffer than these are instruments such as canes fashioned of reeds or bamboo, or the flat faces of sabers and paddles. Along with all of these devices, the practice of whipping and beating naturally finds good use for chains and cords; indeed, a glance at the literature shows that both erotic and ascetic fantasy know scarcely any limit at all to their utensils. Erotic stimulation tries out all possible gear, all of it to some extent symbolically charged through the mere fact of its normal daily use. Meanwhile, religious flagellants use nails, iron stars, or bone chips to sharpen the cords that they draw across their naked backs. Along with all of these objects, we should not overlook a spent historical force that has now lost its niche even in the bordello: the practice of *urticatio*, or beating with stinging nettles, whose history as an aphrodisiac reaches back into ancient times. This *urticatio* seems to have been no less beloved in, say, the English prostitution trade of the eighteenth century than blows from birch branches are in the Russian bathhouses of our own era.

Along with all of these beating tools, we should also mention symbolic devices such as scepters, wizards' wands, bishops' staffs, and marshals' batons, which are in some sense the metonymic cousins of flagellation devices. They espouse the same gestural language of unlimited power that belongs to the whip, though without being used. That is to say, they belong to the class of instruments in which practical form is bound to a symbolic, imaginary value: without this value, such tools would be unable to perform their functions. The imperial link between hand and scepter or the peremptory bond between boot and riding crop are no different from the Passion symbolism of the scourge linked to the torture of Christ that is so stirring to the imagination of the penitent.

There are scarcely any boundaries to the sorts of performance found in flagellation, though there are of course certain predominant traditions and preferences. First, there are the simple scenes and poses in which the victim presents some part of the body: usually the back or buttocks, sometimes bent over the lap or the knee. More complicated than this is the manifold assembly of stools, posts, ladders, crosses, frames, whipping benches, tables, and sawhorses in which the body is harnessed for the purposes of torture, punishment, or erotic stimulation. In the medieval form of religious flagellation, the figure of Christ bound to the column provides a foundational paradigm. The most famous instance in the erotic literature is surely the "Berkley Horse" ordered by the London brothel madam Theresa Berkley in the seventeenth century to use on her customers, which was the prototype for an entire series of appliances still built and sold today. In passing, we should also mention the whipping machines that are said to have been on the market in various countries since the eighteenth century, whose advantages seem to lie above all in the ability to modulate and regulate the blows. Whether these machines have ever really existed or are only figments of pornographic imagination does not need to be decided here. Whatever the case may be, fantastic constructions of this kind repeatedly surface in texts of the nineteenth century, in early scientific literature on sexuality, and in today's pictorial realm of dirty comic strips and pornographic animated cartoons.

Although it lies beyond the scope of this book, we should not avoid all mention of what is doubtless the most horrifying equipment from the realm under discussion. I refer to appliances devised primarily for the purposes of torture — and not only, as is sometimes believed, in the medieval and early modern periods. Often enough, we not only find the same instruments in the bordello and in ascetic practice as in the torture chamber, but even the same styles and devices of staging. Torture chambers and well-furnished sadomasochistic "dungeons" can barely be distinguished at first glance. And yet the difference is absolute, even when the aim of the ritual is to deconstruct it. What distinguishes torture from other forms of flagellation is the determinate boundary where the freedom of choice is cut off. However, it is not easy to establish where this boundary lies, since the excitement of staging in erotic and even religious rituals consists quite often precisely in a simulation of boundlessness, a place where freedom seeks to reach beyond the dichotomy of choice and compulsion.

But scenes of flagellant drama contain more than spaces and instruments. Even more important than these elements are the participants and their bodily senses. The primary subject here is the skin, with its keen sense of touch and feeling, its sensitivity to excitement. Shoulder, back, buttock, and thigh are the preferred bodily parts to be struck and aroused. As a rule, it is the naked skin, especially when only partly uncovered, that is delivered over to the blows. In this way, both tactile and visual perception are entirely focused upon a specific region of the body, yielding an intensity that increases with every blow. The increased reddening

22

of the skin becomes a stimulus in its own right, one that evokes urgency and concentration even in purely visual terms. All of these blows, moments of contact with the skin, and rhythmic sounds lead to a state of arousal not unlike a trance; indeed, it often takes precisely this form. In his critique of the sense of touch, Saint Jerome already warned that the excitement of intense tactility is what most arouses humans, what renders them most lascivious and in the drunkenness of the senses is most easily capable of depriving them of their reason. As the medieval flagellants demonstrate and as the ecclesiastical critics of excessive ascesis also knew, this is just as true for the spiritual experiences of pain as for the erotic sensory rush of the modern flagellant. Both cases are based in comparable degrees of synesthesia. Aristotle observed that the primary organ of tactile arousal is not the skin, but rather the "heart" and the "flesh": the body as a perceptual whole, which is deepened and transfixed in immediate fashion as a synesthetic unity.

Despite the great importance of tactile intensity in flagellation, which we will encounter in the works of Sade, this type of excitation is not what is most central. What *is* central is the other sense that, since Empedocles and Democritus, has been granted a privileged place along with the tactile: vision. It is not enough to speak of the active and passive participants who take part in flagellation scenarios or of the occasional scapegoats who allow themselves to be beaten in someone else's place for a bit of gold. It is also necessary to speak of the voyeur. This term is not meant in a pejorative sense, just as the concept of pornography will not be used pejoratively. Indeed, the voyeur stands at the hidden center of this book, since the texts to be discussed are concerned with the figure of the voyeur more than any other. The voyeur in question is the *reader* of all these texts, who is exposed to them in such a way that they become an imaginary present of ritual and hence of arousal.

The voyeur, then, is already on the scene, even when he or she never openly appears. Public whippings were of greatest interest to both men and women in medieval and modern times alike. Whenever the whip entered into the secret realm of the tribunals

23

of the Inquisition or into prisons, contemporary sources (as well as pornographic novels) report that certain spectators obtained entry to these events by payments or other stratagems. A gaze that views both the tormented body and the whipper is fundamentally inscribed within the scenario of whipping. Along with the gesture of beating itself, this gaze is what structures the theatrical space in which flogger and victim operate. This is true even when the agent, patient, and spectator are all the same person: for example, when the hermit in his cell or his desert refuge maltreats himself, seeking to be cleansed of sinful fantasies. Peter Damian, of whom we will have much to say, imagines God as the spectator in such cases, with the gaze of God determining the gestures and establishing the attitude of the body.

Yet the torment that the hermit inflicts upon himself does not play out solely before the eyes of God, who is supposed to take such delight in it. It also unfolds before the eyes of an imagination whose liveliness and monstrous productions are displayed so concretely in early modern depictions of the temptations of Saint Anthony. These paintings make it evident that the blows of a whip aim less at cries of pain than at an arousal that lets emotion and fantasy take form and pass beyond themselves into an imaginary unity with God. In the Christian culture of the second to the fifth centuries, the intended cleansing of the misleading *phantasmata* or fantasy images already meant that increasingly greater attention would be paid to such images and the passions related to them. When the self-flagellating ascetic gazes at himself, he not only sees his position before the eyes of God: he also witnesses the unfolding of an inner world of manifold desires, even while gaining liberation from it. For this reason, the ascetic desert hermit has been taken as a model for the cultivation of the imagination not only by medieval biographers, but also by Flaubert, Dalí, and Buñuel. In this cultivation of the imagination, the soul constructs itself, its desires, its passions, and its anxieties, experiencing them intensely in an unfolding of images at the very moment that it tries to overcome them. As can be seen in Flaubert's *Tentation de Saint Antoine* and the Dalí/Buñuel film *Un chien andalou*, the figure of the hermit becomes the model of a fascination that gains freedom from the everyday realm through the same form of arousal that one finds in the medieval biographies.

Fixation on the Passion of Christ, which forms the basic model of all Christian life, enters a realm where it is less a question of belief than of repeatedly staging a history of suffering through a dramatic unfolding of the passions and images in the soul. Every text that reports on these matters, every *vita* of the ascetics, is not just an exemplary narration of such spiritual arousal, but also the most important cause of it. It is precisely the text and the scene it portrays that provoke the fascination that flows into arousal.

This link between fascination and imagination is what speaks in the key texts that we will consider. In the Middle Ages, it is the eye of God that is pleased by the spectacle of nuns and monks beating themselves. At the same time, it is these very monks and nuns who take the greatest pleasure in the exemplary texts on suffering, which they imitate through their desire for a liberating unity and intensity. In modern times, this praxis is then transformed into lascivious behavior — into the images belonging to a pornographic culture of arousal. Even Jacques Boileau, author of the *Historia flagellantium* and the harshest critic of voluntary self-flagellation, cannot entirely conceal his voyeur's satisfaction in relating piquant anecdotes to the curious reader in vivid detail. The same holds true for the physicians Johann Heinrich Meibom, Thomas Bartholin, and Kristian Paullini, who in the seventeenth century were interested in flagellation from a medical point of view. Their treatises are first and foremost collections of vividly depicted short stories, clinical cases, and historical examples, laid down as the basis for the formation of medical theory. In these texts, theological and philological scholarship are linked in exemplary fashion with scientific and anthropological curiosity, physiological research, and the pleasures of the voyeur through all of the details and anecdotes that stimulate fantasy.

Of a similar cast is the form of historical imagination that, in the compendia of historical and medical cases, always serves to supplement the "true" event. Above all in the flagellation literature of nineteenth-century France, such as Pierre Dumarchey's *Les grandes flagellées de l'histoire*, the style of exposition occasionally recalls the historiographical art of Michelet, for whom "history" was something supplemental to the event itself, which cannot actually be grasped. In scientifically grounded narratives, the historical event is threatened with transformation from anecdote into a universal exemplar stripped of all individuality. For Michelet, historiography is concerned with reversing this transformation so as to let the singular event emerge in all its captivating force. As a rule, the moderns who speak of flagellation do the same thing, turning what is narrated into an irrecoverable past happening, one that should not just become the object of a historical report, but that as a past event should also become an object of fascination. This is especially so in the case of voluntary flagellation, since it possesses actuality only in its performance. There is no script or musical score that would be able to point to the performance or partially anticipate it. As can be gathered from both ascetic and erotic texts, flagellation is nothing other than an event of arousal for the body and for fantasy alike. By contrast, the texts that bear witness to this process are merely the trace of a trace — the trace of an illegible writing that the scourge has left behind on the body. This trace leaves its residue in the scenes fabricated by those texts, in which the ritual of flagellation is repeated in literary form. The texts considered here always narrate precisely the same anecdotes and turn them into arousing examples. In this way, they restore the initial fascination that was lost along with the event itself.

Flagellation literature as a whole can be divided into four types. The two most important groups are the genuinely pornographic literature of arousal familiar since the seventeenth century and the theological or spiritual texts on religious flagellation originating from the eleventh century onward. Then there is the medical-scientific literature on flagellation of the early modern period. Finally, there are the more historical expositions of flagellation, along with the various compendia of anecdotes: the earlier texts of this kind speak of flagellation in scattered passages, while

those written since 1700 do so more systematically. The boundaries of these four classes of literature often bleed together; in
practical terms, they are often more inseparable than would appear at first glance. The libraries of French-speaking, German-
speaking, and English-speaking countries in particular contain a
great number of volumes that blend all four perspectives and
employ the cloak of historical, theological, or medical interests to
conceal what would have been denounced as "lascivious material"
well into the nineteenth century. Even at the beginning of the
twentieth century, scientific books often contained a full gallery
of sexually arousing anecdotes and examples. Moreover, many of
the numerous passages on flagellation in historical books or in
lives of the saints have actually been mined, since the seventeenth
century, for the raw material for pornographic works. Even when
flagellation is discussed in the writings of ancient authors such as
Herodotus, Lucan, or Ovid or when it is described in Heinrich
Meibom's medical texts of the seventeenth century or Pierre
Brantôme's *Vie des dames galante* circa 1600, one can detect a certain lascivious curiosity — an attitude shared by their readers in all
times and places, who take great satisfaction in racy and titillating
stories. We are indebted in no small measure to such curiosity for
its contributions to a written tradition of endless varied examples
of the passions of flagellation.

Above this mass of widely dispersed traditional material and
compendia of anecdotes, there arise those great and genuinely
historical treatments of flagellation of a more or less systematic
character. Among them, the following books are worthy of special mention: Abbé Boileau's *Historia flagellantium*, Abbé Thiers's
*Critique de l'histoire des flagellans et justification de l'usage des
disciplines volontaires*, William M. Cooper's *Flagellation and the
Flagellants: A History of the Rod in All Countries, from the Earliest
Period to the Present Time*, Giovanni Frusta's *Der Flagellantismus
und die Jesuitenbeichte*, Ernst G. Förstemann's *Die christlichen
Geißlergesellschaften*, Georg F. Collas's *Der Flagellantismus im
Altertum*, and also Ian Gibson's 1978 book *The English Vice: Beat-
ing, Sex, and Shame in Victorian England and After*. These works

offer vastly different approaches and perspectives. Although the aforementioned list is far from complete, most of the other significant books will be addressed in the coming chapters.

In view of these texts and the widely familiar case histories, we can speak of transformations and metamorphoses of ritual reflected in the most varied discourses in which flagellation takes shape. Given this great diversity, the present book is meant to serve as a sourcebook of flagellation literature and to some extent as an anthology. We are compelled to adopt this genre insofar as the object of our pursuit always withdraws from view in a peculiar way. It never fully enters our field of vision, is never capable of being subject to true narration, and we never actually know how to represent it — and nonetheless, it is always there. But it is there not so much as an event that becomes real only through participation and ritual than as an exemplary literary case of the arousal of fantasy and hence as something complementary to the event, something that if necessary can be analyzed, rejected, or affirmed in the light of reason. Often, even usually, it is hard to know what is true, what is fabricated, what is real, and what is imagined or invented. Every narrative of flagellation in what follows is an anecdote that once served as a means or example for the affirmation or deterrence of the arousal of fantasy; every history of flagellation is a compendium of such means and examples. From this it becomes clear that flagellation cannot and should not be narrated, but rather that the event itself and its power of arousal demand to be awakened by narrating them. In this sense, the meaning of narration is imitation, even if it is merely an imitation in fantasy and the arousal of the fantasy as if it were something truly present. Only through this arousal of fantasy does narration regain its singular character as an event and actualize its meaning. It becomes the site of an experience that can be measured against "real" experience. More than this: it becomes the possibility of an experience that otherwise cannot be, at least not in the realm of the "real." It registers an intensity in the imagination and the affects that does not need to trouble itself with the "real" and that is always far ahead of it.

28

Taken as examples, anecdotes stimulate fantasy in precisely this way, whether in the religious or erotic realm. They become objects of imitation in the life story of a saint or libertine. That is to say, the arousal of fantasy through narration becomes the condition of possibility of intensive experience; experience in the text becomes the condition of a manifold experience of life itself, quite apart from all dealings with texts and images. The exemplary function of flagellation naturally has special relevance in religious and pornographic literature, but also in the medical and psychopathological literature, since we are concerned with compendia of case histories. This is also true in cases where the goal is not religious or erotic stimulation, but rather sheer mental amusement at the multiple tendencies of the human imagination. In all of these cases, the "real" is subverted by arousing the imagination. It is not only subverted, but freed up into an intensification of experience — one that points to nothing other than intensity itself. It is this process, I contend, that becomes legible in exemplary fashion in all the different elements of this history of flagellation.

The presentation and historiography of the praxis of flogging offered here, which builds upon a series of traditional texts, is actually not a description of past facts, but rather a montage of the narratives and anecdotes on which all historiographical effort is based. This montage tries to do justice to the heterogeneity of historical material that emerges in the texts and to give the structural outlines of the ritual, without which it remains unintelligible. This should also help to illuminate the descriptive gesture lying at the basis of the various texts that discuss flagellation, which attempts to capture the singular, unrepeatable, and unique aspects that distinguish all scenes of flagellation. Hence, the present history of flagellation is actually a literary history. It is a history of the texts that speak of flagellation, a description of the way they present it, and a genealogy of the archives of stories that nourished all the various histories of flagellation. What we ask about in this historical topology is not primarily the historical reality of flagellation, but rather a simultaneously real and imaginary space of bodily staging, one opened up to us when we read the texts on flagellation. In this reconstruction of the various aspects of flagellation, there is an overlap between the event itself, the understanding of the text that reports it, and the imagination that comprehends the event in a specific way.

I have referred to flagellation as a ritual. This means not only that it is a matter of staging or of a living image, but also means that *within* this staging the performative moment is of greater significance than any representation of it. In other words, the performance is more important than any explanation we might give of it, and with this performance, with the effect of a living image on participants and observers, something happens that cannot be perfectly grasped by words or descriptions. As we will see, this is true of both religious and erotic flagellation and also of the texts that treat of flagellation and turn it into an emblem of their own desired effects. In these texts, whether they have religious or erotic motives, flagellation serves as an image of the stimulation of fantasy. For the female mystic, it is the site of a unification with the "spirit"; for the libertine, of a unification with the "flesh." If we could state any specific thesis that emerges from this overview of flagellation, it would be that voluntary flagellation and the texts that cover it are concerned not so much with "sexuality" (as all the sexual psychopathologists hold), but with the arousal of emotion and imagination. If we do not take the primacy of sexuality as our basis (as all of the moderns do), if we do not trace religious self-flagellation back to some sort of "repressed sexuality," this is because erotic and religious flagellation emerge as rituals that aim to unfetter desire, imagination, and the passions. In both the erotic and religious realms, what is at stake is an ecstatic experience through which imagination — whether through the experience of God or the drunkenness of the senses — attains absolute freedom and transcends the finitude of the real. This ecstatic experience is the shared agenda of religious mystics and the disciples of Sade. In one case, the ecstatic arousal of passion has an erotic-sensual character (though not in the modern, normative sense of "sexual"), while in the other, it is erotic-spiritual. But in both domains (with Sade and Teresa of Avila as the extreme boundaries) there is a surpassing of "nature," of life as something finite and demarcated. Flagellation is the ideal example of this process, a staging of the body along with the fantasy that is thereby aroused. But at the same time it is also a radical affirmation and negation of all images of finitude, all forms of radical spiritualism and radical materialism. Flagellation becomes a site where, in ritual and in the image of ritual, the deterritorialization of desire is displayed in exemplary fashion and remains dissatisfied with the moderate solutions of reason, shifting by extremes from one rousing image to the next. At the terminus of this path, unattainable though it may be, there stands — whether for the ecstatic female mystic or the prophet of apocalyptic cruelty — a resurrection of man beyond all deconstructed finite nature, in an absolute divine freedom capable of converging with death itself. When such perspectives are reduced to the naturalistic logic of "enlightened sexuality," then we misunderstand the dynamic of motion that is the meaning of libertinage and asceticism alike.

Naturally, these are the extreme cases. By no means do they express the characteristics and motives of flagellation in all possible cases and situations. Yet it is already evident that voluntary whipping and flagellation are always bound up with an unfettering of the imagination and with a corresponding intensification of experience. In our own time, this may well entail an ecstatic transcendence of the "sexual." Or at least this would appear to be confirmed by the striking advertising slogan "You will never want to have sex again!" as announced in the S and M establishments of Los Angeles and other cities. In this way, the slogan defines the experience of flagellation as a kind of deterritorialization. It is defined as an experience that perhaps refers to the transcending of finitude through its radically tragic, playful, and ironic affirmation: through beatings and pain. We might doubt whether this sort of theatrical staging is still comparable to the projects of Peter Damian or the Marquis de Sade. But this perhaps has less to do with their practical worth as examples of arousal than with their impoverished literary value.

PART ONE

Ascesis

CHAPTER ONE

Suffering, Transfiguration, and the Scourge

A medieval manuscript housed in the municipal library of Colmar contains the life histories of a series of Dominican nuns of the convent of Unterlinden. Written at the turn of the fourteenth century by a sister named Catherine von Gebersweiler, its hagiographic tone stylizes and transfigures the stories of these nuns into something like the biographies of saints. Catherine had lived in the convent since childhood. In her description of daily life there, she emphasizes the significance of voluntary poverty, as well as the strict rule of silence to which the nuns had to submit. She speaks of the role of liturgy and song in the lives of the sisters, and also — while describing daily church attendance and prayer — the significance of flagellation.

Whipping was a part of the strictly ordered rhythm of convent life, as reflected in the daily schedule, in prayer times and Masses, and even in gestures of the hands and movements of the body. In this way, the lives of the nuns made constant reference to the paradigm of the Christian story of salvation. Not only time itself, but every individual action was clarified in relation to this horizon of existence. Voluntary flagellation (and this is what we are speaking of) is mentioned by the author in the same breath as the "inspired devotional song" of the nuns, with which flagellation was closely connected.

At the end of matins and compline, the sisters remained together in the choir and prayed until they received a sign, upon which they began the most rapturous forms of worship. Some tormented themselves with genuflections while praising the power of God. Others, consumed with the fire of divine love, could not hold back their tears, which were accompanied by rapturous crying voices. They did not move from the spot until they glowed with fresh grace and found the one "whom his soul loveth." (Canticles 1.6.) Finally, others tortured their flesh by maltreating it daily in the most violent fashion, some with blows from rods, others with whips equipped with three or four knotted straps, others with iron chains, and still others by means of scourges arrayed with thorns. At Advent and during the whole of Lent, the sisters would make their way after matins into the main hall or some other place devoted to their purpose. There they abused their bodies in the most acute fashion with all manner of scourging instruments until their blood flowed, so that the sound of the blows of the whip rang through the entire convent and rose more sweetly than any other melody to the ears of the Lord. For God takes pleasure in these exercises of humility and worship and does not fail to hear the groaning of those who are filled with penance. Some of them, inflamed with divine fire, would spend the entire night in deepest prayer and nonetheless take part in early Mass with as much devotion as the rest. Still others, even if they were weak and brittle, did not withdraw after matins, but remained sunken in prayer without stirring. Their cravings were not in vain, for they were filled to the point of overflow by the drops of grace that flowed over them. To those who came closer to God in all these ways, their hearts were illuminated, their thoughts became pure, their sentiments burned, their conscience was cleared, and their spirits were raised toward God.[1]

These Dominican nuns of Colmar were not the only ones who scourged themselves, but belonged to an entire context of late medieval spirituality in which self-flagellation and other forms of castigation were part of everyday ascetic practice. Catherine of Siena, according to hagiographic texts and other sources, trans-

formed herself into "an anvil for the blows of God" (figure 1.1).
The Dominican nun Elizabeth von Oye from the Oetenbach Convent of Zurich whipped herself mercilessly, according to the
reports in her *vita*. Adelheid Langmann, a sister from the Engelthal convent near Nuremberg, reports a vision in which God
required not only that she pray, but also that she actually rend her
own flesh:

> One Sunday, eight days before Shrove Tuesday, the nun contemplated
> the washing of God's feet by his disciples. Our Lord then appeared to
> her with his twelve disciples and said to her: "I have come with my
> disciples and with your beloved, John the Evangelist." To this, she
> replied "Oh Lord, why have you given him to me as my beloved? You
> do this solely out of hatred toward me, since you do not want me
> yourself." Our Lord answered: "I well know that you love him, and
> this is why I speak tenderly to you about him." She retorted, "Lord, I
> would invite you to take me." Yet as soon as she said this, she regret-
> ted it. He said, "I will come, you will not regret it." And he told her
> the specific day, namely the Annunciation. To this she answered "I
> cannot wait until then. It is too long." And he replied "Then choose
> Whitsun, or one week thereafter." To this she said: "Lord, then I
> invite you, your mother, John the Evangelist and the twelve apostles,
> John the Baptist with all of the patriarchs and prophets, my master
> Saint Dominic with all the confessors, saints, and angels, and also
> King David with his harp." Thereupon she turned again toward the
> Lord and his disciples: "Lord, what honor should I now bring you?"
> He then replied, "In honor of my divine power, you should pray a
> thousand ... [gap in text] ... with the antiphon "Te deum patrem
> ingenitum," in honor of my divine wisdom a thousand times the
> "Pater noster," in honor of my divine goodness a thousand times
> the "Veni sancte spiritus," in honor of my incarnate body thirty
> times the "Beati immaculati," in honor of my mother a thousand
> times "Ave Maria," in honor of the angels ten times "Te deum lau-
> damus," in honor of all the saints a thousand times "Gloria patri," for
> the souls of all believers a thousand times "Requiem eternam." While
> praying three times "Miserere," you should punish yourself three

Figure 1.1. Saint Catherine of Siena flagellates herself before the image of Christ on the cross (Raymond of Capua, *Life of Saint Catherine of Siena*, fifteenth century, Paris, Bibliothèque nationale, MS AII 34, fol. 4v).

times with a scourge studded with thorns [*mit einer hecheln*] so that it bleeds, and you should weep with sweet tears.[2]

Just as in the first example, God's command to the nun to whip herself is embedded into the liturgy itself. Song and prayer are equivalents that provide the affective ground for flagellation. Such flagellation, by imitating the physical suffering through which Christ redeemed humanity, allows for an increasing intensity of relations between humans and God, as displayed in the daily rituals of the nuns. While the first example concerns a compulsory structure of daily monastic life in which flagellation belongs as a complement to the morning and evening prayers, the case of Adelheid Langmann gives us a visionary image of cosmic hierarchy. With its theme of the gathering of God and all the saints, it recalls paintings such as the Ghent Altarpiece (1432) of the van Eyck brothers, in which the history of God's saving grace appears as the community of saints gathered around the Easter lamb — a visionary projection of simultaneity. The same thing occurs here, though in this case, the command of God aims less at the practice of repentance than at an eschatological presence of the anticipated contact between humans and God. The prayers that the nun is supposed to utter are a preliminary answer to her desire to possess God as the beloved to whom she will submit (figure 1.2). Yet the effect of prayer consists mostly in projecting the essence of God into the space of her spirit, memory, and fantasy and in evoking the hierarchical unfolding of the divine (the Incarnation, Mary, the saints, and all the faithful). The authentic meaning of prayer consists of this construction of an imaginary presence of God, which is not fantastic and unreal, but pictorial and quite real. And it culminates in flagellation, the singing of the psalm "Miserere," and the prayer of the psalm of repentance. A bridge is thus built between the divine power evoked in the first prayer and the nun's own body, from which the desire of the divine beloved arises and that is therefore also included in the hierarchical unfolding of the divine as construed by the visionary image.

A similar connection between the most ardent desire and the

39

Figure 1.2. Christ strikes a nun or Beguine with rods (*Christus und die minnende Seele*, fifteenth century, Einsiedeln, Klosterbibliothek, Codex 710, fol. VIr).

praxis of prayer, visionary imagination, and voluntary flagellation may be observed in numerous late medieval lives of various saints. We need only mention Christina Ebner, a nun from Engelthal, who mortified her flesh to the most extreme degree,[3] as well as the nuns of the convent of Töß, near Winthertur, who are mentioned frequently in the lives of various sisters. Chronicles from monasteries in Töß and from Katherinental (near Schaffhausen) speak of Katherina Pletin, Beli von Winthertur, Adelheid Zirger, and many others, who flagellated themselves and generally made use of ascetic practices to become "earthly angels" (as the texts themselves put it in hagiographic fashion). They become figures in a drama of a celestial, cosmically unfolded hierarchy.[4]

Tormented Bodies

These nuns, in particular, whose behavior was regarded as "hysterical" and "overwrought" by historians of the nineteenth and twentieth centuries,[5] were certainly not the first to reach for the whip. But contrary to what is sometimes believed, they were also not heirs to a long tradition of ascetic flagellation stretching back to late antiquity. "Novum supplicii genus," "a new form of torture and castigation," seems to have been employed by a hermit named Dominicus Loricatus (Dominic the Armored) four hundred years before the text from Colmar was written as the name for a device involving bundles of rods affixed to whips furnished with leather straps ("virgarum scopas in corrigarium scuticas vertit"). For the rest of his life, Dominic is said to have tormented himself with leather whips to an inconceivable degree, a form of whipping that his biographer Peter Damian informs us was not at all customary, even though Peter normally insisted on a lengthy historical tradition of flagellation with rods. The hermit occupied himself in this way throughout his final years while praying twelve times through the entire Psalter. A hagiographer of the nineteenth century writes as follows:

> Among those who pushed [self-flagellation] to the point of extremity, but who nonetheless managed to reach an advanced age, was the

41

blessed Dominicus Loricatus, known as "The Armored." He took this name from the iron armor that he wore on his naked body for many years as a form of penance. After he entered the clergy, his parents presented the bishop with a goatskin so that he might ordain their son as a priest. Dominicus was so shaken by this sinful act of simony by his parents that he never performed service at the altar in his life. He turned his back on the world, became a monk, and submitted to the most rigorous acts of penance: first in the hermitage in Ponte Rezzoli (Luceoli) in Umbria and a few years later in the retreat of Saint Peter Damian at Fonte Avellano. Only on Sundays and Thursdays did he eat more substantial dishes along with his bread. The rest of the time, he allowed himself nothing but bread and water and slept only little. Along with his iron armor, he wore numerous iron chains about his body, and in this painful iron garb he would undertake one thousand genuflections during the Psalter. Yet even this was nothing compared with his flagellations with rods and, a few years prior to his death, with straps. Scarcely a day passed without his whipping himself relentlessly while meditating on the Psalter twice in succession. Often, especially during the fourteen-day fasts, he would extend his flagellations to the length of three Psalters or even complete twenty Psalters in six days amid this painful form of repentance. On one occasion, during Lent, he carried out two hundred Psalters' worth of repentance. And when he was unable to expose himself for reasons of good manners, he would strike the instrument of penance against his head, neck, legs, and feet. All of this aimed not only at the absolution of his own sins, but those of others, as well, for which he offered himself as a kind of sacrifice. He would always calculate the payments of canonical penance according to the number of blows that he deemed fitting, in conjunction with the praying of the Psalms. By his calculation, ten psalms with one thousand blows amounted to four months of canonical penance, thirty psalms with three thousand blows came to one year, and an entire psalter (150 psalms) with fifteen thousand blows came to a total of five years of canonical penance. This explains how, according to Saint Peter Damian, he often took upon himself the penance of a hundred years. Peter was quite astonished by the enthusiasm of our blessed Dominicus, despite being rather devoted to mortification in his own right. Even on the night before his death, the blessed one prayed matins and lauds with his brothers; but during prime, he departed blissfully into the Lord in the year 1161 (others say 1160).[6]

In Peter Damian's life of Dominicus Loricatus, we encounter the drama of a life devoted utterly to "spiritual exercises" and to a mathematized form of penance, culminating in the fusion of self-flagellation with the reciting of psalms.[7] Here, too, as with the nuns, flagellation is not only an ascetic performance or the means for a quasi-mercantile accumulation of grace. Rather, it is the basis of a dramatization that incorporates the body as a necessary element in the process of a return to God. Obviously, it is always a matter here of an imagined, pictorially staged body. The model is not only the brutalized body of Christ, but also the bodies of all martyrs and ascetics, and even the body of humanity itself as fallen creatures. In the case of Dominicus Loricatus, we also see that the body is not merely part of a hierarchical unfolding through which the path back to God is both sought and staged; the body is also the site of a symbolic exchange between the sacred and the profane. In one sense, the blows of the whip are a praxis that brings to presence the Passion of Christ. In another sense, they form a sort of compensatory act, one invested with the power to actualize salvation and hence to transform the profane into the holy. The praying of the Penitential Psalm, which makes up the liturgical basis of this praxis, is translated and reworked by the blows of the whip into a means of reproducing the lost cosmic harmony, the integrity of the once-divine body in paradise. To some extent, it does this *more mathematico*, in mathematical fashion.

We have seen that flagellation is sometimes compared to music and (especially in the case of the Psalter) to David's strumming on his harp, a comparison made by Peter Damian as well as the sisters of Unterlinden. In one sense, this signifies that the body forms an emphatic space in which the Psalms resound. But it also signifies that this translation of the Penitential Psalm into a gestural performance of one's own body grants bodily access to the restoration of harmony — the promise of Christian salvation aimed at in the desire of the monks and nuns. Hence, the theater of nuns and monks flagellating themselves seems to have only an incidental relationship to the experience of pain and the salvatory force of suffering. Rather, it is a ritual of visualization in which the relation between humanity and God is grasped in quite specific fashion and in which the immediate nearness to God and its tragic impossibility are staged as a form of praxis.

Flagellation in the Middle Ages and Modernity

As already mentioned, Adelheid Langmann, Christina Ebner, the sisters of Unterlinden, and the hermit in the Umbrian mountains were not the only ones who made use of the whip with great spiritual enthusiasm. Certain early modern books on flagellation — such as the treatises of the Jesuit Jakob Gretser (ca. 1600), the *Flagellum salutis* of Kristian Frantz Paullini (1698), and Boileau's polemic against religious flagellation (1700) — not only refer to individual figures as isolated curiosities of religious enthusiasm, but contain countless names of flagellant saints and other devotees of the whip. According to these works, such devotees included Ignatius of Loyola (the founding father of the Jesuits), as well as Francis Xavier, Charles Borromaeus, Catherine of Siena, Mary Magdalen de' Pazzi, and Teresa of Avila. According to Paullini, all of them "whipped themselves with passion ... in order to liberate themselves from temptation." Saint Teresa, "although she was slowly wasting away, tormented herself with the most painful whips, frequently rubbed herself with fresh stinging nettles, and even rolled about naked in thorns." And "the first flower of holiness in equatorial America, the lovely Rosa of Lima, stitched small needles everywhere within and beneath her *cilicio* [a hair shirt worn on one's naked skin]. Every day she wore a crown of thorns, stuck quills into her head, and girded her loins with a triple iron chain."

Along with these thoroughly modern saints of Paullini's time, the *longue durée* of the phenomenon was demonstrated by the

44

Franciscans and Jesuits, the "Syrian Flagellants," and the medieval European processions of flagellants, all serving to exemplify the great diversity of this trend.[8] The list drawn from the seventeenth century can easily be extended backward into the Middle Ages and forward into modernity. The hagiographer of Saint Clare of Assisi tells us that she "tore apart the alabaster container of her body with a whip for forty-two years, and from her wounds there arose heavenly odors that filled the church."[9] According to his *vita*, even Saint Dominic, founder of the order that bears his name, submitted himself each night to long and bloody flagellations with a whip affixed with three iron chains. Occasionally, when his own strength failed him, he would have himself whipped by one of the brothers. According to the reports of Jordan of Saxony, Dominic's pupils followed him in practicing flagellation, as well.

Teresa of Avila and John of the Cross, despite the questionable nature of the evidence, are also said to have ranked among the devotees of flagellation, and the same is said of other saints. This is not to say that pious laymen avoided the practice. Saint Elizabeth of Thuringia had herself whipped by her servants; the French king Saint Louis was flogged every Friday by his attendants or his Dominican confessor, a schedule expanded during Lent to include Monday and Wednesday, as well. Saint Hedwig of Silesia, upon her entry into the Cistercian order, was whipped by her fellow nuns (Figure 1.3). The *vita* of Margaret of Hungary relates the following anecdote:

> After whipping herself along with her fellow nuns, she would whip herself still further after they had left, including with rods and thorn-covered branches. She would strike herself until the blood flowed. These acts of penance, which ran throughout the year, would intensify during the last three days of Holy Week. At all hours of the day and night, she tormented her body with blows that led to great loss of blood.[10]

Some would bend on their knees, others would stand, or sit with uncovered backs, especially in the monastic tradition of

Figure 1.3. Flagellation scenes from the *vita* of Hedwig of Silesia: self-inflicted flagellation and flagellation administered by another nun (*Hedwig Codex*, 1353, Los Angeles, J. Paul Getty Museum, MS Ludwig XI 7, fol. 38v, detail).

punitive whipping. In individual flagellation (as can be gathered from the *vita* of Dominicus Loricatus), the blows fell not only on one's back, but also on other parts of the body, especially on the legs. The blows were motivated, according to historical theories as well as the testimony of medieval documents, by a strict ideology of penance that began in the tenth century and continued to grow throughout the Middle Ages, the period in which we find the greatest number of flagellants. Yet this phenomenon cannot really be explained by the ideology of penance. Nor can we say that the visualization of Christian salvation, penance, and the mortification of the flesh for spiritual purposes always stood in the foreground, as might initially be supposed. This is indicated by Saint Francis de Sales, one of the modern defenders of flagellation and a spiritual authority up into the twentieth century. On October 14, 1604, he wrote to Madame de Chantal:

> It would be good if you would sometimes give yourself fifty or sixty blows with a whip, or even thirty, according to your disposition. It is surprising how much good this did to another soul of my acquaintance. There is no doubt that the outer sensation generated by this practice will drive away inner troubles and sadness. In this way, the mercy of God is evoked. The devil sees how one treats his comrade the body, and he flees from it.[11]

Francis also considers flagellation in his *Introduction à la vie dévote* in the context of mourning and melancholy, which are his primary themes in this work. Mourning and melancholy turn the soul into the playground of evil and of temptations that can be driven away through prayer, song, and ultimately through "external exercises." Among these exercises are flagellation, for it "heats up the heart and purifies it" of the depressive mood that "proceeds from the dry and cool temperament."

Here, a physiological account of whipping replaces the penitential motive almost completely. This account is based on the pathology of humors that held sway from ancient times on into the seventeenth century and that is so prevalent in medical texts

47

of the period that were concerned with flagellation.[12] Whipping stimulates the flow of the humors and hence also the mood of the soul. It is an effective therapy for the melancholy that seizes and cripples the soul. Yet at the same time, it also excites the imagination, the production of fantasy images that are able to lead the soul out of melancholy. In this connection, Francis de Sales counsels "moderate flagellation," whose psychophysiological effect he regards as consisting primarily in accelerating the flow of the humors. By this means, pain is diverted from inner mourning, and ultimately the soul opens up to an inner, imaginative experience of consolation and divine fullness.[13]

As we know from medieval biographies of nuns and "autobiographically" structured books of revelations (as in the case of Margareta Ebner — no relation to Christina), the experiences of desire, of hopelessness, of pain, of being overpowered by grace, and of tears of joy are correlated in a manner that gives flagellation a central role.[14] Along with prayer and song, whipping deepens the affective experience of desire and stimulates the soul, which in this way opens up and allows itself to be overpowered by joy. The "pleasant odor" occasionally mentioned in this connection by the lives of the saints belongs to a synesthetic unfolding of a sensual-spiritual experience that leads the soul back to God.

Although penance fades into the background for Francis de Sales in favor of a psychological and physiological account of flagellation, penance remains important in the *Spiritual Exercises* of Saint Ignatius of Loyola, among the "outer exercises of repentance" that are closely bound up with the testing of conscience. According to Ignatius, flagellation should always be done in secret and should be limited to "summoning pain into the flesh, but not into the bones." For this reason, Ignatius recommends that penance and the exploration of conscience should make use of whips with relatively thin straps so as to injure the surface of the flesh, but not the interior of the body.[15] The "outer" exercise of penance performed on the body, which includes flagellation as well as fasting and sleepless vigilance, complements inner repentance. Its meaning is not only penance itself, or merely the performance of penance through pain, but the opening of oneself to the grace of God, which can be expressed (such as with Margareta Ebner, who follows stock images from the rhetoric of spiritual life) in the intensive feeling of penance, in a flood of tears, or in the elimination of religious doubt. "Pain and consolation" are closely connected. And according to Ignatius, they are connected through flagellation, connected in a manner for which everyone must find his or her own appropriate rhythm and degree.

This view of flagellation as a gesture of repentance, of *imitatio Christi*, and as spiritual therapy for the arousal of weakened affects was especially widespread in Jesuit circles and was adopted in the eighteenth and nineteenth centuries by pious laymen, as well. Even as late as 1957, it served as the inspiration for Émile Bertaud's article entitled "Discipline" in the third volume of the *Dictionnaire de spiritualité ascétique et mystique*. When practiced in moderation, he believes, flagellation permits "those who practice it to come closer to the humility of the body of Christ during his flagellation." He continues: "The practice of flagellation in no way belongs to primitive monastic spirituality or to early Christendom, for which the actual exercises of penance included fasting, chastity, and vigilance in prayer. It must therefore be seen as a commendable exercise, since it was practiced following its spread by the saints and belongs today among the basic features of religious life."[16] The Benedictine Louis Gougaud, who is the source for many of Bertaud's remarks, insists in his classic 1925 study of ascetic praxis that self-flagellation is firmly established in contemporary monastic usage and to some extent even in the rules of the orders. As he puts it, "even today [it] is practiced in most of the orders. For the most part, it entails that according to either written or unwritten rules, flagellation will be practiced on specific days, such as every Friday that is not a high feast day, and on specific days during Lent or Advent — the two most important periods of penance on the church calendar."[17]

As late as the middle of the twentieth century, then, we are confronted with documents that make up the provisional culmination of a long tradition of voluntary ascetic flagellation. As

Bertaud accurately remarks, it is not an archaic, "primitive," early Christian practice aimed at one's own body, but one of relatively late invention, an invention of the medieval and modern periods. It began to spread in the Middle Ages through the efforts of the Benedictine hermit, monastic reformer, and eventual cardinal Peter Damian. Yet with this new ascetic technique (as can already be loosely gathered from the various passages cited), it is not simply a matter of discovering a new and harsher form of penance. Instead, the body, the imagination, and the affects are staged in a highly specific way and bound up with systems of ritual action that have retained their practical significance to this day. A handbook of pastoral medicine from 1887 also suggests the real reason why the practice of self-flagellation was able to attain such a privileged position and to endure even into the twentieth century:

> It is no accidental coincidence, but an inner necessity, that those men who are supposed to have scaled the greatest heights of Christian perfection attainable to humans were always great ascetics, even passionately so. Ascesis is the practical solution to the psychological paradox that the purest, most ideal form of happiness is — pain. One must have reflected for a long time on the nature of Christian perfection to know that it is not a higher degree of pious enthusiasm or the sickly whim of an overexcited brain, but a perfectly rational need of the soul, a justified and irresistible longing, which has led some of our great saints, in the course of their quest for perfection, voluntarily to assume the most severe deprivations and to rejoice in the greatest pains as if they were the most desirable pleasures. By this view, ascesis is the most ideal expression of the love of God and humans. The more bitter the pain, the more valuable it is as a sacrificial offering, laid down before the throne of the Lord, and as a gift of love offered in the name of love of our neighbor. A saint of love such as Saint Francis of Assisi was able to say: "I love you, brother, and I suffer, as you suffer, voluntarily, from love of you, and am thus overjoyed to prove to you how deeply I feel with you!" That is ascesis in the most ideal sense of its Christian conception, as grasped and practiced at bottom only by ascetics. The ascetic who reaches such

perfection must be dominated by a feeling that makes him blessed, like the joy of the Redeemer at his work of atonement.... If we ana- lyze the nature of ascesis by placing the main weight on the moment of the voluntary assumption of pain, this aim can clearly be pro- moted by the most varied forms of renunciation. Human existence displays feelings of pleasure of the most various kind, all of them able to provide starting points for ascetic technique, and in historical terms, they have already done so — not to mention the thousandfold possibilities of redeeming painful sensations through direct and active forms of intervention. The pleasure of satiation is transformed by ascetic practice into fasting, the enjoyment of one's tongue and palate into abstinence, the contentment of sleep into nightlong vig- ils, the pleasant sensation of rest on soft cushions into the boardlike beds of the Carthusians, the lovely charm of staying in large, bright, airy rooms yields to stays in narrow, dark, musty cells. One's feelings can be chastised by harsh habits, tight iron cordons, hair shirts, and scourges, by hours on bent knees on the hard stone of the church, by throwing oneself on the floor, by praying with arms stretched out. The eye will be chastised by bare cell walls, the ear through monot- onous choral songs deliberately stripped of any modulation, and the impulse for camaraderie via solitude. The desire for human speech and reciprocal exchange will be chastised through a rigorous law of silence. And for so many ascetics of the strictest observance, this mixture of pain, reluctance, and deprivation has not sufficed, leading them to employ the most refined cleverness to invent even more forms of self-torment! We read of enthusiasts of ascesis so commit- ted that they find welcome amplifications of the practice of mortifi- cation — by torturing themselves by sitting in cold winter frost in light clothing, or by torturing themselves in the sweat and parching glow of the scorching heat of summer by sitting in an unshaded field under their heavy thick habits of bulky cloth. Some add bitter herbs to their meager meals in order to transform the last remaining trace of palatable enjoyment directly into its opposite; they stand through- out their mealtimes, or they eat while squatting on the floor, using this burdensome predicament to render impossible even *involuntary* comfort that the one who is eating might be able to snatch for himself. Even the peculiar type of dwelling chosen by many saints of the Eastern Church, to which many of them lent a characteristic name (e.g., Simon Stylites), on a platform atop a column of up to forty meters in height, is doubtless of ascetic origin. The Western Church, despite its absence of pillar saints, can offer instead the so-called *reclusae*. Pious virgins or widows would receive the permission of ecclesiastical authorities to be walled up in a small room connected to the church by a small window. They would enter this room with grand ceremony, and there they would spend the rest of their lives until death, in prayer and meditation. Parisian chronicles report that Agnes du Rochier, a very beautiful girl, the only daughter of a rich merchant from the Rue Thibautodé in the parish of Sainte-Opportune, entered the church of the same name as a recluse under the eyes of the bishop on October 5, 1403. This pious hermitess, amid the wildest bustle of the great city, reached the age of ninety-eight years, and at the time of her death had spent eighty years in this voluntary captivity.

The author concludes: "Of all these forms of asceticism, many have a purely individual value. For the great mass of believers, they will seem incomprehensible, monstrous, and bizarre if they are not considered according to the conception that in my opinion is the definitive one for the correct judgment of the essence of all asceticism." According to the author, moderate fasting is an adequate form of ascesis for normal "Catholics," since flagellation tends to blast apart their bourgeois way of life.[18]

The Invention of Flagellation
The practice of flagellation as described here, like the judicial use of the whip, is commonly known as *disciplina*, following Augustine. Although it certainly ranks among the harshest forms of ascesis, it does not rank among the techniques of voluntary Christian mortification that were used from the earliest times. The first evidence of the use of flagellation as *disciplina* seems to appear in the life of Saint Pardulf (d. 737). His biographer reports that during Lent, he had himself whipped by his student Theodenus: "He

lay down completely naked and had his student strike him with rods. At night, whether in winter or summer, he lay on the floor with outstretched arms and remained fixed in prayer for as long as possible. The rest of the time until morning was spent reciting by heart the scriptural readings that he had heard. After matins he meditated...singing songs of praise for the martyrs and confessors."[19] Similar stories are related of other figures such as Saint William of Gellone and Saint Kentigern of Glasgow, yet the lives that give us these portraits come in both cases from the twelfth century and thus contain typical biographical projections and stylizations of the period, including the introduction of the motif of self-flagellation. Only in the tenth century do we find the widespread practice of abandoning oneself to flagellation so as to achieve repentance with a determinate number of blows according to an exact system of tariffs. This can be gathered not only from the somewhat later *vita* of Dominicus Loricatus, but also from books of penance such as that of Regino von Prüm (d. 915).[20]

As stated earlier, the penitential practice of voluntary self-flagellation received the name *disciplina*. Yet *disciplina* in the monastic and scholastic tradition does not primarily signify bodily ascesis, but more generally a kind of training that aims at a determinate conduct of life and leads to true knowledge. For the Christians who adopted this pedagogical ideal from the tradition of late antiquity, this meant actualizing the teaching of Christ, the *doctrina christiana*, for the conduct of one's own life. It was a matter of transforming the self, of a pedagogy of existence, of a "self-fashioning" that made humans Christ-like and thereby led them back into the divine economy of salvation.

A central role was played here by the overcoming of evil as a constant lifelong struggle against demonic temptation, as we will see especially in the arguments of Peter Damian during the dispute over the meaning of flagellation. Only through *disciplina* is Christ victorious, for only in this way does he empower the choice of good over evil. The ancient pedagogy of self-control and the Stoic ideal of *ataraxia* (even in antiquity there was talk of the struggle of reason against the passions),[21] was transformed by the early monks into an agonal concept whose basis was formed by the *exercitia* — the exercises that characterize discipline and the manner of struggle that brings monks and demons into conflict. As Athanasius already said of Antonius, who spent his life as a hermit in the desert, "he became a martyr each day in his spirit and ceaselessly fought the struggle of faith."[22] The reference here is to the struggle against the temptations that steer us away from God, a struggle consisting of a permanent exercise of all psychic capacities, of a transformation of the soul and its passions. Especially in the Eastern Church, such as in the writings of Evagrius of Pontus and of Pseudo-Macarius, we encounter refined models of spiritual life centered on the struggle against the demonic passions. In the West, by contrast, we find great esteem for the passions in the *Divinae institutiones* of Lactantius or in the *De Iacob et vita beata* of Saint Ambrose. When considering the ambiguity of the affects, these works emphasize the positive more strongly and thereby differentiate themselves from Stoic ideas: the affects allow us to mimic the Passion of Christ.

Numerous medieval mystics (one is reminded of Mary of Oignies or Henry Suso) followed the spirituality of the desert fathers and lived as ascetics and martyrs whose lives merged entirely into their struggle with and concomitant arousal of the passions. For them, the imitation of this struggle and the self-stylization connected with it became a program of life that the medieval biographies depict and narrate in connection with the earlier descriptions of the lives of martyrs and hermits. They were exemplars for the following generations of faithful enthusiasts, who sought to imitate the example in their own lives through various exercises. Here, however, it was not a question of the domination of the passions by reason with reference to God, but of a specific unfolding and orientation of the passions and hence of a productive transformation of the affects and their arousal with respect to an ultimately unattainable exemplar. Even the practice of prayer, whose visionary model we encounter in the life of Adelheid Langmann, must be read as an ascesis of this kind, one that transforms the soul and leads humanity back to unity with God by imitating an example.

According to this model of religious life, only the struggle with various exercises makes a human being virtuous and ultimately holy. Here, the message of Scripture converges with the sacramental ordering of church, ritual, and liturgy. Through the exercises, through the ritualization of existence (i.e., strictly governed schedules, prayers, and the bodily practice of ascesis) the meaning of the Gospels, which is promised but not yet fulfilled, is ultimately inscribed in the body and in the temporal existence of the person through acts of repetition. Beginning especially in the high Middle Ages, with the period's widespread concept of the imitation of Christ and his Passion, the body is what bears the promise of the Gospels, whose fulfillment is awaited by humankind. Conversely, this also means that a person reaches beyond the bounds of his or her own existence by way of ascetic spiritual exercises and inscribes them within the horizon of an objective account of salvation as postulated by the Gospels.

Every spiritual and ascetic exercise must be understood as a work of memory, as a memorial gesture in which the message of Scripture and the life of Christ are made present. Here, making present does not refer to an expository form of knowledge, but to a subjective and objective transformation in which Scripture is inscribed in the life of the believer through spiritual practices — readings, prayer, song, liturgy, ascesis, and even the passing of the day and the church calendar. The secret meaning of Scripture, which contains the saving moment of the life of Christ and the divine promise of salvation, thereby becomes present in the body of the believer.

In addition, every spiritual exercise is a staging of human finitude that brings our natural boundaries before our eyes, thereby emphasizing that the passage into the promised freedom — which is transcendent, yet also perfectly immanent — is situated in this passage through finitude. The connection produced by the nuns between desire, the pain of the whip, and tears of joy is an emblematic image of such correlation, one that stages finitude, mystic death, the transcendence of nature, and the return homeward into unity with God.

Such a theatrical formation of human existence through spiritual and bodily exercises, such a conscious awareness of staging, appears most clearly in monastic life. This is the kingdom of discipline, founded in humility and the denial of what is one's own as monk and nun are delivered to the rules of their order and to monastic discipline. For this reason, monasteries and religious disciplines are often described as "schools of Christian philosophy" in which the concept of philosophy implies not just a discursive form of knowing, but — just as in antiquity — the adoption of a specific way of life.[23] "Christian philosophy," as represented for instance by Henry Suso, refers to a transformation of existence involving body and spirit alike, resulting in the birth of a new person. The suffering and death of God on the cross becomes the reality and the very form of human existence.

Also connected with these thoughts on ascetic formation is the use of the concept of *disciplina* for the type of flagellation employed in monastic life. This word is used for a blow that one either receives or inflicts upon oneself. Beginning in the twelfth century, *disciplina* also refers to the instrument itself: the scourge, whip, or rod. As we will see, here, just as with other elements of Christian discipline, it is not merely a question of instruments of punishment, penance, and atonement, but of a technique of staging the story of salvation in the body by relating this history to the body. To this end, monks and nuns try to resemble Christ in his function as savior (the concealed meaning of the whole of Scripture) and to lead body, flesh, and matter back to a state of integrity that can never be reached. The act of becoming similar to Christ determines the way in which embodiment is understood. In the monastic understanding, the "true body" is the one that in bodily resurrection will be united with the resurrected body of Christ returned from the grave. The view of the body considered here — the one displayed in monastic spirituality — is characterized by such a tension. It is expressed in the ambition not only to be the successor of Christ by believing in him, but also to become the very image of Christ.

The tension between interiority and exteriority, between the spiritual cultivation of interiority and the affirmation of the body (a tension belonging to all *disciplina*) remains characteristic for flagellation, as well. Flagellation can be regarded as the epitome of the staging of this tension, as we encounter it in Peter Damian. All self-formation in the name of spiritual freedom and all interiorization of the image is tied to corporeal exercise. And this signifies a simultaneous denial and affirmation of the body, a *mise en abîme* without end that dissolves the supposed opposition of inner and outer. One can certainly speak here of a radical individualization. Every gesture is both affirmation and negation at once, tormenting the body in the name of a spiritual freedom that ultimately wishes to be nothing other than the absolute affirmation of the body and the spirit in the moment of resurrection and victory over death. Every gesture of *imitatio Christi* points simultaneously to another gesture, which in turn points to still others. What forms in this way is a chain culminating in the never fully graspable, never fully imitable bodily and spiritual suffering of Christ — a suffering that in the eyes of God is both the most individual and the most universal. Christ marks the advent of a model of existence by which all those who refer to this model are imitators who become models in their own right. A line can be drawn from the *Historia lausiaca* of Palladios (419–420), which describes in exemplary fashion the life of the Egyptian desert saints, to the medieval and early modern ascetics.

Flagellation is one of the gestural practices in which such a shaping of existence is set forth in exemplary fashion. It is an example of ascetic exemplarity insofar as it imitates the suffering of Christ and simultaneously places before us the way in which this imitation should be carried out. As mimesis, as imitation, it aims at something other than mere representation and similarity of suffering. What flagellation signifies instead (and here is its exemplarity) is a making present that breaks through symbolic similarity and historical relations and seeks to produce for us a "real" immediate presence to the suffering God — an immediacy made possible through suffering, but also shattered by it.

Body and Scripture

Here we return once more to the cultural context of the nuns of Unterlinden, Oetenbach, and Engelthal. Henry Suso, pupil and defender of Meister Eckhart in the first half of the fourteenth century, has left us a work of great conceptual refinement entitled *Exemplar*. It contains, among other things, his *vita*, the *Büchlein der ewigen Weisheit* (Little book of eternal wisdom), the *Büchlein der Wahrheit* (Little book of truth), and the so-called *Briefbüchlein* (Little book of letters). In this work, Suso describes how one should conceive of the *imitatio Christi*, the complex blend of interiority and exteriority, Scripture and body, mimesis, representation, and performance of which we have been speaking. Although in his pastoral work Henry Suso criticized such practices of excessive chastisement as those pursued by the nuns in the Colmar manuscript, he often appears in his own texts and illustrations as a true athlete of suffering. He tormented himself, wore iron chains on his body, had an iron cross fixed with nails pressed into his back, and whipped himself until the blood flowed. In this respect, he was not merely a penitent or the defender of a specifically late medieval "penitent ideology," as is often believed. Rather, as an imitator of the passion of Christ, he presents a complicated model of such an *imitatio*. In this connection, the torment of the body plays a significant role, yet the body is the site where the Christian message of salvation (the message of the resurrection of the body in its original integrity) is to be incorporated and inscribed through suffering. What is intended here is not the representative inscription of the relationship to God. What is intended is *suffering*, which must become actual in the body and transform this body into a likeness of God in his Passion.

The most important divine message to which Suso submits himself runs as follows: "No one can reach the heights of the divinity or unusual sweetness without first enduring the bitterness I have experienced as a man. . . . My humanity [i.e. the humanity of Christ] is the path one takes; my suffering is the gate through which one must pass who will come to what you are seeking . . . all my suffering has to be endured by you as far as you are able."[24] Or in another passage: "You must fight your way through by means of my suffering humanity if you are really to come to my pure Godhead."[25] Hence, what is announced to us in Scripture and in the image of the suffering Christ is meaningful not as a form of knowing, but as a praxis of mimesis through suffering, one by which the human is to become godlike. The resurrection of the body and the victory over death, the joy that will ultimately be experienced in God, can be reached only by becoming like him in suffering. In this way, it is in the body, not merely the intellect, where Scripture and its hidden meaning become actualized.

Thus, when Christina Ebner cuts the cross deep into her breast, when Henry Suso tattoos the name of Jesus on his chest so that his blood runs to the ground,[26] this has more than a merely symbolic significance. What proceeds from such passionate love, what forms such measureless love, receives here an immediate bodily expression that binds Christ mimetically to the body by way of pain and blood. Historians often discuss this in terms of a genuine "ascesis of blood" or "blood mysticism." A good example is found in Elsbeth of Oye, a Dominican nun of Zurich and a contemporary of Suso's, who whipped herself so violently that bystanders in the chapel were splattered by the blood. "They wished that their blood," says church historian Arnold Angenendt, "would mix with that of the Savior, so that God the Father would look upon them with the same pleasure as upon his own Son."[27] The observation that her blood stained her neighbors in the chapel, the walls, or the floor is a stock literary topos encountered even in the twentieth century. It is the trace of blood that bears witness and gives witness in the eyes of the others: it testifies to the reality of atonement, for it is regarded as an exchange of blood with God-become-man, who lost his blood in similar fashion. In this act of atonement, the ascetic nun becomes one with Christ and the martyrs. In the eyes of the pious spectators, she assumes the role of atonement to which the flow of blood bears witness and thereby becomes an element in the theater of redemption.[28]

Flagellation in particular is defined through this mimetic relationship of likeness to the suffering Christ. Unlike fasting, it not only places the body in a state of the tensest vigilance, but actually performs again what Christ suffered at the whipping column. It is therefore not only "atonement by blood" in the ritual sense, and a blending together with the blood of Christ,[29] but an actual inscription of the message of the Gospel in the ascetic's body. The meaning of blood thus fades into the background without altogether disappearing. The pain that rouses vigilance is accompanied by traces of the whip left behind on the skin. These traces are not merely identical with those left on the body of Christ, but mark the site where the promise of resurrection becomes reality. In this way, the body of the ascetic is placed at the center of the cosmic drama of salvation. It is the body that displays the marks of redemption, as Suso makes especially clear in his *Exemplar*. "Blood mysticism," which aims at unity through symbolic exchange, thus is superseded (as was already the case for Peter Damian) by a genuine corporeal staging, one centered less in exchange or in the mixing of blood than in a gesture of imitation. Hence, any explanation that merely relates flagellation to blood mysticism does not go far enough, since it grasps only a peripheral, ritual aspect, and not the theatricality of these bodily gestures.

For Suso, the flow of blood fades into the background in favor of a staging of Scripture in the body itself. This emerges most clearly from the relation of text and image in his *Exemplar*. The images depicted and commented upon in his text (figures 1.4 and 1.5) lead to the image of the stigmatization — a perfect concordance between the bodies of the late medieval mystic and Christ himself. Just as for Saint Francis of Assisi, what is realized is the imitation of Christ lying at the basis of the text, which aims to actualize the secret meaning of the Gospel. Like the tattooing of "IHS" on Suso's breast, as depicted in a further illustration and in the various "IHS" symbols scattered throughout the manuscript pages, the body is the site where the concealed meaning of Scripture, the facts of salvation and resurrection, are made actual. While Suso's *Exemplar* reflects this limitation of the existential and hermeneutic aspects of the relation of image and text,[30] both

Figure 1.4. The "servant of eternal wisdom" kneels before Christ in the shape of a seraph (Henry Suso, *Exemplar*, fifteenth century, Einsiedeln, Klosterbibliothek, Codex 710, fol. 86r).

Figure 1.5. The "servant of eternal wisdom" in prayer (Henry Suso, *Exemplar*, fifteenth century, Einsiedeln, Klosterbibliothek, Codex 710, fol. 88r).

aim at the same thing: the actualization of the message of the Gospel in the image of the body.

In this way, flagellation as a pictorial imitation of Christ becomes a necessary point of passage toward union with God. The passages of the Gospel that speak of suffering must take form in the body, must become actual in an affective-imaginative way, in order that humans be able to transcend themselves and enter the divine tranquility. Much like Mechthild of Magdeburg or Johannes Tauler, Suso states that we pass "beyond images by means of images" and must "dispel images with images." This entails the theatrical staging of suffering in the body, the imaging of the body, which must be viewed as the necessary incorporation of Scripture. In this sense, it becomes part of the Passion drama in which word becomes flesh and flesh again becomes word.

In her investigation of torture, Elaine Scarry puts it as follows:

> imaginary vivacity comes about by producing the deep structure of perception. On one level this is wholly inspiring: if imagining is a mimesis of perception, then successful imagining will of course come about through the accuracy of acuity of the mimesis. What is perhaps less self-evident is the fact that what is imitated in perception is not only the sensory outcome (the way something looks or sounds or feels beneath the hands) but the actual structure of production that gave rise to the perception, that is, the material conditions that made it look, sound, or feel the way it did.[31]

This imitation of the "deep structure," which according to Scarry enlivens the imagination, is also found in Suso's work and his model of the *imitatio Christi*. In the mimesis of perception, in which representation becomes lively and the human becomes the image of Christ, the reader of Suso should be led by the example of the lives of the fathers, the so-called *Vitae patrum*. These are imitations of ideal types: not only in a symbolic sense, but precisely as a mimesis of perception through which the desert hermit becomes the imitation of Christ. In such mimesis, and especially in flagellation, the ascetic undergoes the same experience of pain that was endured by Christ. Hence, for all those who are not actually slaughtered and become martyrs, the imagination becomes the site of an existential transformation in which the sufferer becomes one with the pain of Christ and the martyrs. Here, bodily ascesis, which even in its most radical form was never supposed to be suicidal or to produce martyrdom by its own hand, is not the stimulus for affect and imagination. Instead, it is a supplement that turns real pain and suffering into the foundation of an imaginary unity with Christ. The imagination, guided by Scripture and by the *Vitae patrum*, enters the successorship of Christ not only in a literary-rhetorical way, but in a line of actual unbroken bodily continuity in which even the bodily resurrection promised in Scripture takes root. What arises is a tactile, material horizon of Scripture in which the imitation of successorship is no mere voluntary "daydream" or deliberate illusion,[32] but a lively and sensual image of something else: an image of the suffering Christ that enlivens consciousness from that point onward.

The history of imaginative and affective techniques of prayer and meditation that aim at such realization remains to be written. It begins long before the *Spiritual Exercises* of Ignatius Loyola, and often enough the forms of such exercise and transformation were more radical than Loyola's own.[33] Among the medieval figures worthy of note are Bernard of Clairvaux, Bonaventure, David of Augsburg, Jordan of Quedlinburg, and Suso himself, along with the authors of any number of anonymous texts that develop models of affective-imaginative realization, especially in connection with the Passion story. The path generally leads from *rememoratio* (memory) to *compassio* (pity), from *oratio* (prayer) to *imitatio* (the imitation of Christ). A summation of all these efforts can be found in the *Vita Christi* of the Carthusian named Ludolf of Saxony, arguably the most popular devotional book of the fifteenth and sixteenth centuries. In systematic form, the book depicts the arousal of the imagination that takes place through the remembrance of suffering, an arousal in which images and dramatically embellished scenes have an essential role. Bodily pain and rather specific acts of torture belong to this affective congruence with Christ (figure

64

Figure 1.6. *The Penitent,* Albrecht Dürer, 1510, woodcut (London, British Museum).

1.6). Here, too, flagellation has a privileged status, for here we find the convergence of the arousal of body and soul alike.[34]

The link between flagellation and prayer, encountered not only in monasteries, but also in numerous devotional books of the late Middle Ages (figures 1.7–1.9) offers a radical variant on such techniques.[35] It ultimately signifies that for the self-flagellating ascetic, the resurrected body (that is, freedom in unity with God, or the perfect convertibility of word and flesh) is placed in continuity with his or her actual body — a relation that cannot be conceptually grasped in the here and now, but that is repeatedly made actual in the paradoxical limitation of affirming and negating represented by flagellation. This limitation is based in a reading of Scripture that regards its concealed meaning (the allegorical meaning of Scripture as the container of a spiritual meaning that first becomes real with the resurrection of the body) as actualized in affective and imaginative incorporation. Without this basis, according to Suso, the passage to union with God "beyond images by means of images" is unthinkable.[36]

The Konstanz Manuscript of the late fifteenth century, our source for Suso's *Exemplar* and some additional texts, is not merely an example of this reading of Scripture and of the tendency of the concealed scriptural meaning to arouse the imagination and sensual experience. It is also a psychagogy and an initiation into the reading of Scripture. It is a model of how to translate Scripture, of how concealed meaning is to be realized in such a way that the promise of salvation becomes affectively and imaginatively experienced by believers and thereby becomes pictorial actuality.

Nanna's Reading
This model of reading and of the experiences induced by the text holds good for much more than *spiritual* experience. Already in the early modern period, it held for the *erotic* domain, as well. This is proven by the *Ragionamenti* (Courtesan dialogues) of Pietro Aretino in 1534. In this text, composed some fifty years later than the Suso manuscript, we find that reading and voyeuristic observation are regarded as sites of arousal — an arousal that

Figure 1.7. Christ with a scourge and a praying figure (Thomas à Kempis, *Imitatio Christi*, Strasbourg 1489, title page).

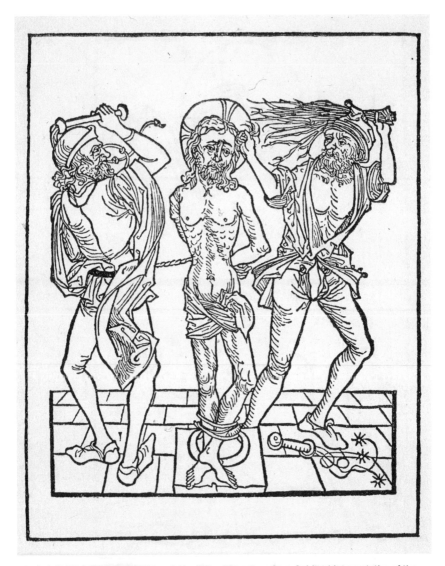

Figure 1.8. Christ at the whipping column (fifteenth century, from *Spiritual Interpretation of the Life of Jesus Christ*, Leipzig, 1922, p. 40).

Figure 1.9. Spiritual scourge (Stadtbibliothek, Nürnberg, MS Cent VI 43e, fol. 198v). Text: "O in-habitant of the cloister, take note / How you lead your life / You have fled from the world and the devil / So that you could come into the cloister. / But you still have your greatest enemy by you. / That, say I to you, is your own body. / You should strike it with this scourge / So that it does not overcome the soul. / You may well make it suffer, / But you should not, however, kill it completely." [Trans. Jeffrey Hamburger, in Jeffrey Hamburger, *The Visual and the Visionary*, p. 462.] Allegorical meaning of the parts of the scourge: Love of God, Brotherly Love, Humility, Patience, Obedience, Generosity [to de-spise riches], Moderation, Chastity.

Closter mensch merck gar eben
Wie du fuerst dem leben
Du pist der werlt mit dem teufel entrunen
Daz du pist in daz closter thumen
Du host dem grosten veind noch pey dir
Daz ist dein eygner leib daz sag ich dir
Du solt in mit disem geisel slagen
Daz er die sel icht werd vbermagn
Du macht in wol noten
Du solt in doch nit gar ertoten

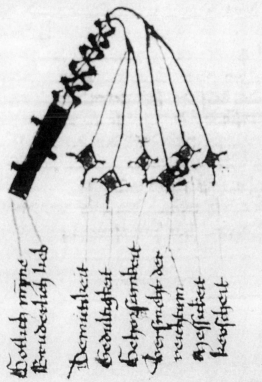

Gotlich mynne
Brüderlich lieb

Demütikeit
Gedultigkeit
Behorsamkeit
Armuecht der
reichtum
gelassenheit
keuscheit

leads to a frenzy of lust that is unleashed in the imagination and even experienced physically. In this work, which remained the gold standard for pornography up to modern times, the paradigmatic case of such arousal is a nun. This is no mere accident or literary commonplace of the kind found well into the modern period: instead, it is Aretino's specific rebuttal of a particular form of reading. His refusal of Petrarchean rhetoric and of Petrarch's transfiguration of woman as an unreachable creature is expressed in the book no less clearly than his dismissive parody of Baldassare Castiglione's *Cortegiano* (The art of the courtier). In this respect, Aretino opposes both Petrarch and Castiglione when he links images and temptation to the experience of materiality and fleshly enjoyment. In other words, monastic rhetoric and its relations with image and text function in Aretino's work as a subversion of courtly or Petrarchean idealization in the name of an ecstatic embodiment expressed by the desire of the nun.

For Petrarch (who was Suso's contemporary), the act of vision is what unleashes passion and imagination; far from depriving vision of such power, Aretino presents it in its most powerful form. The monastery that Nanna enters in the first part of the work (entitled *Vita delle moniche*, Life of the nuns) is a place filled with voyeuristic desire and with erotic readings and recitations. The pictures on the walls, the meaning of Scripture, the meditation on exemplary texts — all these typical elements of monastic life are now put to pornographic use. Nanna and another nun read a book that is not a breviary, but is instead "crammed with pictures of people amusing themselves in the modes and postures performed by the learned nuns." This reading, like the recitation and listening that follow, leads to the desire "to try the painted positions." To this end, a nun clamps a glass dildo between her thighs, and Nanna reports "I flung myself down on my back... and put my legs on her shoulders, and she poking it now in the good way, now in the bad, soon made me do what I had to do."

This sort of arousal by pictures and words is shown repeatedly in Aretino's book. Hence, Antonia asks in the midst of the dialogue: "Do you know, Nanna, what happens when I hear you talk?" And somewhat later she continues: "Yes, I tell you, your stories are so natural and vivid that you make me become wet, though I have not eaten either truffles or artichokes."[37] With its arousing use of pictures, Aretino's book was a model, one encountered again in later pornographic novels of the eighteenth century such as *Thérèse philosophe*.

Word and image are stronger than any aphrodisiac, for they arouse both passion and fantasy alike. The desire for arousing pictures can also be found in the graphic arts of the Renaissance, which often depict the motif of flagellation (figures 1.10–1.12). For Suso, the body becomes a site where Scripture is pictorially displayed, and the same is true here. In both cases, we can speak of an ecstatic embodiment induced by images and texts; in both cases, this ecstasy is based on an arousal of fantasy and the affects by images and by the bodily imitation of an exemplary image. Spiritual and erotic experience are both characterized by intensity of experience, by intensification and amplification, without one form being entirely derivable from the other. Instead, both forms of experience alert us that arousal is induced by the relation to exemplary images and texts and is transformed into an ecstatic corporeality through an affective-imaginative *imitatio*.

As we will see, it is in precisely this sort of transformation that flagellation plays a multifarious role. It highlights the fact that in order for the image to become the site of a truly intensive experience, it must be negated as body and become a pictorial imitation. This occurs successfully, in somewhat different ways, in the ecstasy of Nanna and that of Suso and his readers. Both texts, the *Ragionamenti* and the *Exemplar*, use fantasy and the affects to provoke imitation. For this purpose, ritual flagellation plays an exemplary role.

Figure 1.10. A satyr whips a nymph (Agostino Caracci, 1557–1602, Lascivious Series, London, British Museum, Department of Prints and Drawings).

Figure 1.11. Satyrs and nymphs (Marc-Antonio Raimondi, ca. 1514, Berlin, Staatliche Museen Preussicher Kulturbesitz, Kupferstichkabinett).

Figure 1.12. Bordello scene with a man wielding a whip in his hand (*I modi*, Venice, 1527, illustration of Francesco Aretino's Sonnet 9, woodcut after Marcantonio Raimondi and Giulio Romano, Italy, private collection).

CHAPTER TWO

In Praise of the Whip

About three hundred years before Henry Suso, the Benedictine hermit Peter Damian (born ca. 1006 in Ravenna), actively defended flagellation as a Christian practice acceptable for the church. He did so quite successfully, as can be seen from the survival of this tradition into the twentieth century. At the time, his contemporaries rightly viewed the practice as something new. This was especially true of Damian's opponents, who referred to his "novel" and "unheard of" penitential exercises.[1] They rejected this practice due to its modernity and began by ridiculing it, as Damian himself describes in his letters.

Damian spent the years from 1035 to 1036 in a mountain valley of Umbria; he later became a cardinal and an active monastic reformer. What he had in mind with his defense of flagellation was not a *new* form of ascesis, but a spiritual tradition of whose authenticity he was quite convinced. In his own era, as may be gathered from descriptions found in the biographies of ascetic saints, flagellation was already practiced as an innovative ascetic form. We could cite, among others, Guido, the abbot of Pomposa (d. 1046) and Saint Poppo, the abbot of Stablo (d. 1048). It is said that Gautier, the abbot of Saint Martin de Pontoise (d. 1098) may even have flogged himself in public.

To be sure, Damian's defense of flagellation was not just a matter of establishing a modern ascetic lifestyle. Nor was it a question of granting renewed legitimacy to flagellation, practiced since the origin of the church as a punishment for transgressing the rules of the order. Instead, it was a matter of a radical, voluntary self-chastisement with a very specific ascetic-mystical aim, as already practiced earlier by individual monks. Apparently the spirit of the age was open to these thoughts. Damian writes (if somewhat in the spirit of propaganda) that not only the clergy, but also the laymen of his Umbrian region were devoted to flagellation.

This does not mean that the whip and the flog had been used rarely until then: flagellation was a widely known form of corporal punishment within the orders, beginning from the time of Saint Benedict. It was only the *ascetic* use of self-flagellation that was relatively new. I will therefore begin with a brief sketch of the practice of punishment, since it forms an important background for the ascetic flagellation ritual, which borrowed various elements from the punitive use of the whip. Such use was rooted in the legal traditions of Judaism, late antiquity, and early Christianity — in disciplinary forms drawn from Roman punishments and from scattered passages of the Old Testament.

The Whip as Punishment

In the Roman era, it was not only schoolmasters and slaveholders who used the whip: flagellation was often the prelude to execution. In the punishment of students and slaves, whips were generally made of knotted rope, braided thongs, or leather straps. But for those condemned to die, the leather straps were also furnished with splinters of bone, fragments of lead, or iron barbs. This was the form of punishment suffered by Christ, according to the Gospels, and of numerous martyrs, according to various legends. Typically, this was the model of ascetic mortification that occupied the minds of medieval flagellants, as we know from observing a good deal of iconography. Beginning in the ninth century, the depiction of the whipping of Christ spread into Western art as a whole. The first occurrence of this may have been in the Psalter; later, it was especially found in cycles depicting the life and Passion of Jesus.[2]

Whenever one spoke within the church of punishments involving scourges and rods, the concepts employed included *virgarum verbera* (striking with rods), *corporale supplicium* (bodily punishment), *ictus* (blows), *vapulation* (flogging), *disciplina*, and *flagellatio*. Initially this concerned the lower clergy and later the higher-ranking clerics, but especially the inhabitants of monasteries. Even in the papal legislation of the sixteenth century and the synodal resolutions of the seventeenth, clerics were threatened with whipping for such offenses as blasphemy, simony, and concubinage. Widespread use of flagellation can be assumed to have been a punishment among monks and nuns, as already stipulated in the early monastic rules of Pachomius and Benedict of Nursia. In the Middle Ages, it was surely customary, and must be regarded as one of the basic forms of monastic discipline in every order. Hence, the proceedings of the bishop's council of Douzy in July 874 report the disciplining of a nun called Duda who was said to be guilty of conspiracy, false witness, and rebellion against her superior. The judgment ran as follows:

> She is to be struck with rods on her naked back, not in the presence of men but before the eyes of her abbess and fellow sisters, so that the torture may serve as an example to others, and so that the flesh that led her to this misconduct will be forgiven, and so that the blows that cause blood to appear on the skin will also cause the blood of the soul to flow by causing the flow of tears.[3]

As a rule, the number of blows levied in such a punishment was strictly limited, as was already true for Judaism and in late antiquity. The sources speak most frequently of thirty-nine blows. Saint Columban limited the number of blows for both monks and nuns to twenty-five. Yet even with these limitations, flagellation was never a mild punishment, since — as Peter the Venerable reports from Cluny in the twelfth century — whipping would continue until the blood flowed.[4] In these sorts of punitive procedures we encounter not uncontrolled gestures of revenge and punishment, but strictly ritualized forms described quite precisely by

77

the handbooks of each particular order.[5] One particularly wide-spread model took the following form. After judgment and the sentence were pronounced by the prior or abbot, the guilty party was to remove his shoes, expose his upper body, and present himself at the fore of the chapter hall. As a general rule, he himself had to bring the rod that was used to beat him. The guilty party would then throw himself to the ground in a gesture of submission and humility and not rise again until commanded by the abbot to do so. He would then seat himself on the ground, and the abbot would select a monk to inflict the blows. While being flogged, the guilty party had to repeat the words "Mea culpa" constantly. The punishment would come to an end only at the abbot's discretion. Normally, the brother responsible for supplies was required to maintain an assortment of rods of varying strength, and the abbot would select which was to be used in each case. According to medieval sources, the most terrifying of these by far were the birch rods, used only in cases of especial severity. The individual orders differed only slightly among themselves in how the flagellation was carried out: in some places, the guilty party was not whipped while sitting, but while lying on the floor. They were evidently never tied up while receiving the blows, unlike in the army or on ships, where whipping was widespread well into recent times.

In addition to clerics, monks, and nuns, church law also required laymen to submit to punishment by the whip. It was used, for example, in cases of failing to observe the Lord's Day, soothsaying, blasphemy, bigamy, and even for dissemination of the Talmud. We may presume that such forms of bodily punishment were practiced by the church on laymen well into the eighteenth century. In the monasteries, by contrast, it seems that the practice had been in decline since the eleventh and twelfth centuries, especially in orders that were founded beginning in the twelfth century. Yet simultaneously with this decline, voluntary self-flagellation gained a place in spiritual life that it had never before possessed.

Spiritual Struggle

The form of self-flagellation defended so vehemently by Peter Damian had two aspects that were particularly novel. The first was that flagellation would not always be carried out in public space by the hand of another, but quite often in private and by one's own hand. The second was that flagellation was no longer viewed merely as a ritual of punishment, penance, and atonement, but as part of an eschatological drama performed within human life and aiming at the bodily presence of the suffering of Christ. In this way, self-flagellation was no longer seen merely as a way of atoning for guilt, or as a manner of punishment, or as a way of earning merit, as for example in the thought of Peter the Venerable.[6] Instead, it became a true focal point of spiritual life and of *imitatio Christi*. The reform ideas of Peter Damian were inspired by a mystical-ascetic piety that emerges clearly from the lives of the saints that he authored.

Among these ideas we must include the spread of ascetic flagellation, although modern theological handbooks tend to downplay this point. Damian, celebrated in Dante's *Divine Comedy* (in *Paradiso* 21, 106–142) and honored by Petrarch and Boccaccio, was the author of a total of five life histories, including those of Dominicus Loricatus and Romuald of Camaldoli. In addition, a life of Damian himself was composed shortly after his death (ca. 1076–80) by John of Lodi. We find here a dense interweaving of texts that mutually imitate one another so as to construct a model of human holiness: in Damian's work, ascetic bodily practice is connected with a textual tradition. In both text and ascetic practice, as already seen from our reading of Suso's *Exemplar* and the lives of the nuns written in German, the moment of exemplarity is decisive, since text and ascesis aim at imitation. The goal of this process (human equivalence with God-become-man) is ultimately unattainable and even lies beyond words. Nonetheless, it stands at the point where text and bodily ritual converge, precisely when the text becomes an experienced actuality in the life of the monk or nun. This is also what Damian pursues in his lives of the saints, whose model is the ascetic practice of the church fathers and their concept of exemplarity; Damian's goal is both to represent and to perform this practice in exemplary fashion.

The men we encounter in these biographical accounts — Dominicus Loricatus, Romuald of Camaldoli, and Peter Damian himself — are stylized figures fashioned after the early Christian martyrs, and they become the paradigm of an imitation of the saints that hinges on the body or the flesh. Damian's hagiographies are marked by a strong interest in conversion that can be experienced physically, through a turn toward the very hermetic form of life that he chose for himself at age twenty-eight by withdrawing into the high Umbrian valley of Fonte Avellano.[7]

The description offered by John of Lodi is our only source of information on this period of Damian's life. This text, too, is marked by obvious hagiographic stylizations, yet this fact also allows us to determine what is supposed to count as exemplary. John's text is not to be read as a description of Damian's life, but as a hagiographic project that transforms this life into an exemplary rhetorical type. In its structure and content, this transformation reflects the model of Romuald, who (like Dominicus Loricatus) had been honored by a "monument" in the form of a life history written by Damian in about 1042.

What emerges here is a kind of family history and a horizon of rhetorical reflection on exemplary life. Damian's most important life project, the reform of monastic life through recollection of the hermetic and ascetic life of the tradition, was deeply bound up with such reflection. Mirroring or reflection is the guiding principle of the texts, which are defined by the goal of ascetic performance through perfect imitation. Marinus, the teacher of Romuald, was not the sole model, although he did withdraw into a swampy region of the Po Valley and wander each day in solitude from tree to tree while praying the Psalter. Damian was more concerned with the Egyptian desert fathers of Nitria, whose lifestyle he recognized in a still more rigorously structured form that was introduced by Romuald among the hermits of the Pyrenees.[8] As Damian tells us in his writings, he knew the life histories of the early monks and hermits such as Antonius, Paul, and Hilarion, already translated into Latin in the early Middle Ages by Jerome and Athanasius. It is they who are to be imitated and mirrored anew by each succeeding generation of monks.

In this appeal to the spirituality of the desert fathers, we encounter models marked by a highly complex and diverse staging. Here, the striving for heaven is no longer just a hope for the time after death, but is something that unfolds in complex form in the lifestyle of the hermit. Every hermitage in Fonte Avellana — where as a rule *two* monks would sojourn, serving one another as reciprocal models and as prods to improvement — was a microcosm or minimalist society in which the monks read, prayed, and pursued handicrafts and small-plot farming. They fasted and remained silent. Cooked meals were provided only on Tuesdays and Thursdays. They went barefoot, allowed their hair and beards to grow long, and clothed themselves in scraggly robes that were seldom washed. They often shut themselves up entirely in their cells, as for example during the forty-day fast. In order to mortify their flesh, some of them would throw themselves amid thorns and nettles every now and then.

Along with these practices, there was also the evocation of a world filled with images of temptations and struggles with demons, as familiar from the numerous depictions of Saint Anthony (figures 2.1 and 2.2). Such depictions — indeed, the world of images in general — became here an integral element in staging the tense relationship between heaven and earth in the life of the hermit. The struggles take every possible form, including women and men, vipers, dogs, monsters, and prodigies. All are spawned by a fantasy that seeks to regain paradise through the body and the arousal of the imagination and that first must pass through the demonic realm. Here, too, the ascetic path leads "beyond images by means of images" (Buñuel, among others, plays on this theme in his 1965 film *Simon of the Desert*). As the medieval mystic Mechthild of Magdeburg writes, only through the most radical self-alienation, only through the deepest fall "beneath the devil's tail," do we reach the point at which divine plenitude reveals

Figure 2.1. *Temptation of Saint Anthony* (Albrecht Dürer, drawing, 1502/1515, Vienna, Albertina Museum, Inv. 3143, D1161515).

Figure 2.2. *The Temptation of Saint Anthony* (Félicien Rops, 1878, Musée Félicien Rops, Namur).

itself to the soul.[9] What this means is that no path leads to direct union with God beyond all affect and imagination. These must be fathomed to their most radical depths before they can be transcended. Only in depravity and pain, only in the abject (as clarified by Bataille, both in his theory of inner experience and in his own obscene literary works) do we experience desire in its full strength, so that it becomes the possibility (or the realization of the impossibility) of absolute fulfillment. In similar fashion, the life of the hermit is also a site where the cosmic spectacle of desire and plenitude takes on imaginative and affective form — a spectacle that the Bible tells us has always raged between good and evil, God and the devil.

In his hermitage, the hermit both forms a bond with his fellow monks and remains separated from them through the vow of silence. The hermitage itself is both linked to a monastery and geographically separated from it. In this way, hermit and hermitage alike must be regarded as parts of a highly compressed scenario and as a spectacular staging of the struggle carried out in the practices of hermetic life. Solitude and community, abandonment by God and familiarity with him, demonic temptation and prayer — all of these extremes are brought together as closely as possible. We might speak of a system of temptations, of a genuine "artificial installation" that becomes the projection screen of a psychic struggle embodying the drama of salvation. Life as a whole thereby becomes an exercise and a form of ascesis in which body and spirit (in a merely apparent paradox) can no longer be considered separately, since every spiritual exercise always means a staging of the body through highly specific gestures.

It is not only liturgical gestures and forms of prayer that belong to this scenario. For instance, the paradoxical overcoming of the dualism of body and soul also means precisely an insistence on the body through the radical reduction of needs, as well as an insistence on the material present of the figural world of psychic life in the lives of the saints, often dismissed as fantastic. In this way, the real and the imaginary are fused into a single point where in pain one grasps the unattained absolute freedom and unity with

84

God. The ascetic who withdraws into the desert lives the life of the desert, transposing his own life onto this stage. Through his acts of self-overcoming, all forms of demonic fantasy become directly present in highly dramatic form.

The hermit is a spiritual athlete, as described by Damian in a sermon entitled "De spirituali certamine" (On spiritual struggle).[10] In turn, John of Lodi's biography portrays Peter Damian himself as an athlete of this kind. Only through such a struggle does the hermit attain the inner calm and freedom aimed at by ascetic life: fasting and in silence, dead to the world, calmly contemplating, and living "like an angel" while experiencing the full plenitude of freedom.[11]

As for Romuald, whom Damian presents as a contemporary model due to his style of life and his founding of hermitages, there is some dispute as to whether he ever practiced flagellation. One indication in his *vita* seems to suggest that he did, and evidence from the period hints that flagellation was already practiced at this time by hermits. But above all, it is the idealized life of the hermit as visible in Romuald's example that suggests the framework for Damian's invention. Along with strict fasting, uninterrupted silence, and a lifestyle especially difficult in the winter months, his rules for the hermitage of Fonte Avellano included self-flagellation. Damian thereby became the first enthusiastic defender of a practice that may already have been known in certain hermit circles, but that had apparently never been carried out in a systematic way. Damian now stylized self-flagellation into an ancient tradition.

Ultimately, the hermits of Fonte Avellano established not only the custom of whipping themselves, but a total system of penitential praxis — as already noted in the case of the greatest ascetic athlete of them all, Dominicus Loricatus. The blows of the whip were tallied and reckoned as punishment for sins, a practice that can be seen as a mathematization of spiritual life and the introduction of a culture of achievement among the ascetics. Damian depicts ascetics as unwashed, unkempt figures wearing scraggly, tattered garments, deathly pale, with deep-set and burning eyes;

he tells of many who have clearly overexerted themselves in their efforts. As a means of refreshment, he allowed for the moderate consumption of wine, and he limited the total number of blows of the whip to 40 per day (60 during Lent), up to an absolute maximum of 100. Yet in one of his letters we also find the contrary observation that any increase in the number of blows should be welcomed.[12] In a letter to the hermit Stephanus that contains a detailed description of hermit life, we read that the severity of flagellation should be left to the discretion of the individual.[13] As has often been noticed in the case of the hermits of Fonte Avellana, we find here a peculiar sort of quantification that dominates penitential exercises and that simply instrumentalizes the body with a view toward the pursuit of grace. Here, the ever-increasing intensity of the ascesis becomes less a moment of ecstasy open to liberation than a means for eliminating the body. It seeks to overcome and "translate" earthly existence directly into the spiritual realm through a negation of the corporeal.

Yet this is only a deceptive foreground. It is somewhat tempting to speak here of a Gnostic movement of spirituality and an absolute negation of the material realm. Yet this is false, for if flagellation appears to be the negation of the body, it is also its radical affirmation. There is no salvation, no freedom, no contemplation without the body, even if the body supposedly acts as an obstacle to all freedom. Only on the basis of this insurmountable condition does flagellation, as an ascetic practice and as the decisive element in the reform of spiritual life, attain the central role. In this way, the moment of self-salvation or self-redemption meets with a gesture that aims at a total dissolution of the body, which belongs to us more than anything else. It is a gesture that seeks to abandon the body to the divine through an anticipation of apocalyptic freedom. In Damian's understanding, the Last Judgment and the resurrection of the body promised for the final days is already performed in each individual body in the act of self-flagellation, an act that mystically binds and unites both body and soul with God. It is therefore not surprising that flagellation, as Damian writes in his letters, was practiced even in his lifetime

86

not only among hermits, but also among monks, clerics, and lay-men in his Umbrian region.[14]

Eventually, flagellation came to be practiced in almost every order and every monastery in Europe. As can be gathered from a remark by Paullini in the seventeenth century, flagellation seems to have played a role in the lives of numerous early modern saints. It is surely no accident that the flagellant movements of the late Middle Ages originated in Perugia, not far from Fonte Avellana. They arose as one element of a mystical-ascetic fashion that marked a unique fusion of spiritual desire and bodily experience — the awaiting of the Apocalypse and the hope of redemption.

In Defense of the Whip

Damian's reformist zeal and his proselytizing on behalf of flagella-tion seems to have had a rapid effect on monastic life far beyond the eremitic movements. This can be seen above all in the adop-tion of stricter rules, such as a three-day fast at the beginning of Advent and Lent during which the monks prayed the Psalter bare-foot and received flagellation in the chapter hall. In some monas-teries, the Benedictine reformers arranged for every Friday to be a day of fasting in honor of the Holy Cross, along with the prac-tice of flagellation.

Yet the spread of self-flagellation beyond the hermit cloister of Fonte Avellana near Pesaro (where Peter Damian became prior in 1043 and where he composed his rules for the life of hermits) did not go unchallenged. Numerous monks found the traditional rules of Benedict to be more than sufficient and felt that they could dispense with any innovations. This is confirmed by the numerous writings in which Damian found it necessary to defend flagellation. Hence, in a letter written around 1055, he addresses himself to the clerics of Florence to defend the penitential prac-tice of self-flagellation against a group of "city hermits" (*urbici heremitae*) from the monastic community of Johannes Gualbertus, who had openly mocked the practice. Above all else, Damian tries to undermine the accusation of his opponents that he has intro-duced a new practice foreign to the ascetic tradition.[15]

In a letter from about 1055 he takes up this objection once more, seeking to refute it with references to the tradition. "For according to the Gospel," asks Damian, "did our Redeemer not endure scourging?"[16] Is it not the case that the apostles and many saints were flogged? That Jerome and other church fathers speak of flagellation? Is it not true that Jerome, in a letter to Eustochium, insistently described a vision in which he was whipped until he renounced his preference for Cicero and finally began to love the rhetoric of the Bible?[17] Damian concedes that these saints were flogged by others and never laid hands on themselves. But the same could be said, he continues, of the sufferings of Christ in general: hence, if this argument were used against self-flagellation, it would nullify the entire doctrine of the imitation of Christ. A glimpse into the writings of the desert fathers, which Damian uses as a model, shows the radical extreme to which imitation is conceived in terms of suffering and provides a thorough justification for the practice of making oneself suffer.

In a letter of 1058, Damian emphasizes further that this form of discipline is not conditioned by "modern notions" or invented in keeping with the spirit of the age. Rather, it owes its legitimacy entirely to the authority of Holy Scripture. Christ, Paul, the apostles, the saints, and the martyrs all bear witness to this in exemplary fashion and thereby allow the practice of flagellation to be anchored in an authoritative text. Deuteronomy 25.2–3 is cited in greater detail than before as proof of the correctness of whipping as a punishment. At the same time, in keeping with the Christian notion of overcoming the letter in favor of the spirit, it is no longer read as a judicial prescription, but as an allegory in which flagellation is now found to be hermeneutically embedded:

> In Deuteronomy, Moses commanded, "If the guilty man is sentenced to be flogged, the judge shall cause him to lie down and be beaten in his presence." And then he added, "The number of strokes shall correspond to the gravity of the offense, so that they give him forty strokes, but no more; for if he is more cruelly beaten, your brother may die before your eyes." But what was then a rule of law for this

people is for us a mysterious allegory. The number forty, indeed, means the span of human life. Thus it was that Israel wandered forty years in the wilderness, and so, too, Moses and Elijah and the Lord himself extended their fast for that many days. And just as the Lord lay dead in the tomb for forty hours, he was likewise in the company of his disciples for that many days following his resurrection, so that the good master might teach us, his members, that by walking in the footsteps of our leader, we should be dead to the world and dwell like strangers in this life. In the law, moreover, it was mystically commanded that when a guilty man was scourged, it was forbidden to go beyond forty strokes, because whoever does perfect penance in this life will not be made to suffer punishment for his sins afterward. The number three also relates to the faith, because of the mystery of the blessed Trinity, while the number five, referring to our five senses, concerns its implementation. And since in sinning, everyone either errs in faith or fails in its execution, it was fitting that Paul, who had sinned in both regards, was beaten three times with rods and flogged with forty blows five separate times to achieve perfect expiation. In saying "less one," the Jewish judges meant no doubt to lessen the number forty by one blow, so that by not coming up to the legal count, they would not go beyond the prescription of the law in this regard. And since they stayed on the near side of that number, they would not go beyond it.

Damian continues with the assertion that "not only the authority of the old law, but also the grace of the Gospel recommends the use of scourging, sometimes by command and other times by example." Hence, the apostle Paul writes that "I bruise my own body and make it know its master" (1 Corinthians 9.27), and thus we as imitators should bruise ourselves, as well:

> Moreover, since the hand of the executioner is now withheld from being laid on the martyrs, what objection can be raised if fervent devotion should inflict upon itself something that makes one worthy of being a partner of the blessed martyrs? For when I freely scourge myself with my own hands in the sight of God, I demonstrate the

same genuine and devout desire as if the executioner were here in all his fury. For if from love of Christ the punishment is so dear to me when the persecutor is not present, how ready would I be to accept it if he were on the scene? If I should wish to suffer martyrdom for Christ, yet do not have the opportunity to do so because the time of battle is over, by afflicting myself with blows, I can at least show my heart's fervent desire.

Indeed, if the persecutor should flog me, I would be beating myself, because I would of my own accord be offering myself to be scourged. Now if one carefully reads the Scriptures, one finds that Christ, the king of martyrs, was handed over not only by Judas, but also by his Father and by himself. For the Apostle says of his Father, "He did not spare his own Son, but gave him up for us all" [Romans 8.32]. And elsewhere he said of the Son, "He loved me and gave himself up for me" [Galatians 2.20]. Therefore, if I punish myself with my own hands, or if the executioner applies the blows, I become the actual author of this ordeal if I voluntarily present myself to be tested. Moreover, since the tambourine is made of dry skin, in the words of the prophet, he truly praises God on the tambourine who, when weakened by fasting, scourges his body with the discipline [See Psalms 149.3 and 150.4].

Obviously, the sacred canons also sometimes order those who have sinned to be flogged. Thus, many holy pontiffs commanded that some penitents first be scourged in their presence and then sentenced them to further penance. And before our own time, this disciplinary norm was not unknown in most holy monasteries, even if it was not often used. Accordingly, it was the custom to commute a year of penance into a thousand blows of the discipline. Yet what you denounce is not so much the use of the discipline, but its prolonged application. You do not forbid us to administer the discipline while reciting one psalm, but gaze in horror at someone taking the discipline while chanting the entire Psalter.

But tell me, brother, if I may speak with your good leave, do you detest the disciplinary practices that usually occur in chapter? Do you also, perhaps, condemn the custom whereby a brother who has admitted some slight offense is often required to undergo twenty blows, or at most fifty? But since this amount of discipline is hardly oppressive and is easy to bear and generally meets with the agreement of the brothers, it is clever of you that you do not oppose or condemn the practice, lest you appear to challenge the common custom of our holy order.

But now let us get to the point. If, as we said, it is permissible to impose fifty lashes, why not also sixty, or if I may dare to go so far, why not a hundred? And if one is allowed to approach a hundred blows in this offering of loving devotion, why not also two hundred, why not three hundred, four hundred, or five hundred? Or why can we not proceed to a thousand and beyond? For it is truly absurd to accept freely a minimal part of a thing but reject a greater measure. And it is most foolish to believe that we should be allowed to begin something good, but not permitted to intensify it. Is it really possible that if a small amount of discipline is purifying, its increase will pollute us in the sight of God? For if fasting for one day is something good, fasting for two or three days is better.[18]

In this way, Damian instructs the monk Peter Cerebrosus, his critic and the recipient of this letter, that the practice of flagellation is not only justified, but should be seen as the authentic ascetic activity and imitation of the suffering of Christ.

But flagellation signifies more than this. The most important evidence comes from a letter written by Damian to the monks of Montecassino in May or June of 1069. This letter, which used to be published as an independent treatise with the title *De laude flagellorum*, is less a treatise than a treatiselike letter in which Damian calls on the Benedictines of Montecassino to resume the use of flagellation on Fridays. Evidently the problem of nakedness or of partial exposure had led to abandonment of the practice. Damian tries to undercut this objection in his long letter to the monks that culminates in the following assertion:

A holy nature does not fear taking part in the suffering of Christ, even in flagellation, nor does it blush before shameful bodily nakedness. Christ himself has said: "For whoever is ashamed of me and of my words, of him will the Son of man be ashamed when he comes in his glory and the glory of the Father and of the holy angels" [Luke 9.26]. That is to say, whoever carefully reflects on the promise of future reward will never be confused by his bodily nakedness.

Damian continues by pointing to the theatrical character of this scene, which at first might be regarded as thoroughly dubious:

> What a joyful, unique spectacle, if the heavenly judge looks down and man flogs himself to his depths for his shameful deeds. In this manner, the accused himself presides in the court concerned with his soul and occupies a threefold office. His soul is the judge, his body is the accused, with his hands he joyfully becomes the torturer, and the holy penitent says to God: it is not your task, oh Lord, to command me with your violence, to punish me, even if it should happen that you cast me to the ground with the blow of your righteous judgment. I bring myself before the court, I pronounce my own punishment, I myself recompense my own misdeeds. This is also what is meant when the apostle Peter gives us the following speech: "But let none of you suffer as a murderer, or a thief, or a wrongdoer, or a mischief-maker; yet if one suffers as a Christian, let him not be ashamed, but under that name let him glorify God" [1 Peter 4.15–16]. In fact, the demons flee wherever this happens, and they shrink back in terror before what belongs to the honor of Christ but to their own shame. By contrast, the angels watch this spectacle, rejoice over the turning of the sinner, report to God joyfully about it, and the invisible judge gladly takes note of it. This is the sacrifice, offered in such lively fashion and delivered by the angels of God — and thus, in an invisible way, the sacrifice of the body of man is blended with that unique sacrifice that was offered at the sign of the cross. Thus in one place the entire sacrifice is united, both that of each individual member and that of the head of all the chosen.[19]

According to Damian's explanations, self-flagellation is not only an exercise of penance and mortification of the flesh. It is also a play before the eyes of God in which the soul plays all roles in the eschatological tribunal — which, in fact, already happens in this life. In this way, the ritual of penance becomes a staging of the Last Judgment and also the symbolic self-sacrifice that repeats the divine sacrifice in a rectification that begins by destroying and desecrating the holiness of the body.[20] In view of this truly cosmic dimension of the tragic affirmation of divine-human existence in flagellation, the shame of blushing is hardly a good reason to dispense with the exposure of the body or with the whip. Along with fasting, flagellation is the most decisive moment of self-sacrifice — one through which humans become Christ-like in their suffering.

Yet flagellation does not prevent struggles with demons. Like a harpy and a vulture (here Damian refers to Genesis 15.11, in which Abraham scares off a vulture from his sacrificial site) the devil awaits the sacrifice that the body becomes in the drama of flagellation. According to Damian's startling theory, it can be no one but the devil who flusters the monks so greatly that they cannot strip naked before one another. Who could it be but the devil "who caused our ancestors to blush before their nakedness?" For before the devil caused them to succumb to temptation, they were not ashamed. With these arguments, Damian seeks not only to dispel the misgivings of the monks with respect to nakedness, but also to characterize their embarrassment as something owing to the work of demons and opposed to the primeval condition of Adam. As we will see later, this primeval state is supposed to be reawakened by flagellation. Only the sinner is ashamed and conceals his or her naked body, as did Adam and Eve after the Fall in paradise (Genesis 3.10). Only pride, the demonic cause of the Fall, is the basis of the shame sensed by the monks. Freed from pride, everyone will submit naked to flagellation and not be ashamed of their nakedness.

In this way, Damian associates the nakedness of the flagellant with that of the first humans in paradise. The flagellant is the new Adam, no less than the new Christ. The shameless nakedness lost by Adam is reinstated by the naked, suffering Christ as embodied by the flagellant. Who, then, should be ashamed to imitate the

Passion? On the contrary: those who will not bare themselves and allow themselves to be whipped are in fact mocking the suffering of Christ, since Christ was publicly stripped and hung on the cross. Damian proceeds further, revising his views on the End of Days:

> What would you do if you saw those whose shame you now witness seated as judges on the fiery throne of the ultimate tribunal? As judges who will pass terrible and righteous judgment on the human race? The sun will darken, the moon will be swathed in darkness, the stars will fall from the heavens, the mountains will tremble, the sky will fill with terrible lightning, earth and air will be consumed, and all elements will be mixed together. And you, well-clothed, well-furnished, and soft: what will you do in the midst of all these things? How do you believe, what hubris permits you to believe, that you will take part in all this glory, whose shamed and maltreated visage you have not deigned to support? You tender creatures and weaklings: who will accept you in the community of martyrs, whose transfigured bodies display the welts of rods and countless scars? Christ did not blush before the shame of the cross — yet you are ashamed of the nakedness of your sagging flesh, which will one day be eaten by worms?

According to 2 Corinthians, Damian continues, the apostle Paul was flogged in public. On five occasions, he received "forty blows of the whip less one," the maximum punishment under Jewish law. There were three instances when he is supposed to have been struck with rods (2 Corinthians 11.24) and rejoiced over it. A similar fate befell Peter (Acts 5.40–41). In addition, Damian uses a whole series of passages from the Old Testament, especially from the stories of David, Isaiah, and Samuel, to prove that nakedness should be perceived with a humble mind (*humilitas*). He therefore asks his brothers not to bow to the flustering caused by the devil, but to take up the flagellation of the naked body as a genuine form of imitation of Christ, of the Last Judgment, and hence of the transfiguration of the body. Even in the letter of 1055, the

94

dominant trope was that in the act of self-flagellation, a person becomes simultaneously "accuser and torturer, the rigid judge as well as the executioner."[21] This trope now became the genuine key to the practice of flagellation, which it defines as the radical anticipation of the eschatological transfiguration of the body. This entails an archetypal nakedness, free of shame.

Rituals of Flagellation

Peter Damian's letter to the monks of Montecassino was successful; they seem to have resumed regular use of flagellation as a result of Damian's arguments. Moreover, flagellation spread rapidly in the following decades as a generally accepted form of religious practice. From the statutes written by Peter the Venerable, we know that it was customary in Cluny. Among the Carthusians, Cistercians, and Premostratensian canons, it became customary from about the twelfth century on. In Cluny, communal flagellation sometimes took place in the chapter hall, sometimes in the church. We may also presume that the monks whipped themselves privately in their cells. Beginning in the thirteenth century (as seen from the examples in the first chapter of this book), flagellation eventually became general practice among monks and nuns, even among lay brothers and outright laymen. As seen in the report from Unterlinden, rods, whips with leather straps, knotted cords, iron chains, and various instruments furnished with hooks and barbs were used.

The practice of flagellation should be seen as linked to the course of time as regulated and ritualized by the church, whether in the ecclesiastical calendar of the year, in the course of any given day, or in the prayer times observed by a monastery. But above all else, flagellation is closely connected with the praying of the Psalter. It was not uncommon to be whipped every day, as at Unterlinden, or every other day, as among the Carmelites. Flagellation usually took place on Fridays, especially on Good Friday, and in most orders (not just Unterlinden) at Advent and Lent. During these seasons, it was also practiced by the Carthusians, usually for the duration of seven "Pater nosters" and the hymns

"Veni Creator Spiritus" or "Veni Sancte Spiritus."[22] Flagellation often took place on Mondays, Wednesdays, and Fridays throughout the year, except on particular feast days and during Easter Week. This can be seen in the rules of the Spanish Minorites (*Constitutiones fratrum discalceatorum ordinis trinitatis redemptionis captivorum*), who practiced flagellation after compline — that is to say, following night prayers and the examination of conscience.[23]

As a general rule, flagellation was often connected with confession or soul-searching, as in Montecassino, where they struck themselves after confession, or in the congregation of Bursfeld, where the monastic superior struck the brothers on Fridays after they blamed themselves for their misdeeds. The whip was also taken up when special occasions required special forms of penance.[24] We may presume here an original connection between individual confession, mandatory penance, and flagellation. As I will argue below, this connection is constitutive for the specific development and significance of flagellation without exhausting it. But contrary to what is often believed, what is paramount here is not a calculus relating penance and pain, but the affective intensity evoked by flagellation, one that corresponds to the flowing of tears in confession.

As to the exact methods of voluntary flagellation at the hands of a fellow brother, we find some information in the *Liber ordinarius* of the Saint Jacob's Monastery of Liège, which compiles liturgical prayers and customs from the years 1284 to 1287. From it we learn that the monk who wished to be flogged would normally ask a priest to carry out the flagellation. In the ritual that followed, the monk would sit down and draw back his clothing to expose his back. He positioned himself in such a way "as to be able to receive the blows unhindered" — "ut commode suam valeat recipere disciplinam" — and would pray the "Confiteor," the general prayer concerning sins, three times. During the first two prayers, the priest would answer with "Misereatur tui" and at the same time strike at least three blows. On the third occasion, he would do the same thing while also pronouncing an "Indulgentiam," the brief formula of priestly absolution, and finally the

"Absolve Domine" (or "Dominus Christus te absolvat"). There followed three additional blows accompanied by the words "In nomine Patris et Filii et Spiritus Sancti." The priest would then conclude with three additional blows. Each monk was permitted to ask for three such penitential sessions daily, whether in immediate succession or at intermittent times. According to the report of the monastery in Liège, flagellation was especially popular in times of fasting and privation, although we cannot exclude the possibility that individual monks might have had themselves flogged daily throughout the year. The text emphasizes that the whipper was obliged not to hit too hard, unless the one being whipped asked for greater intensity due to the fervor of his devotion ("ob instinctum devotionis"), wordlessly and through the motion of the body alone.[25]

This highly ritualized performance of flagellation, which followed the basic features of the churchly penance ritual,[26] complementing it solely through gestural action and bodily pain, also provided the model for private practice. Flagellation that monks and nuns performed on themselves in their cells was generally accompanied by the incantation of the "Miserere" psalm or some other prayer. In Fonte Avellana, as we have seen, the Psalms were recited during flagellation. Today, this practice is governed by the "Rules for applying the discipline" (*Ordo ad disciplinam faciendam*) in the monastic breviary. What is prescribed is the recitation of the psalm "Miserere," two prayers, and finally one "De profundis." During the last three days of Easter week, flagellation would close with a "Respice."

Numerous religious orders developed their own flagellant practice and related liturgy as variants of this basic pattern. The regulations of the order of the Hospitallers of San Giovanni di Dio, approved on April 15, 1617, prescribe the following procedures:

> All of our members submit to the discipline every Friday. The only exceptions are at Eastertide and on Fridays that happen to be feast days. For Advent and Lent, the brothers must whip themselves three times per week without exception. Each time, flagellation takes the

following pattern: after the early service, matins, and after the lauds for Mary, the flagellation takes place in the prayer hall if the hall is large enough. Otherwise, the community will move in a procession into the church while loudly reciting the psalm "Domine ne in furore tuo arguas me" [Psalm 6]. In the church, the brothers fall in a row on their knees until the psalm is finished. Then all lights are extinguished. Once this has happened, the prior can, if it seems appropriate, make a brief oration to the brothers about the mortification of the flesh, encouraging the brothers to suffer joyfully for our Lord. Then he will say, or have someone else say, the following words: "Dearest monks and brothers, we take this flagellation upon ourselves in remembrance of the blows of the whip received by Christ our Lord, and also as penance for our sins and as an intercession for purgatory."

After this, the leader says: "Praised be God."

The superior answers: "The suffering of our Lord Jesus Christ should be always in our hearts."

There follows a reading in Latin: "Let us remember, dear brothers, that our Lord Jesus Christ was sold for our sakes ... that he was brought before Pilate, where he was bound to a column and flogged, that a crown of thorns was placed on his head, a purple mantle slung around him, that he was pelted with stones and spit upon ... led to the mount of Calvary, and crucified along with two thieves, one to the left and one to the right of him, that he received a sponge soaked with vinegar when he said he was thirsty, and that he said 'it is accomplished' before his head sank and the spirit left him. Thereafter a soldier opened his side with a lance, from which water and blood poured forth, and finally he was taken down from the cross and buried. On the third day, he was resurrected. Oh Lord, have mercy on us."

All respond: "Thanks be to God. Serve God in terror and praise Him in trembling." The flagellation then begins as the following psalms and prayers are recited with loud voices: "Miserere" and "Gloria Patri," "De profundis" and "Requiem aeternam."

There follow three invocations on behalf of the members of the order, all the faithful, and humanity as a whole. After this, the prior "by his own discretion would let the flagellation continue a little bit longer" and would end it with a clap of his hands.[27] The flagellation would end with communal song and prayer as the lights were put on again.

In other monastic orders, flagellation occurred in connection with the silent vespers prayer, such as in the community founded by Filippo Neri in the sixteenth century, where whipping took place every Monday, Wednesday, and Friday, along with the afore-mentioned feast days. Here, too, the motif was "recollection of the blows of the whip that the innocent Christ took upon himself for our sakes." Following the "silent or spiritual prayer, the supe-riors immediately rise up and pass out flogs made of cords with a row of knots, send away the boys (if any are there), carefully close the doors and windows, and extinguish all lights so that darkness reigns, aside from the light of a small lantern placed on the altar that illuminates the cross of Christ and nothing else." After this, the same words follow that are already known from the previous text, and finally the actual flagellation, which follows the same pattern and ends with the same words.[28] In the rules of the hermit brothers of the Order of Saint Jerome we encounter a similar sort of flagellation.[29]

We find here a correlation between prayer and the whip, and especially a connection with the Fiftieth Psalm (the Fifty-First, according to the new numbering), which David is supposed to have sung after his affair with Bathsheba. This correlation con-cerns a structure established in the time of Peter Damian that touches on the seven penitential psalms (Psalms 6, 32, 38, 51 [50], 102, 130, and 143), along with the ritual of confession. In his letter to Petrus Cerebrosus (*Letter 56*), Damian also compared the blow of the whip with the harp playing of David evoked in the psalm. The sisters of Unterlinden followed this image when they imagined the ear of God opening to the sound of the whip and their bodies resonating with the text of the psalm. Even Martin Luther, who condemned the practice of flagellation, often refers in his theory of justification to the Fifty-First Psalm, which in this context becomes the model of a purification ritual staged anew in flagellation. The voice that bemoans its sins and asks for forgiveness thereby sees itself returned to its materiality or bodily constitution in which it makes itself the "victim" referred to in the text and in the gesture of self-annihilation awaits the grace of God and the onset of the new Jerusalem (Psalms 50 [51], 18–21). But the voice also goes further, evoking the word that will finally become reality in the body oppressed by the whip in the ritual of flagellation. In penance and in flagellation, what becomes present is the entire temporal horizon stamped by remembrance of the suffering of Christ and eschatological awaiting. The ritual of flagellation does not embody eschatological temporality by giving it symbolic expression. Instead, in the ritual of flagellation, the eschatological time of the connection of sacrifice and resurrection becomes the life of the soul, which is entirely absorbed by this ritual. In the resonant space of the body, the promised meaning of the word becomes actual through the earthly horizon of the experience of time.

CHAPTER THREE

The Theater of the Flagellants

"Priest and count, knight and serf participated ... as well as monks, burghers, farmers, and professors." This was the impression of the processions of flagellants recorded by Hugo Spechtshart of Reutlingen, in his chronicle of the year 1349. Yet he also complains that numerous swindlers, rogues, and madmen also took part in the processions, which appeared almost everywhere in Central Europe during 1349 and 1350. Here Hugo is describing an event that must have made a strong impression on contemporaries, perhaps writing in its immediate aftermath:

> Let me tell you in detail what has taken place in this world, even if the things and times of which I write are already known to you. In those days, the flagellants moved about the land in great throngs. They tortured their bodies with gruesome whips whose effect was increased by the presence of knots in the straps. Whoever goes with them places himself under the sign of the cross, for as Scripture teaches us, all those who bear the cross are worthy and acceptable to the Son of the Virgin. They wore crosses on the front and back of their coats, also on the front and back of their hats. All of them wore coats and overclothes of this kind, and only their underclothes were not marked with a cross. If someone brought them something to eat, they would cover themselves with their hats. They even wear hats while flagellating themselves in a circle, so that while eating and

101

whipping, the cross is constantly before their eyes. The cross was reminiscent of the golden scepter that Ahasuerus held out to those who sought access to him [see Esther 4.11]. No one was allowed to approach him who did not submit to this sign. And yet he was a good and just king, as we read in the Book of Esther. In similar fashion, one needs a sign to enter into the life of Christ, and Scripture teaches us that this is the sign of the cross (figure 3.1).

I now return to the scourge and the knotted straps. Two criss-crossed pieces of sharp iron were stuck through the knots, so that four points would bore into the penitent's back when he struck himself. Priest and count, knight and serf participated, even teachers of various schools, as well as burghers, monks, students, and farmers. They would spend each night in a new place. They stayed overnight at various sites, often quite impoverished ones, and would move about for a total of thirty-four days, since Christ spent exactly that many years on earth. The last day is only a half day, then everyone returns home. Nonetheless, this final day also symbolizes a year, for the final year of Christ was shorter before he ascended to the kingdom of heaven.

Once at night and twice during the day, they tormented themselves with blows of the whip before the eyes of the astonished crowd, and together they sang hymns while moving about in a circle and throwing themselves to the ground in the form of a cross. They did this six times, remaining on the ground each time until they had prayed two "Pater noster." Then they rose up, again singing hymns and flogging themselves more severely than before, and again went in a circle, barefoot, covered from navel to ankles with a miserable cloth, the shameful parts covered, but the upper body naked except for the head. Each of them also whipped himself once at night until having prayed seven "Pater noster." In this case, too, he was required to cover his head with a hat. Before sitting down at the table, each prayed two "Pater noster" while kneeling and three after mealtimes. There were no servants here who brought water. Rather, a container of water stood there for all to wash their hands in common. The brother flagellants were permitted no bath and could not wash their hands with soap. No one could associate with women or trim their

Figure 3.1. Flagellant procession, ca. 1380 (Paris, Bibliothèque nationale, lat. 757, fol. 155).

beards unless their leader permitted it as a special exception. No one
was allowed to wash his clothes before the allotted period had
elapsed. They kept the Sabbath and went nowhere alone, yet each
of them slept in separate quarters. Where one slept today, another
would sleep tomorrow. They used no bed and merely threw a cloth
over a heap of straw, yet they were permitted to use a pillow for
their heads. Everyone fasted on the sixth day. On that day, they were
flogged three times in common, meaning that they threw themselves
nine times to the ground.

Seldom does one see such a great number of people as in these
processions of flagellants. Sometimes thousands of them are in a city
together, sometimes it is small bunches, and sometimes they split
into small groups if the crowd becomes too large. They are always
welcomed by the other people. Although many reasonable folk join
in, one also finds a good number of madmen and crazy misfits, to the
annoyance of the clergy and the righteous, who are concerned with
eradicating the bad and promoting the good.

Along with all of this, everyone connected with these flagellant
orders had further duties, which we will not discuss here for the sake
of brevity. Whoever went to the latrine was required to take off the
cross, which otherwise never happened. Only those who had confessed were accepted into the community. Whoever injured someone with words had to make amends to that person. If he did not do
so, he was regarded as condemned by Christ and as a captive of sin,
no matter how high his social position. No one was allowed to enter
a house, not even to buy something that he needed, unless he was
first asked to do so by the head of the household. If the flagellants
were not asked into the house by anyone, they would remain in the
fields or on the street until someone offered them entry, nourish-
ment, and a place to stay for the night. The groups had two or three
leaders whose authority they recognized. They carried flags with
them that also bore the sign of the cross. While on the path engaged
in communal flagellation, they walked in side-by-side rows, like sib-
lings, and sang songs as if they were scholars. As soon as they entered
a place, the bells would ring and the people would stream out to
gape at them and their fascinating, terrible wounds. But they also

came to beg of Christ, the crucified, to fend off terrible and sudden death, and to give grace to the dead, peace to the living, and heavenly joy to the close of their lives.

Often on these occasions, other people would join the flagellants. Shimmering groups formed out of the most diverse sorts of men. Even women gathered in the throngs — indeed, this happened every day. Crowds of men formed, and after a while they disappeared and no one knew any longer what had become of them.[1]

Public Staging

What is so fascinating to Hugo of Reutligen here, what he describes so grippingly, pertains to the year 1349. Following the appearance of the plague and its trademark "sudden death," processions of flagellants appeared everywhere in Europe. This was not the first time that such movements formed, some of penitents loyal to the church and some of anticlerical groups. An earlier wave of the "flagellant movement" already had entered the annals of history from 1260 to 1261. At that time, in Italy, self-flagellation became a mass spiritual movement for the first time. This began in Perugia, amid economic insecurity, struggles between the Guelphs and the Ghibellines, raging epidemics, and perhaps even a Joachimite expectation of the Apocalypse. There suddenly appeared one Raniero Fasani, a layman and member of a penitential brotherhood, as the founder of the first flagellant movement. In May 1260, with the approval of the city authorities, he and a few companions had whipped themselves publicly. While doing so, he is said to have proclaimed that "the voice of an angel had informed him that Perugia would be destroyed if the inhabitants did not repent."[2] Perhaps through the efforts of Fasani's followers, the city council declared a one-month work stoppage, during which the residents of the city and its surroundings were to give themselves over to penance: especially to confession, processions, and also to public self-flagellation. On September 4, a genuine peace procession set out for Bologna, its participants publicly submitting to the type of flagellation advocated by Fasani (figure 3.2).

Figure 3.2. Flagellant procession (*Belles heures de Jean, Duc de Berry*, New York, Cloisters, fol. 74v).

This was the trigger for a general European movement. It began not far from Fonte Avellana, where Peter Damian himself had defended flagellation, and took shape against a general background of Franciscan spirituality. A legend from the fourteenth century that celebrates Fasani as the originator of the rules of the "battuti" in Bologna (a Bolognese penitential brotherhood) gives a stylized account of the origins of the movement:

As brother Rainerius once flogged himself in the middle of the night and raised his eyes to the cross and to a picture of the Holy Virgin, he saw a boy standing on each side. Between them there appeared a girl who bore a letter in her hands. She set the letter down and disappeared once more, along with the boys. The brother, however, broke into tears and was very confused. He said to himself: "Praise be to God in his gifts and blessed in all his works." Then Saint Benvignay appeared and asked him: "Why are you crying and so troubled?" Brother Rainerius answered: "Because of things I have just seen." Saint Benvignay answered: "Do not be troubled, for what you have seen comes from God. One of the boys you saw was Michael, and the other is Gabriel. The girl was the mother of our Lord Jesus Christ. And I say unto you, because of countless and shameful sins... God wanted to destroy the world. But through the pleas of the Holy Virgin, our Lord Jesus Christ came down to allow time to repent. And he wills that flagellation, practiced until now only in secret, should from now on be carried out in public. Therefore, go this morning to the bishop of Perugia and deliver to him the letter so that he might announce its contents.".... The bishop opened the letter immediately and took it in his hand to the steps of the city hall of Perugia. There he declared to the people the origin and contents of the letter. Among other things, he read as follows: "take upon yourselves the discipline [i.e., self-flagellation] if you do not wish to be struck by the wrath of God and depart from the path of salvation." As soon as the letter was read aloud, many began to strip bare and whip themselves. So it happened that, by the grace of God, on the following day, there was no man left in the city who had not publicly whipped himself while naked.[3]

The sources report that the people threw themselves to the ground, implored Mary for her intercession, and called out "Misericordia! Misericordia!" or "Peace! Peace!" The legend indicates that what Raniero initiated was not just a radical actualization of the suffering of Christ as a sign of individual piety and repentance. He established the basic features of a people's movement that became characteristic of a public staging of a ritual of penance, purification, and spiritual actualization previously exercised only in private. What was central was the notion of the angry God who had threatened to destroy the world out of rage at the sins of man, but who might be placated with the aid of Mary and with blows of the whip. Here it was not only a question of a penitential gesture, but of a system of actions in which the salvation of the world would be attained through flagellation and through a radical likeness to Christ. Thus, every flagellant would work on the spectator like "a new Christ" and thereby actually change the entire population into an image of Christ.

In the fall of 1260, the movement began to spread, with a series of new flagellant processions leading from city to city on the Italian peninsula. Lacking any clear concept, leadership, organization, or any sort of homogeneous structure, the flagellants can be traced through Imola, Bologna, Reggio di Emilia, Parma, Modena, Genoa, and in the Marches and the region of Romagna. Salimbene of Parma reports somewhat formulaically (much like Hugo of Reutlingen in the following century) that "the unimportant and the important, knights and commoners," moved "naked in processions through the streets" while whipping themselves. As chronicles of the time attest, to look upon them was *horriblis et miserabilis*. "They groaned and wept as they whipped themselves until their blood flowed." Bishops and monks often led the processions. From this we may conclude that the movement was initially loyal to the church and fully in keeping with the long tradition of ecclesiastical processions. Yet "astonishing things" are also said to have happened, which hints (at least in the view of the chronicles) at the connection of flagellant rituals with apocalyptic expectations and a vision of universal reconciliation. "Peace agreements were made," the sources report. "Stolen goods were returned, and people confessed their sins so eagerly that priests barely found the time to eat."

In addition, as already seen in the text of Hugo of Reutlingen, the flagellants composed "hymns in praise of God and the Blessed Virgin," which they sang while whipping themselves.[4] Belief, confession, and penance were thus transformed in such a way that the content of Christian confession was actualized in a spontaneous public performance pointing to one's reconciliation with other humans, as well as with God. The explicit emphasis on the performative moment of linguistic and gestural action, which is established in various parts of the church liturgy and which generally lies at the basis of it, suddenly gained the upper hand. What stands at the fore is not the representative and repetitive aspect of liturgical ceremony, but the promise immanent in the liturgy of a transformation of the world — one put into action by the flagellants themselves. The total sacramental performance is projected onto this gesture of the imitation of Christ, which thereby becomes the authentic site of redemption, indeed, of the self-redemption of Christ.

A chronicler from Padua reporting on the first processions of flagellants tells us that women were excluded from public self-flagellation, in which "nobles and commoners, old and young, even five-year-old children took part." Yet women flogged themselves "in their chambers, and in all virtuousness."[5] The same observer again emphasized the social success of the flagellant movement. Enemies were reconciled, entire families and cities made peace agreements, stolen objects were returned, jails were opened, slaves and captives freed, and exiles allowed to return. Throughout the length and breadth of the land, one heard nothing but the singing, beseeching, and weeping of the flagellants.[6] We could speak of a moment of social utopian catharsis here, even if the report's rhetorical and propagandistic tone cannot be trusted literally. Nonetheless, we can surmise the existence of a social drama of reconciliation under the auspices of an imminent Apocalypse. The author of Santa Giustina in Parma also emphasizes the moment of apocalyptic angst that prevailed at the time. It seemed "as if they were afraid that the power of God would otherwise consume them with fire from heaven or swallow them up in a crack in the earth or [annihilate] them with a mighty earthquake and other disasters."[7]

Observers have often stated, and rightly so, that this penitential movement can be viewed as a peace movement stemming from fear of the Apocalypse (the "Dies irae") and the Last Judgment. This is certainly the case, yet the use of the whip cannot be seen only as a sign of penance and punishment. Instead, it is a ritual performance that translates the meaning of Scripture immediately into self-perception, affect, and vivid imagination through the bodily staging of a drama of salvation. Hence, the affective arousal that the flagellant produces in himself also aims at arousing the other, who is thereby moved to the same state of spiritual trance and hence becomes a flagellant himself.

The same phenomenon can be observed north of the Alps, as well. The ritual of collective flagellation, whose origin according to some contemporaries was "not to be found in any kind of reasonable conceit," spread across Europe in 1260 and 1261 like a brushfire.[8] In Friuli, cities and towns were gripped by flagellation mania by the end of the year. From there, the movement reached Carinthia, Styria, and finally Hungary, Bohemia, Moravia, Silesia, and Poland, as well as Bavaria, Franconia, Swabia, and ultimately as far as Strassburg. In Strassburg during Lent in 1261, over twelve hundred flagellants gathered in the city, gaining an additional fifteen hundred adherents during their stay. According to the report of the *Chronicle of Heiligkreuz*, for example, a pattern had been established even with these first flagellant processions: in each case, the participants would take part in the parades for thirty-three days. Their public example would lead to further participation by others, ultimately unleashing a social chain reaction (see figures 3.3–3.14).

No less astonishing than its initial dynamic was the end of the movement. Having scarcely begun, the wave of flagellants simply dried up. Already by the autumn of 1261 we encounter only spo-

Figure 3.3. Flagellant procession (Aegidius li Muisit, *Chronicle*, Corpus chronoricum Flandriae, vol. 2, p. 349).

Figure 3.4. Flagellants (Vitale da Bologna, ca. 1350, Rome, Pinacoteca Vaticana, detail).

Figure 3.5. Predella with flagellants (Bartolomeo Caporali, Giustizia Triptychon, 1475–76, Perugia, Galleria Nazionale).

Figure 3.6. Predella with flagellants (Bernardino Fungai, altarpiece, altar of Saint Catherine in Frontbranda, Siena, 1497–1516, detail).

Figure 3.7. Initial with Mary, Christ, and Flagellants (1345, Udine, Biblioteca Civica Vincenzo Joppi, MS 1228/III, fol. 16).

Figure 3.8. Initial with two flagellants (fourteenth century, Udine, Archivio Capitolare, MS 24, fol. 32r).

Figure 3.9. Mother of God with flagellants (Perugino, Madonna della Consolazione, 1496–98, Perugia, Galleria Nazionale dell'Umbria).

Figure 3.10. Flagellants (marginal illustration from a book of hours ascribed to the brothers of Limburg, 1407, Oxford, Bodleian Library, MS Douce 144, fol. 110).

Figure 3.11. Flagellant procession, from a Hungarian chronicle (*Magyar Muvelodestortene*, vol. 1, p. 419).

Figure 3.12. Flagellant procession in Doornik (1352, Brussels, Bibliothèque Royale, MS 10376-77, fol. 16v).

Figure 3.13. Flagellant procession (*Konstanz Chronicle*, Munich, Staatsbibliothek, fifteenth century).

Figure 3.14. Flagellant (Pietro da Montepulciano and Arcangelo di Cola, fresco cycle of the New Testament, S. Nicolo, Osimo, c. 1420, detail).

radic flagellation movements north of the Alps, and they lasted only for brief periods, such as in 1296 during a famine in Strassburg. In the region north of the Alps, we certainly cannot presume either an organized recruitment of flagellants or a ubiquitous apocalyptic mood (as in the theories of Joachim Fiore) that might serve as the trigger for a mass flagellation movement. Nonetheless, such a mass movement is precisely what occurred, gradually spreading thanks to various sociological and ideological factors. Among the important reasons for this were the radicalization of the mood of penance and the changing state of piety since the twelfth century, as expressed in other cultural phenomena that are generally regarded by historians as responsible for the rise of the flagellant movement. But as already stated, what is most noteworthy is not so much the new ideology as the fact that the theology of confession, penance, and reconciliation was transformed. What was now central was the public performance of what otherwise used to belong to liturgical practice within the church. In other words, the displacement was less a matter of theory than of practice. Although the movement cannot really be described as an emancipation of laymen, it still implies a theological transposition that aims (just as for Damiani and the nuns of Unterlinden) at a ritual embodiment of redemption. In this way, what comes to the fore is a specific imagination of the body as a site of living performance, and not just a symbolic one — a place where Scripture and liturgy converge.

Even when the flagellant movements did not behave in anticlerical fashion, the church lost a certain degree of power, for with public self-flagellation, we encounter a theatrical ritualization in which the layman, his body, and the gestures of flagellation replace the other liturgical forms that served to mediate salvation. Hence, what was being evoked here was by no means any sort of "original corporeality," but a vivid presence of the body and a ritual commerce with it. All of this is drawn partly from the ascetic tradition, but also contains something fundamentally new that posed a threat to the official ecclesiastical forms of penance and confession. For this reason, the church and the authorities always

123

required flagellants to be advised by clerics and stipulated that individual flagellants had to submit to regular confession. The goal was to prevent the processional theater of self-flagellation from replacing supervised penitential rites and the official forms of reconciliation with God.

The surmounting of the narrowly delineated sphere of the church, the act of wandering about the land, the adoption of strange styles of behavior, and the gestures of reconciliation all surely had a subversive effect on the traditional norms of the church. They loosened individuals from their niche in the social-institutional scheme, integrating them on a different, egalitarian plane of existence with their group as a whole and its penitential practice. Or at least this was the case for as long as any given procession of flagellants endured. The already cited theme of deterritorialization is hence just as important as flagellation itself, through which a human being becomes like Christ and also becomes a redeemed element in the theater of the world — a theater that exists in the imagination and is also inscribed in one's own body by means of flagellation. In the ritual performance of flagellation, the Christian experience of time, as shaped by the original loss of wholeness and by the expectation of the Apocalypse, becomes the life of the soul itself. This experience is no longer abandoned to time, but lives it and imprints on the world as a whole the newly structured time found in the processions of flagellants.

A similar, yet more radical phenomenon can be observed in the following century. During 1348 and 1349, the fashion of flagellation arose once more as a mass phenomenon in Europe, some eighty years after this first occurred. Unlike the first wave of flagellant processions, no precise origin can be determined for this second movement. The first areas gripped by the new movement appear to have been Styria, lower and upper Austria, and Hungary. It later seems to have spread to Bohemia, Poland, Meissen, Saxony, Brandenburg, and finally Thuringia. In Würzburg, for instance, it was reported that a flagellant procession entered the city on May 2, apparently coming from the north. Somewhat later, we encounter the flagellants in Swabia. In June and July, they entered Strassburg and then spread farther along the course of the Rhine. They surfaced in Basel, as well as in Speyer, Mainz, and Cologne. In August, the movement reached its zenith in the Netherlands. From Holland, they spread to northern France and England, though by this time the phenomenon was already ebbing. Aegidius li Muisit, the abbot of the Benedictine Abbey of Saint Martin, described the arrival of the flagellants in Doornik (the French Tournai) as follows:

> In Doornik, the rumor circulated that in Hungary, Germany, Brabant, etc., great communities had formed who carried out their penance in public. Later they came to Flanders. At Lent in 1349, there prevailed in all of Christendom a general voluptuousness exceeding all measure, the greatest splendor and lack of chastity among men and women, laymen and clerics, despite the warning sermons of priests and monks. There followed persecutions of the Jews, the appearance of the flagellants, and the plague. At the time of Assumption (Saturday, August 15, 1349), the first flagellants arrived in Doornik — approximately two hundred men from Bruges. They gathered in the great marketplace, and the crowd assembled before them and watched their work of penance. On Sunday [August 16], the flagellants from Bruges entered the Saint Martin Abbey, where they twice performed their ritual of penance. On Tuesday, a great procession took place at which the Franciscan Gerard of Muro gave a sermon, but the inhabitants of Doornik were angry that he did not pray for the flagellants. In the same week, there came a throng of approximately four hundred flagellants from Ghent, a second group of approximately three hundred flagellants from Sluis in Zeeland, and a third group of four hundred from Dordrecht. They all flogged themselves twice per day, sometimes in the great marketplace, sometimes in the plaza before the Saint Martin Abbey. On August 29, a group of approximately one hundred eighty flagellants came from Liège, headed by a Dominican. They remained for two days and performed their work of penance. The Dominican was permitted to give a sermon in the Saint Martin Abbey, and such a great

crowd of people streamed in that the square of the monastery was almost too small. The Dominican criticized the Franciscans violently for rejecting the flagellant movement. Moreover, he expressed a number of suspicious thoughts. In this way, the population of Doornik was stirred up even more against the Franciscans and the local clergy. The dean and assembly of canons of the Cathedral of Our Lady, which at that time governed the diocese, since the bishop's chair was unoccupied, gathered there to discuss the sermon. They ordered a great procession as well as a sermon for the following Tuesday [September 1]. This was given by the Augustinian Robert, yet the people did not appear in great numbers. As he began to speak about the Dominican's sermon, he was interrupted by heckling, and thereafter it was almost impossible to restore order. In this way embitterment against the Franciscans and the local clergy increased further, and this same Robert sought to calm the people with a sermon at yet another procession. But in the meantime, the Dominican of Liège had moved on to Valenciennes, where he once more delivered his bold sermon, as he had everywhere else. He was once again confronted by the clergy, yet they did not dare to try anything against him for fear of the crowd that accompanied him. In the meantime, the example of the strange flagellants had also encouraged the population of Doornik to imitate them. Approximately 565 men received permission from the government to leave the city for thirty-three days. Around the feast of the Birth of Blessed Mother Mary [Tuesday, September 8], they were ready, having first whipped themselves in Doornik in the great marketplace. They marched first to Lille in Flanders and returned to Doornik on Saturday, October 10. They gathered again in the great marketplace. The next morning, they went to Mont Saint-Aubert, one hour north of Doornik, and flagellated themselves along the way. After consulting among themselves, they chose four capable leaders: Squire Johann of Lyancourt, Johann Mackes, Johann Wauckiers, and Jacob van Malda, the latter at the request of the city government. The flagellants were also accompanied by a prior and a monk from the Doornik Augustinians, by two lay clerics, and (at his own request) by the monk Aegidius, canon of Saint Nicholas de Pratis in Doornik. The clerics went along with the flagellants in order to hear confessions and to give sacraments.[9]

In this way, the flagellant movement, which initially threatened public order in Doornik and was even viewed by li Muisit as an apocalyptic sign no less foreboding than plague and the persecution of the Jews, was ultimately reintegrated into society. From Doornik, just as from Bruges, we have statutes of the flagellant communities that confirm that the movement had attained a socially acceptable form. What becomes evident is a strongly authoritarian, ecclesiastical, and monastic influence. This was especially true in the Netherlands, the only place where it survived into the early part of 1350 and where the movement found perhaps its strongest support among the clergy.

Here once more, the fashion of flagellant processions had gripped all of Central Europe within a few months, only to disappear as quickly as it came. We have only scattered reports of the appearance of flagellants in the ensuing years: Würzburg in 1370, various parts of Germany in 1372, Franconia in 1379, Heidelberg in 1391–92, and the lower Rhine region in 1400.

It is indisputable that this epidemic phenomenon of flagellant processions was at least in part a response to another sort of epidemic: the plague. The flagellants, whose arrival as a rule preceded that of the plague, prayed in one of their songs "daz got daz grozze sterben wend" — "that God deflect mass death from us," in reference to the plague.[10] Along with other natural catastrophes, the plague was a terror that seized all of Europe and one that the flagellants sought to fend off with their self-chastisement.

Acting as representatives for everyone — this might be an initial explanation of public self-flagellation — they produced atonement in their own bodies for the misdeeds of all. By repeating the flagellation of Christ, they established a relation to God that would move him to liberate humankind from the evil of the plague. As stated in the so-called *Letter from Heaven* (more on this later), it was a matter of restoring harmony and reconciling with God. A similar wish rings out from the songs chanted by the flagellants

during their processions. Thus, the crowds who submitted to flagellation were perhaps more strongly inspired by the desire to put
the divine economy of salvation back in order and to secure their
place in it than by the deliberate social upheaval that is sometimes
imagined in their actions. Nothing in the sources indicates that
the flagellants around the year 1350 were social revolutionaries,
as many claim. There is also no evidence of a spontaneous expression of people's religiosity against the ecclesiastical structures of
repression and control, as is also often claimed.

Yet the numbers of participants cited in the medieval documents are considerable. They testify that even if the people did
not explicitly turn against the church, we are at least dealing with
a sort of alternative theology, one inspired by the flagellant practices of spirituality and the rituals of staging encountered since
the eleventh century, especially among the monastic elite. In general, the broader people's movement adopted an elite ascetic
praxis and made it the means for expressing a new spirituality.
Even if the numbers in the sources cannot be taken literally, they
are still evidence of a noteworthy phenomenon. In Austria, the
texts speak of throngs of forty, sixty, or one hundred people; near
Erfurt for the church festival, three thousand people gathered;
near Grünstadt it was six thousand. From Würzburg and Augsburg, there are reports of between one and four hundred. In
Tournai, according to reports from 1350, processions of four hundred members arrived from Dordrecht and four hundred and fifty
members from Ghent. In Tournai itself, it is said that 565 flagellants formed and marched away. Charles IV, who had wished to
be crowned in Aachen in June 1349, had to yield to the power of
the crowds and did not dare enter the city until the flagellants
had left. There were in fact thousands participating in flagellant
parades in 1349–50, even if the estimates of a French chronicler
of eight hundred thousand flagellants in Flanders and Brabant are
obvious exaggerations. Naturally, all of these numbers, like the
texts we have been citing, are not to be taken literally. Yet in their
rhetorical power, we can glimpse through all the typical imagery a
sort of hazy initial picture of the situation. This picture is enough

to tell us that we are dealing with a phenomenon whose scope was estimated highly by contemporaries.

Unlike with the first wave of flagellants, many sources report of 1349 that not only were men of every social rank involved, but also that women organized their own processions, with men and women sometimes communally whipping themselves in unison. A chronicler from Magdeburg writes: "In certain regions, great crowds of women could be seen entering into processions while chanting their songs and whipping themselves in the same way [as the men]. Their backs were fully bared, while their faces were veiled, and they wore a cloak that covered their sex and their breast."[11] A French source states that "it should not be left in silence that many honorable women also practiced this form of penance with the whip. They went from place to place and from church to church while chanting their songs, yet they gave it all up again quickly."[12] And from Liège it is reported that "very haughty women came from Germany who laid aside their clothes and struck one another with rods and biting whips, while also chanting strange songs in the same manner [as the men]." But these women, the chronicler concludes, "soon disappeared again and scattered throughout Saxony."[13] A Polish chronicler also records in 1349 as follows:

In this year the mortality was unbelievably high in the Kingdom of Hungary. Many settlements and towns were depopulated, and great throngs of people from Hungary and neighboring regions marched through the land while whipping themselves. They threw themselves to the ground and summoned others to repentance and atonement. Young and old women from the towns were also there, with close-cropped hair, moving about in the processions as if in a state of mania, whipping themselves. They spent nights in the woods with a certain Gregorius, whom they regarded as a saint. Seduced by the devil, many of them were led to hell.[14]

All questions of credibility aside, these texts remind us of the observation of Hugo of Reutlingen, who said that these flagellant events became a social magnet that offered everyone a means for rising up and breaking away from the usual course of things. Everywhere they went, the flagellant processions offered a theatricalization and ritualization of communal existence as a possibility of such liberation; indeed, this may sometimes have been more important than the penance that aimed at an explicit self-staging. Yet when considering the phenomenon of flagellation, we should be cautious in making statements about the intentions of the participants. These are to some extent known from the songs that have partially survived or from contemporary descriptions. Yet it remains to be demonstrated that the ritual of flagellation, and hence the theatrical performance, makes up the genuine core of the historical movement and that this theatricalization has left its traces in other realms of medieval urban culture.

The Ritual of the Flagellants

The general duration of a flagellant procession was thirty-three and a half days. As we have already seen from Hugo of Reutlingen, the number was meant to correspond to the number of years of Christ's life on earth. This points to the fundamentally commemorative character of this penitential action. In the words of a French flagellant song, they wished to "beat [their] flesh in memory of the Passion of the Lord and of his pitiful death" — "en remembrant la grant misère / De Dieue et sa piteuse mort."[15] Hence, it was initially a matter of recollection and its communal staging. These flagellant processions must be viewed as throngs that pursued the goal of recollection by marching from place to place, forming after the lapse of a certain period of time a new procession that followed the established model. This can be seen from the flagellant sermon reported by the Strassburg chronicler Fritsche Closener. In this sermon, we find a genealogy of the flagellant throngs: those who initiated the train moved "from Eisenach to Würzburg, those from Würburg marched to Halle, those from Halle to Esslingen, those from Esslingen to Kalwe, those from Kalwe to Wil, those from Wil to Bülach, and those from Bülach finished the pilgrimage by going to Herrenberg, Tübingen, and Rotenburg. They also proceeded along the Rhine, arriving in small and large towns and finally in Alsace. At present we, the people of Lichtenau, are leading the pilgrimage."[16]

We can also determine from Closener's text that not all of the penitents quit and went home after the specified period, but that a few people at the end of each flagellant journey began anew and made an enduring lifestyle of it. Through this kind of propagation, the movement spread quickly and turned the whole of Central European space into a stage of ritual theater that enlisted the imitation of the Passion of Christ, along with the bodies of the flagellants and, to some extent, the geography and the very body of the earth. It was not only the church that was a site of memory in this way, and not merely the region of the church congregation or pilgrimage site ritually entered by a procession, but the landscape, rivers, roads, and cities themselves. Through the gesture of penance and generalized pilgrimage, every site was linked to every other site, and the atlas was entirely assimilated by the wandering flagellants, who thereby actualized evangelical memory as a kind of topography, annexing the world with their blood.

As a rule, the individual groups that took part in these actions, rarely comprising more than fifty or sixty members, were organized according to the model of the lay brotherhoods. They had one or more elected leaders, whom each flagellant was required to obey. As can be seen from the consitutions of a flagellant order in Tournai in 1349, members had to follow the rules of the group and were not permitted to carry weapons. When it came to sleeping (and here the chronicles agree with Hugo's observations), the flagellants did not sleep in a bed, though a pillow was permitted for the head, and they had to spend each night in a new place. They limited their bodily needs and praised chastity, and they were obliged not to beg, not to abandon the sick, and not to be a burden on their hosts. They usually marched in ranks of two, following the model of other ecclesiastical processions. Their heads were covered by cowls, then covered in turn by hats. Their hats, coats, and the back part of their overclothes were adorned with red crosses. Often the flagellants would carry torches and flags amid or ahead of them when they entered a place. They sang songs, some of which have survived. Each flagellant carried a scourge in his or her hand, whose straps were furnished with knots and sharp points of iron. When the flagellants entered a place, the bells would be rung. They would begin by marching into the church, where they would throw themselves to the floor. The people gathered to watch the drama. "It must be said," wrote Fritsche Closener in his Strassburg chronicle, "that everyone came running, and everyone's tears flowed at this devotion, which was of a kind never seen before."[17]

Following their entry into the city, the public flagellation ritual was performed twice daily. According to several sources (which here deviate slightly from Hugo of Reutlingen), it began with a ceremony of confession and absolution. The participants threw themselves to the ground in a circle with their upper bodies bared. By means of their bearing or through a mimed gesture, each one let it be known what he or she thought needed to be repented. Perjurers, for instance, extended three fingers in the air, while adulterers would press their lower bodies to the earth. The master of the throng then stepped over the first one, touched that person with the scourge, and absolved the penitent of his or her sins with a phrase of absolution. The absolved party then rose and, along with the master, stepped over the body of the next one. This was repeated until all were standing. The entire throng whipped themselves subsequently through three rounds while chanting prayers and songs. As we know, many participants in the movement also flogged themselves a third time privately at night.

After the dispersal of the flagellant procession and the return to bourgeois life, every member was bound to self-flagellation as a lifelong duty, at least on Good Friday. On that day, they would flog themselves three times during the day and once at night, continuing as a rule until the blood flowed, although (as seen in the statutes of the flagellant brotherhoods) serious injuries were supposed to be avoided. Communal flagellation followed a ritual filled with numerous gestures, with the flagellants falling to their knees, throwing themselves to the earth in a cross-shaped figure, and finally praying with raised hands to be protected from "sudden death." A layman then read the *Letter from Heaven*, which is already known from the flagellant movement of the thirteenth century in Perugia and which was followed by a sermon expressed in the vernacular.

The Strassburg chronicler Fritsche Closener reports on this sermon in some detail. After the end of their performance, the flagellants had covered themselves again, and:

> one of them, a layman able to read, stepped onto a piece of high ground and read the following letter: This is the message of our Lord Jesus Christ, which fell from heaven to the altar of Saint Peter in Jerusalem, written on a marble tablet from which a light emanated like that of lightning. The tablet was produced by an angel of God. As the people saw it, they threw themselves to the ground on their faces and called out "Kyrie eleison," which means "Lord have mercy on us."
>
> The following was the message of our Lord: you human children, you have seen and heard what I have said to you, yet you have not followed it. You are unjust and unbelieving. You do not celebrate my holy Sunday, nor do you repent or improve yourselves, nor desist from the sins you have committed, although you have heard from the Gospel: "Heaven and earth will pass away before my word passes away." I have sent you more than enough grain, wine, oil, and fruit wine, yet I have taken everything from you again because of your wickedness, your sin, and your pride, for you have honored my holy Friday and my holy Sunday neither with fasting nor with celebration. Therefore I have ordered the Saracens and other heathens to make your blood flow and to take many of you captive. In just a few years much bad luck has occurred. Earthquakes, famine, fire, locusts, ravens, mice, hailstorms, frost, storms, and numerous wars. I have sent all of this to you because you have not kept Sunday holy. Since you are obviously blind and deaf to the words of my voice, I have sent you much pain and trouble, even letting the wild animals devour your children. I have sent drought, hard rains, floods, and I have made the earth infertile. I have sent the heathens to you to

kidnap your children. I have made it so that you must eat dry wood, that there was no bread in many places, and that out of hunger the people had to eat pine cones and grass from the garden and the edge of the road. And all of this because my holy Sunday and Friday were not honored.

Oh you disloyal unbelievers, you do not perceive that my wrath, the wrath of God, has come over you because of the wickedness that has now become customary for you. I intended to destroy the world because of your disbelief, that is, because you did not wish to understand my holy word in the Gospel, that "heaven and earth will pass away, but not my word." This you have forgotten, for you have honored my holy Sunday and my holy Friday neither with fasting nor with other good works. Oh you miserable ones, you do not think of the cross of God when you say "We are brothers, but we are not true brothers." You are enemies to one another, and when you are bound to one another, you do not behave as you should. For this reason I intended to scatter you across the world so that you might no longer find one another. Yet I repented of my decision and revoked it, not because of you, but because of my holy angels, who fell to my feet and pleaded with me to withdraw my wrath from you and to exercise my mercy upon you. Oh miserable race: to the Jews, who belong in hell, I have given the old covenant, the law, on Mount Sinai, and they honored the Sabbath. But to you I have given the new covenant of baptism with my own soul. And yet you honor neither the holy Sunday nor the holy Friday nor other feast days of the saints. For this reason I will unleash my wrath on you until the wild animals devour your children, until you die in youth, until the Saracens trample you under the hooves of their horses and thus avenge my holy resurrection on you. Verily, I command you: honor the Sabbath, from midday Saturday until early Monday. I ask the priests and monks that on Friday you follow the stations of the cross and that you fast and pray. Believe me, if you do not follow this command, I will let bloody rains fall, more horrible than hailstorms. On the tenth day of the seventh month — that is, on Sunday after the Feast of the Birth of Blessed Mother Mary — I intended to kill everything that lived on the face of the earth.[18] I was turned from this resolution by my dear mother Mary as well as the holy cherubim and seraphim, who ceaselessly begged on your behalf. For their sake, I have forgiven your sins and had mercy on the sinners. I swear to you by my angels that I will send you animals and birds that you have never seen before, and that the sun will grow dark, and that one man will slay the next. I will turn my face away from you, and an inhuman wailing will fill the earth with many voices. Your souls will wither endlessly in the fire. I swear to you by my right hand, by my divine power and greatness, that I will completely extinguish you if you do not keep the Sabbath, so that you will never be thought of on earth again. But I also say unto you: if you turn away from sin, then I will speak my holy blessing upon you, the earth will become fertile, and the entire earth will be filled with my greatness. I will send you my joy, so that you do not live any longer in sin, and I will forget my wrath at you so that all of your places will be filled with divine goods. And if you come before the Last Judgment, I will be merciful with those who are chosen for the eternal kingdom. Amen.

I say that whoever does not believe this message will fall under the notice of my heavenly Father. Whoever believes it, his house will be filled with my blessing. Behold: whoever lives in strife with his neighbor should reconcile with him before he receives my holy body. He who pressures or coerces someone to swear an oath on Sunday is cursed, along with the one who swears the oath. Whoever passes judgment on my Sunday is banished for all eternity. Know that I hold lordship over all creatures in heaven, on earth, in the underworld, and everywhere. And yet you are so unfaithful! See how you do not understand, and receive neither penance nor absolution for your sins! For you do not honor my holy Sunday and my holy Friday, and you also do not obey the other commandments, since you are so stupid and lacking in understanding and therefore understand neither eternal rest nor eternal joy. All days are mine, for I have created not just them, but time as a whole. Everything that you possess, I have given to you, yet you perceive neither time nor me, although the other creations serve their creator and are thankful to him. Yet you miserable and foolhardy ones are not. Therefore it would have been better if you had never been created and never received life. Understand: my days are always in eternal rest, and the creature who wills to serve me must be worthy of receiving this eternal rest. But you miserable ones will not receive this rest, for you do not honor the holy Sunday and other feast days of my saints.

Any priest is the enemy of God and his commandments if he receives this letter with my message but withholds it from the people and does not read it to them. Yes, there are many who become priests so that they might wallow in eating and drinking without proclaiming the word of God. For this they will repent when they come before God. Yet if you hear my voice, follow my commandment, and turn away from your sins, I will never curse you. Verily, I swear to you also by my left hand and by my arms and by my angels that I shall fulfill everything that I have promised to you if you honor my holy Sunday and my Friday. Those who go to church, give alms, and honor me, I will reward them on Judgment Day and at the end of time. Yet God's wrath will come to all profiteers and interest takers if they do not improve themselves. Verily, all adulterers, both male and female, will go together to hell and be eternally damned if they do not improve their ways. All who speak the Lord's name in vain will be eternally damned, for they torture God. Oh you miserable ones, if you do not pay your taxes honestly, the wrath of God will fall upon you. But whoever goes to church on Sunday and other holy feast days and gives alms to the poor gains the mercy of my Father.

After this message was read aloud by the angel and held again in his hand, there sounded a voice from heaven that said: "Do you believe with penitent heart in your creator and in the good message that I have proclaimed to you? For even when you wish to flee, you cannot hide from my eyes." Then the patriarch, the priests, and the people all rose. Whereupon the angel said: "Listen all, for I swear by the virtues of our Lord Jesus Christ, by his mother the pure maid, and by the virtues of all the angels and the crown of all the martyrs that this letter was not written by human hand, but by the very hand of the king of heaven. Whoever does not believe this will be damned and banished, and the wrath of God will come over him. Whoever believes it will attain God's mercy and eternal life will be granted him. Whoever copies the message and carries it from house to house, from place to place, and from town to town will partake of my blessing. All priests who hear this letter, write it down, or proclaim it to the people will receive my blessing and will eternally rejoice in my kingdom with the other chosen ones. Amen."

Now be silent and listen, for I will now tell you where this flagellant brotherhood and its procession began. That is, I will tell how it took its origin from the angel of the almighty God, through whom God announced to the world that they had enraged him, and wrote this on a marble tablet that he sent with the angel to Jerusalem. The angel knew the contents when he held the tablet high and said: "Oh you miserable ones, why do you not know your creator. You should know that he will unleash his wrath and his power upon you if you do not fear him." When the people looked at the tablet containing the message, they saw that it illuminated the church like a lightning flash. The people were terrified and threw themselves to the ground. But what did they do when they came to themselves again? They turned to one another and consulted about what they should do in order to honor God and assuage his wrath. They spoke about this and turned for advice to the king of Sicily so that he might tell them how God's wrath might be assuaged. He advised them to fall on their knees and to beg of the Almighty to tell them what they should do to become reconciled with him and assuage his wrath against wretched Christendom. They did what he said, and fell on their knees, and prayed to God fervently for advice. Then the angel said: "Man, you know well that God spent twenty-four years [sic] suffering on the earth — I am not speaking of the great torment that he suffered on the cross — yet you have not shown him thanks for this, nor do you will to do so. In order to reconcile yourself with God, you should undertake a pilgrimage of twenty-four days. And you should spend neither the days nor the nights pleasantly, but should let your blood flow — only then will you appreciate the blood that he let flow for you, and he will assuage his wrath against wretched Christendom."

The king of Sicily put these requirements into action. Together with his people, he undertook a pilgrimage as far as the king of Krakow, who for his own part marched to the king of Hungary, who proceeded to make pilgrimage to Würzburg. They then marched further to Halle, from Halle to Esslingen, then on to Kalwe, and from Kalwe to Wil, from Wil to Bülach... and finally to the large and small places along the Rhine into Alsace. And now we of Lichtenau continue this pilgrimage and ask God, so that he might bring us strength, endurance, and understanding, to accomplish all that suffices to honor God, his dear mother Mary, and all angels and heavenly hosts. And we ask that it should be a consolation for the body and soul of all those who have undertaken the pilgrimage, undertake it now, or will undertake it later, and all those who do or have done good things, so that God might reward them, and their souls this very day should be freed from all of their troubles. In this may we have the help of the Father, the Son, and the Holy Ghost. Amen.[19]

The flagellation sermon ends with a brief remark relating the *Letter from Heaven* and the genealogy of the flagellant processions to the immediate circumstances of the time: to death from the plague, which raged everywhere in Europe. When the sermon ended, the flagellant procession reentered the church in two columns while singing the song of entry again. There the flagellants once more threw themselves to the ground in a cross-shaped figure before the ceremony ended.

In the *Letter from Heaven*, which lies at the basis of the flagellant sermon and which is also found in the Raniero Legend from the thirteenth century, we are dealing with a text that was probably composed in Latin in the sixth century and that has been available in all European languages almost without pause on into the twentieth century. It was highly popular during the Middle Ages and underwent a true renaissance at the beginning of the twentieth century — above all at the time of World War I. In the Strassburg sermon, this letter, which may have played some role in the flagellant movement from the very beginning, served as the framework of a true genealogy of flagellation pilgrimages, reaching from its mythical origins up to the time when the sermon was delivered in 1349. What is unique about the flagellant version of this letter is the importance it lays on the holiness not only of

Sunday, but also of Friday, which was especially important to the flagellants as the day of the Passion. More than this, the letter is of the greatest importance for our understanding of the flagellant movement as a whole, for it gives evidence of the attempt to create a genealogy reaching back into the earliest history of the church and treats the penitential ritual of the flagellant not merely as a normal institution of salvation, but instead as a radical and indispensable emergency measure. As such, its remembrance of the Passion of Christ tries to put a halt to the historical time of the alienation of man from God and his divine punishment. By the same gesture, all time is transformed into eschatological time. The emphasis on keeping the holy days holy, especially Friday and Sunday, should be seen not only as a requirement of duty and as the accomplishment of a spiritual time of memorialization in place of the worldly time of normal life. It also must be interpreted as the blazoning forth of the two most important bodily moments of the Christian drama of salvation: the Passion on Friday and the Resurrection on Sunday.

With God's "letter," whose manner of indictment recalls Old Testament prophetic rhetoric and Yahweh's gestures of punishment against his people, the central command concerns ritual memory. It is the disregard of commemorative realization that transforms the cosmos into a world of horror and absolute loss of origin. On the other hand, the turn away from sin signifies not only divine sacrifice, but also the presence of divine benefits. The doubling of the message in the letter and in the words that follow aims at emphasizing both their eternity and also the moment in which the letter is read as a point in time when everything is decided. In this way, the *kairos*, the present in which the throngs of flagellants carry out their ritual, is not only genealogically bound up with the history of true repentance, it is also the unique confrontation with the drama playing out between God and man, which is grasped not only as a framework, but also as a performance effected by itself, as a staged event and a new order of time. The embodiment of this confrontation, the making present of the drama of salvation, is expressed in the flagellant journey and in

the communal shedding of one's own blood. Through this procedure, every flagellant not only sets aside his or her everyday social
status and its hierarchical inscriptions, but enters into the egalitarian ritual of reconciliation that plays out between humans and
God.

Spectacle and Song

As can be seen from the chronicles, including those of Hugo of
Reutlingen and Fritsche Closener, the flagellants not only sang
songs while moving through the cities and whipping themselves,
they actually performed a bona fide play. The concept of a play
was already used by the medieval chroniclers, who described the
appearance of the flagellants as "magna spectacula" or "grand theater" absorbing the attention of the people. In the writings of
Henry of Herford, we find a good example of delight in spectacle
and theatrical gestures aiming to affect the observer:

> As they began to sing and as they reached the place where the Pas-
> sion of Christ was being taught, they suddenly threw themselves
> down, whether on clean ground or in dirt, whether in thorns, brush,
> nettles, or on rocky ground. Nor did they bend down to the ground
> or first kneel to it — no, they fell down like pieces of wood, throwing
> themselves onto their stomachs, faces, and outstretched arms, and
> prayed, where they lay stretched out in the shape of a cross. It would
> take a heart of stone not to burst into tears when seeing this. Later,
> after someone gave a sign, they would all stand up again, continuing
> their procession and their songs just as before.[20]

In the chronicle of Matthias of Neuenburg from the year 1349, we
find a similar report that gives us some sense of the effect such
spectacles had on those nearby:

> Shortly after the plague appeared in Germany, men began to whip
> themselves and to move throughout the land. In the middle of June
> 1349, seven hundred of them marched from Swabia to Strassburg.
> They had a leader and two other masters who were obeyed by every-

one. As the first of them crossed the Rhine and the people hurried out to see them, they formed a circle that was quite large. In the middle of the circle they threw their clothing and their shoes, so that they wore only leggings resembling stockings from their hips to their feet. They then threw themselves to the ground in the shape of a cross, one by one while moving in a circle. In so doing, those who stepped over those who had already fallen to the ground would touch them with their whips, whereupon those who had fallen would rise up again and begin to flagellate themselves. They used instruments whose straps were furnished with knots and with sharp iron points. The gestures of the flagellants were accompanied by vernacular songs with multiple verses in which they made implorations to God. In the middle of the circle, three of them stood whipping themselves while pleading loudly and singing, as the others answered.[21]

As we already know from other sources, what followed was a shifting play of processional rounds, genuflections, songs, and communal falls to the ground.

In the ritual of public flagellation, as can be gathered clearly from Fritsche Closener, the songs were a rather striking element, quite impressive to spectators. They were not an independent component of the spectacle, as Closener also makes clear, but must be regarded as part of a genuine liturgy that can be termed a liturgy of flagellation. In Italy, there was usually a basic repertoire of songs having a close typological connection with the stock chants of established brotherhoods, with the tradition of the so-called Lauds, and, above all, with the songs concerning Mary and the saints. In the German-speaking world, a proper repertoire developed, closely linked to church songs. These included songs to be sung during flagellation itself and others to be sung during arrival and departure at any place. The texts of these songs have been recorded in detail by Fritsche Closener and Hugo of Reutlingen and in the chronicles of Magdeburg and Limburg, the *Magdeburger Schöppenchronik* and *Limburger Chronik*. Anton Hübner undertook a painstaking investigation of these songs, which he eventually published in 1931. However, there is no longer general agreement with his judgment that they represent an anonymous repertoire or "people's poetry of the purest variety."[22] The notion of "the people" is as much a projection here as all the Romantic and social revolutionary projections were.

Yet it must be noted that even the medieval chronicles regarded the songs as something altogether new and remarkable. They often emphasized, sometimes with contempt, that the songs (Hugo of Reutlingen even records the melodies for us) were sung in the vernacular and hence marked a vulgarization of liturgical song practices. The texts stood in specific connection with other songs from which they originated and with which they remained in close contact, such as the tradition of processional and pilgrimage songs, but also spiritual formulae of supplication and invocation, as well as songs concerning Mary and the Passion. In many cases, the closest connection is obviously with the Good Friday liturgy and the "Stabat mater." We have seen that the Psalms (especially the "Miserere") had played a central role in individual and private flagellation since Peter Damian. For the flagellant processions, it was instead the commonly chanted songs that gave additional depth and figure to the ritual, together with the accompanying gestures of suffering and the sight of flowing blood — all of which had a strong emotional effect on spectators. Recent scholarship has backed away from the former opinion that the flagellant songs were composed by the hypothetical leaders of the movement, a belief that led one to ascribe a programmatic and revolutionary theological content to them. Just as the flagellant trains had no central leadership or purpose, so, too, the songs were an expression of the sheer multiplicity of this movement and developed from existing forms of song and supplication.

No genuine or unified doctrinal view speaks from the songs, and likewise, the rituals that we are able to reconstruct are by no means unified. Nonetheless, it is always evident that we are dealing here with forms that possessed a certain liturgical-sacramental force, as emphasized further by the fact that the verses were generally recited by a lead singer and repeated by the entire throng. The meaning of the songs thus has less to do with their content (which is often quite conventional) than with their use, or with their intended effect in the public ritual of flagellation.

For at least some of the flagellant trains of 1349, we can reconstruct an authentic flagellant liturgy from the aforementioned German sources. On this basis we can say that during the flagellation ceremony, which consisted of three rounds with the whip, a three-part song was sung. The theme of the first part was the Passion of Christ and its status as a model for the flagellants; the second concerned the wrath of Christ at the world, along with Mary's intercession; and finally the third dealt with the sins of humanity. This song was not a simple accompaniment of the flagellation ritual, but an integral component of it. It begins with an introductory verse that calls one to join in and—just as with the ascesis of the desert saints—pushes the struggle against the devil to the forefront in programmatic fashion. During the first flagellation, the principle of the struggle is defined: penance as a form of imitation of Christ, more specifically as an imitation of the pain suffered on the cross. This theatricalization of penance aims explicitly at an exchange in which the flagellant takes the place assumed by Christ in his suffering for humanity. In flagellation, then, the penitent fuses with the redeemer. The first round ends with the words:

Jesus was nourished with bile,
And thus we fall in the shape of a cross!
Raise your hands to the sky,
Ask God to protect us from the black death!
Raise your hands to the sky,
Ask God to have mercy on us!
Jesus, in the name of Trinity,
Free us from our sins!
Jesus, by the force of your bloody wounds,
Protect us from the sudden death!

According to the chronicle of Fritsche Closener, after the first concluding verse, the throng fell to their knees, remaining silent

143

for a moment on the ground and finally raising their hands toward heaven in a gesture of supplication while singing the last eight lines. This intermezzo was also repeated after the third part of the flagellant liturgy. In the second round, central place was given to the song of Mary, the wrath of Christ, and Mary's intercession. In the third round, the song presented a list of sins, ending with the remark that those people will be saved who devote themselves to true penance and to the imitation of Christ. What is crucial here are motifs taken from the evangelical crucifixion scenes, such as the crying, the pain, the wailing, and the quaking of the earth.

As we already know, the flagellation ritual was embedded in a processional pattern, which according to Closener began and ended in a circle, with everyone successively kneeling and then rising. Songs were sung both before and after the flagellation, as the throng of flagellants moved in double columns or stood before the cross. What is still preserved from all of this are an entry song, two songs of Mary, and a handful of fragments. The entry song characterizes the framework of the flagellant journey as a "journey of supplication" whose programmatic basis is the entry of Jesus into Jerusalem. This introduces the motifs of the cross, the flowing of blood, penance, and supplication for the assistance of Christ, linked with prayers of supplication to Mary. The concluding lines repeat the central concept of supplication that was linked with the penance. As Hugo of Reutlingen reports, after the performance of the flagellant ritual, the entry song was first repeated, after which the flagellants gathered before the cross and fell on their knees while singing a song of Mary. In general, Mary assumed a central position in the flagellant liturgy as the helper of humanity and the mediator between sinners and God, flesh and word. She appears here in her function as the "pure maid ... full of grace," as the intercessor who intervenes for the salvation of human souls and leads them back to God.

After the recitation of the song of Mary, the lead singer turned and made a call of supplication to Mary ("Ave Maria, sweet mother Mary, have mercy on poor, wretched Christendom"), which the others repeated. He then said simply "Ave Maria," whereupon they threw themselves to the ground in the shape of a cross. Finally, there followed another call to Mary, with everyone rising up and saying "Consoler of our sins, have mercy on all mortal sinners, both men and women!" The speaker repeated his call to Mary, after which they threw themselves in a cross shape to the ground once more. They spoke as follows: "Ave Maria, rose of the kingdom of heaven, have mercy on us and all believing souls and all things in holy Christendom." Finally the leader ended the ritual with the words: "Dear brothers, ask of God that we accomplish our sufferings and our pilgrimage in such a way that God protects us from the fires of hell, that the souls of the poor believers should be released from their suffering, and that we and all sinners earn the grace of God, and that in grace he stands at the side of all well-meaning people. Amen."[23] In closing, the flagellants all moved again in double columns away from the site of the ritual, perhaps repeating the entry song, but certainly singing some song or other.

An additional aspect of this dramatic performance should be mentioned here. The Strassburg chronicler writes that "those who had the most beautiful voices began the song, and the others followed — just as happens in a dance." The reference to dance is not irrelevant, but touches on an aspect of the flagellant procession that has previously attracted scant notice. The very heart of the whole event, from the moment of lying down in a circle to the moment in the sermon when everyone stands up again, can to a large degree be understood as a dance. A connection may perhaps be drawn with the "dance epidemics" of the Middle Ages, barely understood even today. But it will still be necessary to distinguish between the highly ritualized behavior of the flagellants and the apparently disorganized and ecstatic action of "dancers." For the most part, contemporaries viewed the "dancers" simply as possessed, while the reaction of the public and the church to the flagellant movements allows us to recognize that from the start, they were viewed as a phenomenon in which theatrical forms served to link a specific theological understanding of visualizing memory with the message of the Gospel.[24] If the flagellation ritual is thereby in some respects similar to dance, we think above all of the spiritualization of dance found in Mechthild of Magdeburg, which (following motifs from the Song of Songs) embodies a drama of love — an intersection of suffering, consolation, and joy.

Secret Apocalyptic Cults

We have seen that the praxis of the flagellants aimed not only at penance, but also at reconciliation and at the evocation of eschatological awaiting. Through flagellation, time was brought to an end, since the event and its emotional content link salvation and sacrifice to the Last Judgment. It is difficult to reconstruct whether Joachimite ideas of apocalypse played any formative role for the Italian flagellants. In any case, the chronicle of Salimbene of Parma already had noted the connection between flagellation and the awaiting of the Apocalypse in the earlier movement of 1260. Salimbene remarks that the torment of the whip should be grasped as a passage into the age of "the eternal gospel" — the "evangelium aeternum." [25] In this spirit, according to Salimbene, the first flagellants called out. "we are the voices of God, not of men" (Acts 12,22).

Yet this eschatological horizon, in which the Apocalypse was viewed as imminent, was perhaps not quite as significant in the Italian movements of either the thirteenth or fourteenth centuries. At least initially, it was typical only of the so-called Crypto-flagellants, who appeared in Thuringia in the late Middle Ages. Nonetheless, the significance of eschatological motifs should not be underestimated for the other flagellant movements. Either they were influenced by such motifs or their opponents linked them with the appearance of the Antichrist. A prophetic message handed down to us by the Annalista Saxo (Abbot Arnold of Berge and Nienburg) contains a prediction linked with the appearance of the flagellants that openly ascribed an apocalyptic significance to them. In a Dutch source of the fifteenth century, it runs as follows: "It is said that a long time ago a prophet already predicted the coming of these people: 'A people without a head will appear and whip themselves for their sins.'"[26] Headlessness was generally interpreted as referring to the cowls worn by the flagellants so that their heads could not be seen. In light of this prophecy, the flagellants were identified by many contemporaries (especially in the various antiflagellant polemics) as forerunners of the Antichrist and heralds of the approaching end of the world. Portions of the flagellant movement did view themselves in this way, even in the absence of an explicitly Joachimite context, both in the first wave of 1260 and the second wave of 1348. Nonetheless, the eschatological motif might have been less a program than a diffuse background and a mentality — one whose content is hard to reconstruct, but that left a deep imprint on the spirit of the participants.

Far more radical and explicit were the views of the so-called Cryptoflagellants, a sect especially widespread in Thuringia. Following various late medieval bans on flagellant processions by the ecclesiastical and temporal authorities, the members of this sect whipped themselves secretly in small groups. Their name was coined by Ernst G. Förstemann in his book on Christian flagellant movements, *Die christlichen Geißlergesellschaften* (The Christian flagellation societies), in 1828. Most interesting here is the fact that these groups of flagellants acted in secret until being discovered by the Inquisition. From the documents preserved by the Inquisition, it may be presumed that there were individual groups and sects that practiced flagellation either in connection with the flagellant movement or in distant relation with it. This entailed a concrete rejection of the church's monopoly on mediating salvation. Instead of ecclesiastical hierarchy, what is central here (just as with certain theologians and heretics of early Christianity) was the pneumatic community, the congregation of ascetic-enthusiastic saints.

The roots and sources of such heresy lie in distant history, even if it is less a genealogical relation than a typological one. Above all, there are the so-called "agnostici" or Circumcellions of the fourth century, a late Roman movement of wandering, mendicant, social revolutionary ascetics. According to Augustine, their members often chose to die as martyrs in a sort of radical ascetic gesture. It is also possible (the ecclesiastical documents paint in this direction) that they formed a model for the perception and assessment of numerous late medieval heretic groups, especially groups of radical flagellants.

One of these groups was discovered in Nordhausen in 1369 by the Dominican Walter Kerlinger, who was active as papal inquisitor in Erfurt beginning in 1364. He had already made a name for himself through the condemnation of the Beghard preacher Hartmann of Erfurt, who was burned at the stake in 1367, as well as the banishment of two hundred Beguines. Here we can speak of a genuine wave of persecutions that had their genesis in a specific image of heretics. During these persecutions, the flagellants, too, were "discovered," persecuted, and finally condemned.

The leader of the Thuringia flagellants (our main interest for the moment) was Konrad Schmid, who openly declared himself a prophet and predicted that the world would be destroyed in the year 1369. It is unclear whether he was executed like the aforementioned Hartmann, though later flagellant movements sometimes seem to have associated the two. Perhaps Schmid died of natural causes, as might be surmised from a document of the Cryptoflagellants unmasked in Sangerhausen in 1414.

We find information on the Cryptoflagellants in numerous documents: the *Prophetica* of Karl Schmid, a document of the Inquisition about the Nordhausen case of 1369, one concerning Sangerhausen in the Halberstadt Diocese in 1414, another about the Sondershausen persecution, and still another on the Nordhausen Inquisition of 1446.[27] In Sangerhausen on January 15, 1414, with the Erfurt theologian Heinrich Schönfeld presiding, thirty-four men and women were brought before the inquisitor. Thirty-one of them recanted, while three did not and were burned. History has preserved the protocol of their interrogation.[28] On March 21, another fifty people were examined, of whose fate we hear nothing more. When we speak of the Cryptoflagellants, it may be presumed that we are speaking of a considerable number of people. Yet it remains unclear how homogeneous the movement was and whether it was related to further persecutions of heretics, such as in Mulhouse in 1420. There are indications that the Cryptoflagellants or a similar group was revived around 1446 in Toba, near Sangerhausen. In the same year, they surfaced in Nordhausen through an investigation by the inquisitor Friedrich Müller, and in 1454, they were subject to renewed persecutions in a number of places.

From documents of the Nordhausen Inquisition of 1446, where five men and eight women were arrested and interrogated, we are able to gather the following information from the words of the Inquisition. Supposedly the subjects of the investigation whipped themselves on Good Friday and on Fridays more generally; they believed that only through flagellation would all sins be forgiven; that with the emergence of the flagellant processions, baptism by blood had replaced the customary kind; and that all sacraments of the church had been abolished and replaced by the sole ritual of flagellation. Moreover, the protocols of the Inquisition are always histories of temptation, as well, in which the practice of flagellation stands for a conspiratorial attitude that would also be expressed in the person's opinions. Förstemann gives us the following paraphrase from the protocol:

Gertrud Becke confessed that ever since one particular Friday at age fourteen she had whipped herself every day. Her husband had said that the flesh and blood was not the host that was raised up during the Mass, but the hand of the priest that raised it. Her mother had taught her to believe in flagellation instead of all the sacraments, then Heinrich Rebening had taught her this as well. This man seduces the people to such heresy and instructs them in it. For this, he receives gifts and is held in great esteem. On the second day of Easter of this year, Becke, her husband, and Hemelstoß mutually whipped one another because they had apparently gone to Communion like other people. They had heard from their grandmother that the church service of the clerics was idolatrous and sheer insanity. Christian Weyner explained that from childhood onward he had whipped himself as directed by his parents. He had spoken about flagellation with Johann Trockenbach, and both agreed that sins could be repented in this manner alone.

We also encounter short life histories of Schwenhild Hemelstoß, Konrad Stockhausen, Katherina Dymerod, Mechthild Volker, Heinrich Schelle, Nikolaus Billeben, Dietrich Herzey, Osanna and Johann Trockenbach, Berthold Becke, Heinemann Curdes, Christina Berge, Albrecht Froß, Kunna Weyner, and Ayla Weyner and her husband Christian Weyner. Their names give us an indication of a network of people for whom flagellation played an important role as the core of a temptation to heresy. For members of the sect, flagellation was openly regarded as a liberation from an errant sacramental praxis of the church. Only through flagellation, they believed, can we restore the immediate relationship to God, which was lost by the church. These findings are confirmed through the report that the interrogated parties often believed that thanks to flagellation, they would return immediately to God after their deaths.[29]

A Magdeburg chronicler describes the Thuringia flagellant group as made up of "diehard" heretics,[30] yet this is a stereotypical judgment that tells us nothing about this particular situation. This is always the case with medieval proceedings in which specific groups are identified as heretics. From the persecution of the Sondershausen heretics, we have a collection of twenty-five articles that document the heretical views expressed in interrogation. They give us a certain degree of information, even if only from the standpoint of the interrogator.[31] In the course of this wave of persecutions, which encompassed a number of other cities and regions in Thuringia, hundreds of people were questioned, condemned, and finally some of them were delivered to the temporal authorities and burned at the stake. The last cases of this kind stem from the 1480s, and the name of Konrad Schmid, prophet of the Cryptoflagellants, remained infamous. He was even familiar to Martin Luther, who used him as an example of the "most horrifying" heresy.

Despite the large scope of the movement suggested by the sources, we know little as to the actual views of those concerned. If the whole flagellant movement was strongly influenced from the beginning by the involvement of laymen, in the person of

Konrad Schmid, we find a remarkable lay prophet. He and his message were central for at least some of the Thuringia Crypto-flagellants, a sect in which flagellation became the single most important ritual. This meant not only that flagellation should be grasped as a radical form of penance, but that "this bodily torment [should produce] a new faith." In this sense, flagellation should be "understood as a new baptism ... in which the flagellant makes himself a Christian anew by means of the blood struck from his body." This means that in this eschatological transfiguration of the present, the sacrament of baptism is replaced by the act of self-flagellation, which holds good as a new and conclusive baptism of the chosen. For Konrad Schmid, the understanding of flagellation as a penitential praxis embedded in the tradition of the flagellant processions (one thinks here of the *Letter from Heaven*) played an important role from the outset.

A sense of apocalyptic expectation can immediately be gleaned from the *Prophetica* — a text that survived in a late medieval manuscript in Middle High German with a Latin gloss. "This is the prophesying that Konrad Schmid has spoken, and with which he deceived the world." Thus begins the document, which is impossible to separate from the inquisitorial suggestion and interrogation of "true" Cryptoflagellant convictions. The prophesying is notable for its immediate expectation of the end of the world and the Last Judgment. This entails a duty to keep the torment of Christ more firmly in mind than ever before and also to end our submission to temporal authority. The prophet says: "You should serve only those who have no master above them." This means that humans should submit themselves directly to the angel called Trona, their advocate at the Last Judgment. As the gloss remarks, at that point, the tenth choir of angels — the choir of the angels that have fallen into hell with Lucifer — will be reconstituted by the men and women who are saved. Thus, the flagellants form a group of angelic humans who will replace the lost choir of angels and establish the original cosmic harmony. They are the saved ones who save the world in turn, as long as they remain active and oppose their own new sacramental practice to the deception of humankind by the clergy.

The absolute certainty of being chosen finds its clearest expression in Schmid's appeal to his disciples not to be led astray from the path. In this way, the Cryptoflagellant movement was related to older flagellant movements and equated with the relation between John the Baptist and Jesus Christ. What was evident in all earlier forms of voluntary flagellation should now be fulfilled in the renewed movement in view of a radicalized awaiting of the Apocalypse. Consequently, great emphasis was placed upon the identification of the Cryptoflagellants with Christ and the apostles.

Konrad Schmid saw himself as a kind of "new Kaiser Friedrich" whose coming had been foretold by previous prophets and who had now become the head of Christendom with a view to the approaching end of times. The only ones to be saved would be those who "move their arms, and thus regain their purity," hence those who flagellate themselves. In this gesture, we are to find absolution, a true honoring of God that at the same time liberates us from our sins. With their interpretation of the miracle performed by Jesus at the wedding in Cana, the flagellants demonstrated that "authentic baptism consists in the flowing of blood, just as Christ turned water into wine." To legitimize their position, they also referred to the story of Jesus throwing the moneychangers out of the Temple. According to the interrogation protocol, they believed that the same thing needed to be done in the church at the present day. Moreover, citing many passages from Holy Scripture, they argued for the necessity of flagellation, especially by referring to episodes from the life of David, whom they regarded as a prophet of flagellant praxis. An important part of the mentality of Schmid and his movement was that he often referred to the Book of Revelation and to the gathering persecution that the flagellants would eventually overcome.

What is characteristic for the flagellants here, as was already the case for Peter Damian, is the relation to David and to a specific understanding of the Penitential Psalms. But apparently far more important for Konrad Schmid and his followers was the connection between an immediate expectation of the Apocalypse and the concept of a new baptism in the blood of the flagellant.

This radicalization of the meaning of ritual is what first constituted their group consciousness and made them feel certain of being chosen, as can be gathered from the sources. Flagellation is not just penance, but the performance that turns the flagellants, both male and female, into angelic creatures who already enter the heavenly hierarchy, even while still on earth.

Above all, the rejection of any ecclesiastical-sacramental means of salvation and the replacement of all other liturgical rituals with the single sacrament of flagellation is found in the protocols of Sangerhausen and Sonderhausen. Once again, what is produced here is a relation to the genealogy of the flagellants, to the *Letter from Heaven* and the anchoring of the movement in a divine message that was once given to humans directly and now awaits fulfillment. This message strips the pope and all church institutions of their authority. This is why the interrogated parties emphasized (or rather, the interrogators heard them say such things after suggesting them within the framework of their questions) that the mediation of grace and the institutions of salvation of the church were all "merely fabricated," that the church could be cleared away, just as Jesus cleared out the Temple, and that a man could be freed of his sins only "though the spontaneous flagellation of his body performed in inner repentance." In the Sonderhausen protocol, we also read that "baptism by water [should be] abolished and replaced with baptism by blood," which would be the only means of freeing humans from their sins. This was supposedly the true meaning of the miracle at Cana, where Christ changed water into wine. They said that "a drop of blood that stems from flagellation is far more welcome to God than all baptism by water. And in exactly the same way, a drop of blood is worth more than the extreme unction, which was regarded as shameful." They believed, the protocol remarks, "that after death, those who make their own blood flow with the whip will go directly to heaven."

Like other medieval and early modern heretics who were interrogated according to similar structures of questioning, the flagellants supposedly challenged not only the validity of the sacraments, but also transubstantiation, confession, purgatory, icons, and the swearing of oaths. Moreover, a second manuscript containing the articles of the Sonderhausen investigation of 1454 stresses that these groups met in cellars, where sisters had sexual intercourse with brothers, fathers with daughters, and mothers with sons.[32] This corresponds with other reports (which also hark back to the stock figures of heresy from late antiquity) in which it was regularly insinuated that medieval heretics did things such as gathering in secret, praying to the devil, and finally extinguishing the lights so that everyone might have sex randomly with everyone else, every man enjoying without limit his mother, sister, or daughter.

Here it is no longer a matter of some sort of diffuse apocalyptic angst, but of a specifically prophetic gesture that obviously stood in the center of the movement and that was meant to replace ecclesiastical authority. Schmid's position, although lacking in any social revolutionary program, can also be described as free-spirited and revolutionary. It seems that he radically denied spiritual and temporal authority, saw himself as the head of the Christians, and taught that self-flagellation was the sole means of salvation. In the Sangerhausen document, too, we read of the flagellant belief that only self-flagellators could attain salvation. The Roman Church was thereby declared to be utterly worthless. It was identified with the Antichrist, who had reigned for a long time and who, since the appearance of the prophet Konrad Schmid, was opposed only by the true spiritual church of the flagellants. The Sangerhausen text identifies Schmid as "Henoch" and a second prophet as "Helias." Occasional attempts have been made to identify the second prophet as the Beghard preacher Hartmann, burned at the stake in Erfurt in the late fourteenth century, but this has not been historically verified.

Given the meager availability of sources, all of them tinged by the views of the inquisitor (and I have sought to assemble them in a unified picture despite their highly fragmentary character), it is impossible to speak of an authentic movement whose outlines might be adequately sketched. All that can be identified, if we believe the ecclesiastical protocols, are simply gestures and elements of alternative theological practices that undermined the legitimacy of the church, placed it explicitly in question, and created their own ritual around the new sacrament of flagellation. The church reacted to this provocation not only by persecuting flagellants, but also by delivering many of them to the temporal authorities to be burned at the stake.

Theological Critique

But it was not only the Cryptoflagellants who were a thorn in the flesh of the church. Other groups who occasionally or frequently used the whip as an instrument of penance were criticized and persecuted. This began with the first appearance of the flagellants in the thirteenth and fourteenth centuries,[33] yet the denunciations grew increasingly stronger. An important treatise against flagellation dated June 18, 1417, was composed by Jean Gerson, chancellor of the University of Paris. One might initially be inclined to suppose that this treatise was meant to oppose tendencies that always had been visible in the flagellant movement (or at least had been *ascribed* to it, as with the Cryptoflagellants) since the thirteenth century — especially north of the Alps. Unlike in Italy, where the flagellant movement as a penitential movement was always under the strong influence and strict control of clerics and monks (above all those of the mendicant orders), observers north of the Alps often noticed a strongly anticlerical tone. Aegidius li Muisit speaks repeatedly of the discontented masses, describing them as acting with a rebellious tone ("cum magno murmure").[34] From early on, the flagellant movement in the North (even in contemporary eyes) was also a forum for the emancipation of laymen as many flagellants assumed the rights of lay preachers and lay confessors.

"Day laborers, millers, and butchers proclaimed the Gospel, secretly conspiring against the clergy. The shoemaker is the confessor and imposes penance. The weaver and the smith both preach and conduct the mass." This report comes from an Austrian chronicle from the very first wave of the flagellant movement in 1260.[35] There is also a Breslau manuscript that closely links the flagellant views with heretical concepts and anticlerical polemics, though it was written only in the fifteenth century and therefore reflects the moralizing perspective of the author far more than that of the flagellants or their contemporaries. According to this source, "the flagellants asserted that they could entirely free themselves from purgatory. Everyone who would take part in flagellant processions for thirty-three and a half days would thereby free himself and seven other souls from the punishment of purgatory. Those who were completely mad even asserted that they could also save other souls from the fires of hell, and even empty hell of everyone but Judas, Pilate, and Herod." In their sermons, the flagellants did three things especially: "They slandered the lifestyle of all priests and even of many monks and nuns. To this end they mocked the mystery of the Mass and the sacrament of honoring the body and blood of Christ in the most disgraceful way."[36]

As a rule, such assertions always draw on the stereotypical stock descriptions of heretical movements in the Middle Ages. Whatever they might tell us, neither for the first nor the second wave of the flagellant movement is it possible to speak in general terms of a genuine social uprising, a class struggle, or an early bourgeois and deeply anticlerical or anarchist movement, to use terms sometimes found in the literature. This remains true even though certain flagellants or groups of flagellants may have had traffic with such elements, ultimately provoking a harsh response by the spiritual and temporal authorities. During the second flagellant movement, as may be seen from the chronicle of Aegidius li Muisit, the authorities sought to implement a greater number of violent prohibitions than had been the case in 1260. The intervention of Charles IV and Philip VI of France and the critique of the theologian Johannes Du Fayt of the University of Paris finally inspired Pope Clemens VI to take a stand against the flagellants and forbid public processions, as announced in the papal bull *Inter sollicitudines* of October 20, 1349. However, the pope also made it clear in this bull that it was not a matter of banning flagellation as such. He made an explicit exception for self-flagellation "if it be practiced, whether under instructions or spontaneously, at home or elsewhere, and if with right intention and honorable devotion — but simply not in connection with the just mentioned superstitious groups, associations, and movements." The "groups, associations, and movements" that were condemned and to which the pope refers were subject to an "everlasting ban," and both clerics and laymen were threatened with prosecution and jail for participating in them. The pope speaks in this connection of a group of people who "in Germany and its vicinity," inspired by the devil, had invented "a new, hollow, and superstitious religion." This religion had seduced a great number of people "against all reason" to follow false rules of life and "to do things that are entirely foreign to life, customs, and faith." At the same time, he used this bull to blame flagellants for the horrific pogroms against Jews, as often occurred during times of plague.[37] Even if this accusation cannot be established historically, in view of the likely fanaticism of the movement (to judge from the explosive speed with which it spread), it must be assumed that such attacks against Jews did indeed occur. Yet it is also not possible to see the flagellants as the sole parties responsible for the anti-Jewish pogroms, as the papal document suggests.

The papal ban, then, was explicitly *not* aimed at the individual practice of ascetic flagellation, but only tried to establish social control over the flagellant processions, with their rebellious tone. It was published only north of the Alps, where individual bishops, cities, and secular authorities had already enforced draconian measures. In places such as Lübeck and Erfurt, the city gates were closed to the flagellant processions. As for the papal intervention, one has the impression of a policelike action initiated at the request of the temporal authorities, who had lost the ability to control this mass movement. The arguments brought against the flagellants all belong to the stock repertoire of traditional complaints against all heretics.

Despite the draconian measures (especially in the fifteenth century), which included numerous executions, the flagellants never entirely disappeared in the late Middle Ages. In 1353 and 1357, there had been renewed proceedings against the flagellant groups by the provincial synod of Cologne. There was renewed talk of flagellants in Utrecht in 1355. Around 1400, yet another wave of flagellant processions appeared in the Netherlands and along the Rhine. In northern Italy, Spain, and southern France, there was also great enthusiasm for flagellation, often stimulated by passionate preachers, which was sometimes revived and would occasionally achieve the dimensions of a mass movement. One reaction to this phenomenon is found in the text written by Gerson referred to a bit earlier. In June 1417, together with Peter of Ailly, he beseeched the Dominican penitential preacher Vincent Ferrer to bring a halt to flagellation.

Ferrer was a native of Valencia, in Spain, and was eventually canonized in 1458. Moved by a miraculous cure and strengthened by a vision in which Saint Francis and Saint Dominic appeared to him (in 1398), he began to travel as a penitential preacher throughout central Europe — especially through France, western Switzerland, and northern Italy. Enthusiastic flagellant groups openly attached themselves to this charismatic preacher, groups that were a thorn in Gerson's side. In a letter to Ferrer, Gerson wrote that he "greatly [esteems] your sermons, but must also mention those sects of the ones who beat themselves, who in the past were often banned in many places." Certainly, Gerson continues, Ferrer must not approve of the behavior of these people, yet he does not sufficiently "distance himself" from them.[38]

Gerson argues by using the same passages that were cited by the defenders of self-flagellation. He refers to Paul, who was regarded by the flagellants as the advocate of a strict discipline of the flesh, yet he quotes him as using the following words: "for the weapons of our warfare are not those of the flesh" (2 Corinthians 10.4). Accordingly, the Christian sermon uses words, not the public chastisement of flesh as practiced by the flagellants surrounding Ferrer. Gerson insists on this point, thereby anticipating Protestant critics of flagellation, as well as Jacques Boileau's polemic against the practice.

Shortly thereafter, in his treatise *Contra sectam flagellantium* of July 18, 1417,[39] Gerson stressed with satisfaction that Ferrer had politely bowed to the decision of the Council of Konstanz, in a letter considering the question, that once again banned public self-flagellation (as opposed to private flagellation).[40] In this text, Gerson's argument is more detailed, making clear that he is rejecting flagellation not as a penitential practice, but as a quasi-sacramental practice — one that did in fact count as a new sacrament in the eyes of many flagellants. Gerson realized that this was the claim made by portions of the flagellant movement and that it was precisely *public* flagellation, with its quasi-liturgical context, that appeared as a sacramental action. For this reason, he writes that the "law of Christ is love," and according to Gerson, the established number of sacraments corresponds to this simplicity. Even in the law of the old covenant, self-mutilation was already forbidden for precisely this reason and was linked with superstition or idolatry. In this sense, Christ's sacrifice for us should be seen as a one-time act through which we are justified and saved. The flow of blood stems from the mercifulness of God and is made present in the sacraments that arise from the new covenant, which leave no room for flagellation. Whatever goes beyond these sacraments, especially when they go beyond the sacrament of confession, should in Gerson's view be rejected. "Many flagellants," he continues, "do not concern themselves with the sacrament of confession and with sacramental penance, but assert instead that flagellation is a stronger means of purification of sin than all confession." They compare themselves to the martyrs, and from this they gain an inappropriate justification for their actions. Gerson especially opposes the notion of the clerics whipping themselves, as well as the fact that blood flows during flagellation. He thereby aims to destroy the egalitarian relationship produced between laymen and clerics through flagellation and to prevent any equating of the blood that flows with that of Christ and the martyrs, as the flagellants implicitly or explicitly claimed.

Both lines of argument attempt to unmask what the church regarded as the pseudosacramental character of flagellation and to strip it of all legitimacy. To this end, Gerson tallies up all the evidence that speaks against it. Each paragraph of his treatise begins with the phrase "Lex Christi." Against the flagellants, this "grisly and bloodthirsty sect," he opposes the commandment of love and mercy and also the authority of the church, which has always opposed such movements. Nothing is legitimate unless it can be derived from the law of love, rather than from the radical spiritual materialism that the flagellants tacitly were defending. With respect to flagellation, Gerson, too, (like the critics of Damian in the eleventh century) speaks of *novitates* or "innovations," of a new practice established in the Middle Ages and mostly successful only in the context of heretical rebellion. He also makes insinuations about the "secret love affairs, the adultery, and the whoring" that was ascribed to all heretical movements and fringe groups since the Middle Ages.

Despite such stereotypical invective, Gerson's case before the Council of Konstanz is motivated not only by antiheretical zeal, but by his concern for those who mutilate themselves in opposition to the command of Christ. This is a form of idolatry that in his opinion makes the Christians equivalent to those who "in India . . . baptize themselves with fire." Only at the outset does Gerson speak of the apocalyptic attitude that in his view forms the basis for the self-concept of the flagellant movement and their spiritual lifestyle and that for him is so reminiscent of the practices of "Indian" ascetics. He decisively rejects the "new" and "fantastic" tales and miracles relating to the flagellants. As in the case of the sacraments, where Gerson insists on preserving the hierarchical and sacramental position of the clergy and firmly linking the means of salvation to established ritual forms, the authority of the church is established once more in connection with the expectation of the Apocalypse.

While making criticisms on this point, Gerson keenly perceived that it was not only the radical and openly anticlerical flagellants who posed a danger to the church. Neither was it a question, as is sometimes supposed, of some resurfaced archaic and superstitious movement reminiscent of the mystery cults. By practicing a new public ritual that claimed to be both a fundamental gesture of penance and also the most intimate imitation of Christ, all flagellants were actually subversive — even those who did not openly oppose the church. They were subversive by establishing what amounted to a de facto new penitential liturgy and a new sacrament, one that went so far as to produce a direct relation between the suffering of Christ, one's own body, and the Last Judgment. Even if numerous documents attest that the flagellant movements often took care to remain loyal to the church and encouraged their members to partake of confession and penance, their implicit effect was a genuine transformation of thought about penance in the Late Middle Ages.

It was perhaps as a direct result of the dispute about the Cryptoflagellants (for whom the transformation of the concept of penance and the Last Judgment were the very core of their program) that two small treatises were written against the flagellants by Johannes Hagen, a Carthusian monk of Erfurt. In one of these treatises, which dates from 1468, he laid out the argument that the law of Christ is not flagellation, but mercifulness, and that if flagellation were carried out as a private penitential exercise, it could in no case be allowed to make blood flow. The meaning of Christ's evangelical message is not the "Judgment," he wrote, but "mercifulness" and consolation, "for ye that labor and are heavy laden." Hence, Christ does not command his believers to flagellation, but to do good works.

Behind this line of argument, which owes a great deal to simple Christian common sense, there is concealed an objection to the central node of the flagellant ritual: the anticipation of the Last Judgment and the new baptism in one's own blood. Here Johannes Hagen detects idolatry, as well as a moment of self-justification that essentially undermines the meaning of the sacraments and delivers the means of salvation entirely to the whip and to the arousing ritual of flagellation. Hence, his critique is aimed at arousal through the image and against the gesture of self-absolution. Both accusations had been leveled against the flagellants from an early date, and both would return to the fore in the sixteenth and seventeenth centuries in the Protestant and Catholic critiques of flagellation alike.

The Theater of the Battuti

During the Late Middle Ages, the flagellants were often banned, but this signified neither the end of the flagellant movement nor the end of individual flagellation. Just as the practice had survived the ebbing of the first wave of the movement in 1261, it did so during the following waves, as well. When public flagellation was forbidden, as at Ferrara in about 1269, the flagellants withdrew into private orders, founded communities, and continued to whip themselves. In general, the Italian flagellant movement in Italy (unlike north of the Alps) was a genuinely urban early modern phenomenon, with all the expected urban forms of organization. In Italy, penance as an urban practice took a form that went hand in hand with new lifestyles and that included self-flagellation until at least the eighteenth century. Numerous brotherhoods of so-called "battuti," "disciplinati," "scopatori," "verberatori," or "bianchi" — as the flagellants were called in Italy, due to their white garments — formed in the late Middle Ages. They continued to practice flagellation with the tolerance and even encouragement of the church.

Through the formation of such flagellant associations, as with the Congregatio devotorum Beatae Virginis in Bologna, a preexistent community of religious penitents often developed into a community of battuti or disciplinati — in other words, flagellants. The Bologna group, which we have already encountered as the sponsor of a life of Raniero Fasani from the fourteenth century, regarded him as the founder of their rules. This is mostly the stuff of legend, yet the legend is not just some sort of baseless founding fiction. If penitential communities were initially formed in Perugia that were devoted to flagellation, communities that perhaps began at Fasani's own initiative, this soon happened in other Italian cities, as well. In the wake of this emergence of sedentary forms of the flagellant movement, other traditional penitential practices became just as important as whipping, including charity work, prayer, and spiritual song. In Bologna, we can follow the rapid growth of such a "compagnia di battuti" beginning in 1261.[41] While the members first had informal meetings in the Church of the Eremitani, by 1262, they seem to have already had their own headquarters and statutes. To this was added a hospice for the sick, and ultimately — as with many other flagellant communities — an actual hospital. In this way the battuti were established as a society in the city, and achieved a status altogether embedded in the ecclesiastical and worldly structure of society. It was no peripheral movement, but an important political and cultural force in the community. In the ritual of flagellation, the community possessed the form in which its origin and its unity were newly confirmed in both the religious and worldly spheres. To an increasing degree, women were accepted into the societies, even if mostly as associates of their husbands. Yet it seems that they never took part in public flagellation processions.

A similar urban integration of flagellant practices can be traced in the history of countless communities of "battuti" or "disciplinati" in numerous Italian cities. Bologna is used here as just one example among many. As can be seen from the statutes of the Bolognese community, it is no longer flagellation as such that stands in the spotlight, but communal penance, pious communal belief, and communal feast days. The members of the community were obliged to follow an orthodox ethical life consistent with church doctrine and thus were not allowed to pass their time in "taverns or in other, more shameful places." They went to confession, commissioned Masses, cared for sick brothers, and if necessary would pay the cost of proper burial for each other. Moreover, the community had a genuine peacemaking and peacekeeping function within the city, and most of their surviving statutes gave especial emphasis to this aspect, along with that of "brotherliness."

Moreover, the members sometimes whipped themselves within their community and sometimes also arranged flagellant processions through the city: "We thus order that all members should gather at the community headquarters every Sunday and on all feast days of the Blessed Mary and all apostles. There, they should put on their penitential garments. Thereafter, they should move through the city, visiting the larger churches of each neighborhood.

As they go through the city, they will flagellate themselves in honor of our sweet Christ, who let himself be flogged and killed for our sins."[42] Private flagellation was depicted in the following manner:

> All lights were extinguished except for one candle on the altar and another near the leader of the community. After everyone had thrown themselves to the floor, the leader began to recite the Sixty-Seventh Psalm, "Deus misereatur nostri et benedicat nobis [God be gracious to us and bless us, Psalms 67.1]" in solemn and humble fashion. He would chant the individual verses, which were then repeated by the others in the choir. In the meantime, they passed out the scourges or thongs that lay ready on both sides of the altar. Following additional songs and the recitation of the so-called "Remembrance of the Passion of Christ" — a part of the second chapter of Paul's letter to the Philippians — the leader then said: "Servite Domino in timore, et exultate ei con tremore [Worship the Lord with reverence, and rejoice with trembling, Psalms 2.11]." Thereafter he commanded "Apprehendite disciplinam [Pick up the whip]," and hardly had he said the words before the brothers would begin to flagellate themselves while they answered with a "Miserere nobis [Have mercy on us]" the supplications that the leader directed to Christ.[43]

During their flagellations and their processions through the city, most of the flagellants wore cowls and coats with crosses, as already known to us from the earlier flagellant processions of the thirteenth century and as still used even today during Holy Week in Spain (Semana santa, figures 3.15 and 3.16). These insignia, together with the ritual of flagellation that took place sometimes while walking on the streets, sometimes in public squares, and sometimes in the private rooms of the brotherhood, contributed to the theatrical radiance of the flagellant brotherhoods in early modern times.

Even in the processions of the brotherhoods, flagellation as an imitation of the Passion aimed less at representation than at a spe-

Figure 3.15. Holy Week (Francisco de Goya, *Semana Santa en tiempo pasado en España*, 1824–25, Ottawa, National Gallery of Canada).

Figure 3.16. Flagellant procession (Francisco de Goya, c. 1816, Madrid, Royal Academy).

cific form of mimesis (as we will see in the Counter-Reformation's defense of such processions), one already encountered in medieval ascetic practice and that here affects both actors and spectators equally. The radiance of the dramas staged in this way is quite ambiguous in its arousal of fantasy, as is confirmed by Marcel Proust, who in *Sodom et Gomorrah* mentions the "shameless spectacle" that is called "the Passion" and is displayed during Holy Week ("ces indécents spectacles qu'on appelle *la Passion*"). The reason I speak of ambiguity here is because Proust, as we will see, was still fascinated in *Le temps retrouvé* (Finding time again) by the spectacle of flagellation and by no means condemns the blows of the whip. Instead, he turns them into a counterimage of the experience of intensity that stands at the beginning of *A la recherche du temps perdu* (In search of lost time).

In a few communities of southern Italy — such as Guardia Sanframondi, Nocera Terinese, and Verbicaro — a comparable ritual endures to this day. Nocera Terinese in Calabria is a good example of the liturgical theatricalization of a small city during Lent and Eastertide. A dense structure of liturgical practices, processions, and popular customs is thereby extended across everyday life. The finale consists in an Easter Sunday procession and the appearance of the *vattienti* or *vattenti*, as the flagellants are known in this place. They are not actually part of the procession itself, which moves with an image of the Pietà through the streets, but form a second and complementary pole of the event. The flagellant first prepares himself privately for public flagellation by wounding himself on the legs, especially the calves, to the point that the blood begins to flow. In public, wearing a shirt and short pants, he is accompanied by a young man — an *ecce homo* figure wearing a crown of thorns — who evokes the exemplarity of Christ and defines flagellation as a specific mimetic practice. A second young man, who carries a bucket of wine, pours it on the wounds of the *vattente* from time to time in order to wash away the blood and to prevent clotting. In this way, three people move through the streets, often first passing the house of a friend, where the flagellant whips himself before the door. Only after this do the flagellants meet in various parts of the city with the processional train, kneel before the Pietà, and strike their calves until they bleed. Thereafter the *vattente* kisses the Pietà and moves away along with his two comrades. He often passes by additional places, moving to individual churches or specific places in the city where he flogs himself further. Along the way, the wounds are regularly washed with wine and kept open so that the blood flows and leaves behind traces at each place visited. At the conclusion of all this, the flagellants wash themselves with a rosemary fluid that acts as an antiseptic, don festive clothing, and return to the public procession.[44]

Such forms of individual flagellation are only loosely connected with public processions and should be seen more as signs of personal devotion and ascetic performance. By contrast, flagellation within the behavioral framework of late medieval and early modern penitential communities largely possessed a socially integrative character. With often quite precise prescriptions that determined individual daily prayer, church attendance, and the prayer schedule of holidays through the statutes of the community, the life of the individual member was entirely harnessed to the community's culture of remembrance and this in turn to the Christian story of salvation. To a far greater degree than with the flagellant processions, we should speak here of the spiritual culture of an elite aiming at the formation of social groups. The rituality at the basis of such integration consists in theatrically actualizing and scenically configuring the relation to Holy Scripture and the remembrance of Scripture: especially the Passion, redemption, and the function of Mary. This becomes possible by structuring the entire life of the individual members of society.

Ricordare, memoria, and *commemoratio* are central concepts of the statutes of these brotherhoods, which are closely connected with the ritual practices of the flagellants. Within the brotherhoods, each person becomes an example for the others — an example not only of ethical life, but also of remembrance of the Passion and of redemption. As concerns the outer world, it is the task of the brotherhoods "di fare memoria della passione di Jesù Cristo," to recall the Passion of Christ, "per tutta la terra," over the entire

168

Earth. The means of doing this are procession and public flagellation, which are organized on special church feast days and which
extend memory in a highly practical sense over the whole of common life, including houses, churches, streets, and crossroads. In
this way, the life of a flagellant community member is not only
bound up with a weekly rhythm through the duty of attending
Mass and flagellation on both Sundays and Fridays, but also
through the rhythm of the church year itself, which makes the
entire history of the Gospel present. We can speak of a theatricalization not only of the message of Holy Scripture, but even of the
daily lives of the brothers.

The so-called lauds developed in parallel with dance songs and
gained their towering significance above all through the "iocula-
tores Dei," the "minstrels of God," as the brothers around Francis
of Assisi were called. From the time of the 1260 flagellant movement, the lauds were already the center of their vernacular
liturgy. Song, as well as the theatrical elements of the church liturgy, was brought into the streets and squares, turning these
places into scenes of a lay religious enthusiasm. Like the German
flagellation songs, the lauds were chanted by a lead singer and
answered by the community. This singing developed into a vernacular liturgy in which the dramatic elements came increasingly
to the fore. The events reflected on during the church year were
thereby made present and dramatically expressed through anti-
phonal singing (as was already the case in the collection of lauds
from Perugia). These began at Advent with the representation of
the Antichrist and the Last Judgment, passing from there to the
birth of Christ, on to his Passion, and finally to the resurrection.

Terror and consolation, longing and fulfillment coalesce in
these texts, which reach their most effusive and beautiful form in
the lauds of the Franciscan Jacopone of Todi. In one of his most
famous texts, *Donna del paradiso*, (Lady of paradise), he passes
entirely to the dialogue form and creates a drama of the suffering
of Christ and his mother. In the first scene, a messenger (perhaps
John the Evangelist) announces to Mary the sufferings endured by
her son; in the second scene, we hear the final exchange of words

between mother and son. In the meantime, she expresses her own pain and makes a passionate appeal to Pilate. As in the "Stabat mater" and "Dies irae" (which are said to have originated with Jacopone or with Thomas of Celano and which were beloved within the flagellant movement), what is central here is a passion raised to the level of drama. Christ no longer sits enthroned above humanity, as was usual in earlier medieval iconography. Instead, as a man of suffering, he is presented in dialogue with his mother. In this way, the relation of the faithful to the Gospel becomes less a matter of the content of their beliefs than of an affective and imaginative envisioning whose essential meaning lies not in what it presents, but in the performance of the drama itself. One impressive document concerning this affective spirituality is the lauds collection of the flagellant brotherhood of Assisi from the fourteenth century (*Laudarium Frondini*). It contains a dramatic dialogue between Mary, the faithful, Mary Magdalene, and John, or, in other instances, between the Jews, Caiphas, Judas, Pilate, Christ, and a young maiden.[45]

Flagellation was inserted into precisely these sorts of paraliturgical forms. From an early date, they also took the form of processional plays, Advent plays, Passion plays, and Easter plays. Such plays were already produced in the twelfth century by lay groups and religious lay communities, as is still often true even today. But what is new with Jacopone, for example, is the portrayal of the figure of Christ and of the Passion. The Passion is presented in all its human drama and tragedy through the examples of Mary and Christ, even if Christ is the one who ultimately triumphs over death. The entire life of Christ was dramatized in the collections of lauds from the Umbrian flagellants and presented on the most important feast days of the church year. Here the Passion obviously plays a special role, ultimately leading to the resurrection scene of Easter. Christ says: "I am birth and life for those who believe in me. Whoever dies, lives without knowing, yet whoever lives in belief and believes in me cannot die [Io so' nascemento e vita / a chi à en me credenza / e se la vita sua è finita / ancor vove sanza entenza, / e chi vive avendo fede / non può morire, s'egli en me crede]."

The site of flagellation is the connection of pain with the absolute affirmation of life embodied by Christ as God-man. By establishing itself as a religious practice, it turns into an integral part of the liturgical drama lying outside the Mass proper and the expression of a mystical spirituality. What becomes apparent here is an identification of humanity with God that, beyond the dramatic staging of the Passion and the death of God, ultimately knows that it is bound to the suffering of God and the joy that answers it in turn. In a Franciscan spiritual context, this means that ultimately only this bondedness, only the imitation of suffering, can allow us to discover an overcoming of death and the beauty of this world. This is not so much an expression of a "spontaneous people's piety" as of a new economy of life that privileges specific aspects of the relation between humanity and God and redefines them anew. It is still questionable whether this historical constellation allows us to speak of a "newly discovered subjectivity," as has often been claimed since the Romantic period, at least with respect to the so-called German mysticism of the fourteenth century. But naturally, the depiction and exhibition of individual penitents before God is a paradoxical consequence of the egalitarian gesture of flagellation. This evokes and lays bare an "I" that is simultaneously negated in favor of an overarching continuity of reconciliation between humanity and God. Here we cannot speak in any genuine way of autonomy and subjectivity, not even if a radical liberation can be detected. Yet this very liberation entails a departure from all subjectivity. As concerns embodiment (more specifically, the imagined and aroused embodiment that is staged here), I would prefer to speak of a spiritual materialism that ultimately takes individuality to extremes in the form of pain, dissolving it in pain and grasping the human as a part of the promised bodily resurrection. This is not a site of subjectivity at all, but of objectivity that seeks to overcome in theatrical fashion the separation of word and flesh, an objectivity of which the "I" is only the peripheral movement of an encompassing drama.

A portion of the spirituality that devoted itself to such (originally Franciscan) theatricalizations of existence found adequate

form in the late Middle Ages and early modernity in the organized
and highly disciplined flagellant societies. Through the compagnie dei battuti and their own brand of theater — a sanctification of
everyday life and of the world as expressed in the lauds and especially in the "Canticle of Brother Sun," by Francis of Assisi — a
radical gesture of the affirmation of suffering was established in
the religious life of the late medieval cities. This may seem paradoxical, since flagellation at first seems to amount to sheer contempt for the world and an absolute denial of the body. Yet what
stands at the horizon in flagellation, just as in Franciscan spirituality, is *laetitia*, and hence joy, with the affirmation of creation in all
its multiplicity. The course taken by flagellant theater in early
modern times displays this tendency, even if — especially on the
Protestant side — it was generally criticized not so much because
of its gruesome character as because of its wealth of presentation
and its delight in theatrical arousal.

Later collections of lauds confirm that the theatrical gestures
already found in *Lamentations of Mary for the Body of Christ* from
the twelfth century and in the early lauds developed rapidly, but
not without opposition. One such collection comes from Orvieto
in 1405. Here, a practice of staging had been developed that was
denounced as *vanitates*, or "joy in spectacle." In 1421, this led to a
total ban on the performance of plays in the churches of Orvieto.
Church authorities decreed that "all *Representationes* or *Devotiones*
that in truth and deed primarily serve to entertain and that have
as their theme the deeds and events of the life of Jesus Christ, his
mother, other saints ... or even miracles ... are forbidden ... in
the aforementioned church of Orvieto or in any part of this
church ... under penalty of a fine." What caused annoyance was
the digressive form of the plays — the increasingly luxurious complexity with which they brought biblical events before the eyes
and made them into an outright spectacle. In the eyes of church
censors, this no longer corresponded to the ideal of piety, but
only to a gesture of self-representation by the well-off bourgeoisie. In the view of the clergy, the practice of piety that sacral-
ized everyday life through the staging of suffering had begun to

generate a theatrical world in which, even within an ostensibly spiritual play, secular desire predominated.

The reading aloud of the lauds, which had begun as a simple scene or dramatic relation between the choir and individual voices, had now developed into a complicated play. From a rather early date, they had begun to use costumes and finally a vast panorama of sets and actions that were foreign to the original Passion spirituality of the lauds. New figures came into play, drawn from the Old Testament, the Apocrypha, and the ever-popular lives of the saints. The performance of the staging and the recitation of the lauds together with flagellation aimed at an immediate possible connection with the divine. But the later forms of the dramatic staging of the lauds bore a closer resemblance to theater. From a theatrical actualization of the inner relation of the faithful to God, which consisted in the ritual of flagellation accompanied by the singing of the lauds, matters had evolved into a theatrical representation in which even flagellation had an increasingly symbolic effect. This is confirmed by changes in the use of the scourge as recorded in the late Middle Ages and in early modern times. To an increasing degree, a symbolic flagellation was practiced in the flagellant communities, one that took care not to inflict any severe pain. Increasingly, the word *disciplina* was used in a way that referred to exercises of piety more generally.

Apart from isolated cases, the battuti and disciplinati were certainly well integrated into society and official religion. Nonetheless, the flagellant societies and their methods of staging Holy Scripture came under discussion at the Tridentine Council. Yet instead of leading to a restrictive politics, it resulted in an authentic renewal of the movement under the overall control of Charles Borromeo. The cardinal himself was an advocate of private self-flagellation and defended the practice in other contexts, as well. Commenting on the foundation of a new penitential brotherhood that he had helped organize in Bergamo in 1575, he noted: "of all the penitential brotherhoods in our diocese, that of the Disciplinati is certainly the most pious and exemplary," for the flagellants "show us ... in their *imitatio Christi* ... the true way of salvation, which consists in avoiding the satisfaction of the world, subordinating the flesh to the spirit, and repenting for sins by penitential exercises and self-chastisement." In such exercises, they made use of:

> whips with straps, for these recall the rods with which the Lord, fettered to a column, was whipped for our sins. In the process, they strike fast and hard, for they do not whip themselves for their own sins, but for those of the whole world. They flagellate themselves every Sunday during Advent, from the third Sunday before Lent to Whitsun, during the three great processions, on Holy Thursday, and on specific days, such as during Carnival, when God was especially abused.[46]

Here, too, the proper compass of flagellation, as Borromeo writes, is the length of a "Miserere" psalm, recited while kneeling and while one strikes oneself on the naked back. As numerous sources attest, the flagellant brotherhoods who followed this ritual in private and brought it to the public eye in parades continued to survive even into modern times. From Italy and Spain especially, countless paintings of processions and theatrically staged church feasts of the seventeenth and eighteenth centuries have been preserved, paintings that depict flagellants. Yet we must assume that flagellation (aside from renewed flare-ups of Cryptoflagellant movements and a number of secret Congregations of Mary) increasingly took the form of a symbolic praxis before finally disappearing from sanctioned public penance altogether.

CHAPTER FOUR

Arousing Images

Whatever the judgment of the pope or the Council of Konstanz, the question of flagellant processions was still alive in the late Middle Ages. In the following centuries it was discussed repeatedly, whether in light of the Reformation, of Counter-Reformation strategies, or in the seventeenth century within the church in France. It was now generally not a matter of mass processions of laymen following charismatic preachers such as Vincent Ferrer, but of the theatrical activities and productions of bourgeois flagellant brotherhoods based in the cities.

Ascesis Rediscovered

Flagellant brotherhoods existed from the fourteenth century on in all of the larger Italian population centers and in numerous places in France and Spain, as well. The flagellants wore habits of various colors: according to their association, origin, or neighborhood allegiance, they were known variously as white, black, gray, green, violet, blue, or red penitents. Usually their parades simply enlarged upon the traditional church processions, yet they also arranged their own processions, especially during Holy Week, and made a decisive contribution to the theatrical or pantomimic manner of presenting the Passion story in the more traditional processional forms. In this way, a paradigm of the pictorial-scenic imitation of the Passion was instituted in the Catholic countries, but most especially in the nations of the Romance languages. It was a paradigm already carried out in germ by Dominicus Loricatus as he whipped himself in imitation of Christ. The high point of such flagellant imitation can be seen in two specific trends. First, there were the Passion plays of the del Gonfalone brotherhood, which took place on Good Friday in the Coliseum in Rome, unsurpassed in terms of their wealth of magnificent spectacle. Second, there was the general upsurge of self-flagellation among laymen in the sixteenth and seventeenth centuries. Everywhere in Catholic countries, on specific feast days, there were nighttime processions in which laymen moved through the streets by torchlight while flagellating themselves; everywhere, people flagellated themselves in private, as well, to express their piety.

Contemporary reports affirm that the processions were emotionally moving for participants and spectators alike, as was already the case with the Strassburg flagellants described by Fritsche Closener. We learn that spectators broke down in tears and were moved to scourge themselves, as well. Intermittent ecclesiastical measures directed against such aroused forms of piety were seldom effective. In this spirit, the Spanish episcopate sought to intervene in 1565 against the flagellant processions "in defense of public morals." But they were unable to gain significant influence over a movement that blossomed on the Iberian Peninsula on into the twentieth century and that quickly took root in the colonies.

As for Italy, the Passion plays produced by the Gonfalone Society in Rome sometimes degenerated into pogromlike persecutions, with aroused masses of people actually whipping the actors and those who represented Jews. For this reason, Pope Gregory XIII banned "sacre rappresentazioni" on January 26, 1574, though he permitted the Jesuits to continue with their own form of didactic theater, which played on the emotions of the audience in more controlled and deliberate fashion.

In France, flagellant and penitential brotherhoods were revived during the reign of Henry III (1574–89), even gaining a certain degree of political influence. Here again, flagellation was defended by a Jesuit, Edmond Auger, Henry's confessor and the author of a *Discours sur la pénitence* (1584). Under Edmond's spiritual leadership, the eccentric favorite son of Catherine de Médicis not only took part in public processions, but actually *initiated* them. Henry, whose "excessive temperament" was proverbial,[1] always endeavored to proclaim his religious devotion to the public, and to this end (reversing the decree of his predecessor, Charles IX, who had outlawed penitential brotherhoods) he founded the Congrégation des Pénitents de l'Annonciation-de-Notre-Dame. The members — including the king, who appeared as a brother among brothers — wore penitential garments of coarse Dutch fabric, floor-length and white, with a flat cowl that covered the face entirely except for two eye slits. On their belts they hung a rosary and a scourge. In processions beginning on Annunciation Day, March 25, 1583, the king and a number of devoted members of the nobility and urban middle class publicly whipped themselves in a procession from the Grands-Augustins monastery to the Cathedral of Notre Dame under pouring rain. Contemporary sources report malicious ridicule of this action, especially among opponents of the king's luxurious lifestyle.

A short time later, in 1585, Henry founded the Confrérie de la mort et de la passion de Notre Seigneur Jésus-Christ, a private penitential society. This group gathered every Friday evening in the Louvre, and members would whip themselves during the prayer of the psalms "Miserere" and "De profundis." For all the critique and ridicule of Henry III, his involvement in the penitential involvement spurred numerous imitators. Other brotherhoods quickly formed — termed blue, black, or gray penitents in accordance with the colors of their garments — that also organized processions and public self-flagellation.[2] In these societies, which were found both in Paris and the French provinces, flagellation was practiced well into the eighteenth century, except during periodic bans or times of political difficulty.

Their flagellation observed the forms already known from monastic life. According to the intensity of religious devotion, the whipping could be either *sec* (dry) or *sanglant* (bloody), either individual or communal. The practice of flagellation was pursued above all on certain days of the week, on ecclesiastical holidays, during Advent, Lent, and Holy Week, and during processions more generally. In many cases, communal flagellation during ritual gatherings of the brotherhoods followed the model already familiar to us. According to the rules of the White Penitents of Puy from 1778, they gathered in the chapel, whereupon the lights were put out at the beginning of the ceremony. Only two lanterns continued to burn, one on the altar and another next to the rector, who began by calling the brothers to atonement and penance. He then spoke of the Passion of Christ and the meaning of the imitation of his suffering through flagellation. The brothers took the scourges from the altar and began the flagellation, accompanied by a series of prayers and the reading of Scripture, all in perfect darkness, all accompanied by the chanting of further prayers and the psalm "Miserere." The lights were turned on only after everyone was dressed again, and the ceremony closed with a series of prayers. This ritual, which is documented up to the end of the eighteenth century, is also said to have been practiced by various brotherhoods throughout France. It is only in the nineteenth century that we finally lose track of it [3]

If the Jesuits were already important for the resurgence of flagellant passion in France, they were even more important in Germany. Here, self-flagellation had entirely vanished since the fifteenth century, but it was revived under the influence of the Jesuits in the second half of the sixteenth century. Starting in 1600, in almost all the Catholic cities of Germany, flagellant processions took place during Lent and on Good Friday. Here, too, following the Italian model, the Passion story was expressed both through figures carried in the procession and in living images. As late as 1719, it is said that over one thousand people took part in a flagellant procession organized by the Jesuits: they held skulls in their hands while wearing chains around their necks and crowns of thorns upon their heads.

This Catholic staging of a Christian world of images (a world of spiritual tableaux vivants capable of arousing the emotions) did not go unnoticed by critics and polemicists on the Protestant

side. For example, a violent dispute between Catholics and Protestants arose just before Good Friday in 1605 as to whether a penitential procession would be permitted in Augsburg. From this
dispute we can determine what motivated the advocates and opponents of flagellation. On the Catholic side, there was an especial degree of intervention by the Jesuit Jakob Gretser, who took
a stand on this point. His pugnacious and polemical involvement
led to a treatise with the title *De spontanea disciplinarum seu flagellorum cruce* (On the spontaneous use of the discipline or the
whip in imitating the Passion), which was published in 1606 in
Ingolstadt and translated shortly thereafter into German. A supplement to this work followed in 1607 under the title *Spicilegium
de usu voluntariae per flagra castigationis* (Treatise on self-castigation by the use of the whip). When the Protestant side attacked
him on this matter, the combative father struck back with an
entire series of polemical treatises. In 1607, there appeared *Praedicans vapulans et disciplinatus* (The flogging and flogged preacher);
in 1608, *Virgidemia Volciana* (Volcian floggery); in 1609, *Agnos-
ticum spirituale* (Devotional witness); and finally, in 1612, *Athletica
spiritualis gemina, legitima et illegitima* (The athletic sighs of devotion, both legitimate and illegitimate). All these documents served
as apologia for an ascesis that was at once pictorial and imaginative and physically arousing. Teamed up with Gretser in the con-
troversy was the Jesuit Konrad Vetter, who ridiculed his opponents
in a pair of colorfully named treatises. One was entitled *Geißlung
Procession, welche im Lutherthum nicht allein am Charfreytag, sonder
das gantz Jahr hinumb gehalten wirdt; mit sampt einer andechtigen
Letaney* (Flagellation procession, which among the Lutherans is
practiced not only on Good Friday, but throughout the year;
Including a prayer litany). Another was called *Volcius Flagellifer.
Das ist: Beschützung und Handhabung fürtrefflicher und herlicher
zweyer Predigten von der unleydlichen und Abschewlichen Geyzel Pro-
ceßion, erstlich gehalten, hernach auch in Truck gegeben durch den
Kehrwürdigen, unnd Wolgekerten Herrn M. Melchior Voltz Luthe-
rischen Predicanten zu Augspurg bey Sant Anna* (The whip-carrying
Volcius. That is: Defense and propagation of two excellent and

praiseworthy sermons regarding the abominable whipping processions; First delivered, then published by the respectrious and
illustable Melchior Volcius, Lutheran pastor of Saint Anna in
Augsburg). On the Protestant side, the main opponents of flagellant practices and the Catholic processions were Melchior Voltz
(a pastor in Augsburg), Jakob Heilbrunner, and Georg Zeaemann.
Their polemical writings, which first appeared around 1607, were
republished in 1613 and 1614 in Wittenberg under the title *Carnificina Esautica: Quatuor libri spontaneae flagellationi oppositi*
(Esau's butchery: Four books against devotional self-flagellation).
Obviously, there was great interest in flagellation as a genuinely
Catholic practice, one that appeared especially worthy of censure
in the eyes of the Reformation.

In the foreword to his *Praedicans vapulans*, Jakob Gretser speaks
in absolute tones against the Protestant criticism: "discipline and
the scourge are our teachers, without which the flesh does not
recognize sin." Gretser's line of argument is primarily polemical,
historiographical, and philological and accuses his opponents of
lies, misunderstanding of the sources, inversion of the facts, as
well as confusion and self-contradiction. In this way he wants to
prove that "disciplina" as a praxis of voluntary self-flagellation is
already found in the Bible and is therefore justified. The heart of
his argument is based on philology and a correct reading of Scripture, but also on the right understanding of the concepts of self-
mortification ("mortificatio" and "crucifixio") that Paul outlines
in his letters to the Christian community. The Protestants are to
be unmasked not just as false and immoral theologians, but also —
on their own territory — as bad philologists. "Should one, for
example," Gretser asks polemically, "mortify and crucify his flesh
by following Luther and, in the most shameful way, taking a nun
as one's wife?"

The Jesuit argues to the contrary that "the spirit of mortification through prayer, fasting, and bodily ascesis" should be like "an
architect who lays a new foundation and lets a new house take
shape." Through flagellation, the "heroic soul" does just what Paul
asked us to do when he demanded that we mortify the flesh with

the spirit. Gretser objects decisively to the view of the "Protestant preachers" that the divine spirit pervades only the language with which humans relate to God, but not the other (bodily) "gestures and images employed to this end: for example, penitential belts and garments, fasting, tears," and other devotional practices. A system of corporeal gestures thus becomes paramount and is equated with the meaning of words, without which, in Gretser's view, we cannot do justice to Paul's call for mortification. Perhaps the word alone reaches the spirit of humanity, yet it does not establish an immediate relation with the crucified God to the same degree as does the chastisement of the body. This is not contradicted by the point made by the critics that flagellation arouses the body and leads to dangerous desire. After all, for Gretser, this ambiguity cannot be the criterion for banning a practice, since this would introduce a radical dualism. What he demands is a reading of the Biblical passage that takes *castigatio* or chastisement literally (1 Corinthians 9.27), as involving the body, thereby working through the ambiguities of arousal evoked by the devotional practices. Luther opposes this completely.

In one of his table talks on marriage, Luther comments on this passage by saying "the more I chastised and macerated myself, and the more I disciplined my body, the more I burned." With such statements, which refuse the corporeal enactment of chastisement and the imitation of the cross in relation to the body, Luther becomes in Gretser's eyes the author of a "fifth Gospel." Even for Gretser, the imitation of the cross can take many forms, since he says that everyone should bear "his own cross; all that remains obligatory is that the Christian should follow the example of Christ." The exemplarity of Christ, which always remains a "mystery" (1 Peter, 2), however, according to Gretser, is not something simply to be "believed," but something to be actualized in bodily form in physical gestures of imitation. This is what flagellation aims at, along with other techniques of mortification. They make the suffering of Christ both tangible and visible in the flesh. Johann Eck, in his attack on the Protestant iconoclasts in 1522, had already emphasized that this visualization and embodiment proceeded immediately from the theological paradigm of the Incarnation and through this paradigm was not only legitimized but actually demanded.[4] In this way, among others, a specific form of late medieval piety emerged once more into prominence.

The same concern guides Gertser's 1608 work *Virgidemia Volciana*. Here, he defends himself against two arguments stated by Melchior Voltz, the Protestant pastor of Saint Anna in Augsburg, in his *Geißlung Procession*. Here once more, in the debate with Voltz and with Jakob Heilbrunner, a defense is made of the Christian work of self-chastisement. (Heilbrunner had published a treatise against flagellation in 1607 under the title *Flagellatio Jesuitica: Jesuiterische Lehr vom genannten freywilligen Creutz* [Flagellatio Jesuitica: The Jesuit doctrine of the so-called voluntary cross].)

This all seems to have been primarily a matter of confessional polemic. Gretser gives extensive citations from the writings of Luther, as well as his critique of the so-called Catholic piety of works. Yet this is merely the surface level of the treatise. Basically, the discussion is not determined by confessional polemic, but by a different theological understanding of exemplarity and the validity of images. Thus, for example, the statement by the apostle Peter that Christ died for our sake and provided us with a model must in Gretser's view be related to suffering in a quite specific way — a way that the Protestants are incapable of understanding. Gretser explains that being a Christian does not consist so much in believing that Christ did this or that. Just as little does it consist in "doing what Christ did." It is not a matter of literally imitating history, but "of suffering what Christ suffered" ("ut patiamur ad imitationem Christi quod Christus passus est"). Gretser thereby opposes the mimetic moment of experience to the representative moment of achievement that Volz and the other Protestant critics pressed to the fore in their polemic against the Catholic-pictorial form of imitation, which in their eyes was idolatrous and which in their eyes was also characteristic of the Catholic position.

According to Gretser, this was not the case, since the staging of suffering aims at the intensity of experience and at identity in experience, not at representation or the charging of a payment in the economy of salvation. In self-flagellation, "man forms himself ... into an example of suffering that the suffering Christ bequeathed to us" ("conformat ergo se ad exemplum patiendi, quod nobis à Christu passo S. Petrus relictum affirmat").[5] Here it is a question of neither a literal imitation of Christ's example nor an ascetic performance that heaps up the greatest possible number of justifying works, but of a temporal experience of suffering that creates a relationship to God and grants a space of action to justifying grace.

According to Gretser, this exemplary and experiential relation cannot be actualized if, as Luther demands, we turn the tradition of chastisement into a Stoic practice of daily moderation in which life is perhaps characterized by fasting, work, and modesty,[6] but never reaches intensity in the imitation of suffering. The relation succeeds only when the arousing quality of the image is taken as a basis and one accepts the ambiguity of the death of God, which is repeatedly restaged in the practice of the flagellants.

Mimetic intensity — and not the Stoic ideal of self-control — is the object of the ascetic example that Gretser sets forth in his writings for purposes of illustration. What is important here is no longer philosophical argument or exegetical and dogmatic theses, but the tradition, the chain of exemplary images. It becomes a baroque picture gallery in which the flagellants and ascetics gather before the eyes of the reader as examples of imitation. Here we have what is doubtless one of the high points of the Catholic history of flagellation, as Gretser presents ascetic monks and nuns in an imaginary museum of exemplarity and an imaginary history of the Catholic tradition. All the figures are examples both of *how* to imitate and *what* to imitate. They are examples of a history of arousal in which each narrative of a marvelous ascetic life is also an example of the force that is able to affect such a life.

Moreover, the figures referred to are examples of how one should be led by images, examples of how the Christian is unified with Christ through arousal. Thus, every life of a saint is both image and example: it is an arousing model, not merely a venerated one. It would be idolatry if the exemplary nature related merely to imitation — and thus to the imitation of experience as the experience of imitation, rather than the imitation of the experience of suffering itself. This would turn religious experience into a merely aesthetic experience, while Gretser insists that every aesthetic experience (that is, the experience of the arousing image) must be transparent in its experience of the suffering embodied by Christ, which is able to save those humans who are truly affected by it.

Image and Affect

How this affective imitation should be conceived and how strongly the power of images is to weigh within it is shown by a treatise of the Spanish Franciscan Philippus Diez. This work was translated in 1610 by the Jesuit Konrad Vetter, a colleague of Gretser; Vetter also provided a polemical foreword targeting Jakob Heilbrunner, Gripus von Lauingen, and Melchior Voltz. The three Protestant critics of flagellation, who were already targeted by Gretser in his *Praedicans vapulans*, were supposed to learn from this work "so that they could understand the flagellant processions in Augsburg and other places, not watching these processions as blockheaded idiots, but with the ability to contemplate them and to be moved."

The title of the treatise, reprinted numerous times at the beginning of the seventeenth century, was *Der Evangelische Lauttenschlager. Das ist: Zwo schöne unnd über alle Lautten liebliche Betrachtungen, bey dem Himmel Räyen und Englschen Tantz, deren so in der Charfreytags Procession sich selbsten Discipliniren...* (The evangelical lute player. That is: Two beautiful and exceedingly pleasant-sounding meditations on the heavenly roundelay and angel's dance of those who whip themselves during Holy Friday processions...). The point here is to instruct us on how to interpret the flagellant procession, for it is explicitly a question of the role of seeing and of visual meditation. Furthermore, the text allows us to recognize that we must understand the function of the visual with a view to the imitation of Christ, which is so

184

important for Gretser and which is subjected by his opponents to a thorough critique. The author writes:

> In Greece there were many open spaces, called fighting places by the young men who were occupied there with wrestling, fencing, and boxing. In these places, they displayed statues and sculptures of noble and famous fighters in specific poses, as if one were going to kill the other or try to overturn him. They did this so that the young would have these images before their eyes while they engaged in exercises of fighting and wrestling, so that they would imitate them, that they would become fearless and courageous, and that they would win their matches.

"The life of a Christian," the text tells us, should imitate this example, since it is "also called a fight." It is not a fight against other humans, though, but against the powers of darkness:

> O what terrible, cruel, and horrendous enemies of mankind there are, which have great power and might. And although we exercise ourselves in fighting and in battling the flesh, this is not the decisive battle, since the apostle says: "For our struggle is not against flesh and blood, but against the rulers, against the authorities, against the powers of this dark world and against the spiritual forces of evil in the heavenly realms." The fight against the flesh is nothing compared with the fight against the evil forces. It barely merits to be called a fight.
>
> On the place of the fight that Christians have to wage, the Holy Church arranges statues, sculptures, and images of exemplary fighters in similar fashion before our eyes. They represent fighters who have won victories against the evil spirits, the flesh, and the blood. The church does this so that these images might fortify us when we look upon them with our eyes in contemplation and that they might lead us toward the spiritual victory for which we hope.
>
> These statues or images are nothing else than the lives and examples of many saints who have shown and preached to us about how to fight, above all the most excellent and glorious example of all — that

of Jesus Christ, the Son of God, who fought a great victory against the powers of hell and all the evil demons.

The glorious saint Jerome relied on this example when he called Saint Hilarion his fencing master. He trained himself to be a fighter through his contemplation of Hilarion's ascetic life and penance, and thus he made himself fit and courageous in his spiritual battle against his own body and the temptations of inverted nature.

The contemplation of the gruesome torments, tortures, beatings, and whippings that our most holy captain Jesus Christ suffered in his death should incite and excite us to do the same, whenever we look at his example with our inner eyes.... He wanted that we, his soldiers, should do the same when he willingly suffered, when he let his body be pierced, whipped, wounded, and cruelly beaten. He says that we should "follow" him and "do the same" in times of temptation and battle, that we should engage our enemy and break our bodies with whippings and beatings, with canes and discipline, and with other forms of penance.... These should excite our minds and hearts and terrify our enemies, so that we can follow the example of Christ and be victorious.

Diez and Vetter, the authors of this text, quote examples from the Old Testament that anticipate this type of Christian battle, emphasizing that they form patterns and figures of imitation for how we should use "whips, canes, and chains" to treat our bodies and excite "Divine Love." Here again, as in earlier texts, David appears as one of the key examples, since he is the one who "desired such suffering and pain with the highest affective intensity," which he expressed in his songs. The example of David, the paradigmatic performer of the Psalms, above all of the "Miserere," should be imitated by all those who take up the whip. He is the one who "tortured, whipped, and disciplined himself," the lute player who made his body into his instrument.

Diez and Vetter emphasize that we are painters and sculptors of ourselves when we engage in these practices of imitation. These performances not only create a new foundation of our existence, as Gretser pointed out, but they give shape to a new body in ways that are quite similar to the Greek athletes who imitated the exemplary fighters in their exercises. Here the text offers a rather surprising and original reading of Paul's statement that "the mind of the sinful man is death, but the mind controlled by the spirit is life" (Romans 8.6). In his view:

> the apostle meant that the difference between body and soul can be compared to the difference between a painted image and a carved image. From a carved image, you take things away; to a painted image, however, you add various elements. With a carving, you work and cut and strike until it has a perfect shape. With a painting, you add different colors until it is perfect. A carver takes a piece of oak or another kind of hardwood, then he works on it with his hands, sawing, cutting, carving, and taking the wood off until it is a perfect image. A painting, however, takes shape when it is painted with a brush and when all kinds of beautiful colors are applied. You have to work and to add until it is finally finished. The painter starts with an empty surface, then he adds a first, a second, a third, and a fourth layer, working with artificial materials, disposition, light, shade, and coloring, until he has a perfect painting and artifact before him. God has created our mind in the same way. The mind is an even, clean, and absolutely empty surface, and there is nothing on it, neither written nor painted. He gave us the power to decorate it and to paint it with the most beautiful and dignified colors. This is the reason why God praised all the other creatures after he created them (as is to be read in the book of Genesis, chapter 1), since they were created perfect and meant to stay the same from the beginning until the end of the world. He did not praise mankind, though... since he gave the freedom to mankind to shape itself and paint itself with beautiful colors (i.e., with the beauty of virtues). Thus, man has to create the beauty of his mind, his heart, and his soul himself. He has to produce his perfect form, so that God can praise him at the end of times. This is the reason why God praised all the other creatures at the beginning, but he was not willing to do the same with mankind.

If we look at ourselves and think of our bodies as carvings that

begin as nothing else than blocks of hard wood, we understand that
we have to work the wood and to shape it by forming it, cutting it,
sawing it, and planing it. Chips, splinters, and pieces have to be cut
off. A lot has to be taken off our bodies, namely, the pleasures of
food, sleep, luxury, pleasure, etc. The body has to be shaped like a
piece of wood, with beatings and whippings, with canes, scourges,
and discipline. The body has to be tortured and starved, so that it
submits to the spirit and takes perfect shape.

Diez and Vetter point out that all this happens before God's
eye. He is the one who looks at the humans who torture themselves and make their bodies into the stage of a sacrifice that gives
us a new shape. And just as in the case of Peter Damian's depiction of the monastic scene of self-flagellation, here, as well, the
penitent becomes the judge who anticipates the Last Judgment
and performs its work, as well as the work of salvation, individu-
ally and self-reflexively. "Oh what a sweet and consoling message
for all the penitents this is," they write, "to know that God,
whose majesty is infinite and beyond our understanding, has his
eyes fixed on them, that he considers them to be the elected and
the most beloved, that he looks at them as his beloved friends, and
that he will never have enough of this spectacle." In the scene of
self-flagellation and of ascetic self-fashioning, the penitent transforms himself or herself into the likeness of the Son of God, who
sacrificed himself in a "most unbelievable spectacle of suffering
and death." To succeed in this, penitents keep their eyes fixed on
"this spectacle, which the Holy Church puts this very night before
our eyes."

In other words, by looking at the display of the suffering of
Christ in the Passion plays and by experiencing the liturgy of the
Holy Week, penitents should not only learn about the mysteries
of Christian faith, but transform themselves into a part of this
spectacle. This happens wherever someone follows in the steps of
Christ, wherever someone "imitates his example when he takes
up the exercise of whips and canes, discipline and castigation."
Then, and only then, the "affection" that has been shown by God

188

in the sacrifice of his son will be mirrored by humans. And only then, as well, will the fight against the demons be won. This presupposes, however, the staging of the spectacle in processions and ecclesiastical rituals:

> Everyone, the princes of the court, the aristocracy, the priests, and the leaders of the peoples should spend the night [of Holy Friday] in supplication and processions...adorned in their royal purple, that is, covered in their own blood, and walking in this way through the streets, places, and corners of the city. We should show ourselves dressed in this royal garb, which is the garb of our master and king Jesus Christ...since he showed himself dressed in royal purple, that is, dressed and covered with his rose-colored blood from head to toe. Thus we will chase away the demons, since they will recognize our high standing with the Divine Majesty in the fact that we wear the same purple garment of honor.

What follows is an even more intense emphasis on the necessity that human blood should flow during these processions. They embody the sacrifice of Christ not insofar as they *represent*, but only insofar as they *emulate* the scene in which Christ has been "whipped with cruel strokes, in the way strong rain strikes the earth and covers it and in the way hail roughs it up." Only this turns human gestures of piety into true gestures of imitation and true acts of memory.

> Even the pagan, wild, and barbaric peoples teach us in their ceremonies and rituals how we should sacrifice our blood. We hear about the Indian Mexicans that they were not content with blood alone when they sacrificed a human for their gods. Rather, the pagan priest takes a knife from his belt, opens up the breast of the victim, takes out his heart, lifts it up to heaven, and sprays the blood from the heart into the air. They believe that their gods will not be happy with the blood alone, but that it has to come from the heart, and that the heart itself has to be sacrificed. This, as well, has been shown by Christ. He was not content with the fact alone that he sacrificed his

189

most holy blood for the sins of the world . . . but he wanted that they opened his breast and side after his death. There, in his side, lay hidden the most valuable part, that is, his most beloved, most tender, and most holy heart, which burned beyond measure in his love of mankind. He wished that even the last drop of blood in his heart should be spent. Thus he wished to show that he gave not only the blood in his body, the blood in his limbs and vessels, but the very blood of his own heart.

"God asks us that we sacrifice our blood in the same way, namely, the blood of our heart," when we imitate the "incomprehensible torture" of his own "incarnate son, who suffered this for us." Thus we ask God to accept our sacrifice in his "infinite goodness," the sacrifice of "all the drops of blood and rivulets of blood that flow from the nations and peoples of this earth who are part of the Catholic Church overflow during this night [of Holy Friday]." What we find here is the model of the Good Friday liturgy as a spectacle of sacrifice that offers up not only the human body, but the soul, as well. The text offers no mere explanation or justification of the flagellant procession on Good Friday, but a spiritual meditation that gives form to the spirit and stimulates the powers of imagination. In this respect, the theatrical elements are quite significant. The text clarifies that the procession and its commerce with images is concerned with staging a transformation of one's disposition and with actually performing the *imitatio Christi*. At the same time, the text itself practices this transformation: it abandons the level of sheer explication, and in a movement of *mise en abîme*, it traces the meaning of the image not to something standing outside of the image, but to an ordeal of meditative mimesis in which the soul becomes entirely image and — to use an expression of Eckhart of Hochheim — finally "loses its own being."

The second spiritual meditation from the same volume follows this model, as well. Here again, what is central is the meditation on the figure of the suffering Christ:

The good Jesus stands stark naked bound to the post...his body bent now to one side, now to the other, since he suffers the most cruel and unimaginable pain from the whipping.... Oh you, delight and praise of the angels, how terrible and lost you look when I gaze at you! Which heart could be so hard and unbreakable that it would not be torn and split apart when it looks at this inhuman pain, when it contemplates and feels the torment and torture that you suffered.

The catalog of ascetics that Gretser depicts in his *Virgidemia Volciana* in the manner of a picture gallery has the same role and value as the aforementioned intuitive presentation: they, too, give pictorial form to what will be imitated. Moreover, they shed retroactive light on the tradition of exemplarity and imitation lying at the basis of flagellation from the start, from Peter Damian onward. The theatrical scene produced by the flagellant, in which he or she simultaneously imitates both Christ and all the ascetics who preceded him or her in imitating Christ, allows the flagellant to become a tableau vivant or living picture. Through suffering and through the gesture of flagellation, the flagellant is the mirror image of an original suffering that can no longer be grasped — one that has its place solely in a history of imitation that in its own right is nothing other than an exemplary mirror of imitation provoking further imitation. For this reason, Diez writes that the divine affect that moved the Father to sacrifice himself as man for humanity is reflected back on God by humans who themselves suffer — both by the flagellants and by their spectators.

Every life of a saint presented by Gretser should be seen as a mirroring image of this kind. It is both an example and an individual mutation; each life is a monad in which the relation to God is reflected both perfectly and in absolutely unique form. It is in this sense that each life is also an example of the practice of imitation that takes form in a unique way in each and every new image. For self-flagellating ascetics, this signifies that they translate themselves in the image and that, with the aid of flagellation, they transpose themselves into a state of affective arousal and imagine themselves as "another Christ" and "another imitator of Christ."

At the same time, they recognize themselves, see themselves as individualized: that is to say, as a new image. In the unavoidable failure inherent in such a translation, the ascetic becomes aware of what is his or her own. In the gesture of flagellation, which can never reach the goal that it sets for itself in the horizon of earthly temporality, which never manages to produce unity with Christ, it nonetheless remains visible as an example. Through this paradoxical gesture, ascetics (like Dominicus Loricatus and the anonymous medieval flagellants) turn themselves into imitable human examples. As such, they enter the gallery of imitators, who are both perfect yet in their humanity ever imperfect. Hence, the image of the ascetic becomes the object of imitation, which aims at becoming aware of its own finitude through the performance of flagellation and also aims through this affective and intellectual experience at attaining the suffering that characterizes the death of God as man — the God exhausted within finitude.

The exploration and examination of one's own soul as taught by Ignatius of Loyola in connection with the medieval techniques of prayer (above all in the *Vita Christi* of Ludolf of Saxony) gives us the logic of this ordeal. It presupposes the activation of the imagination and the intensification of the affective life of the soul, which Gretser and Diez here turn into an essential element of flagellation as the imitation of an image. Only in a peripheral sense can this be considered as the ascetic achievement of suffering. Rather, it attains its significance by concretely staging the relation to God and thus allowing the soul and body to be absorbed in an imaginary space of exemplary images that transport the soul back to God through the suffering of God as man. Hence, the processions that Gretser defends against Protestant criticism are "nothing other ... than a public prayer." They are signs that "publicly witness ... and declare ... faith" and also a means of "edifying the viewers." The visual elements that play a central role in this process (the "figures" and "portraits") are supposed to "inflame" the participants or arouse their emotions.

In this concept of arousal by images, what we encounter is the Jesuit interpretation of images as expressed in the concluding

192

decree of the Council of Trent in 1563. In the words of the
decree, the image should "instruct and move" ("docere et movere").[7] That is to say, through a form of meditational practice
grounded in images, which Ignatius of Loyola sketched in his *Spiritual Exercises*, the soul should also be led back to God by way of
the senses and the emotions.

Like Gretser, Louis Richeome grasped this understanding of
images in an especially systematic way. In 1597, Richeome first
published a treatise that quickly spread throughout the Catholic
world and that bore the title *Trois discours pour la religion catholique: Les miracles, les saints, les images...* (Three discourses in
defense of Catholic religion: The miracles, the saints, the images
...). What especially interested him was the effect of the image
on the one who meditates on it. The image does not summon up
adoration in the viewer — which would justify the accusation of
idolatry by the Protestant critics — but instead leads the viewer
beyond himself or herself. This happens because the image, unlike
the word, mediates all information in a single instant and thus
does not unfold slowly over time, since it affects humans in such a
way that their souls rise up from the visible to the invisible.[8]

This ascent is induced not only by inner spiritual images, but
also through actual pictures. As evidence of this it is sometimes
noted that Ignatius of Loyola (similar to what we have learned
from Henry Suso's *Vita*) kept a collection of pictures in his cell
and was moved to meditate by pictures.[9] Jerónimo Nadal, who
published the *Evangelicae historiae imagines* (Images of the story of
the Gospel) by order of Ignatius, realized this project of an affec-
tive-pictorial translation of Scripture by transposing the text into
images that would serve as the basis for meditation and as a point
of departure for inner reflection (figure 4.1).[10] The *docere*, the
learnable message and the content of faith, is realized in the
movere — that is to say, in the inner movement and arousal of the
soul that mirrors God not only intellectually, but in a visionary-
affective way. Thus, in Nadal's way of presenting things — in the
Adnotationes et meditationes in evangelia (Annotations and meditations on the Gospel) and in the *Evanglicae historiae imagines* — the

Figure 4.1. *The Flagellation of Christ* (Jerónimo Nadal, *Evangelicae Historiae Imagines*, Antwerp, 1593, CXXI. Explanation of the references that are meant to guide the contemplation of the image: "A. The loggia from which Pilate observes the flagellation. B. The column to which Christ is fettered. C. The block on which the condemned is beheaded. D. Romans and Jews. E. Jesus is whipped severely. F. At Pilate's command, his henchmen cease the whipping. G. The Virgin Mother feels the traces of the blows. Meditate on how terribly she experiences the blows in her soul and in her heart."

entire church year is encompassed and wholly transposed to this level of meditation on images. With respect to the images that fill the church, images of the crucified,[11] the martyrs, and the ascetics, this means that the viewer himself experiences the drama presented in the image — as in the procession that stages the image once again.

What Jakob Gretser and Konrad Vetter defend in their *Procession Buch* (Procession book), which bears the subtitle *Von dem Dsciplinieren und Geißlen in den öffentlichen Processionen* (Of discipline and flagellation in the public processions), is supported theologically by more than this understanding of images. The significance of the images is related to the doctrine of transubstantiation and thereby submitted to the horizon of the concept of real presence. The monstrance set up during the feast of Corpus Christi forms the paradigm of a making present to which the other figures, images, and stagings of flagellation also belong.[12] These represent or symbolize not just the relation to God (which according to Gretser is already done by the Ark of the Covenant with respect to the old covenant).They are a performance of sensual presence, both spiritual and bodily, just like the sacrament of the Eucharist. The effect of the ritual, as of the sacraments, is to be found in its performance, rather than in the charisma or inspiration of the performer (in theological terms, *ex opere operato*, not *ex opere operans*). Thus, it has the power to affect both participants and spectators and to integrate them into the "holy imitations of the cross" that have inspired the Christian world since the death of the Savior.

Gretser and Vetter emphasize that everyone who saw the flagellant processions of the thirteenth century immediately wished to take part in them and to participate in a real presence of the divine. This doctrine has its basis in the paradigm of visualization represented by the Incarnation. Such real presence was instituted by the flagellant processions — obviously not by the "heretical" flagellants — that were customary beginning in the thirteenth century and that are presented here as the background of the Augsburg processions. Gretser constructs a genealogy of the praxis of flagellant processions that begins in Perugia with an "attack" of the Holy Spirit among laymen, which formed an "example ... through which all the others were inflamed and enamored."[13] Hence, the heretics are not those who become images in their suffering as flagellants. Instead, the heretics are those who avoid such imitation of the Savior's example and who criticize the mimetic process of recollection — a process instituted in the forms of "inflammation" and arousal in the Good Friday procession in Augsburg after the model of Italian and Spanish communities.

Gretser describes it in the following terms: "A new form of supplication has been introduced for the night of Holy Friday. Three years ago a member of the aristocracy led a small group of men, dressed in sackcloth, into battle. Following his orders, they carried certain figures, statues, and scenes from the life of Christ in front of them, as if they were living images. This year the Brotherhood of Our Lady was invited and took part in this procession, as well." There were seventy people dressed in "black sackcloth," and one "counted twenty-six heavy wooden crosses, which they carried on their shoulders in imitation of the example of Christ."

> Over one hundred people were walking with candles and torches.... The first in the procession was the Brotherhood of Corpus Christi in red clothes. They carried a figure of Christ praying on the Mount of Olives, his sweat falling to the ground like drops of blood. The figure was illuminated by four burning fires they carried along ... and his miserable face was clearly visible. Four boys were walking in front of this figure, singing and crying over the fate of Christ in a song of lamentation. A second figure followed, showing Christ attached to the whipping post and whipped by strong soldiers.... This, too, was accompanied by sad music. A group of flagellants followed, dressed in red sackcloth and whipping themselves so that their backs were covered in blood. The third figure showed Christ when he received the crown of thorns from the soldiers... confronting us with a vivid image of this. The fourth figure showed Pontius Pilate....

The fifth figure wasn't a painted image, but a living man who represented Christ carrying the cross, accompanied by a captain on his horse and followed by his mother the Virgin Mary and the apostle John. This was the end of the brotherhood in red cloth. They were followed by the aforementioned Brotherhood of Our Lady in black sackcloth. They carried an image of the cross on a pole ... and four boys dressed up as angels were singing a sad song. They, too, were followed by a group of flagellants who slashed up their backs with whips. Behind them was a figure of the Holy Virgin with her son in her lap. Again, an angel accompanied this scene with sad song and music. And this was all followed by a large group of flagellants who tortured their naked backs with all their might.

The third and final figure showed the body and the burial of the Lord. This was accompanied by four angels singing a sad lamentation. This was followed by the last large group of flagellants, who already had whipped themselves so much that they had to be told to cover their backs because their bodies were already covered with blood....

The last part of this army of soldiers [of Christ] consisted of those who carried the large and heavy wooden crosses ... followed by the members of the clergy, the aristocracy, major families, and others. They were all dressed in black and carried wooden blocks on their shoulders. Those who walked barefoot made an especially deep impression on the bystanders.... The end of the procession was formed by the citizens in their ordinary garb, carrying the Holy Cross. The procession reached from Holy Cross to Saint Ulrich and from there to the Perler Square and to the church of the Jesuits. Everyone was quiet and calm, and even the heretics [i.e. the Protestants] were deeply touched, either because they were truly moved or because they were terrified by the power of this spectacle, as the evil demons were.

In addition to this procession, the Brotherhood of Our Lady did not only spray their blood onto the streets of the city, but they attracted others who had not participated during the procession ... and so seven groups formed who whipped themselves in churches on the last day of the Holy Week.[14]

The procession through Augsburg as portrayed here is obviously also a political demonstration. It is a war parade against the Lutherans, one that aims to convert them to the Catholic faith through the power of images and exemplary piety. The fact that the processions, which apparently included all social classes and thereby encompassed the entire city, both began and ended at the church of the Jesuits is as much a part of the rhetoric of this passage as are the "figures" of which it speaks. This text of Gretser and Vetter, so thoroughly imbued with a polemical tone, declares itself to be not just one pamphlet among others, but the evocation of a radically different type of conversion. This is established not least by means of the images employed in the text. Like the processions themselves, the images are elements of a logic of the pictorial-affective return to God, a logic that sees its emblematic defense in the scene of voluntary flagellation. "Moved," "terrified," and "frightened" are the distinguishing words here, words marking the fact that from this standpoint, faith is inconceivable without an affective turning toward the image of the suffering God and his imitators.

Abbé Thiers's Defense of Flagellation

A final great debate over the meaning of flagellation as a spiritual practice occurred within the Catholic clergy around 1700 — about a century after the discussions in Augsburg and 130 years after the astonishing revival of the flagellation processions under Henry III in Paris. In 1703, Jean-Baptiste Thiers, "Doctor of Theology and parish priest of Vibraye," wrote the dedication to his *Critique de l'histoire des flagellans, et justification de l'usage des disciplines volontaires* (Critique of the history of the flagellants, and justification of the voluntary use of the whip). There we read the following words: "Monsignor, since voluntary discipline has a long tradition and is authorized by the church, it is all the more surprising that, for some time, efforts have been made to give it a bad name among the public."[15]

What Thiers is referring to is the work *Historia flagellantium* (History of the flagellants), by Abbé Jacques Boileau, "Doctor of

Theology of the House and Society of the Sorbonne and Canon of the Sainte-Chapelle of Paris," who despised and condemned this "most holy practice." According to Thiers, Boileau's book is pleasing only to heretics and libertines, and in this spirit he attempts to refute Boileau's arguments over the course of twenty chapters. Thiers's three primary complaints are the misleading title of Boileau's work, his poor literary style, and his deficient command of Latin. Furthermore, Boileau's manner of citing authors is said to be "too affected," and the text as a whole is said to have been composed in too wild a manner.

All of these points fill up four comprehensive chapters. Only then does Thiers come to the point and try to refute Boileau's arguments. This amounts primarily to the accusation that Boileau conflates heretical groups of late medieval flagellant sects with groups loyal to the church that flagellate themselves in a true spirit of penance without the support of erroneous opinions. Another problem is that Boileau regards flagellation "sursum" (on the back) and "deorsum" (on the waist and buttocks) as a shameless and disgraceful practice, and in Thiers's view this is based on false assumptions by Boileau. Finally, Thiers tries to show that Boileau's assertion of the pagan origins for flagellation does not entail that it cannot be a legitimate Christian penitential practice. There is always the possibility, for Thiers, that the early Christians adopted pagan customs for their own rites.[16]

His position is comparable to that of Gretser, who argued in a similar way against Martin Luther's critique of bodily ascesis. Much like the Spaniard Philippus Diez, who gives an example from "pagan Mexico," both Thiers and Gretser begin by assuming the possibility of a Christian transformation of pagan practices and defend such possibilities against accusations of idolatry. As Thiers asks:

> How then could one more gravely slander the saints who beat themselves *secundum sub* [on the loins and buttocks] than to assert that they were guilty of idolatry and superstition, that they had lost all reason and all sense of shame, that they were trapped in ignorance

and deviant belief, and in short, that they were wrong? Could one possibly do more dishonor to the saints, or at least to those who flagellated themselves, than Monsieur Boileau does here?[17]

What is most notable about Thiers's critique is a new accusation that had never played such a role in previous assessments of flagellation and that touches immediately upon Boileau's text. What is at issue here is the vivid presentation of the problematic in the text itself — that is to say, of Boileau's *narration* of all conceivable flagellation histories and the description of all possible scenes, especially the erotically tinged ones. Thiers emphasizes that "the sense of shame, even if contrary to Monsieur Boileau's intentions," is nonetheless lacking in his depictions ("la pudeur souffre un peu, quoique contre l'intention de M. Boileau"). In the earlier discussions of the ascetic significance of flagellation, this "erotic" aspect had not yet played any role. As we will see later, it is only with Boileau that it comes to the forefront as a central topic of discussion. Suddenly, the ambivalence of the flagellation images becomes thematic in such a way that it openly seeks to do justice to the Protestant critique and also to sweep it aside. What Boileau censures in the practice of flagellation, the weight and significance of pictorial arousal, is now turned back against him by Thiers, who accuses Boileau of arousing the imagination with his critical discussion of the example of flagellation, an arousal that marks the secularization of pictorial imitation that we find in the work of Gretser.

According to Thiers, almost every sin, almost every crime and transgression, can be named and narrated without danger, without the reader or hearer of the story being at immediate risk of being seduced by it. But as concerns the themes now under discussion, this is not the case, since readers and listeners are immediately affected — mental representations are stimulated by words, and through these representations the passions are aroused. Whenever there is talk of flagellation, whenever any sort of *impureté* is so much as mentioned, the speaker and hearer are stimulated by the word. In this way, Thiers holds Boileau guilty of the same act that he criticizes, since through "the stories that he relates, he teaches the very evil that he despises."[18] The narratives of flagellation that are supposedly meant to promote a sense of shame actually arouse the movements of precisely those passions that Boileau wishes to suppress. According to Thiers, Boileau becomes entangled in his own critique — which aims at suppressing a specific form of pictorial imitation but is incapable of doing so, since he is unable to subordinate the images that are evoked to the goal of exemplary imitation. Hence, in Thiers's view, the narratives that Boileau offers as horrifying examples of exaggerated ascesis and ambiguous casuistry are not so much examples of a misguided piety. Rather, they are a kind of seduction by means of a vivid language that no longer views itself as in the service of ascetic imitation and the sense of shame postulated by it. Hence, what Boileau produces is a libertine text that increases the arousal of the example by freeing it from its spiritual relation to the *imitatio Christi*. In this way, it unleashes pure arousal as such.

Harking back to Damian, who had already emphasized the same point, Thiers writes that when imitating ascetic models, it should be a matter of turning the body into an instrument ("like a drum with a tanned skin") on which blows are struck in praise of God. Here once more, mortification of the flesh with the whip can be seen as a kind of music, one that recalls the suffering of Christ and the apostles and the martyrs when the monks and nuns of all orders flagellate themselves.[19] As an expression of the *imitatio Christi*, of the wish for martyrdom, of the mortification of the flesh and its submission to the spirit and ultimately to penance, flagellation is simultaneously an act and sign of humility and shame. The catalog of holy flagellations and the constitutional structure of many orders, which Thiers takes as the authoritative foundation of his arguments, has the function of forming the actuality of life through examples. Yet the argumentation is more complex here than in the late medieval texts; Thiers thus reflects in a critical way the standpoint of Boileau, a matter to which we will return later. He explains that the examples, as allegorical images of human existence, are endangered in their spiritual status if any room is left for Boileau's critique. If we no longer accept exemplary vividness or the imitation of a model as a valid paradigm of our own existence (and Thiers is surely correct to say so), then we destroy the foundation of spiritual praxis to which flagellation also belongs. Flagellation will then appear as a sign of penance, with increasingly grotesque effects, and lose its character of the real performance of imitation. In this way, the images of flagellation become deeply ambivalent, because their potential for imaginative-affective arousal is no longer related to the *imitatio Christi*, but instead is released into a dangerous sort of freedom — one that breathes the air of the libertine.

For Thiers, the ambivalence of the images unleashed by Boileau becomes an important theme. This is especially true when considering nakedness or the concrete description of flagellant praxis. Thiers is quite clear that any Catholic theology of imitation cannot aim at a thorough condemnation of the ambivalence of arousal (which can be expressed as both a pictorial-affective devotional imitation and as a libertine ecstasy) through a total renunciation of pictorial-imitative ascesis, as was attempted by Protestant critics of the practice as well as by Boileau. Instead, it is a matter of regarding ambivalence as a possibility of being transformed by the image of Christ as presented by the tradition of the lives of the saints and as practiced in the spirituality and rhetoric of the Jesuits. Only in this way can we see the radical realization of finitude in the death of God as also marking the possibility of the liberation of humanity.

In this way, Thiers defends the flagellation of the naked flesh as a type of ascesis able to achieve precisely this. Following the example of Saint Anthony, it unleashes arousal while also binding its demonic force in a relation to God, the Passion, and the Crucifixion. Thiers repeats Damian's argument that Christ and the martyrs were not ashamed of their nakedness and that "no one should be ashamed of baring their flesh, which will one day feed the worms."[20] Instead, nakedness is a radical relinquishment and renunciation, a realization of finitude.

In fact, one suffers more strongly and therefore earns greater merit, when one beats flesh that is fully exposed instead of covered by a cloak. For this reason, the monks and nuns today receive the blows of the whip on the shoulders, somewhat lower near the kidneys, or even on the naked thighs. But they do this not before the eyes of their brothers or sisters, but alone in their cells, in the chapter hall, in the choir of the church, in the church itself, or in some other place set aside for this purpose. As they do so, the windows are closed and perfect darkness prevails. In this way they prevent the shamelessness that might appear when flagellating oneself while naked.[21]

Despite this apparent limitation to the private realm, what Thiers especially defends is public flagellation. He even defends its exemplary-pictorial effect against the critique inspired by Gerson. Vincent Ferrer, whom he cites, is not assigned to the realm of heresy, but instead is regarded as the one who, in the debate initiated by the Council of Konstanz, grasped better than others the "fruits" that flagellation is able to produce "in the spirit of the penitent." This signifies in turn an apologia for the image, which moves, which arouses, which affects the spectator and thereby gains its legitimacy.

Saint Vincent Ferrer wished that those who followed him, in order to repent of their sins, should arrange processions every day through the cities and the places where they were. While doing so, they should sing hymns that he had composed for these occasions, and move through the streets with naked shoulders while flagellating themselves.... Everyone should declare with loud voices that this was happening for the sake of the remembrance of the suffering of Christ and for liberation from our sins. These flagellation processions were so pious and edifying, so full of groaning and wailing, that not only did the spectators break out in tears, but more than this — deeply moved by this impressive example — they would immediately attach themselves to this follower of God and those who accompanied him.[22]

It is precisely this effect, which Gerson found disturbing insofar as it excludes the word and reason in favor of an immediate effect upon the affective part of the soul, that is most important for Thiers. Stated concisely, we might say that for Thiers, there is no salvation through the word alone. Salvation happens only in the complementary relation of word and flesh, which is constituted through the arousing force of the image and the gestures of imitation. According to Thiers, Christian salvation presupposes the formation of life through images that function in exemplary fashion and that make the body, imagination, and the affects into integral parts of this transformation in the face of divine suffering.

"Cet humiliant spectacle," this humiliating drama, is an expression that continually resurfaces in the work of Thiers. It refers to a theatricality without which he would find Christian life inconceivable. This theatrical shaping of life was put into effect by the flagellant communities whose rules are cited by Thiers: for instance, from the provincial council of Milan in 1569 and an entire series of similar stipulations in seventeenth century France.[23] Also cited are resolutions on ecclesiastical penance rituals. These come from Evreux in 1606, Arras in 1628, Beauvais in 1637, Rouen and Chartres in 1640, Orleans in 1642, Bourges in 1666, and from other places, all of them demonstrating that flagellation was one of the most habitual and useful forms of penance. Even if there is no evidence of voluntary flagellation before Peter Damian (a thesis that both Thiers and Gretser seek to refute with numerous arguments), the list of examples makes clear that flagellation, like many other ecclesiastical customs and rituals, had been established over the course of time as an important means of recollection and penance.

It drew its legitimacy from its function. Even the "tradition" that plays such an essential role here can ultimately be traced back to the *function* of flagellation, since this consists in nothing other than the tradition of exemplary gestures and forms of life, indeed, in the appropriation of all tradition as an example that either attracts or repels. Hence, the spiritual-ascetic tradition is ultimately not dependent on Scripture, for "who can prove that Saint

Romuald and the blessed John of Mont-Férêtre [two hermits] did not learn this pious practice from other hermits who lived before them, and these hermits in turn from still others?"[24] What becomes evident here (as was repeatedly remarked in the apologetics of the flagellants) is a possible genealogy of the praxis of flagellation — one whose origin is entirely separate from Scripture and that owes its existence to an imitation practiced in living examples, thus to a purely pictorial-bodily imitation. Its (fictional) origin ultimately lies nowhere else than in the immediately moving sight of the suffering God.

The theater of hermits and ascetics since the eleventh century includes not only Damian and Dominicus Loricatus, but also such figures as Saint Guido, the abbot of Pomposa, Saint Poppo, the abbot of Stablo, and many others reported by both Damian and Thiers. For Thiers, this becomes an interface with the history of salvation, one through which bodily mortification with the scourge finally enters public consciousness and thus changes from a secret ascetic practice into a general spiritual resource. From this point onward, recollection of the Passion is in his eyes necessarily bound up with the gesture of flagellation. It is the place where *memoria*, the engaged memory of the suffering of Christ, converges with individual penance, through which humanity achieves salvation and is adopted once more by God.

Thiers does not locate the high point of this pious praxis in the Middle Ages, but in the seventeenth century, from which he draws most of his examples, especially those taken from the constitutions of orders and brotherhoods. The portrait that Thiers paints of the orders and congregations that institutionalized flagellation confirms that both the communities of Augustinian origin and those of a Benedictine persuasion provide a genuine tableau vivant or living picture of the *imitatio Christi* and penitential imitation. This includes both monks and nuns, but also pious laymen. Accordingly, wherever one looks, what is customary is flagellation on Friday after matins, performed during the recitation of the psalm "Miserere," the antiphons "Christus factus est pro nobis" and "Respice." Often during Advent and Lent, flagellation

took place on Mondays and Wednesdays, while in the week between Palm Sunday and the Saturday before Easter flagellation
was a daily event. Beyond this, all the various orders had their
own specific regulations, while individuals were often left free to
give themselves additional whipping at their own discretion.

In his book, Thiers assembles a catalog of all forms and regulations known to him. He does so in such detail that one has the
sense that he wants to be part of the production of this tableau of
flagellants and expand it further — a tableau whose exemplary status in all its possible variations later found even more imitators.[25]
The gallery of individual ascetic destinies, which encompasses
clerics, monks, nuns, and laymen, and whose lives Thiers depicts
both vividly and in detail, is here transposed into a universal
gestural praxis.[26] One is tempted to conclude with Thiers that
wherever we look, those who are actually pious will flagellate
themselves, thereby situating themselves in a gallery of exemplary
figures who use flagellation to transmit the image that, in the
exercise of penance, fuses affect and imagination with the model
of Christ.

According to Thiers, this is the solution that "true" Christians
oppose to the ambivalence inherent in all pictorial arousal. Unlike
the Protestants, "true" Christians do not abolish the ambivalence
of images and their affective power and transform the *imitatio
Christi* into an always experimental exercise of pictorial-affective
arousal. For Thiers, flagellation has legitimacy as an exemplary
praxis of imitation amid the series of imitative images that stretch
from antiquity into early modernity, images that produce a bodily-
experiential relation to the first figure who was beaten: Christ.
Through imitation, the painfully rousing sight of Christ's suffering is uninterruptedly transmitted. In this way, flagellation is the
deepest expression of imitation ("plus sensible témoignage") and
of the longing for martyrdom ("marque du desir sincère et ardent
du martyre").[27] It kindles the "fire of devotion" ("feu de la dévotion") in which Christians become like the lamb of God and are
freed from their sins.[28]

Abbé Boileau's Critique

This form of pictorial-bodily exemplarity, which imitates the suffering of Christ, is addressed primarily to the affects and the imagination. It is precisely this sort of exemplarity that is central to Jacques Boileau's critique of flagellation. Yet Boileau's initial claim is more deeply rooted and more practical:

> What caused the author to write this book were the various opinions held concerning the use and abuse of "discipline" as received either on the back or on the hindquarters. Even the scholars who were drawn into the discussion by several popes and who were offered great reimbursement for their reviews were not of one opinion. Who does not wonder in amazement as he watches otherwise rational men display a grisly and barbaric side that leads them to tear up their skin with blows of the whip, which they do as though it were part of a simple, holy, and pious life?

The preface to the French translation of Jacques Boileau's 1700 book *Historia flagellantium* notes that we are dealing with a "sujet assez piquant de lui-même," a "piquant subject." The preface tells us that the author speaks here not as a theologian, but as a critic and intellectual who is concerned by the abuse of the practice. In this book, which first appeared in Latin and then the following year in French in Amsterdam, Boileau's accusations against flagellation range from perversion to madness, from shamelessness (especially in connection with the "lower discipline") to superstition. On July 9, 1703, the book was placed on the church's *Index librorum prohibitorum*, its list of prohibited books.

Boileau had returned somewhat earlier from a trip to Flanders, where he had noticed the fashion of "shameless and lascivious necklines," leading him to publish a treatise entitled *De l'abus des nuditez de la gorge* (On the excessive fashion of low-cut dresses). His critique of flagellation is likewise aimed at its "abuse." As stated in the first chapter of his book, "abuse" refers to flagellation in cases where it is "detached from other practices of mortification" and lays claim to some sort of special status. Even if Boileau distinguishes his own position from those of the Lutheran and Calvinist critics and emphasizes the significance of the Catholic tradition (especially that of the church in France), his views still have numerous points of contact with the Protestant position. This is most true as concerns the meaning of figurality and the visual display that addresses the passions and that so appalled him in the necklines of Flemish women. His target in this critique of fashion (which was translated into English shortly after its appearance) is the arousal that begins from the sight of the "pretty swelling breasts" and that passes through the eyes to inflame a boundless "sensuality" and "libertinage."[29]

In his eyes, the same thing happens when the lives of the ascetics become the object of visual contemplation and intensive sensual experience. Like Martin Luther before him, Boileau speaks with astonishment of the spirituality of the desert hermits and their ascetic achievements. And like Luther, he remarks that such achievements deserve our respect, though not in the literal sense that they actually ought to be imitated.[30] Here, too, the critique aims at a specific concept of exemplarity and figurality: "I find that the life of the hermits of Thebais [in Egypt], Syria, and Palestine should be respected, rather than imitated. For these holy men have, in a unique way and in guiltless virtuousness and through much trouble, laid the path into paradise and transformed themselves into angels." But flagellation played no role in this process, as Boileau aims to show. Indeed, it is sheer innovation when flagellants voluntarily torment themselves "on the back or hindquarters" with "whips, cords, and rods." Both "the upper discipline" of the shoulders and back, as well as "the lower discipline" on the buttocks were not customary in the early history of the church; according to Boileau, the latter is of especially "recent date." For him, these practices contradict both piety and any sense of shame. They arise from "idolatry and superstition" and could have been introduced only with the "beautiful semblance of piety and mortification."

Boileau points to the same sort of ambivalent figurality that was already criticized by the Protestant opponents of Jakob

Gretser. Like these critics, he believes that there is something essentially misleading about the effect of images.

> It seems to me that the painters with their pictures have contributed not a little to establishing this practice and helping it make its break-through. For Pope Gregory I . . . wrote that pictures "are the libraries of unlearned Christians." In any case, the painters have scarcely ever painted a hermit of olden days without placing either a scourge or rod somewhere on the canvas, even if the good hermits in question had never used such an instrument or even thought about it in their lives. As a result, in the past century, many good writers have con-flated the "discipline" with other forms of bodily ascesis and propagated it as such, without differentiating all of these forms.

Meanwhile, Boileau emphasizes in highly ironic fashion that it is "not [his] goal to fight against these great men, the towering members of the Jesuit order and the scholarly world." The point for him is more to criticize the "ignorance and pushiness of the painters, of whom Lucian said in his *Dialogue on Paintings* that they are just as free as the poets." A further point is to criticize the custom of hanging in the churches paintings that contain both fables and outright lies. Truth and lie stand opposed here in a way that counters the seductive image, which "remains fixed and immobile in the center of all the confusions of the human spirit" ("elle demeure fixe et inébranlable au milieu de tous les égare-ments de l'esprit humain").[31] It should be added that when he speaks of the painters, Boileau is referring to the Jesuits, whose rhetorical strategies he holds in low regard.

Boileau begins by demonstrating that self-flagellation cannot be justified on the basis of the Old Testament, since in the Mosaic law God forbids self-mutilation. In his view, the Old Testament agrees with the standpoint of natural reason, which commands humans to abstain from such practices. Of the eleven passages in the New Testament that speak of flagellation, Boileau says that not one of them can be interpreted in the sense of the self-flagellation advocated by Jakob Gretser. Even the philological argument that

Gretser imports from 1 Corinthians 9.27 ("but I pommel my body and subdue it, lest after preaching to others I myself should be disqualified") cannot be maintained, in Boileau's view. The Greek word *hypopiazein*, which according to Gretser signifies that one "leaves welts on the body with a whip," has additional meanings that have nothing to do with flagellation. Moreover, according to Boileau, neither the Greek nor the Latin church fathers understood the text in Gretser's sense. Hence, Boileau explains that the passage can be interpreted entirely in terms of fasting and other ascetic practices of the mortification of the flesh, but not self-flagellation, as Gretser asserts.

In the next chapter of his work, Boileau shows that flagellation is actually of pagan origin, whether considered as a form of punishment or as voluntary flagellation within a ritual framework. He draws the needed evidence from Tertullian and Plutarch and also refers to Cicero, Lucian, Philostratus, and Herodotus, who are cited in evidence that flagellation originated in the Isis cult of Egypt, where men and women mutually whipped one another. He also describes in detail various cults of Diana, as well as the Roman Lupercalia festival, which prove that flagellation in antiquity and late antiquity was typical among the pagans, but not the Christians. Once more it is Gretser's arguments that are targeted when considering the relevant passages that justify flagellation in the eyes of the Jesuits. Boileau takes aim not just at Gretser in his capacity as philologist and theologian, but also at Gretser's model of exemplarity and imitation:

> I have found only a single example of voluntary flagellation in the early history of Christendom. It concerned a virgin who dressed as a man and lived under the name of Joseph. The Jesuit Gretser took this story from a manuscript of 1538 and told it in the thirteenth chapter of his book on discipline in the following words: "She was filled with such penitence over all the terrible satisfactions that she had earlier enjoyed, that her spirit found no rest. She found this only in the mortification of the flesh. Intoxicated with the sweetness of the flesh of the Easter lamb, and inflamed by a holy enthusiasm, she

cut out pieces of her own body, which she despised, and buried these in the earth." Yet the Christian faith forbids us from following such strange examples.[32]

With this brief final remark, Boileau takes a distance from Gretser not only through his ironic philological critique (the reference to the dating of the manuscript), but above all with a view to the significance of the image and of exemplarity. Jakob Gretser is the rhetorical painter of whom Boileau spoke at the outset. His examples are more closely related to the pagan practice of flagellation and to idolatry than to the Christian ascetic practices that Boileau draws from the church fathers.

Nor is Gretser the sole target. Whenever Boileau looks at translations, he finds that the Jesuits use the words "flagellate," "whip," and "beat" in their translations and make use of pictorially evocative verbs in places where the texts speak of chastisement, penance, and mourning in a much less specific sense. According to Boileau, it turns out that in the entire literature of the early lives of the saints and of Greek and Latin theologians, there is not a single passage that speaks of voluntary flagellation, even though mention is made of all other possible ascetic practices. The early founders of orders and their rules do not speak of voluntary flagellation. In short, flagellation during the first thousand years of church history belonged neither to the church's means of salvation nor to the ascetic methodology of Christian perfection or forms of holy life. As Boileau repeatedly emphasizes, it was a praxis that contradicted both Christian life and the ideal ascetic pursuit of perfection, one whose success had been due solely to a specific rhetoric. It is this rhetoric that invented flagellation as an ascetic praxis that can be depicted in painting and is able to cause arousal by pictorial means. It is a question here of a history of seduction.

Hence, the introduction of flagellation by Damian "in the year 1047 or 1056" (Boileau ascribes it to Damian's models Dominicus Loricatus and Rodulf of Gubbio) already meets with Boileau's resistance. In the examples given by Damian, a "superhuman" flagellation praxis that no normal human would be able to imitate is linked with a "dubious political engagement" by Damian on the side of Pope Alexander II. According to Boileau, the new penitential praxis arose from a diffuse enthusiasm and from the opportunism of Damian, who with this new practice also wished to create a kind of monument for the pope.[33] From the relevant surviving letters, Boileau gathers that numerous monks rightly opposed flagellation from the start and also became involved in a discussion with Damian, who eventually had to concede that on a scriptural basis it was only flagellation as a praxis of *punishment* that could be justified, not as a voluntary *ascetic* praxis. His observations are supported above all by the correspondence of Damian with Petrus Cerebrosus and the brothers of Montecassino. From Damian's tone and style, Boileau concludes that he respected differing opinions, that he was conscious of the radical modernity of the policy he advocated, and that he in no way wished to establish it as a prescription and a necessity. In this passage, Boileau returns once more to the work of Gretser, now clearly recognizable as his most important opponent. He is the "learned Jesuit who wrote numerous books in defense of voluntary flagellation, conflating it with all other techniques of chastisement that our predecessors practiced."

This mixing of flagellation with other, more moderate ascetic techniques is a thorn in Boileau's side. Guided by the perspective of his critique, he works out a genuine deconstruction of the historical gallery of flagellants offered by Gretser in the *Virgidemia Volciana*. In the process, he aims not only to show in a correct historico-critical and philological way that all the lives of the saints presented by Gretser breathe an atmosphere that already presupposes Damian's reforms. More than this, he seeks to pass critical judgment on the supposed exemplarity of the lives and their reception in the first place. Boileau differentiates here between respect or wonderment at the highest ascetic achievements of the saints and the question as to how normal believers should imitate them. According to Boileau, no one should regard himself as actually obliged to imitate these acts, for who could think himself capable of an equally self-abnegating piety? The exemplary figures he presents are not only the great sufferers, but above all the saints who remained steadfast in the sight of naked temptation.

This is precisely what Boileau excludes as a possibility for normal Christians. As we will see, he intends not just to show the overpowering force of eros in every flagellation scenario, but above all to demonstrate and to condemn the seductive power of images because of their ambivalence, which cannot be handled by the common believer. The Holy Fool Simeon of Emesa, Saint Bernardin of Siena, the Capuchin brother Matthew of Avignon all successfully withstood the efforts of naked woman who sought to seduce them. Yet in the wake of these examples, Boileau also presents the example of the "Father Cornelius Adriaensen." According to contemporary sources, in the middle of the sixteenth century Adriaensen assembled a group of women around him and was not content to "strike them with knotted cords," but also "gently touched their naked thighs and naked backsides with rods of willow or birch." This history of Cornelius Adriaensen, to which we will return in the next chapter, forms the paradigm of a danger and an unavoidable abuse that Boileau regards as inherent in voluntary flagellation as such.

This final counterexample cited by Boileau marks a radical historical break, after which flagellation is no longer primarily understood as a spiritual praxis, but as a form of ascesis that conceals an erotic ambivalence, and deliberately so. Not only the critics of flagellation are convinced on this point, but even a portion of its defenders. As already seen, Thiers accused Boileau of treating the ambivalence of images in negligent fashion and of evoking such ambivalence and parading before the eyes of the reader things that give rise to arousal in the wrong sense, rather than a sense focused on the imitation of Christ.

The case of "Father Adriaensen," in which according to Boileau an abuse of flagellation praxis can be grasped in exemplary fashion, points, as he sees it, not merely to the danger of abuse. It also testifies to the pagan origin of flagellation in ancient rituals involving nudity, erotic chastisement, and spiritual-lascivious arousal. From the evidence of Damian's letters and other sources, such as a *Histoire de la table ronde et des faits du chevalier Lancelot du Lac* (Tales of the round table and the deeds of the knight Lancelot du Lac), total nakedness was typical during flagellation even in medieval times. In Boileau's eyes, this links flagellation to the pagan traditions, which do not so much "bear witness to great piety" as form "a source of lascivious arousal." Concerning a scene from the medieval novel, in which the king strips himself naked before the bishops, priests, and his subjects, breaks out in tears, sinks naked onto his knee, confesses his sins, and receives blows of the whip as his penance, Boileau does not speak of a wondrous spirituality, but of "products of straying desire" ("productions d'une volupté desordonné"). Here it is not a matter of following true wisdom, but of performing "exercises of fantastic and misguided piety."[34] Precisely for this reason, since nakedness leads to shamelessness and unregulated desire, the monastic tradition has always prescribed perfectly vain measures to protect against it. Boileau asserts that these measures were regularly undermined by the practice of flagellation, since in his opinion this practice awakens perverse desire by its very nature. In short, every use of the whip has a tendency to awaken not piety, but erotic desire, with which all arousal through flagellation will now be identified. According to Boileau, this is a pagan legacy lurking at the very heart of Jesuit piety.

What Boileau presents is also to be read as an ironic variation on Gretser's gallery of flagellants, even as a parody of it. Here it is primarily a question of (entirely religious) histories in which racy or erotic aspects come to the fore. The lives that Gretser reads with a view to the salvation of humanity as examples of model religious lives now appear in a different light, as examples of a dangerously neglectful ascetic practice that conflates penance with desire. *Voluptas* (desire) and *pietas* (piety) can therefore both arise from or be witnessed by the same gesture of flagellation, the same staging. Yet according to Boileau, worldly desire is no doubt stronger, since flagellation isolates, cultivates, and just barely conceals the moment of arousal in ascesis.

Beyond this, as shown by a whole series of medieval histories presented by Boileau, flagellation must be seen in particular as a superstitious practice whose significance should not be taken seriously in theological terms. He comments ironically on his anti-Gretserian gallery of examples: "In what unbelievable extravagances can the human spirit find satisfaction, especially if it possesses the allure of the new!"[35] Among such extravagances Boileau includes the flagellant movement, which he condemns with the same arguments used by Gerson. Self-mutilation by means of loathsome injuries, a pagan or superstitious understanding of penance, and finally the sensual temptation produced by undressing — these are Boileau's main arguments as to why reasonable men are forbidden to follow such a practice, which, we have seen, had come back into fashion even in Paris in 1575 under Henry III.

Only at the close of his work does Boileau turn toward the medicinal questions that Jakob Gretser had already touched upon. Against Gretser, who had consulted a physician and from this had concluded that flagellation was harmless,[36] Boileau emphasizes that blows on the shoulder are damaging, for they "block up the life spirit coming through the nerves from the brain" and in this way are particularly liable to impair the sense of sight. If such practices are followed excessively, the result will be blindness. "For this reason," Boileau adds, "the Capuchins and various orders of nuns switched to tearing their backs or thighs with thorn-covered rods or knotted cords" and hence no longer whip their backs. However, this solution conceals a far greater danger, for the blows on the lower back and the region of the buttocks "violently drive the animal spirits against the pubic bone [os pubis] and awaken unchaste movements due to their proximity to the genital region."

Thus, at the close of Boileau's volume we have once more returned to where the danger lay all along: to the connection between flagellation and the erotically aroused imagination. To my knowledge, this is the first time this danger was identified in connection with ascetic flagellation, although Luther's derisive remarks on the mortification of the flesh obviously point in the same direction. Physiology now forms an important basis of the argument. Boileau concludes the passage as follows: "The impressions thereby awakened flow into the brain, where they paint living pictures of forbidden desires, which captivate the brain with their deceitful magic and deliver chastity to a life-and-death struggle." Moreover (and here Boileau cites the opinion of the doctor Johann Heinrich Meibom, of whom we will have much to say), flagellation of the buttocks or the loins ("deorsum") heats up the portion of the seminal fluid that, in the theory of his day, comes from the brain and is transported by vessels that lie on both sides of the spinal column. Under the blows of the whip, "the seminal fluid is heated up and forced into the genitals, where it arouses a boundless desire ... and summons us to the raw enjoyment of fleshly satisfaction." According to Boileau, this is confirmed by the tales of men who "were never able to satisfy their raw desire ... and became intoxicated with shameful pleasures" of which they became capable after use of the whip or rod. In the concluding series of examples, Boileau seems to take pleasure in the raciest details of the medical literature, which prove that "discipline d'enbas," meaning blows upon the back and thigh, are not merely a "useless modern invention," but an "exercice mauvais, villain et infame" and thus a "shameful and shameless practice" that contradicts all decency.[37]

Jacques Boileau's brother, the poet and theorist of literature Nicolas Boileau-Despréaux, summarized the critique of the theologians in the following lines:

Qui, sous couleur d'étaindre en nous la volupté,
Par l'austérité et par la pénitence
Sait allumer le feu de la lubricité.[38]

Who, through severity and repentance,
under the cover of mortifying desire,
knows how to kindle the fire of the flesh.

Boileau's arguments do not flatly disqualify the example of the saints and ascetics, but they do draw a distinction that marks an absolute separation between "normal" Christians and ascetics. There is no longer a fine line between the two, and for Boileau, the believer is incapable of living in ambivalence in the same way as evoked by the gestures of the ascetic. A new status is thereby assigned to exemplarity. The example is an image that is not actually supposed to be imitated in a bodily, sensual, and affective way, but instead is to be believed in the context of edifying readings or enjoyed in the context of aesthetic contemplation. Exemplarity does not institute some sort of physical continuity with the original models of Christ, the martyrs, and the ascetics, transformed repeatedly through affective arousal by the image. It cannot become the basis for a ritual realization, one in which men and women push their finitude to the point of excess in the experience of bodily pain even while transcending it in mystical-pictorial fashion through equivalence with Christ. Rather, for Boileau, the ascetic gesture is only representative and symbolic. Flagellation as pictorial imitation, whose meaning consists in exemplary arousal, is in one sense a kind of pagan idolatry and in another sense (given the desire that it arouses) a medium of "pagan," bodily, erotic experience. Hence, for Boileau (who much like Luther paves the way for a strict dualism between the bodily and spiritual realms), it is nothing other than a dubious practice that, promoted by the vivid rhetoric of the Jesuits, arises from an incorrect understanding of exemplarity and imitation. In addition, the medical theory of the humors, which here takes on new authority, proves that flagellation of the loins, thighs, and buttocks always aims at a psychophysical arousal in the sense of fleshly desire and is thus unable to form the basis of a spiritual praxis.

Here we are on the verge of a structural bifurcation, one that in dealing with images no longer deals with the ambivalence of desire, but seeks instead to overcome this ambivalence and therefore demands a new praxis for dealing with images. Thus, what is central is no longer a pictorial-affective imitation, but (even for Boileau) an enlightened and faithful wonderment. This means that what comes to the fore in flagellation is the arousal of lustful images no longer under the control of the model of the imitation of Christ. At the same time, it is condemned as an arousal that withdraws from the power of reason. From this point onward, erotic arousal becomes the "libertine," "pornographic," or "hysterical" counterpoint to spirituality, rather than the condition of possibility of spiritual experience.

PART TWO

Erotics

CHAPTER FIVE

The Priest, the Woman, and the
Divine Marquis

When speaking in modern times of flagellation, penance, and arousal, the first thing that comes to mind is not so much the ecstasies of Saint Mary Magdalen de' Pazzi and Saint Teresa of Avila, but the notorious stories of such figures as the Marquis de Sade. For the modern enlightened understanding, it is only here that we find the "true" reality of flagellation, seen as only superficially concealed in religious practice. This purported true reality takes the form of "repressed sexual desire" or "hysterical extravagance" (especially in the case of nuns), which has been subjected to enlightened analysis by modern medicine and psychology since the nineteenth century. Such activities are consigned to pathology, even though the medieval and early modern religious sources specifically *do not* establish any relation between the effects of flagellation on the body and soul and what is now termed "sexuality." This relation surfaced only around 1700, in Boileau's critique of flagellation. Only there do we pass beyond mere mistrust of the effect of exemplary narratives of flagellation and the blows of the scourge on the body and hear the flat-out assertion that the supposed spiritual transformations seen by the monastic tradition are actually a matter of erotic stimulation. According to Boileau, the danger of libidinous arousal in flagellation (both physiologically and psychologically) reaches such a degree that the practice must be altogether abandoned.

What begins to predominate is a standpoint that criticizes any inclusion of the body and the imagination in the drama of salvation (as referred to by Peter Damian in connection with flagellation) — a critique made in the name of a psychological and medical discourse. This discourse, which to some extent follows the Lübeck doctor Johann Heinrich Meibom, is focused on physical arousal and the absolute primacy of erotic images, which in modern eyes can at best be transformed for spiritual use. Around 1700 (anticipating the modern hegemony of sexual discourse), the critics of flagellation began to suppose that the imagined proximity to God and the images of spiritual voluptuousness staged in flagellation are really nothing but the fulfillment of an erotic-libidinous desire — a fulfillment that is both concealed and sublimated and that draws a perverse connection between desire and pain. The ambivalence of images and their affective impact, which for Mechtild of Magdeburg or Hadewijch of Antwerp allowed for a language in which the erotic and the spiritual are mutually transparent, was thereby abolished in favor of a clear separation.

Lascivious Fantasies

In his critique of the flagellants, Boileau is thinking especially of scenes and narratives (which were already stock scenarios as early as the Middle Ages) in which the priest uses his pictorial-affective rhetoric to seduce the pious sinner or the nun, playing with flagellation in a kind of double game behind which we catch a glimpse of concealed diabolical shadows that first come fully to light with the libertines of the seventeenth and eighteenth centuries. More than this, he is thinking of spiritual arousal itself, which abandons all "reasonable" or literally determinate relation to God. An exemplary case can be found in the practice of flagellation, such as in the image of Saint Catherine of Siena kneeling before the cross.

For the critics, examples of spiritual arousal such as those provided by Damian in the lives of Dominicus Loricatus and the sisters of Unterlinden, with their communal, liturgical flagellation, become nothing but further instances of an apparently devotional desire that is in fact purely physical. They see it as a kind of pagan idolatry that mistakes earthly vividness and bodily experience for the divine. The staging of flagellation here remains an outstanding example of spiritual arousal, yet the condition has disappeared that was obligatory for flagellation from Damian to Gretser and Thiers: exemplarity was not supposed to be taken as a norm or convention of devotional ascesis, but as a psychophysical or affective-imaginative continuity between God and humanity — one that was constituted by the exemplar and that linked every aroused flagellant to the desert fathers, the martyrs, and ultimately to Christ at the whipping column. Hence, the concealed meaning pointed to by the example was the presence of the suffering body of Christ in every ascetic. Like Holy Scripture, the example holds an allegorical sense that was not supposed to be read literally, but simply related to the spiritual presence of the divine. In exemplary flagellation, this also meant that such presence became open to bodily experience as the flagellant became "another Christ" in his or her own body. Once this physical continuity and the constitutive function of flagellation was questioned (as in Boileau), thereby losing its implicit spiritual psychology, all that remained was the stimulation of fantasy as a singular moment that seems suspiciously similar to affective-imaginative arousal without any true connection to its model.

Through his mimetic action, the flagellant was meant to become an enactment of recollection and a "second Christ." However, there was no longer any special status for this enactment. It was now merely a sign of a recollection that represents and signifies a moment in the history of salvation — without producing this moment anew through arousal by the staged image and without creating any supposed continuity with its model. Obviously, this form of arousal is unleashed primarily in the body, especially by means of flagellation or the exemplary image. This physicality now began to inspire mistrust toward the proverbially lascivious monks and corrupted nuns who were devoted to such practices and (according to Boileau and the critical tradition he inspired) who secretly experienced the supposedly spiritual and pious actions as purely libidinous and erotic.

223

Boileau was not alone in this critique. Lecherous monks and lascivious nuns were stock characters of erotic and anticlerical literature. Through countless "anecdotes" and "histories," which managed to circulate despite official suppression, these well-known figures nourished and roused the fantasies of historiographers and collectors. They were also the basis for anticlerical polemics in the Middle Ages and again beginning in the eighteenth century.[1] The historian of human sexuality Iwan Bloch writes in his history of culture and morals that the "truly modern, refined form of illicit sexuality . . . always flourishes best in the specifically Catholic countries, in the places devoted to ascesis and celibacy."[2] In this way, it was flagellation (viewed as perverse, archaic, or sanctimonious) that became the special target of critics of the church, for it apparently displays the duplicitous morality of the church's agents.

Indeed, such critique often took the explicit form of polemical insinuations concerning the secret ribaldry of the clergy. Henry Spencer Ashbee, one of the most important bibliographers of erotic literature in the nineteenth century (of whom more below) notes this connection in his *Centuria librum absconditorum*. At the same time, his commentary also displays the hypocritical attitude of an Enlightenment man in his judgment of supposedly dark prehistory as he turns monks and nuns into examples of unbridled lust. According to Ashbee, "enlightenment and education" are the best weapons "against vice and error." Yet the curiosity of this enlightened erotomaniac constantly aims at those figures in whose shadow carnality and vice blossom to a special degree. These are the men of the church, especially Jesuits, to whom he devotes not just a few pages of his introduction but also large parts of his bibliography.[3] Moreover, as often occurs with critiques of the Jesuit order, his observations concerning the lascivious fantasies of clerics does not exclude rabbis, who in this way are placed in close proximity to Catholic spirituality and its vivid and seductive rhetoric. As his most damning and illuminating example, Ashbee recalls "Rabbi Eleazer" and "Rabbi Solomon Jarchi," who supposedly taught that God created Eve because

224

Adam had already had sex with all the animals of paradise and was still not satisfied.[4] In Ashbee's bibliography, this is supposed to prove the close connection between Catholic and Jewish hermeneutics and rhetoric, for in both cases, the exegetical and parenetic dialogue demonstrates the unleashing of fantasy through an allegorizing-pictorial reading of Scripture.

But according to Ashbee, nothing reaches the level of imagination displayed by the casuistical Jesuits, as expressed for example in the "Catalog of Questions" drawn from the *Disputationes de sancto matrimonii sacramento* (Disputations on the sacrament of holy matrimony) of Tomás Sánchez. Ashby, whose voyeuristic lust for the genealogy of erotic fantasies is barely concealed behind his gestures of enlightenment, tells us that Sánchez considers the following questions: whether it is permitted to ejaculate outside the vagina, whether one may think of another woman while having sex with his wife, whether the man may withdraw while the woman ejaculates, and whether Mary ejaculated when the Holy Spirit came over her. Incidentally, this question was taken up by Samuel Schroeerus in his 1709 *Dissertatio theologica de sanctificatone seminis Mariae Virginis in actu conceptionis Christi* (Theological dissertation on the sanctification of the semen of the Virgin Mary in the act of conception of Christ), which he answered in passing by saying that the Holy Spirit, when it came over Mary, "due to its creative power also created at the same time the semen that she discharged, as belongs naturally to every act of procreation." Ashbee refers to such theological discussions as examples of the lack of inhibition of the fantasies of clerics, who conceal their immoral subversion behind their habits. Their power and their secret intention does not lie in the consideration of a technical question, but in the evocation of an intense visual language that arouses the fantasy.[5]

Today, the work of Tomás Sánchez is seen by historians of church and society as an example of the church's turn away from sexual pessimism of the Augustinian style following the Counter-Reformation.[6] But for Ashbee, it becomes an example of condemnable permissiveness, given the stimulating potential of the imagination. With this background in mind, Luther's critique of the life of the clergy should also be read as a demand that fantasy be subjected to a radical discipline.

This demand may have been sharpened further in the debates between orthodox Lutherans and Pietists. With all due reservations, we can speak with Norbert Elias of a "civilizing process" in the modern period, leading to increased control of drive, affect, and especially the play of affect and imagination. Yet this does not mean, with Elias and against Foucault, that we are faced here with an "oppression of sexuality." The modern development must be viewed instead (with Foucault) from the standpoint of a specific economy of the affective and imaginative capacity of the soul, one that first gave rise to the field from which the "dispositif of sexuality" that dominates the moderns would later arise.

Whatever Ashbee discusses is changed from an individual case into an exemplar — not an exemplar of moral theology or sinful transgression, but of a shameful and fascinating arousal of fantasy whose concealed origin lies in a specific theological discourse. It is precisely this provocative way of relying on the power of the imagination and the vivid evocation that here becomes the primary object of suspicion. What is central is not the figure of transgression (the imaginative sin and therefore one that is all the more desirable), but the perverse stimulation of fantasy, the arousal that lurks behind the mask of the ascetic.

The mistrust of such stimulation, directed against rabbis and Jesuits alike and ascribing the same shameless character to both (as depicted with various tales and graphic anecdotes), endured into the middle of the twentieth century. In the 1930s, it was expressed in such works as Anton Kaiser's *Josephsbrüder: Jesuitengeist und Judengeist* (Joseph's brothers: Jesuit mindset and Jewish mindset) and in Ludwig Engel's *Der Jesuitismus, eine Staatsgefahr* (Jesuitism, the danger for our nation). An entire series of titles could be cited that present comparable analogies emphasizing the shared rootlessness of Jews and Jesuits, the impossibility of integrating them into the nation or *Volk*, their secret sexual immorality, the "devious" or "Talmudic" arousal of fantasy, and hence the

226

common links between Jewish and Catholic "pictorial-allegorical" exegesis.[7] As for the Jesuits, the historian of sexuality Iwan Bloch notes that they were the "masters" of sexual casuistry and of the technique "of clothing their own immoral dealings in a mystical-pietist garment" in order to "satisfy their always considerable sexual cravings."[8]

As we have already seen from the discussions of the religious meaning of flagellation, it had been presumed since Boileau that secret desire and immorality are present whenever voluntary flagellation occurs. It is not only the Jesuits who were objects of suspicion here, but virtually every tradition of Christian monasticism. Around 1843 (150 years after Boileau), Giovanni Frusta writes in his critique of the Jesuits, reflecting on the full history of the church, that:

> on this occasion we must not leave unnoticed that the busy or rather idle fantasy of many monks of the Middle Ages, as described in the histories of martyred saints, have invented a whole series of such martyrdoms or have depicted them beautifully. In the process, something was mixed in that we do not wish to describe, but that entirely agrees with the prevailing inclination to decorate the cells of individual monks with pictures of the penitent Magdalena [figures 5.1 and 5.2], painted in gaudy colors. Zimmerman, in his classical work on solitude, has given us the best psychological information in this respect. For it is he above all who did an injustice to the ascetics when he armed them with the scourge and situated them in such manner that, while trying to drive out a devil, they always summoned up ten more. Only in the case of Saint Anthony was he somewhat closer to the truth.[9]

The name "Zimmerman" refers to Johann Georg Zimmerman, a doctor in the Swiss town of Brugg and later the court physician in Hannover, whose four-volume work *Über die Einsamkeit* (On solitude) covers in great detail the effects of solitude on the imagination. An exemplary role is played here by medieval monastic piety and especially by the spirituality of the ascetics, which according

Figure 5.1. Saint Mary Magdalene penitent (Felice Ficherelli, middle of the seventeenth century, Dublin, National Gallery of Ireland).

Figure 5.2. Saint Mary Magdalene penitent (Giovanni Barberini, known as Guercino, 1649, New York, private collection).

to Zimmerman displays a clear unfettering of the imagination and a lewd world of images in the lives of the hermits.[10] Giovanni Frusta, who cites Zimmerman, follows up by asserting that the whole scope of the *Acta sanctorum*, the collection of lives of the saints, is a "gallery... of dubious material" and demands "a purifying work of editing" of these archives of materials, which are "so overrich in actual poetry." As will be seen from the following examples, Frusta's way of proceeding is anything but "purified." Although he superficially denies this, his procedure is calculated to achieve the sort of arousal through images that Zimmerman had observed in the life of Saint Anthony:

> Either the work of the monks and hermits was not strong enough, or the devil was stronger than their work. Hence, if the monks had gotten married... their damnation would perhaps not have been as great as it necessarily became, since they lived in solitude and transplanted themselves into frightful deserts and limitless temptation. They seemed to do every possible thing in order to smother in their soul that drive for which men so often give up all happiness on earth and in heaven, yet they did not smother it. The quest for holiness regards total abstention from women as the best means of perfection, and of all devils there is none that stimulates these holy men as much as the devil of fornication.... It seems to me that it was just such an evil effect of solitude, in which one abandons oneself mostly to tempting perceptions, images, and thoughts, that gave the Egyptian solitaries all too many temptations of this kind, so that they thought too much about it. Their strife with the devil of fornication was merely a sickness of their imagination. Such sick people are never so unlucky as they are in solitude. There they are pursued by the lewdest of images despite the best of resolutions. Nowhere do they find things more tolerable than in dealings in the world with others, and nowhere worse than in solitude.

In the eyes of the enlightened historian, this becomes the site of arousal amid the praxis of anchorites, monks, and nuns. It is a sort of arousal that blossoms precisely and only under such conditions:

"Lewdness was . . . not at all a bodily need, but a bodily weakness and excessive excitability of the imagination. It maintained an irresistible force over the soul, if nothing distracted these sick people, and if no object worked more strongly on them than the imagination. In this way, their sick and excessively sensitive nerves became ever more excited, and their bodies became increasingly exhausted through these struggles."[11]

In Zimmerman's descriptions, which are based especially on descriptions of the life of Egyptian desert monks in late antiquity and the Middle Ages, ascesis as a practice of imitation, repression, and control becomes the production of a libidinous world of images that can no longer be tamed, since it was never intended by nature. For him, it is "nature" that counts as the ultimate authority and even determines the framework of possible freedom and the form of faithful imitation. Ascetics transgress the norms of nature in their self-discipline, which always aims at playing with the imagination. In the eyes of their modern critics, they do this in the name not of some liberating grace, but of a limitless "overstimulation" that emerges from the world of images along with its poetic and emotional effect. According to the judgment of the Enlightenment, bodily emaciation, "lunacy," and melancholia are the consequences of this "rush of the imagination" seen in the texts of the hagiographic "painter of human souls" who follows the model of the monkish life in Cassian (as well as in the life of the libertine).[12] Even Jakob Hermann Obereit, the author of *Vertheidigung der Mystik und des Einsiedlerlebens* (Defense of mysticism and the hermit life), whom Zimmerman criticizes in his discussion of solitude, stands according to Zimmerman in a tradition that exalts such "overstimulation." The history of this tradition supposedly includes not only the "lunatic Greek" Dionysius the Areopagite, but also Jacob Böhme and especially the female mystics of the Middle Ages, with all their ecstasies of suffering and love.

Yet what most inspires the fantasies of the historiographers of flagellation is not the lives of the saints. Rather, it is tales that give evidence of the "overheated fantasy" of monks and nuns and hence of the supposed ambiguity of spiritual flagellation. What is especially fascinating, according to Frusta, are those places where "sumptuous spiritual mysticism crosses its boundaries and degenerates into a refined sensuality paired with a kind of religious fiddling around."[13]

Here, too, the narration of a supposed historical reality is not just a documentary report that confirms the thesis that enlightened critics of religion take as their basis. Instead, the narration itself becomes an exemplary text, a poetic example of "refined sensuality" that exhilarates the fantasy and that is the only thing that allows the ambivalence of religious flagellation in historical description to arise. The sort of historiography that is undertaken in this way thereby enters a textual field centered on the arousal of fantasy through the exemplar and through narration. As a collection of scandalous histories, it becomes (if rarely in a conscious fashion) a variation on hagiography and its history of spiritual examples. Giovanni Frusta's *Flagellantismus und die Jesuitenbeichte* (Flagellantism and the Jesuit confession) displays the manner in which an arousing example that has lost its spiritual meaning ultimately becomes an erotically dangerous example. Only here does flagellation first attain the concealed "univocity" and "true erotic meaning" of which it had been accused since Boileau.

Not only is the text present in doubled form as both historiographic and erotic, the same is true even of the author: the erotomaniac is concealed behind the man of enlightenment. With "Giovanni Frusta," as with a great number of authors of literature on flagellation in the eighteenth, nineteenth, and twentieth centuries, we are dealing with a concealed figure. The name is a pseudonym under whose protection the author mixes a bit of sexual libertinage along with his anticlerical Enlightenment writing. In short, we find here the same double game that men of enlightenment ascribe to the priests: they assert that priests make a show of proclaiming the religious message only so as to stimulate erotic wishes and be in position to fulfill them. In similar fashion, one can see from reading Frusta that he actually develops his enlightened discourse in order to indulge in the images repressed and forbidden by reason and produced by an imagination that stands entirely in the service of desire. In a text that purports to go beyond the dangers of fantasy by disciplining it with reason in the name of a "healthy," "natural" life and an enlightened corporeality, the world of images turns against this express intention. Unfolding their power as image and narrative, the histories of corruption begin to displace the gestures of enlightenment. Hence the author "Giovanni Frusta" tries in vain to forestall the suspicion that he is merely engaging in lascivious enjoyment when he hides behind a pseudonym and claims to be translating the book from a foreign tongue.

However, he either would not or could not conceal himself entirely. The book was not translated from the Italian, as the title page claims, but was originally written in German. Its true author was Karl August Fetzer, a lawyer and politician born in Stuttgart in 1809 who served in the Frankfurt Parliament in 1848–49 as a member of the Left faction. Along with the aforementioned work, which ranks as both a classic history of flagellation and a classic critique of the Jesuits, he also wrote poetry, a tragedy, another book entitled *Philosophische Leitbegriff* (Main concepts of philosophy) under the pseudonym "Antiromanus," as well as several antipapal and ecumenical writings. As can also be found in other writings on flagellation from the eighteenth and nineteenth centuries, these works mix an Enlightenment standpoint with a more or less free-spirited, sometimes lustful, but more often frivolous and inhibited historiography of the "concealed," "genuine," and "true" side of a world thought to be dominated by the Jesuits.

Aside from the lower degree of literary quality, Fetzer's writing is reminiscent of Romantic historiography — especially Jules Michelet's 1862 *La sorcière*, which treats similar material. Like Michelet before him, Fetzer is fascinated by the "poetic" content of the tales circulating from the "dark" history of Christianity. His critique, which explicitly follows Diderot and Voltaire and thus partakes of the spirit of Enlightenment in both a religious and a pedagogical respect, does not shy away from a certain frivolity that is sometimes ironic. In this spirit, he tries to place the "sensitivity" of religious "enthusiasts" in proximity to sexual libertinage. A somewhat unthematic connection is drawn between an Enlightenment gesture and the Romantic attempt to turn all history into an emphatic image. This attempt makes clear that all history is always a history of imagination — that history, in exemplary fashion (as in the rhetoric of the Renaissance and Middle Ages) is simultaneously also an arousal of the imagination. He thus falls neatly into the tradition of the flagellants' practice of the imagination and the exemplary narratives that belong to it. This can be seen in Fetzer's text in passages where the logic of the example turns against the control of "purifying" reason and becomes able to infiltrate enlightened discourse through a moment of affective-imaginative arousal.

Hence it is a bit hasty to claim that Fetzer's work and other comparable productions bring us to the historical point where the secularization (and discrediting) of flagellation takes place through enlightened discourse. Instead, what we see in the relevant texts on into the twentieth century is that the ritual of flagellation cannot be separated from a spirituality that corresponds to it, a spirituality of excess, imagination, and "inner experience" as described by Bataille (with rather different intentions) a century after Fetzer. Even Bataille, who made an early exit from his intended career as a priest, still appeals here to the archive of stories that feeds the historiography and fantasy of flagellation as well as the pornographic imagination of the moderns, though he does so in the spirit of a radical critique of reason. For Bataille, as for Fetzer, this means especially an appeal to the lives of the saints and to the widespread histories of church scandal of which we will speak shortly. In so doing, Bataille traces the history of pornographic literature, which especially in France developed from a tradition of the lives of the saints and which along with hagiographical motifs has remained determinative for a French style of pornography well into late modernity. One thinks here of Bataille's *L'Abbé C.*, but also of the *Dolorosa soror* of Florence Dugas from 1996, a pornographic novel that harks back to stock themes of hagiographic transfiguration, including the most intense flagellation

scenes. Here we encounter a spiritual image of the rhetorical amplification of disgust, the excessive, and the abject that leads
beyond Bataille back to the arousing narratives that Fetzer transmitted with a rather different intention.

By examining pornographic texts of the eighteenth century,
especially the *Thérèse philosophe*, we will consider the ritual and
theatrical staging of eventful intensity that would be so important
for Michelet's admirer Bataille. Such staging forms a link between
religious and erotic flagellation even where it is not yet linked
with Romantic historiography. *Dolorosa soror* makes it clear that
even at the end of the twentieth century, this intensity was poetically evoked by means of a rhetoric that (mediated by Bataille and
Thérèse philosophe) harks back to a tradition of hagiography and
ascetic mimesis of which flagellation forms the most representative example.

When Karl August Fetzer wrote the history of flagellation in
the nineteenth century as a critique of Jesuit seduction, he by no
means entered the realm of a merely secular and Protestant reason that is critical of the imagination. Instead, he unknowingly
participated in the narrative multiplication of a world of images
that actually (and in contradiction of all reason) stimulate the
imagination. Later, for entirely different theoretical reasons, but
with a view to the same sources, such multiplication would make
up the heart of Georges Bataille's philosophy of excess, arousal,
and inner experience.

Scandalous Histories of Monks and Nuns
One testament of such excess was not only mentioned by Karl
August Fetzer in his polemic against the Jesuits, but was cited earlier in the novels of the Marquis de Sade, by Jules Michelet in the
second part of *La sorcière*, and with them in the entire literature
on the history of flagellation. I refer to the scandalous history of
Father Girard and Cathérine Cadière from 1730. This tale is one
of the stories most beloved in libertine and Enlightenment flagellation literature, along with other anecdotes that shocked and fascinated the eighteenth-century public — such as the stories of the

confessor of Maria Escudero and Father Paulino Vicente Arévalo
in Ypres (both were included in Henry Charles Lea's *A History of
the Inquisition in Spain*). In the Reformation-era critique of the
Catholic Church and its priests, we already find the old topos that
"the first fruit that comes from confession...[is] the fruit of lust"
and that the confessor seduces the one who confesses and turns
her into a "whore" while her husband sits at home "like a fool."[14]
This judgment may be reckoned a commonplace of the modern
critique of the Catholic Church.

In the eyes of the libertine and the anticlerical Enlightenment,
the concealed side of monastic and clerical life, the secret of the
priest or the nun, are evidence of a double game that is always
already underway in the dubious religious practice of flagellation
(figures 5.3–5.6). The secrecy, ritual, and withdrawal that characterize spiritual lifestyles in the monastery more than anywhere
else thereby supplement a projection in which abysmal desire,
tormenting lust, and passionate fulfillment converge with unsur-
passable expression. For this reason (to repeat a timeless stereo-
type that perhaps will live a bit longer), nothing is more salacious
or prurient than the monk and the female sinner, the nun and her
sisters, or the clerical garb that turns out to conceal satyrs and
nymphs.

There were three narratives of excess that especially stirred
the spirits of contemporaries and that circulated widely in the
flagellation literature of modernity. They are the stories of Father
Girard and Cathérine Cadière in Toulon around 1730, of Brother
B. Cornelis Adriaensen in Bruges around 1560, and of the Capuchin monk Achazius of Düren at the beginning of the nineteenth
century. In all three cases, it is stories, rather than actual historical
data, that give rise to anticlerical critique, pornographic fantasy,
and the imagination of the historian of flagellation.

We should follow the trace of these stories. The earliest, if not
the most famous to enter the annals of flagellation, was the story
of Cornelis Adriaensen, which took place toward the middle of
the sixteenth century in Bruges. According to Karl August Fetzer,
whose detailed retelling of the story harks back in many ways to

EXERCICES

DE

DEVOTION

DE

M. HENRI ROCH

AVEC

MADAME LA DUCHESSE

DE CONDOR,

Par feu M. l'Abbé de Voisenon, *de joyeuse mémoire & de son vivant Membre de l'Académie française.*

NOUVELLE EDITION.

A VAUCLUSE,

1786.

Figure 5.3. Title page of an erotic narrative of the eighteenth century with an allusion to the flagellation of the sinner (*Exercises de dévotion*, Vaucluse, 1786).

Figure 5.4. *Punishment of the Sinner* (Charles Monnet, eighteenth century. The engraving was also used as the title page of various printings, Paris, Bibliothèque nationale).

Figure 5.5. Priest and penitent (*The History of Flagellants*, London, 1783).

Figure 5.6. Lithograph for *Gamiani* by Alfred de Musset (A. Achille Deveria, ca. 1848).

the Protestant Enlightenment and especially to the humanist intellectual Desiderius Erasmus of Rotterdam, this story proves that despite the polemic of the Reformation and its sobriety, "even then, enthusiasm, the deceit of the monks, and lasciviousness caused abuse of the doctrines of penance, mortification, and ecclesiastical discipline of the flesh." In order to make his presentation more stimulating by giving it the appearance of authenticity, the nineteenth-century narrator claims to be telling the story from original documents, "both for the sake of the naive honesty with which it is told and also to avoid any accusation of embellishing it into something more beautiful." Nonetheless, the standpoint of "Giovanni Frusta" (Karl August Fetzer) should be suitable for giving "a psychologically important painting of the refined sensuality and art of seduction of the ultra-Catholic clerics." The author generally follows the fashion of his time and speaks of "paintings" when he introduces his examples or when he gives poetic form to an example. As he puts it, the story that follows is painted with a brush comparable to that of certain contemporary painters ("Müller Mahler and W. Heinse"), a brush that brings the power of images into the enlightened discourse of the historiographer.

> Cornelis Adriaensen was born in Dordrecht in southern Holland. After completing his studies, he entered the Franciscan order and in about 1548 came to Bruges and entered the Franciscan monastery located there. He knew how to employ theological knowledge and eloquence in a way that greatly touched the notions of the common people and sometimes flaunted this knowledge and eloquence with sparkling colors whenever this was able to gain him adherents. His Flemish-language sermons drew an unusual influx from the portion of the population that had remained Catholic.... Moreover ... he knew how to work with especial art, using all manner of mystical means of stimulation on the easily receptive fantasy of women, who in Bruges had long been known just as much for their piety as for their beauty. The sense for beauty was not unfamiliar to Cornelis, and he cast his gaze with pleasure on the many devout female visitors

to his confessional and his sermons. Now, in order to please them and himself, as a contemporary put it, he established a very peculiar order among them whose purpose and character comes to light from later reports. But we will now let the story speak, with all its disordered, yet candid details, rather than speaking ourselves. In about the year 1553, among the females who came daily to the sermons of Brother Cornelis, there was a virtuous and highly respected widow, who from time to time brought along her daughter, who was young and lovable both in her character and in her manners. A number of young lasses who had made her acquaintance spoke a good deal about Brother Cornelis and sought to bring her and a few other girls into their religion, as people are usually inclined to do.

This young, beautiful daughter was called Calleken Peter, and at the time she was sixteen or seventeen years old. After she had spent some time with those devout and Christian-minded girls and her mother recognized her increased eloquence concerning matters of God and the church, she permitted her daughter to enjoy their company as often and as long as she wished. Calleken heard a great deal from them about obedience, submissiveness, and fulfilling one's duty and later of secret discipline and penitence. Finally she began to ask: What is the meaning of all these things? The devout girls taught her about everything except for the secret discipline; for, they said, no one can tell her about this except for Father Cornelis himself, who would surely be glad to inform her about it if she would only go to confession with him. Accordingly, she was advised to call on him in person to be informed of the matters of which she was asking.

Cornelis was told that this young daughter wished to apply herself to constant purity and also to enter into secret obedience to him. He arranged with her one day a place where she should come. With him, she met two other girls of great beauty who both attended instruction in the discipline and in the meantime attended confession with Brother Cornelis. These girls were called Aelken van den B. and Betken Pr.

After the first greeting, the monk asked her if she really in all seriousness wished to preserve her virginal purity and cleanliness and would humble herself to this end by obeying him, submitting to him, and being dutiful to him? Calleken answered: Yes, venerable father, that is what I will. He then began to praise the virginal state more highly and emphasize it even more and to deemphasize and belittle matrimonial matters more strongly than in his sermons. And after he had advised her at length and multiple times to remain in this state, he requested of her for the time being (but only with the assent of her mother) to visit him on a specific day every week in order to receive the necessary instruction in holy obedience. Calleken promised to comply with this task to the best of her ability. Her mother likewise gladly agreed.

The next time they saw each other, Cornelis addressed the girl as follows: "Well, my child, now you must obediently let me know all of your vain thoughts and desires and remain silent about nothing. Then I can absolve you both of these thoughts and also of your daily sins, so that you might preserve your pure maidenhood both spotless and clean." Calleken promised to do as he asked.

After six to seven weeks of probation and instruction, the monk ceremoniously accepted her in the role of her confessor. She was required to swear an oath, with her hand on her breast, that for the whole of her life she would confess to no other priest. Once this had happened, Cornelis conveyed to her that she could now be like the other girls in his discipline chamber and could prepare herself for penitence. He had a chamber in a house on the Steinhauersdyk owned by a widow, Frau Pr. Here the virgin named Betken lived, along with a few other girls, in order to learn the art of cooking. Frau Pr. possessed a good mind, a pleasant appearance, and directed her institute very skillfully.

When Calleken entered the chamber for the first time, Cornelis commanded her in the name of her promise of obedience to confess to him all of the challenges and temptations that are so inherent in human nature and especially not to be bashful about sharing with him the unchaste dreams, thoughts, and desires that so afflict virginal purity, for only in this way could he find means of protecting it. But since Calleken seemed not to be open and candid enough, and because it appeared to Cornelis that she knew little of these matters, he said to her as follows: "Bah! I am convinced that you are familiar

243

with all the unchaste impurity that takes place between married, fleshly humans in the world; for the world lies in such disorder and is damned to such a degree that young girls of eight or nine years old know full well the way in which they came into the world. Bah! And a girl of sixteen or seventeen, like you, supposedly has nothing to say of fleshly temptations, desires, and torments. Bah! If you had remained in the world, you would soon have become the mother of three or four children."

After these words from Cornelis, Calleken stood blushing with downcast eyes, incapable of giving an answer, for her mother had carefully shielded her from all vain, frivolous, and dishonorable utterances and dealings. The monk continued "Oh bah! Here I do not believe you. Innate nature, damned and frail, must at your age have taught you of these things; it is impossible that you should not sometimes have had to endure challenges and struggles. But as you are now silent with me out of shame, I am completely unable to absolve you. My blessedness is at stake in this; for this reason, pre- pare yourself better for the next time." Here he again released the virgin and informed her of a specific later day, to which she agreed in the name of God.

On her third visit, Cornelis repeated his earlier speeches to her. She remarked to him: "Venerable father, I ask our Lord God daily with ardent and heartfelt prayers that for the sake of his grace he should protect me from all temptations, anxieties, and challenges of the evil fiend and of the flesh." Cornelis praised this, but added: "You must formally ask the Lord for temptations, anxieties, and chal- lenges. A state in which these are absent cannot be called holiness. To have them is an honor. One must summon up the inner burning heat in such an irregular nature as that of man and woman in order to be able to resist them like a solid block. What merit is there in a matter for which one has no feeling? You, virgin, also have flesh and blood like other humans; you should be quite wary of hypocrisy and spiritual pride." Hereupon he renewed his command that she freely confess to him all prurient thoughts and sensuous dreams so that she might be cleansed and purified with the holy discipline.

Calleken felt ever deeper shame at what she heard. But Cornelis demanded that she imitate the example of the other girls who stood under his discipline and asked her somberly: Was it her full and unhypocritical wish to entrust the salvation of her soul to him? This she forcefully affirmed. "Well then," he continued, "if you trust me with the salvation of your soul, then with much less danger you can trust me with your earthly, perishable body. For if I am to make your soul blessed, so above all else must I make your body completely clean, and capable of all virtues, all devotion, and all penitence. Is it not so, my child?" She replied: "Yes, it is so, venerable father!" He responded: "Well then, so is it necessary that you should submit to me in holy obedience in the way that I will command."

Hereupon Cornelis placed himself at the foot of the bed that stood in his chamber, about two steps away from Calleken. He commanded her, in order better to overcome the shame that posed such a hindrance to the holy discipline and penance, that she should expose her body and completely undress. Calleken answered, shocked: "Oh worthy Father! How could I possibly do this? Truly, I would have to die of shame!" Cornelis: "See, my child, it must be so; the blessedness of both of us depends upon it. Overcome your shame!" Calleken: "Venerable father, I would rather freely confess all of my challenges and fleshly thoughts to you in the future than to do what you require. I would rather die than do what you require. I would rather die. I ask you humbly, release me from it!"

Cornelis urged her impetuously to obey and argued with her that it was impossible ever to become perfectly devout without such self-humiliation. This was the first means to a comfortable reception of the holy and secret discipline. He required of her absolutely the same obedience that all the other daughters of the discipline gave him, and he asked her delicately whether she was trying to be better than they. Sighing, she resigned herself to her fate. She removed her upper and lower garments; but as she was at the point of untying her girdle, bright tears fell from her eyes. Cornelis encouraged her and commanded her to fight piously and cleverly against shame and hypocrisy, to win a victory that would be more glorious than all triumphs and joys of the world. When she was undressed all the way down to her shirt and was about to remove this, as well, shame overtook her to

245

such an extent that the glowing red of her face turned into a deathly pallor. Cornelis, noticing this, rushed to her aid with some spices and herbs that he kept along with some pleasant-smelling essences and other aromas in a nearby cabinet. When the girl again came to consciousness, he let her go with the remark that that would be enough for this time. For the next visit, he promised her the company of other girls who would lead the way for her and provide a good example. Calleken for her part promised to come again and promised total silence about all that had happened.

According to Frusta, in an argument already familiar to us from Damian's defense of flagellation, the overcoming of shame is the first goal of clerical rhetoric and confessional praxis. What Frusta presents is a strategy of seduction that (as in Sade's *Philosophy in the Boudoir*) manages to unfetter a "guiltless" fantasy still free of image or arousal. This occurs initially as a conspiratorial liberation from prejudice and as a descent into the image-world of temptations. Here, too, it is the stimulating exemplar that ultimately leads to transformation — that is to say, the overcoming of the "natural inhibitions" demonstrated in resistance:

> The next time she came to the discipline chamber, she met there the two aforementioned beautiful virgins [Aelken and Betken]. At the first call of the father, these two took off all their clothes and stood entirely naked before him. Calleken was immensely dismayed by this strange piety; but Cornelis praised this glorious victory over the so highly detrimental sense of shame, which inhibited all progress in virtue and devotion; he pointed out the necessity of overcoming inner hypocrisy. But even this time he could not convince her. He tutored the virgin for many months in undressing, like all the others. His basic principle was: she must voluntarily give up her shame and desire the discipline herself.

Here, along with the monk, there stand those young women who have already been brought to his side and who belong to the conspiratorial context of production of a confusing flood of images.

THE PRIEST, THE WOMAN, AND THE DIVINE MARQUIS

This unfolds "through his ceaseless talk of fleshly challenges and worldly, impure dreams; of natural, fleshly desires and inclinations." By these means, the words of the priest stir up such a storm in Calleken's soul "that almost daily there came to her mind those things that she was to guard herself against and for which she was to repent." The priest thus creates the situation that later summons pangs of conscience and ultimately the wish for confession. Only then is Calleken capable and worthy of "receiving the secret discipline." The father "commanded her to buy a broomstick, to make rods from it, and the next time to bring one of them with her."

Calleken was obviously not the only one who had placed herself at the disposal of the father. According to the history transmitted by Frusta, he apparently had succeeded in seducing "numerous wives" in the same way, by himself summoning forth the very challenges under which they later suffered. Only through acceptance in his "order," in which they received adequate "penance," could they be freed from the bite of conscience that went along with it. "He set . . . a rule [for them] according to which they must appear and confess to him each month and freely and exactly utter all of the unchaste thoughts, desires, and actions of which they were guilty, whether through marital duties or otherwise; the more flatly, openly, crudely, and completely they did it, the better for them."

Along with the ritual of declaration and penance, which included confession and flagellation, there was also an oath of silence. Under the shield of this oath, Father Cornelis had each of the women come to the house of a certain Calle de Najeghe, who had his confidence.

As soon as the women came for the first time to Calle de Najeghe she gave them a rod, indicating that they should take it into the discipline chamber. But the next time they were to buy a broomstick themselves, to make rods from it, and to bring one with them each time. Cornelis, arriving in the chamber, used to tell his confessing children with a somber expression: "Well, my daughter, in order to receive this holy discipline and secret penitence comfortably, you must expose your body. Therefore I command you to take off your clothes." The poor women would do so, and when they stood there, they had to give him the rod themselves and ask him in all humility to discipline their sinful bodies. He then did so, but very slowly, with a series of light blows that did not hurt very badly. In the meantime, he would produce all manner of passages from old books that speak of flagellation that said that God preferred the humility of those who would expose themselves, rather than the pain of many hard blows. In the winter, when it was too cold to undress themselves completely, the penitents had to lie down on a great cushion; Father Cornelis lifted up their clothes and flogged them in this position. He sometimes did the same thing to married women who could not remain away from home for long or to widows who had been under his discipline for a long time. Indeed, he sometimes permitted the latter women to receive the discipline instead from Calle de Najeghe, his confidante.

The so-called "gynopygian [i.e., ass-venerating] sect of the beautiful women of Bruges" that Father Cornelis managed to assemble about himself in this way is said to have existed for more than ten years. It was finally revealed in 1558 by sheer accident. After a meeting of his "order," the father (who according to the sources was also an outstanding dancer) had openly exchanged a kiss with one of the women after a meeting. Displeasure became widespread. It was Calleken, in particular, who turned against Cornelis, became mistrustful, and thus in turn aroused the mistrust of the father. He tried to keep her under control by means of cunning, but Calleken finally began to ask about the meaning of the "discipline" and the penitential procedures that Cornelis imposed upon her and that he insisted were so necessary. This launched a discussion between the two in which the young woman became the critical questioner.

Although the priest tried to save himself by means of subtle rhetoric and pious analogies, he was powerless against the "precise, sensible girl," who educated herself by looking "in the Bible, in the Gospels, in the letters of Paul and other apostles," finding

248

nothing anywhere about flagellation. When the father accused her of having become one of the "Erasmians" (i.e., disciples of Erasmus of Rotterdam), who were rampant in Bruges at the time, she answered as follows:

> I have not come from the Erasmians, nor have I spoken with any. I would gladly like to know the truth for myself. And for this reason I ask you if this undressing and nakedness and this secret flagellation is so necessary and unavoidable for blessedness as I have thought up till now. And since you have told me yourself that other ways are open for the salvation of the soul, so, too, do I have the desire to follow one or another of them.

Although the father now took all measures and presented all possible proofs for the necessity of flagellation, Calleken insisted on "proofs from Holy Scripture" and had decided not to trust anything any longer besides Scripture. After she had told the entire story, without breaking her oath, to a brother from Cornelis's order, she withdrew from him and split contentiously with the "gynopygian sect." Only years later, after the full truth about Cornelis had come to light and proceedings had been initiated against him, did Calleken also speak before the magistrate.

> Cornelis, benefited by the fact that no one could prove that he had actually attacked any women and upon whom no other misdeed could be pinned than the purely disreputable exercise of the theory of penance and the confessional, was expelled from the city to Ypres. That is to say, he merely exchanged one monastery for another. But of the many pious daughters of his discipline, many conceived such a loathing for the Roman faith that they secretly converted to Calvinism, together with their families.[15]

In this story of "Erasmian," that is, Protestant enlightenment, the female protagonist fits seamlessly into Fetzer's project *Zur Emancipation der katholischen Kirchen von Rom und zur wahren Gleichstellung all christlichen Kirchen* (On the emancipation of the

Catholic churches from Rome and on the true equality of all Christian churches, 1831). Calleken, who is at first seduced by "mysticism," becomes a critical questioner and finally the advocate of an emancipation of laymen: a Protestant well-versed in the Bible. And "before her marriage [she] told the entire story to the groom and reassured him of her own innocence in the tale."[16] As we will see, with this clearing of conscience in the name of a purified fantasy, she is the antitype of the figure in the *Thérèse philosophe*, who transforms clerical abuse and seduction into libertine enjoyment through the affirmation of flagellation and thereby becomes the radical liberator of fleshly desire. By contrast, Calleken represents the good bourgeois woman who leaves behind both Catholicism and also the unsettling power of arousal of fantasy.

The second spectacular scandal among the clergy is reported by Fetzer not from Bavaria, which this Swabian regards as the "classic land" of Jesuit "fantasies" and hence of self-flagellation, but from the area near Aachen. Here a Capuchin monk, Achazius of Düren, possessed a reputation as a powerful orator, despite "faunlike manners" and "ugly features." What is remarkable, just as in the previous case, is that the clerics in question are fully equipped with the bodily features of ugly satyrs, features that supposedly serve to reveal their true nature. Behind their speeches, behind the subtle rhetoric with which they seduce women, what becomes visible is the body of a faun that lets desire run its course without restraint and that uses theological-spiritual discourse as merely a refined mask. This objection conceals both an anticlerical moment and also the typical Enlightenment mistrust of a pagan rhetoric of images what is at work in the Catholic praxis of the care for souls and supposedly practiced by the Jesuits. "Mystical language," we read of Achazius of Düren and his style of preaching, "especially inclined the women toward him" and prepared them to offer themselves to Achazius and his lusts. The same is asserted of Brother Girard and Cornelis Adriaensen, who are subsumed under the same category of a subtle and abysmal rhetoric of images that aims primarily at seduction.

It is an open question as to what extent the three case histories related here represent "a historical series of events that happened in this way." Except for the case of Father Girard and Cathérine Cadière, this is more than questionable for many aspects of the stories that circulated (regarded all the while as entirely historical reports of true events) beginning in the early eighteenth century in the literature on flagellation. What stands out most of all is the construction of the cleric as a type: as a seducer who stands in subversive opposition to the bourgeois household and its libidinal economy. What is ascribed to the priests who came up with "the idea of passing the time in a worldly spiritual way" is not only a devious rhetoric and wily casuistical reasoning, but frequently even a Gnostic-dualistic theology in which the satyr-priest is seen as the one who is able to possess a skillfully disguised and nearly incontestable position, even amid the ordered and seemingly transparent bourgeois world. In the eyes of critics, there is a pagan lechery surviving amid Christianity in the figure of the Catholic priest. And the Jesuits above all others represent the authentic archetype of the crafty seducer. This was true even in the twentieth century, as in Carl Felix von Schlichtgeroll's re-telling of the case of Girard under the title *Ein Sadist in Priester-rock* (A sadist in priestly garb) (figure 5.7).

In this image, we encounter the simple inversion of the accusation made by the church inquisitors against "free spirits," who were said to be agents of a permissive worldview that derives the freedom of bodily enjoyment from the absolute freedom and lack of restriction of the spirit. The same was true of the seductive clerics, according to their Protestant and Enlightenment critics. In their view, the permissive strategy of Catholic priests was projected through a rhetoric that gave them the power to place themselves beyond the law and beyond the economy of bourgeois life. The bourgeois ideal loses its regulative value wherever "inspired speech" lays stress and priority on intense spiritual experience, instead of on measured emotions. It is precisely this appeal to a rhetoric of the "mystical" image, to confessional and penitential practice, that was supposed to lead spiritually beyond

Figure 5.7. Title page from Karl Philipp Schlichtgeroll's retelling of the scandalous history of Cathérine Cadière and Father Girard (*A Sadist in Priestly Garb*, Leipzig, 1904).

the normality of life, and hence beyond "nature," which is cited by Fetzer as an ultimate authority. In the eyes of the anticlerical critics, it amounts to nothing other than a renunciation of the authoritative reason that guides the bourgeois household and the economy of body and spirit.

"The spirit," as Frusta summarizes the supposed doctrine of Achazius of Düren, "belongs to God, the body to the world." Since humanity is "incapable of taming the desires of the heart," the command of purity can be applied only to the soul, whereas the body must participate in its own proper sphere. These "free-spirited" thoughts were supposedly designed to justify the ritual of penance that Achazius seems to have practiced before his cult was discovered, although the trial initiated against him was annulled by Napoleon's attorney general. Frusta reports of this cult as follows:

> Since the virgin possessed sufficiently magnificent charms to awaken the appetite of the father, he suggested to her a form of devotion that she immediately adopted. After completing confession, she had to kneel before Achazius and humbly beg forgiveness for her sins and then strip down as far as the level of her kidneys. The father now took a large rod and struck her with it; finally, he satisfied his animal desires with her. On departing, she had to promise to win over other women of her acquaintance. This indeed happened. It began with a few friends of advanced age, and thus the way was paved to younger ones, most of them married. Additionally, they also had to bring a number of other clerics into the business. Gradually there formed an Adamite flagellant club in which all manner of dreadful things were pursued, and we would blush if we were to record them.
>
> Normally, flagellation played a central role. Achazius procured an entire bucket filled with vinegar and salt in which the "consecrated rods" were placed. When the spiritual exercises were finished, he would rage about with these rods in an altogether terrifying manner. Then, following all the acts of brutality, they would have a delicious meal.
>
> Only after a few years did all of this come to light, as a result of

confessions that a young nun seduced from her convent felt obliged
to make following her marriage to a French officer. An investigation
was launched that lasted a long while, and it soon encompassed a
great number of individuals, even from the highest-ranking classes,
in a series of thick and complicated files. Among them were some
highly charming women who had been morally pure prior to their
entry into the club. One of them, who had lived there a short time
previously and was the wife of a paper manufacturer, made a confession under interrogation, as well as to acquaintances who had
expressed astonishment at her strange taste for such an ugly man as
Achazius. He had her completely under his spell, so that she was lim-
itlessly fond of him, and she had gone along with everything he said,
as will-less as a child. He had struck her so hard with the consecrated
rods that she sometimes was forced to remain in bed for over three
weeks, giving whatever excuses for this were necessary. The other
things that she reported cannot be repeated — but they would do
great honor to the fantasies of the author of *Justine*.

There were so many details of this kind, and the clerical class was
so seriously compromised by Achazius and his fellow participants,
that for political reasons, Napoleon ordered his attorney general to
put an end to the entire trial. Achazius was confined to close quarters in a monastery, and this was his entire punishment. The documents were later passed along to the Royal Court of Justice in Liège.
But due to bribes from individual families who wished to efface the
monuments of their shame, these documents were thoroughly plun-
dered, so that the strongest *species facti* no longer exist.[17]

Here, too, what seduces is not primarily the sight of erotic licen-
tiousness. Instead, it is words, or "sermons and confessional sermons," through which (in Fetzer's view) the satyr in priest's
clothing gains his "extraordinary influence over the hearts of the
people." Fetzer's retelling of the story is both suggestive and vivid,
even though he asserts that he will "give only the roughest out-
line" of this "publicly conducted trial of the most scandalous
kind," since he must leave the rest aside in the interests of "morality and seemliness."

The final tale that belongs here concerns the cause célèbre that played out in Toulon between the Jesuit Father Girard and the merchant's daughter Cathérine Cadière. The case is extensively documented in the trial records, *Recueil général des pièces contenues au procès de Père J. B. Girard et de Dem. C. Cadière*, which appeared in five volumes in Aix-en-Provence, excerpts of which were swiftly translated into other languages. A collection of the trial documents already appeared in the same year in German in "Cologne on the Rhine" (actually the publishing house of Franz Varrentrapp, in Frankfurt am Main). In 1732, three volumes were published. The first had the title *Factum oder Verteidigungsschrift der C. Cadière wider den Pater Girard* (Factum: Or in defense of C. Cadière against Father Girard). The second was called *Erstaunenswürdige Historie des Jesuiten Pater Johann Baptista Girard ... welcher unter dem Schein der Heiligkeit die Jungfer Cadière, nebst noch unterschiedenen seiner Beicht-Töchter zur entsetzlichsten Unzucht verfüret* (Astonishing history of the Jesuit Father Johann Baptista Girard ... who under the semblance of holiness seduced the virgin Cadière, along with various other girls for whom he served as confessor, to the most horrifying illicit acts). The third was called *Gespräche im Reiche derer Lebendigen, zwischen dem bekandten Pater Joh. Girard, einem Jesuiten, und der Madem. Marien Catharinen Cadière, darinnen der gantze Verlauff von allen denjenigen sonderbaren und erstaunlichen Sachen, was zwischen diesen beyden Personen zu Toulon in Frankreich vorgegangen, entdecket ist* (Dialogues in the realm of the living, between the well-known Father Joh. Girard, a Jesuit, and Mlle. Marie Catharine Cadière, in which the entire course of remarkable and astonishing events that transpired between these two persons in Toulon in France is revealed).

All of these works were published by the same firm in Frankfurt, whose identity was kept hidden. They bear witness to the success of scandalous histories, as well as to the popularity of anti-Jesuit polemics. This material was the subject of renewed historical treatment from August Kurtzel in 1843 under the title *Der Jesuit Girard und seine Heilige: Ein Beitrag zur geistlichen Geschichte des vorigen Jahrhunderts* (The Jesuit Girard and his female saint: A contribution to the spiritual history of the past century). Finally, it was reworked in 1904 by Carl Felix von Schlichtgeroll into the tale *Ein Sadist im Priesterrock* (A Sadist in priestly garb).

Schlichtgeroll serves to illustrate the way in which these scandalous histories were received, even in the twentieth century. He is the author of numerous flagellant texts, of a two-volume monograph with the title *Die Bestie im Weibe* (The animal in woman, 1903), as well as of biographical works on Leopold von Sacher-Masoch and Gilles de Rais. He was best known in the first decade of the twentieth century for joining with Sacher-Masoch's second wife Hulda in sharply criticizing the picture that Wanda von Sacher-Masoch sketched of her life with Leopold in her *Lebensbeichte* (Confessions). In 1901, Schlichtgeroll published the volume *Sacher-Masoch und der Masochismus*, the first draft of a biography. He had also written a *Geschichte des Flagellantismus* (History of flagellantism, 1913) under the pseudonym Georg Friedrich Collas, translated erotica under the name Dr. Georg Cordesmühl, and finally edited the journal *Geißel und Rute* (Scourge and rod) from 1907 to 1908.[18] Hence, his interest in the clerical abuse of flagellation is embedded in a series of texts that celebrate flagellation and that seek to inherit the literary mantle of Sacher-Masoch. Incidentally, it should be mentioned in passing, these are all texts that were suppressed from the list of Schlichtegroll's publications when in 1933 he became a member of the Reichsverband deutscher Schriftsteller, the German writers' association, and in 1943 editor in chief (*Hauptschriftleiter*) in Leipzig.

The scandalous story of Cathérine Cadière and Father Girard reaches its conclusion in the treatment given of it by Schlichtgeroll, the admirer of Masoch. The genealogy of this story shows how it entered the annals of flagellant phantasmagoria and its related exemplars of arousal — a process beginning in the eighteenth century, but one especially strong since the nineteenth and twentieth centuries. Historical reconstruction here is thus not just an object of genealogy and narrative retelling, but also of archaeology — that is to say, of the discovery of hidden textual substrata within and beneath specific layers of the text, substrata in which new possibilities of experience are elaborated. It should be noted that there is a key moment in all the layering and unfolding of the material of Cadière and Father Girard, one whose first literary treatment appeared under the title *Thérèse philosophe* in 1748, reprinted numerous times since then. It was a best-seller, as established by Robert Darnton in his study of French "clandestine literature" of the period.[19] Moreover, the text of *Thérese* is said to have circulated in manuscript form even before being printed. This novel doubtless represents the decisive point at which the case of Girard, with its specific connection between confession, penance, and flagellation, entered into pornographic and free-thinking fantasy, where it has retained a niche up to our own day. It also demonstrates the way in which hagiographic models are employed and poetically redefined for pornographic purposes.

But we will return to *Thérèse philosophe* a bit later, and in some detail. For now, we return to the history of Girard and Cadière as told by Giovanni Frusta in 1843. According to him, Cathérine Cadière, who was born on November 12, 1702, "blossomed . . . as a beautiful and sharp-witted young maid, full of splendid dispositions of spirit and feeling, pure and harmless, distinguished above all her playmates by innocence, virtue, and genuinely virginal attractiveness." What drove her toward her fate was a "mystical," "longing" pull that was averse to worldly joys and that also caused her to reject numerous "advantageous marriage proposals." For this reason, Cathérine had already joined a group of young girls who formed "a kind of order: and devoted themselves to pious exercises." Their leader was none other than Father Girard, who as a preacher "was especially pleasing to the women." According to Frusta, Girard developed "the well-known system of Molinism with a freedom and brazenness that did honor to the shrewdness and savoir faire of the Jesuits."[20] What distinguished the preacher were "mystical ways of speaking" with which he knew how to "make the young ladies completely his own in both spirit and body." Decisive in this scenario of temptation was the theory of confession and penance in which the father progressed from mild punishments of sins all the way up to the "discipline." While most of the young women "did not have anything even remotely bad in mind," there was one among them who, "although in one sense mysticism may have played a role for her," clearly conspired with the father primarily "for sexual reasons." She led other women to the father, who began by "enjoying himself by flagellating [them] in a subtle, Jesuitical, lascivious way" as he devoted himself solely "to brutal drives" and linked "other, highly frivolous acts with these chastisements."

As soon as Girard made the acquaintance of Cathérine Cadière, her charms inflamed his fantasy in the most violent way. According to Frusta, he proceeded with her with the greatest of care and seduced her slowly and subtly by first learning of her "inclinations, moods, and ideas" in the confessional. In this way, he succeeded in bringing her into "hysterical-mystical states" in which she had visions "that only heated her blood all the more and increased her fantasy all the more." The young woman fell in love with the "cunning priest," who also took an interest in the worldly welfare of his penitents, "for suitable meals, for parties in the countryside, for bouquets of flowers."

Over the course of time, Cathérine became increasingly the slave of the priest and displayed extraordinary behavior. She had "spells, convulsions, and bouts of unconsciousness," which Girard used in order to control her even more strongly by posing as the caretaker of her "possessed state." Ultimately, he alone had access to her in the home of her parents and used this situation "for the satisfaction of his lusts, and in the most brutal manner," while Cadière experienced "states of unconsciousness and hysterical convulsions." When she turned for assistance to Mlle. Guiol and the "devotional sisters" who had conspired with the father, she no longer found them supportive. They made fun of her and "told one another of the liberties that Girard was permitted to take with them." And "this consisted always of discipline on their naked bodies and great mockery of their virginal honor."

Cathérine's condition became increasingly "hysterical." She saw visions, became anorexic, and also began to show stigmata. At the same time, the father accused her of pride and arrogance that could be atoned for only by a special form of penance. He ordered Cathérine to promise total silence concerning these matters.

Thereupon he ordered her to climb into bed, where he supported her with a pillow. He exposed her body shamelessly and gave her a few blows on her hips, which he then kissed. Not content with this, he forced her to take off her clothes completely and to stand humbly before him. The young lady fell unconscious; finally, when she came to, she declared herself willing to obey; then, with a childlike piety, she removed her last layer of clothing, kneeled down before him, and once more received a few blows. "To narrate the rest," says the pious Protestant church historian who prepared the German edition of the trial records, "is no longer a secret of the tongue, but of thought alone. Concipe animo!"

To relate these details, Frusta says, "runs against all moral feelings." Cathérine soon became pregnant, had an abortion at Girard's behest, and was placed by him in a convent. Even there, Girard maintained his privileges. He conducted a correspondence with her, using the "enthusiastic tone of one who was in love," revealing "the entire system of Molinism." He also maintained the ongoing right to visit Cathérine, even though the other nuns distrusted him. At the same time, he promoted her reputation as a holy penitent. Only the intervention of the bishop, who permitted her to return home, and the spiritual attention of the prior of another monastery in Toulon finally revealed the "great betrayal and boundless depravity of Father Girard." Before and during the criminal proceedings in Toulon, "the Jesuits" sought to intervene, plotting "the most infamous intrigues" and trying to intimidate Cathérine and to influence the court. After Cathérine withdrew her statement before the court of Aix-en-Provence, *she herself* was initially convicted and was released only after lodging an appeal. To the great outrage of the people, Father Girard was set free. He died the following year, whereupon "the Jesuits, consistently enough . . . seriously considered having him canonized and brazenly compared his fate to that of Christ." Of Cathérine, whom

Frusta emphasizes in closing was a "brunette of well-ordered physique and lovely, subtle features . . . [with] enthusiastically gentle, darkly glowing eyes . . . [and an] extraordinary . . . full and fresh attractiveness . . . [and] beautiful black hair," history speaks not another word.[21]

Seduction in the Confessional

Alongside these figures, whose histories span from the sixteenth to the nineteenth centuries, the imagination of historians of flagellation, the confessional, and pornography are populated by other clerics, monks, and nuns. Along with "Giovanni Frusta" (Fetzer), there is a multitude of authors whose texts spring from the tradition of anti-Jesuit polemic and the anticlerical spirit. At the same time, ranging up to Carl Felix von Schlichtgeroll and other twentieth-century authors, they also indulge in their presentation of curiosities and horrors with a barely concealed lust.

In this connection, *The Priest, the Woman, and the Confessional* should be seen not only as the title of a polemical treatise by Father Charles Chiniquy (first published in London in 1874 and frequently reprinted and widely translated). Instead, we might interpret this heading as the designation for a true literary genre that took a critical position against the history of the Jesuits, above all others, from the sixteenth century into the nineteenth. Here we find a portrayal of the Jesuits as propagators of flagellation, one that also emphasizes that they are entirely conscious of the libidinous, imaginative-affective double game of which they are being accused.

In order to understand more clearly Fetzer's view of the causes of flagellation, we can turn to an additional case that he reports in connection with his portrayal of the Jesuits and the other orders and their flagellation practices. Fetzer assembles a series of received case histories that especially enable us to recognize that flagellation in the nineteenth century had come to be understood as a practice with an ultimately sexual meaning, a meaning that could be adequately understood only as an expression of "repressed sexuality." This does not mean that Fetzer presupposes an alteration of the practice of flagellation and its context, such as can be observed in pornographic novels. Instead, it means that the praxis of flagellation is placed in a new imaginative horizon in which both religious and erotic flagellation are regarded as sexual practices and as part of a perverse system of illusions. Enlightened discourse teaches that flagellation is never anything more than a form of sexuality, and such discourse also replaces the religious and erotic-libertine imaginary with sexual imagery from which the true meaning of a great portion of religious practices is now supposed to be gleaned. Peter Damian saw in the mind of the monk a horizon of confession and penance, especially the image of the Last Judgment and of the plenitude of God's grace. Ecclesiastical critics of flagellation pointed to the integrity of the body and the commandment of love. By contrast, Fetzer introduces concepts that define the horizon of enlightenment primarily on the basis of what he calls "female voluptuousness" and the seduction of women by satyrlike clerics. For Fetzer, then, the paradigm of explanation is Diderot's tale *La religieuse*, which for him makes visible once and for all the "spiritual abyss of hell" of the monasteries and has "painted, more truly and in more lively fashion than the hand of any artist, the dark glow of erroneous fantasy that stems from the unsatisfied sexual urge."

"Erroneous fantasy," "overstimulated senses," and "hysteria" — for Fetzer and other historiographers of flagellation — these are the models of interpretation lying at the basis of their views. Especially significant here are the connections between flagellation, confession, and penance, connections already important for Peter Damian, which bound flagellation closely to ecclesiastical rites of confession and penance beginning in the Middle Ages. This does not mean that voluntary self-flagellation was ever generally accepted in the church as satisfaction for humanity's sins. Yet ever since the Middle Ages, flagellation has been bound up with penance, with the confession of forbidden desire and the purification of it. The evocation of this desire in words and images, as spoken in auricular confession and secretly heard by the father confessor, is directly correlated in the fantasy of historiographers with flagellation itself, for in both cases, it is a question of arousing images. In this process, the father confessor, who imposes penance and has the power of purification, plays a key role. The link between confession and flagellation forms not just the unity of confession and penance, but the evocation of a specific, analogous emphasis on the visual. Here, in the representative exchange between the one who confesses and the priest, a ritual that stages the act of confession, the confession is transformed into penance and the flesh is purified. According to Fetzer, it is in this transfer and theatricalization of the body and its resulting desire (that is to say, in the pictorial narration of secret desires) that the "arousal of fantasy" takes place. This arousal makes confession and flagellation comparable at precisely the point in spiritual praxis where they cannot be explicitly related at all. "Unfettered fantasy" is "fantasy whipped into a frenzy." It "produces sensuality and voluptuous mysticism, as well as delusional errors of the senses and spirit of every kind. Wherever this happens, we see flagellantism in a state of special effectiveness." Hence, confession, according to Fetzer, is the necessary correlate of flagellation, since both practices aim to unleash sensibility by stimulating the imagination.

Fetzer demonstrates this with an additional "true story" said to have taken place during the closing of a monastery in Bavaria — a place that for Fetzer ranks as a veritable abyss of overstimulated Catholic visual culture. According to this tale, as the political shutdown of monasteries was being implemented, a sister was found who had been kept hidden by the other nuns in a wooden crate inside the convent. The other nuns asserted that she was insane. Fetzer relates the prehistory of this "insanity" and in so doing follows the usual pattern of the eighteenth century: tracing the supposed pathogenic route leading from idleness and reveries to the discovery of sensuality, through unsuccessful ascesis, to the ceaseless arousal of fantasy and permanent lasciviousness, and finally to nymphomania, the melancholy of unfulfilled desire, and ultimately manic depression. Tormented by deep melancholia, the nun Alberta, isolated in the convent, is consoled by the fact that "the play of her fantasy fell upon the unhappy images of the delights of the senses previously enjoyed in secret." This *speculatio*, as meditation on seductive fantasy images was known in medical handbooks of the eighteenth and nineteenth centuries, leads to the abyss of endless and inescapable arousal.

> Her entire physique, the peculiar nourishment in the convent (in accordance with the vows of the orders, they were forbidden to consume meat products, which were replaced by sweet, strongly flavored pastries and salted fish) and many other factors worked in detrimental fashion on her humors. Solitary life in a bleak cell, the lack of all communication with the sisters of her order — in short, absolutely everything about her life — contributed to her becoming the hopeless prey of a flaming imagination, wallowing in images of the most heated sensual desire. This state of her soul ultimately took the form of a bodily illness.

The doctor who was called in diagnosed not only "a perfect development of hysteria," but one that "stood at the point of passing into full-blown nymphomania."

What was finally prescribed (and approved by the abbess, but in vain) was the intermittent aid of therapeutic flagellation by the "manly force" of a monk. This therapy missed its mark, and in fact, "heavy use of the scourge . . . inflamed her sensuality all the more." What followed was a sensual delirium that Fetzer portrays to us in a visually graphic manner in no way inferior to the supposedly seductive rhetoric of Catholicism and its "pictures":

> As if in a turbulent sea of sensuality, her voluptuous and ample limbs flamed and arboresced under the rod of apparent penitence wielded by a male hand. All the images of enjoyment were thereby summoned forth all the more, and since actual enjoyment was withheld from her, with calamitous self-deception, she permitted herself secret joys that destroyed her life forces, finally leading through overstimulation of the nerves and through the awakening of conscience to outright madness.[22]

In this tale and others, seduction and mistreatment by priests, monks, and nuns are ranked as the primary cause in a tragic history of abuse. The actual cause denounced by anticlerical polemic is not transgression, but the arousal of fantasy, which according to Fetzer was systematically practiced by clerics and used with the aim of seduction. The priest not only stimulates the production of confusing fantasy images, but (as the examples show) turns himself into an absolute and thereby irresistible phantasm, for in the eyes of the women who honor him, he appears as a beautiful seducer, although he is an ugly satyr. For Fetzer, the men of the church — no less than pornographers such as the Marquis de Sade — are thus the henchmen of a bewildering imagination that circumvents the ordered household and the libido that is economically well regulated in the very family life that the church advocates. What is retained in this model is the ambivalence of Christian ascesis, which always consists not only of the spirit's ability to free itself from the body in Gnostic fashion, but in the affirmation of freedom in resurrection, an affirmation that presupposes suffering and the cross.

Perception, indeed the production of desire through a strong power of imagination, is common to all cases of seduced women presented by Fetzer. All of this is inflamed even more by flagellation, which presents itself merely as mortification of the flesh. The meditation on sin and sinful intentions that is supposed to steer us away from stimulating images is therefore deceptive, since it evokes the very dangers from which it is supposed to protect us. The cleric, who hears the confession of the flesh, becomes the agent of a fantasy that is ultimately stronger than he himself — as with the divine overpowering in the testimony of the medieval lives of nuns — which takes hold of all self-possession as an abyss of erotic delusion. Here, as in the work of Boileau, ambivalence and the arousing commerce with images more generally is nothing but a danger to moderately ordered life and no longer a radical possibility of spiritual experience.

In Fetzer's analysis, one can see confession and penance as one of the sites that give rise to a variation of manifold erotic images, the construction of an *ars erotica*, and the cultivation of desire as a differentiated experience of desire, pain, and forbidden or deferred fulfillment. This experience arises from a staging that supposes in theological terms that reason is at first unable to comport itself to God in belief, but that it is initially assigned to the affective and imaginative world of images, which can be overcome only in a second step and by means of a paradoxical turn. We recall the conclusion of the medieval mystics Mechtild of Magdeburg, Henry Suso, and Johannes Tauler that individuals have to move "beyond images by means of images," that the route to the divine is always at first a descent into the affirmation of fallenness into sin. Images are thereby defined as a site and medium where experience, whether spiritual or erotic, gains intensity through specific forms of staging and rhetorical practices of evocation.

In this scenario, the cleric is the actor who is not integrated into the modern bourgeois household, with its ordered economy of passions, and who becomes (in an only apparently paradoxical connection with the widely scorned love novels of the time, which were criticized for inducing daydreams) the seducer of daughters and wives in the name of an uncontrolled world of images. Hence, critical voices often bemoan the fact that it was or had been customary in Catholic areas for priests and monks, especially Jesuits, to possess the status of "house friends," a role in which they would freely converse with the ladies. Given that these priests and monks also embodied a radical spirituality that was explicitly excluded from the normative attachments of the family, they represented the very model of the seducer, whose vivid and suggestive speech appeared to moderate, economical, household reason as a "lascivious" counterimage. Thus, for critics of the Jesuits, the figure of the priest became the archetypal seducer of wife and daughter — and the champion of a libertine subversion of the normal order of life. To give just one example, in Honoré Gabriel's *Hic et Hec, ou L'élève des RR. PP. Jésuites d'Avignon* (Hic et Hec, or The student of the Jesuit fathers in Avignon, 1777–80) the Jesuit student clothed as an abbot is not merely the in-house teacher at the Valbouillant home, but the agent of a lewdness that ultimately takes over the entire household until it reaches the form of communal orgies.

The supposedly most dangerous scene in which these arts of seduction are played out is no doubt in the confessional. When the priest hears confession, he is at the same time seducer and seduced, calling forth the spirits from which he is unable to free himself, even when he wishes it. Madame de Merteuil, who in Choderlos de Laclos's *Les liaisons dangereuses* (Dangerous liaisons) is initiated by her father confessor, confirms this observation and is only one of many literary figures who could be cited here.

Above all, it was the polemical treatises against auricular confession, which appeared with increasing frequency in the seventeenth century, that viewed confession as a site for the production of lascivious thoughts and an erotically stirred life of the soul. Chiniquy's *The Priest, the Woman, and the Confessional* is exemplary for this entire genre of texts. This book, like the others, can also be read as a collection of salacious tales that in turn become exemplars of arousal. It draws on case histories that make clear how the father confessor carries out "his manipulations on [the wife's] soul" in order "to open her heart . . . and to seek through the hallowed chambers of her innermost and most secret thoughts." What stands at the center here are questions that the priest apparently poses in order to learn of individual sins, but that in Chiniquy's view actually disturb the woman's mind and enable the priest to "hear and see [her] most secret words and deeds" and know her "innermost thoughts and desires."[23] Complete confession of sins, the theological precondition of absolution, is in the Enlightenment view a paramount danger to "wives and daughters" and encourages an alienation of the wife from the husband within the bourgeois household. "The husband may consider the exterior of the palace; he may rest his head on the cold marble of the outer layer of doors; but the father confessor enters triumphantly into the secret, star-spangled rooms and examines their countless unspeakable marvels as he pleases, and to him alone is it permitted to rest his head on the soft pillow of boundless trust, on the unlimited respect and love of the wife."[24]

So goes the judgment of the husband about the priest who hears the confession. Yet the priest establishes himself not only as a counterforce to the head of the bourgeois household, but as a genuine agent of slumbering passions. His questions speak aloud an apparent "depth of the feminine soul" that is unfathomable to the husband, thereby unleashing all the "forces" that are doubtless unsettling to him. The "secret art" of the priests, with which the pope "wishes to conquer the world by means of woman," consists in the fact that the priest not only hears the confession, but through his questions brings her to renounce herself completely. He thereby circumvents "self-respect and chastity" by evoking what is concealed and stirs it to life with arousing images.

Here, too, the metaphorics that we encounter in the works of the critics of Catholic practices is predominantly spatial, theatrical, and painterly. The confessional becomes a stage where what is otherwise kept silent is now freely spoken and imaginatively staged in dialogue and where the passions unfold their independent lives. In the drama of intimacy that is here first genuinely invented and constructed, "father confessor" and "penitent" play their roles, which withdraw more and more from the everyday order and which, behind the curtain of supposedly feigned humility, patience, and piety, conceal a secret stage of seduction and of the most lascivious fantasies.[25]

Auricular confession is not only the construction of this deeper intimacy that overshadows the daily relationship between husband and wife, parents and daughters. It is simultaneously the site where the passions renounce their true nature, bringing forth in the drama of confession the world of "dirty voluptuousness" that is excluded from the bourgeois household. The priest ultimately takes up the scourge in order to correlate the sins of the flesh (whose power he himself evoked with his seductive language) with the corresponding penance and what are known as works of satisfaction, the making of amends. In this way, to play on an image familiar since antiquity (and that appears in Fetzer as a counterimage of bourgeois moderation), he becomes a satyr who weds the nymphs (see figures 5.8 and 5.9).

L'AUTEUR REMPLI
DE
SON SUJET.

Figure 5.8. Title page of *Dom Bougre ou Le portier des Chartreux* (Frankfurt, 1741).

Figure 5.9. Monk and nun before the altar of Priapus (frontispiece of the second part of *Thérèse philosophe*, London, 1783).

Here, even "the banker's wife," seduced during confession, is lost in an abyss of voluptuous delirium. According to Fetzer, the consequence of this abysmal link is a "raging enthusiasm" of a type found, for example, in the life of Saint Teresa:

> Teresa's character was highly enthusiastic from earliest youth. By nature she possessed an unusually fiery power of imagination. In later years, since her education was neglected, this imagination was only increased by her intake of inverted religious concepts and the bad morality of her century. There was also this Spanish woman's spiritual pride and her taste for the adventurous, a hysterical physical constitution, and a melancholic mood of the soul. What was initially enthusiasm became, in the end, flat-out madness.[26]

Confession and Imagination

The Redemptorist priest Alfons Maria di Liguori was canonized in 1839 and on March 23, 1871 received the honorific title of Doctor of the Church. His moral theology and confessional theory are the most frequent examples cited by anti-Catholic critique of the most deplorable casuistry and probabilist strategies of power in the confessional. A polemical work of 1902 designates this patron of father confessors and moralists as the "gravedigger of morality" and his theory of confession as nothing other than the deliberate construction of a state of mind overpowered by fantasies and estranged from the "natural" equilibrium of the psyche.[27]

According to this anti-Catholic polemic, the confessional practice sketched by di Liguori in his *Theologia moralis* (which became the official doctrine of the modern church through the edicts of Pius IX and Leo XIII) is the culmination of a development that began with the medieval obligation of all Christians to make private confession. Stemming especially from the confessional customs of the medieval Irish monastic tradition, this obligation initially replaced the penance ritual that took public form in the congregation as a whole. It thereby integrated believers into a structure that permitted them regularly to confess their sins and other, smaller transgressions. What was central here was no longer a public ritual of penance and reconciliation, but a private procedure between the priest and the confessor. Ultimately, the Lateran Council of 1215 made annual confession or so-called private penance obligatory for laymen, as well. But already from the fifth century onward (through the monastic traditions of Ireland and Brittany) there had been penitential books or catalogs for priestly use that compiled all the various sins in the form of a schema of questioning. These books contained a diverse variety of instructions for the priests that were developed partly out of local and regional interests. Such instructions defined the priests as leaders of souls and constituted a reference work for interrogation, for specific sins, and for the corresponding acts of penance in the framework of a tariff system.[28]

Such catalogs spread rapidly, and from this we can suppose that the penitential books already belonged from an early date to the inventory of every church community. For example, in the tenth century, Regino von Prüm recommended that every priest should have a penitential book to draw upon as support while conducting private confession, inquiry into sins, and the levying of penance obligations. The practice of private penance and the use of penitential books caught on during the following centuries, and beginning in the twelfth century, when the number of sacraments was definitively settled at seven, confession was fixed as one of them.

With the spread of penitential books, which initially amounted to simple collections of case studies with the recommendation of relatively stiff penitential obligations, a textual tradition was established that reached its summit in the penitential canon included by Burchard of Worms as the nineteenth book of his manual of ecclesiastical law and moral theology, *Decretum collectarium*. There, Burchard gives an extensive and detailed account of forbidden acts and how they should be expiated. Questions concern not just extramarital or adulterous life, but also the practice of marriage itself: "Retro, canico more?" (From behind, like dogs?) "Menstruo tempore?" (During menstruation?) "Postquam infans motum in utero faciat?" (After the child has already moved

in the belly?) "Post manifestam conceptionum?" (After conception?) "Die dominica?" (On Sunday?) "In Quadragesima?" (During Lent?) These are questions placed to married couples to
determine if there had been a sinful act of sexual intercourse, one
not aimed at reproduction. Extramarital transgressions are investigated no less precisely under the headings "De adulterio" and
"De fornicatione" (On adultery and On Fornication).

It is remarkable here that, along with the specifics of individual acts, what comes to the forefront is the exact relationship
between the partners (the sister of one's wife, the sister of one's
brother, one's niece, two sisters?). On the whole, it can be said
that for a long time, the main factor in determining purity concerned ritual matters, rather than ethical ones, and hence concerned the integrity of the congregation before God. What was
central was the participation of individuals in ritual, which was
not permitted in cases in which the believer had been guilty of
some sort of desecration.[29] It is typical here that the sinful actions
that qualify as besmirching are neither related to one another nor
explicitly opposed to some sort of normality. Instead, they are
correlated with specific punishments related to the purification
of defilement and the reincorporation of the sinner in the ritual
community. A decisive role is played not only by the transgression
itself, but by the status of the sinner. In the so-called *Paenitentiale
Sangallense*, handed down from a ninth-century manuscript from
the Saint Gall Monastery, we read as follows:

> A bishop who commits a sexual offense is degraded and must do
> twelve years of penance. A priest or deacon who commits a sexual
> offense in the natural way should do two years.... Whoever sins
> with an animal does one year of penance.... Whoever sleeps with
> his mother is condemned to three years of penance and eternal
> pilgrimage. Whoever sprays his semen into the mouth of a woman
> should do three years of penance. If they do this often and by regu-
> lar agreement, it is seven years of penance. Whoever satisfies a
> woman orally must do four years of penance.... Men who have anal
> intercourse repent for three years, juveniles for two. If they do it

regularly, the priest should give them supplemental punishment. If they satisfy one another with their lips, they will do penance for three years.[30]

The twelfth century witnessed the emergence of a new form of this literary genre: the so-called penitential summa. The summa mirrors the extension of the church's power into all realms of life and at the same time the revaluation of each individual case and its assessment in confession. Unlike in the earlier penitential canons, more attention was now paid to the personal evaluation of sins than to the tariff system that mathematically correlates sins with specific acts of penance. In the genre of the penitential summa (especially in the *Summa confessorum* of Johannes of Erfurt from around 1300), one also cannot fail to notice a more rigorous legal approach — that is to say, a juridical systematization and polished casuistry. In this way, judicial evaluation is intimately linked with introspective disclosure. This allows us to speak of a system in which the exploration of sinful acts and sinful desires through confession is granted as firm a position as the juridically defined proper degree of penance that transfers sin and subjective confession into the objective realm. But now the penitent is neither overburdened by a confusing system of rules nor underburdened by merely schematic external tariffs. This emergence of a system of the actual evocation of sins in which an assessment of their weight should be performed results from a consistently sacramental understanding of the Catholic penitential system in the late Middle Ages that dissolved and replaced the ritual purification of the early Middle Ages.

Absolution presupposed complete confession, along with penance and the making of sufficient amends. For this reason, it was important that the greatest possible number of sins was reflected and included. We have seen that a practice of interrogation arose, along with a corresponding literary genre that aimed at making sins conscious and explaining them in confession to the priest. According to Alain of Lille, for example, such making conscious is the genuine meaning of confessional interrogation, which builds on the penance of the confessor and which should serve as the ultimate basis for the acts of atonement that the priest imposes on the penitent. Ever since the early Middle Ages, penitential books had already attempted to record and classify sexual acts as completely as possible — for all acts were seen as sinful other than sexual intercourse within marriage for the purpose of reproduction. It should be stressed here that we are not speaking of "sex" or "sexuality,"[31] but rather of specific acts that can be included under the title *De fornicatione* (for example in the works of Burchard of Worms or in the *Paenitentiale Sangallense*). *Fornicatio* refers to every type of sexual intercourse outside the single religiously sanctioned form; the concept possesses a classifying authority that makes specific assignments possible. The role assumed by the priest in confession and the assessment of acts is compared to that of a "spiritual doctor" (*spiritualis medicus*). In this capacity, just as in medical practice, he pays attention to the place of the deed, the time, the circumstances, and the penitent's age, sex, conditions of life, physical constitution, and facial expression.

The penitential canon of Burchard of Worms in 1008–1012 already has the title *Corrector sive medicus* (Reformer or healer). Along with this medical analogy, which agrees with canon 21 of the Lateran Council of 1215 that confession is the "healing of a sick person," there also appears at a rather early point (especially in the works of Bonaventure, Richard Middleton, and John Duns Scotus) the characterization of the priest as a judge and of confession as a court.[32] At the same time, penitential obligation (*satisfactio*), which was typical of the early period and was already criticized by Alain of Lille, seems to have lost importance, while in scholastic theology the role of repentance (*contritio*) was increasingly emphasized. Thus, contrition and repentance were to become the decisive moment within the three aspects of the penitential sacrament, contrition (*contritio in corde*), confession (*confessio in ore*), and making sufficient amends, or satisfaction (*satisfactio in opere*). Ultimately, William of Occam and Gabriel Biel would regard making amends as no longer part of the penitential sacrament and would emphasize instead an increasingly subjective concept of penance.

In the developing history of confession, we can speak on the one hand of an exteriorization (from the grieving heart to the confessing mouth and to acts of satisfaction), and on the other hand of a genuine privatization and interiorization that pushes penance and the confession of sins out of public view, unlike what was found in earlier Christianity. Confession was now something that played out between the ear of the priest and the mouth of the penitent in which the private realm constituted by the secrecy of confession was protected by the sharpest of sanctions.[33] We can speak here somewhat paradoxically of a rhetorical figure of privacy in which what is innermost is spoken aloud, but only under the condition of a new intimacy with the one who hears it, shrouded in absolute silence. At the Council of Trent and in post-Tridentine Catholic theology, this strategy of privatized exteriorization was consolidated and formulated in obligatory form. Indeed, this happened in explicit opposition to the Protestant view, where penance was identified with faith itself in a figure of radical interiorization in which Christians define themselves as sinners in their most intimate self-knowledge, abolishing the need for the sacraments of penance and confession as well as for their rhetorical framework provided by Catholic ritual.

In matters of private confession, greater importance now was ascribed to the questions asked by the priest (as already emphasized by the *Paenitentiale Sangallense*, Burchard of Worms, and in the twelfth-century Alain of Lille). What they especially seek to avoid is the possibility that transgressions might remain unrevealed and hence unrepented. The priest must cause sinners to become inclined toward penance with words (*verbis allicere*), he must flatter them (*blandimentis mulcere*) and show himself humble so that shame does not prevent penitents from confessing their sins. Hence it is decisively important to establish an emotional situation favorable to confession. The introduction of the *Paenitentiale Sangallense* emphasizes that the priest should begin confession with a prayer accompanied by "tears, groans, and in sorrow" so as

275

to produce the correct emotional mood. Even for Henry Suso, whose life describes confession as a liberation of the soul along the path to God through imagination and affect, tears are usually the key sign of emotional readiness for passage into a new life.[34]

The overcoming of shame is a decisive moment of confession, the significance of which is emphasized by Burchard of Worms and Alain of Lille. Alain already remarks on this score that the priest should not occupy himself with unnecessary details in the realm of *fornicatio*. This exhortation to caution is precisely what is most important here, since Alain's central interest is not the concrete description of a state of affairs in realistic, representational manner, but rather the clear, categorical grasp that has to proceed from the Seven Deadly Sins or the Ten Commandments and attend to the necessary differentiations between each realm. Alain thereby warns expressly against depicting "the most reprehensible sins," for in this way both men and women will be led astray into committing sins that they had previously never known at all. Hence, writes Alain, who appears to take a critical position here, when dealing with someone who performed sexual intercourse outside the sanctioned form, one should not ask if it was "from the front, from the rear, or the like" and thereby bring them to think of precisely these ideas.[35] Alain strikes from his penitential catalog all those questions from earlier works (such as those of Burchard of Worms or in the *Paenitentiale Sangallense*) that deal with these matters and that in early modern times filled the penitential books and exemplary *Speculum peccatoris* (Mirrors of sinners) under the rubric of the Sixth Commandment, from Tomás Sánchez and Tommaso Tamburini up to Alfons di Liguori and the tradition connected with them.[36] With this work of revision, Alain seems to be taking account of a tension between two counterposed realities. In the first place, full recognition and confession of sins is impossible without the exploration of possibilities and discursive disclosure through a catalog that then also becomes necessary in the second book of his *Liber poenitentialis*. But at the same time, there is also the precise danger of the stimulation of the imagination and desire against which he warns.

Alain explains that it is not merely the catalog that decides the weight of sins and the penalty that should be paid for them. Instead, he differentiates between "causa incontinentiae" (lack of self-control) and "causa solius libidinis exercendae" (a desire aiming at forbidden pleasure itself). In the former case, the sin is *veniale*, or forgivable, since it overtakes the sinner unawares; in the second case, it is *criminale*, since it occurs for the sake of desire. When the sin arises not through desire, but rather through a deliberate stimulation of desire, then it weighs even more heavily.[37]

With all these considerations, the mirror of sinners reflects more than a systematic accounting of possible acts. In the praxis of confession, it also includes a hermeneutics of desire and our dealings with it, which the priest as a "spiritual doctor" has to initiate during his interaction with the penitent. His interrogation is by no means merely the medium through which the forms of *fornicatio* are discursively revealed, related to a systematic catalog, and related to a specific penance. It is also the site where penitents are instructed and led to *explore* their desire, to communicate and thematize this desire as such in their intimate relations with the priest. Hence, one must speak of a double movement. On the one hand, there is a categorical explication and a differentiated construction of the territory of "fornication" as a register of possible acts. On the other hand, there is a rhetorical evocation and phenomenological exploration (which despite all commands of caution is always an imaginative-affective one) of the desire that the classified acts express. Here, the transgression of *fornicatio* is no longer merely a ritual self-tainting, as in the older penitential manuals, but also a window onto the underlying dynamics of desire and the passions that contradict the turn toward God in contrition.

The *Liber poenitentialis* that emerged during the twelfth century also represents a more complex level of penitential book than the older catalogs, since it emphasizes more strongly the penitent's relation to the priest. Alain mentions by way of a warning that it is precisely in this situation, in which the enumeration of acts is linked to a hermeneutics of desire, that the seductive power of mentioning other possible actions is especially great. In this he was not alone. Even in the work of Peter Damian, a strong defender of flagellation, we find a sharp attack on certain penitential manuals. In the aptly named *Liber Gomorrhianus*, he criticizes the enumeration of transgressions related to *fornicatio* in the older *canones*, whose legitimacy he fundamentally rejects. He refers to the transgressions of unchastity that they contain as "figmenta diabolica," "devilish inventions," which behind the veil of piety and conversion seduce the hearts of believers "like the song of the sirens." For this reason, the penitential books must be liberated from "these theatrical fantasy images" ("his scenicis deliramentis"). What Damian focuses on is actually a dialectic or ambiguity of the imagination set free in penitential praxis, above all in private confession and in "the most sorrowful and emotional [dialogue] possible."[38] In this way, he expresses the reservation that became the primary modern argument against private confession, especially auricular confession.

What Damian advocates here is not a radical control of the imagination by reason, as with the Enlightenment figures of the eighteenth century, but rather a strategy for transforming the life of the soul, one that converges with his defense of flagellation and that would be developed in a similar and more systematic form by Ludolf of Saxony and Ignatius of Loyola. According to Damian, what should be opposed to the "selective and momentary pleasure of the flow of semen," to the unleashing of the libidinal sensation of desire, is not the enumeration of all unchaste acts, but rather an imaginative realization of the transitory character of the earthly realm and the terrors of hell. At the same time, again through use of the imagination, attention should be paid to the "promised reward for virginity," and "the eternal Jerusalem" should be contemplated. This strategy of an introspection that ascertains the secrets of the soul ("intra mentis tuae secreta considera") thus permits us to free ourselves from the "passion of desire" and the "plague of libido" ("ab omni peste libidinis") only when a deliberate steering of the imagination gives it proper form.[39] Such imaginative transformation is opposed by Damian to the evocation of

278

all individual sins in confession. Hence, he does not reject imagination completely, but affirms its function even here.

The question posed by scholarship as to whether the catalogues of penance and sin reflect a historical situation (the actual experience of the believer) or a fiction (the imagination of the priests) thus seems to me to be not only unanswerable, but falsely posed altogether.[40] This question misunderstands the status and rhetorical character of the written texts. The first signs of a classification and codification of sinful behavior undertaken in the penitential books and manuals are important not for the usual reason that they provide access to a "mentality." Their significance comes not from their reproduction of a concealed "worldview," but from the way that they organize, segment, structure, and conceptually organize both reality and all conceivable possibilities. In this spirit, the elements of classification are not meant to represent concrete actions that have actually happened, nor do they represent the imagination of the cleric (although both of these can sometimes be the case). Instead, they construct the most complete picture of possible (and forbidden) actions by revealing them and linking them with specific penitential acts of satisfaction. It is only in confession, and hence in concrete performance, that this catalog takes on concrete form. Naturally, the logic of confession and penance is permeated by a primary interest in the repression and control of the libido so that it takes only those forms permitted by the church — virginity on the one side, procreation within marriage on the other. Yet these controls, which aim at ritual purity, rather than at the often bewailed "repression of an originally free sexuality," did not take shape in the Middle Ages through silence. Instead, they emerged through discursive evocation and (as Alain of Lille advises) a cautious, even therapeutic exploration of all possibilities as a framework for assessing human actions.

In light of this catalog, the acts that are confessed are always secondary. They first reflect possibilities of "self-contamination" and later reflect the realm of the passionate and imaginative unfolding of a libido that is constructed in the hermeneutics of confession. This is confirmed in striking fashion in the *Confession-ario mayor y menor en lengua mexicana* of 1643, which is concerned (in relation to missionary work) with Christian self-understanding and hence with adequate consciousness of sins. The explanation and denotation here of actions that were not previously consciously recognized as sins aims at the configuration of a new psychic reality along with its contents.[41]

Perhaps it will be difficult to accept that the penitential catalogs do not reflect a "diverse, open, and freely expressed sexuality" that was then repressed and finally extinguished by Christianity and by church politics, as is sometimes held.[42] Rather, as indicated by Michel Foucault in *The History of Sexuality, Volume 1*, the controls developed in much more complex fashion — one that produced the controlled territory as a differentiated and thus controllable reality. Everyday acts became contaminating, libidinous, compulsive, unchaste, and (in the worst case) motivated by desire alone, and hence they degenerated into the mortal sin of luxury (*luxuria*).

It is actually tempting to speak here of an *enrichment* of the repertoire of libidinous acts and pleasures or even of the invention of an erotic imagination. Hence, we should not proceed from the hypothesis of an originally "freer sexuality," but from an amplification of libidinous and erotic possibilities of experience on the basis of a discourse favorable to differentiation. The fact that this discourse sought to exert controls by no means signifies that an "original" freedom was repressed, but points instead to the definition of a new territory through which new possibilities also could arise. In this sense, the systematic naming of possible transgressions is an excellent example of what Foucault has called the "productivity of power." This culminated, I would argue, almost seven hundred years after Burchard of Worms, in the newest edition of the *Theologia moralis* of Alfons Maria di Liguori, which appeared in its eighteenth edition in 1967–69 under the editorship of Joseph Aertnys, Cornelio A. Damen, and Ioannes Visser.

What Foucault fails to notice in his analysis is a second and complementary plane, one that is of great importance here. In the confession that refers to the word and to truth, the word is not merely "confession of the flesh," but at the same time (and especially) an image that evokes the very sin that it names on the plane of imagination and the affects.[43] The vivid word produces the reality of tempting fantasies and possible acts that Alain of Lille had already warned against, but that unfold in both a practical and theoretical way in the early modern period in confessional praxis. As we will see, confession, contrition, and penance are thereby constituted as the dramatically configured space of an experience of sin and transgression that should not only be recapitulated through words, but actually relived and reenacted in affective and imaginative terms.

If we consider the history of the penitential books from this standpoint, it is evident that along with the paradigm of "ritual purity versus self-contamination" that predominated in church history until modern times,[44] there is a second paradigm related to the hermeneutics of concealed passions — one that more strongly emphasizes the dynamics and the phenomenology of desire. What became central in a way, just as with the ascetics of the old church, was the standpoint of an active struggle with *phantasmata*. Confession became the privileged site where all the forces are evoked that participate in this struggle and where they are constructively unfolded. Arrayed against such affective and imaginative stimulation, we find all the objections raised by the polemics against confession since Luther, polemics that survive in the anti-Catholic and especially anti-Jesuit literature of the nineteenth and twentieth centuries.

In the work of Alfons di Liguori, and indeed already in that of Tomás Sánchez and Tommaso Tamburini (two Jesuits who in modern times were often seen as the advocates of a moral theology noted for its laxness, casuistry, and destruction of all morality),[45] we find a stronger emphasis than in their medieval forerunners on the connection between the interrogation of the penitent and the inner life, and thus with concealed thoughts and desires. This interrogation gives depth to the catalog of sins, which is found here as well, whose very concreteness, along with its casuistical classifications and evaluations, has been a thorn in the side of its critics. Such depth can be understood as the continuation of a dimension of privacy that began to emerge in the twelfth century. Thus, Liguori writes in his work *Praxis confessarii* (The practice of hearing confession) and in his *Institutio catechistica ad populum* (Popular catechism) that penitents should be interrogated with a view to their thoughts and wishes and whether they took pleasure in them.[46] Already in Tamburini's work, the same motif forms the initiating gesture of confession. What must also be investigated is the number of thoughts, their severity, their type, and their date of occurrence. If the thought involves a woman, is it a matter of women in general, or only of women possessing especial beauty? The catalog of questions can be extended. The relevant paragraphs refer to obscene words and dialogues and finally to acts proper, which are disclosed in the most complete and differentiated manner possible. What forms here is a hierarchy leading from thoughts to words and acts. At the same time, we encounter the framework for the exploration of desire that begins with the first question and that is extended during interrogation all the way to the ultimate ramifications of possible libidinous acts.[47]

In Tamburini's work, we already find this meditation on *fornicatio*, prefaced by an introductory selection entitled *De delectatione turpi solum interna, seu, ut dicitur, morosa* (On inward pleasure in shameful things). The most important concepts in these pages are *desiderium* (desire), *consensus* (inner agreement), *delectatio* (pleasure), and *gaudium* (joy). They are characteristic of a growing psychological attention paid to the way of recollecting sins (as "outer" acts) through a subjective exploration in which desire and imagination unfold. This high degree of inwardness is found especially in confession, which presupposes its elaboration in a dialogue with the priest. It is Liguori, above all others, who explains that the model of a struggle with demons (already familiar to us from the ascesis of the desert fathers as well as from Damian and Suso) also provides the scenario for the unfolding and ascertainment of desire and the imagination.[48] In the ritual of confession, everyone is instructed to evoke the demonic realm (*luxuria*, and thus desire or lust) in all its vividness and to name and evaluate all their actions in connection with it. As Liguori puts it, the father confessor is no longer doctor and judge, father and teacher alone. Instead, in confidential and empathetic dialogue, he becomes an agent who assists in bringing desire into a language that he alone is permitted to hear.[49] At the same time, he is the one who stages the discourse that assigns desire to its proper place — or as the anticlerical critics saw it, the discourse that opens up a disreputable space in which the priest can then operate.

This situation, in which intimacy is established between the priest and concealed desire, has been a bone of contention in anti-Catholic and especially anti-Jesuit polemic on up to the twentieth century. In a 1901 tract by Paul Schreckenbach entitled *Römische Moraltheologie und das 6. Gebot* (Roman moral theology and the Sixth Commandment), we find the argument that "in the circles of the moral theologians of Rome, there is apparently no feeling for the fact that a dialogue between man and woman about these things is already in itself an outrage. To ask a woman if she has received or given sensual and impure kisses, has allowed herself to be touched, and the like, is in itself already immoral."[50] The doctrine of Liguori, which is "strongly recommended" by the pope, is to be regarded "as immoral and as ruinous for the people," for it aims at nothing else than the power of the Roman Church.

The problem here is not only the vivid concreteness of the moral-theological handbooks and the evocation of such concreteness in the confessional praxis that stimulates fantasy, which in the eyes of its opponents spurs both penitent and priest to sexual misconduct. In the eyes of critics, what is still worse is the way in which these fantasies are connected with a "casuistry" or "probabilist doctrine" through which practically anything can be justified — especially by Jesuit moral theologians. By way of example, it was often noted that numerous Catholic moral theologians since the sixteenth century defended the view that to have sexual intercourse during menstruation is permitted, as is fellatio — although both are entirely reprehensible and even "disgusting" ("eine Schweinerei") from the point of view of the Protestant ethics of Paul Schreckenbach. In the same context, the question is cited from Tamburini's *Explicatio decalogi* (Explanation of the Ten Commandments) as to whether the woman, after the man has ejaculated and withdrawn his member, can help herself achieve orgasm with her own hand. The (surprising) affirmative answer of the Catholic moral theologians is cited as an example of the most reprehensible casuistry and barely concealed free-spirited attitude, which is said to lead ultimately to the survival of heathen voluptuousness in the garb of Catholic figurative language.[51] There is also the alarmingly easy familiarity of the casuists with nakedness, curious glances, obscenity, jokes, unchaste books, dance, and dubious theater, all of it a thorn in the side of Protestant ethicists. They say that for Catholic moralists (Schreckenbach cites examples ranging from Tamburini all the way up to the nineteenth century) everything is permitted "that according to Luther and the apostle Paul is supposed to be forbidden." For a Catholic, it is permitted to touch the genitals of another person for joking purposes, while Catholic women are allowed to show their breasts if (by means of a casuistical distinction) this merely displays their beauty but does not lead to illicit arousal. This, the Protestant ethicist claims, allows us to recognize clearly the reprehensible nature of Catholic moral theology.

Here we see that it is also a question of moral-theological casuistry, along with the weakening of a clearly defined relation between word and flesh, instead of a rigorous, puritanical erasure of possibly tempting images and their ambiguity. Liguori proceeds explicitly from the plurality of the human glance, of sight, and of images, all of which is supposed to be thematized and explored in confession.[52] By contrast, Protestant polemic advocates a purgation that is not supposed to enter into the danger of the image, but is supposed to drive out both fantasy and anything that is in any way unethical. "Questioning à la Liguori," through which "unmarried clerics [grope about] in the pure souls . . . of German girls" and "in the chaste hearts . . . of German wives," implies that the fantasy employed by such procedures transgresses the boundaries set for them by nature in accordance with reason.[53] Martin

Luther, who is used as a countermodel and is here taken as representative of an anti-Roman, specifically German religiosity, represents "natural morality," which flees in "spontaneous horror" from all the "dirtiness" that the Catholic tradition provokes in the eyes of the polemicists. Hence, auricular confession, "followed according to Liguori's prescriptions, does much more to undermine morality than to raise it up," for it places "natural morality" permanently in question.[54] It calls into question the postulated unity of morality, nature, and reason in confessional dialogue. When the priest seizes hold of the soul by rhetorically enticing it to engage with the manifold images of sin and desire, he produces ambiguous fantasies and deeds that cause the breakdown of the "holiest thing that can be granted to a human, the comfort of home and family life."

Behind this apparent Catholic subversion there stands the double negation embodied by the priest. First, the priest represents the denial of the necessity of marriage as a "requirement of nature." Second, there is a denial that this gives rise to a necessarily perverse and unfettered fantasy running counter to natural morality. This fantasy ruins the institution of marriage and a "sound, natural sexuality" as defended by Luther in the sixteenth century and as recommended since the nineteenth century by medicine and by Enlightenment-inspired moral theories.[55] In the eyes of the anti-Catholic critic, the priest is not an agent of the divine grace and freedom that transcends all that is conditioned or naturally necessary. Instead, he represents a radical negation of the moderation that is supposed to lie at the basis of human life through the postulated unity of natural morality and reasonable insight. Against such harmonious unity, the rhetoric of Catholic priests provokes a world of ambivalent images. In the eyes of their opponents, such images must always refuse reason, even when claiming to be subordinate to it.

The "clear understanding of natural relations" repeatedly cited by critics of the Jesuits and carried out by Luther when he recognized erotic desire as a legitimate part of the encounter between a married couple comes at the price of renouncing the manifoldness of images. Since the legitimacy of desire is entirely bound up with marriage, only in marriage is it willed and permitted by God. Every arousal of fantasy that transgresses this "honorable relation of marriage" fails, according to the divine order, which is circumvented by the Catholic priest no less than by the pornographer. Even the *possibility* of such transgression (and hence the ambivalence that is always vividly evoked on the Catholic side in ascesis and confession) becomes increasingly silent and subject to control on the Protestant side, as shown by Tilmann Walter in his investigation of early modern catechisms and explanations of the Ten Commandments.[56]

Thérèse philosophe, *or: Passion Liberated*

We now return to Father Girard and Cathérine Cadière. In the history of libertinage, their case is interpreted as a rejection of the Protestant notion of "naturalness" by the unfettering of fantasy in the Catholic ritual of confession and penance. It was not only for the "Divine Marquis" (as Sade has been called) that the case of Cadière became the model for a paradigm shift. Rather, by having some characters "discover" the 1748 book *Thérèse philosophe* in one of his novels, Sade staged the way in which the case of Cadière (and its various theological aspects) had become a historical model for pornographic literature. In the third part of *Justine*, he allows the protagonists Juliette and Clairwil to find a copy of "*Thérèse philosophe*, a stimulating book by the hand of the Marquis d'Argens," as they rummage through the library of a Carmelite convent (figure 5.10). The ascription of this anonymous work to the Marquis d'Argens, which remains a matter of dispute, was borrowed by Sade from a philosophical novel by Lambert de Sauméry from 1741 with the title *Le diable hermite*, which mentions the work and the marquis in the same breath. Other sources claimed that the author was Denis Diderot, Voltaire, or even Friedrich II, but such claims can be dismissed. There is in fact much evidence for the authorship of Jean-Baptiste Boyer, Marquis d'Argens, whose father had professional involvement as a judge in Aix-en-Provence with the trial against Father Girard. Sade saw

Figure 5.10. Title page of *Thérèse philosophe* (Paris, 1774).

this book as inaugurating a pornographic literature that he himself sought to complete.

Thérèse philosophe, ou mémoires pour servir à l'histoire du P. Dirrag & de Mademoiselle Eradice (the title contains obvious anagrams for the names Girard and Cadière) is no mere frivolous narrative reworking of what can already be learned from the documents on the case in the version of the story told by Karl August Fetzer. Rather, the novel is in the first place the narration of the life of the protagonist Thérèse, as recorded for her beloved, the count. It should also be noted that the text is a variation on the life of Saint Teresa of Avila and other lives of the saints, since Thérèse begins and ends by saying so. It is not merely the name of the heroine and Sade's staging of the discovery of the text in the Carmelite convent that play on this parallel. Rather, everything portrayed here is analogous to the great nun's life story, but takes the form of a biographical history of the arousal of fantasy. The book is concerned with the same type of stimulation also found in Fetzer when he speaks about Teresa of Avila. Yet the arousal is not described (as in Fetzer in 1843) as a pathological "extravagance," but as the condition of possibility of a still unknown freedom. Hence, the central concept is "passion," not reason or will. More specifically, it is passion in its double unfolding as "love of God and love of fleshly pleasure." According to Thérèse's statement, it was "God himself who allowed the passions in my breast."[57] It was through reflection on images and through reading and ascetic practice that the famous Saint Teresa overcame her temporary "great inner aridity" or lack of intense spiritual emotions. By contrast, for Thérèse, it is the discovery of erotic passion, which has the same goal of experiencing "inner sweetness and occasionally being outside of oneself."[58] At least in structural terms, then, her methods are reminiscent of Saint Teresa's.

Passion determines everything in this work. It is passion that breaks free in ascetic praxis as well as in reading and the meditation on images, to which the young Thérèse abandons herself no less than Teresa of Avila. In spiritual and hagiographic discourse, there is a crisis regularly summoned up at a specific stage in spiritual life, which in most of the lives of the saints is thematized as a mental dryness. Here, by contrast (we are now in the age of Boileau), it is understood in terms of natural and physiological causes. The diagnosis of the doctor to whom the young novice turns replaces the dialogue of spiritual consultation and the discernment of spirits — that is to say, a medical evaluation is put in place of a spiritual evaluation of good or reprehensible forms of emotional intensity. His assessment is not concerned with the cares of spiritual life, but states instead that the equilibrium of humors in Thérèse's body is highly disturbed, for "that divine liquor which gives us our only real physical pleasure, whose taste is without bitterness, that liquor, I say, whose flow is as necessary to certain temperaments as that from foods which nourish us, had flowed out of its proper containers into other vessels which were unnatural for it; which had created disorder through the whole machine." The opinion of the doctor corresponds to the view (derived from the medical theory of humors of that era) that it is lascivious thoughts, the sight of a specific person, or the state of being touched, and hence affective-imaginative influences in general, that cause the increase of *liquor genitalis*, which in turn arouses the vital spirits and awakens "venereal sensations."[59] The *liquor genitalis* is analogous to the semen of the male; at the time, it was thought that it was ejaculated by women at the moment of orgasm. If this did not happen, a disequilibrium of humors would arise in the body. The initial consequence of this failure would be a permanent lewdness and nymphomania and finally melancholia and mania, as Fetzer describes in his nineteenth-century case history.

In view of the diagnosis and the foreseeable course of the illness, her doctor and mother suggest marriage. But Thérèse is not ready for this, for she would "prefer to die rather than displease God." Thus, she turns to the "famous Father Dirrag" and also makes the acquaintance of "his most tender penitent, Mademoiselle Eradice." Initially mistrustful of the especially gratifying experiences reported to her by Eradice (Cadière), Thérèse allows herself to be included in the activities so that she might secretly watch through a peephole to see what plays out between Girard and his penitent. What Thérèse discovers through the peephole is actually deception by the infamous priest, who employs the ritual of penance (including flagellation *secundum sub*, or on the exposed backside) as a preparation for penetration (figures 5.11–5.13). In the meantime, Eradice-Cadière, who stretches her hindquarters high in the air and props her head in her arms on the bench of the confessional, imagines herself in "divine ecstasy, purely spiritual," although "her pleasure was simply fleshly voluptuousness."

This stock image of erotic and pornographic literature — secret observation through a peephole — is the site where "the truth" is betrayed. What penetrates Mademoiselle Eradice is not the supposed "holy cord from Saint Francis's girdle," but the real penis of the actual father. As is so often the case in the relevant literature, this signifies the true nature of the clergy; the faun hiding under the habit begins to speak, and the priest shows his true colors. In the act of penetration, the father becomes "a satyr, his lips foaming, jaw hanging half open, teeth grinding now and then, snorting like a bull about to bellow, nostrils flaring." In an ensuing reflection on physiognomy, we hear that Dirrag has a face "like a classical painter's idea of a satyr — while he was exceptionally ugly, there was something spiritual about his features. His raciness, his lechery were painted in his eyes." He possesses the additional stock trait of "a perfect talent for persuasion," as well as a cleverness expressed through the fact that the priest is able to acquire the reputation of a proselytizer and gather around him a train of penitent females. Even his ugliness is a mask concealing the abysmal power of a desire that permeates all speech.

The figure of Eradice by no means serves as the pure foil or even victim of the priestly deployment of power, destined to slip away from its grasp once she has seen through it. Instead, she is represented as someone so similar to the father "in character and aspiration . . . that their unification could not be avoided." The cornerstone of this similarity is passion, the arousability of fantasy, which makes father and penitent both tempter and tempted at once. They are linked through their shared passion and enthu-

Figure 5.11. Confession. Illustration from *Thérèse philosophe* (London, 1783).

Figure 5.12. Penance. Illustration from *Thérèse philosophe* (London, 1774).

Figure 5.13. Bordello scene. Illustration from *Thérèse philosophe* (London, 1774).

siasm. At first, Eradice thus seems to be entirely the victim of clerical deviousness and violence, as expressed so clearly in the techniques of monastic ascesis. Yet in unfettered sensuality there also lies the liberating moment of the arousal of fantasy that will ultimately allow her to triumph over the father. Once she has grasped what the father is actually doing with her, she liberates herself and unmasks his deeds before the eyes of the public.

Parallel to this story is the tale of Thérèse, who represents in exemplary fashion the liberating transgression against monastic ascesis and its unhealthy buildup of humors. Her discovery of true desire in no way signifies a return to the sexual economy of the family, but rather leads to a "liberated" existence that transforms the ascetic principle into the basis of the experience of perfect freedom in the world and turns spiritual arousal into pure desire. Thérèse's enjoyment is thus related to the rapture of the free spirit that appears in the face of the priest as a satyrlike trait. Yet before actualizing her freedom, she abandons the "mendacious" (or in medical terms, "unhealthy") world of the monastery.

After leaving monastic life for reasons of health, she eaves-drops on dialogues between her new protectors Abbé T. and Madame C., and only this first teaches her how sensual freedom should be conceived. Freedom means primarily the freedom for self-satisfaction. This is established by the art of cultivating passion and fantasy, not by the mere fulfillment of the physiological requirements of nature, as one might first believe from the medical diagnosis. For "nature," according to the clarifying words of Abbé T., is "a word void of any meaning, an imaginary being... nature is a creation of the mind, a word empty of real meaning." Invented by the theologians as a middle ground between man and God, "nature" has been regarded as the origin of misfortune and malice, so that the duality of good and evil can be maintained and God alone can be held responsible for good things. Yet if one considers that "nature" is merely fabricated, one also accepts "that in the view of God there is no evil in the world." In other words, good and evil exist only in the eyes of those who are blind, for as Thérèse learns from the words of the abbé, "God and nature could only be one and the same." What she also draws from the dialogues of Abbé T. (following which she "really began, for the first time in [her] life, to think") is a religious attitude that does not fear God, but loves him, and that teaches humans that "pleasures are pure and innocent" when they do not contradict the general welfare.

Yet this presupposes an art of dealing with passion, which Abbé T., the man of the Enlightenment and the beloved of Madame C., denies to the bulk of the populace. Liberation is only for "a very few people," who are able to pursue their desires while still "respecting the public good." Hence, the greater part of humanity is best left to the guidance of the church. This theory of the enlightened and also elitist abbé includes sexual practices to an especial degree. Thérèse experiences this by observing the love play between T. and C., which is characterized by reciprocity and consideration, the sight of which stimulates her fantasy.

The next phase in the life of Thérèse begins with a sojourn in Paris, where her mother dies immediately following her arrival, leaving her alone. As is so often the case in this literary genre, this leads to acquaintance with a neighbor who is a courtesan and who becomes the procuress for Thérèse, though she never actually loses her virginity during these arranged encounters. The narrative that follows of the life history of Madame Bois-Laurier, the aforementioned neighbor, accompanies the first series of actions in the book. Thérèse learns in the monastery and afterward that humans are defined by their passions and find actualization in an art of enjoyment; she now experiences from the tale of Bois-Laurier the full variety of forms and wishes in which the passions can be expressed in this world.

The private sphere is what dominates in the dialogue between Madame C. and Abbé T., but it is now the standpoint of society that prevails. Everything is possible; nothing stemming from the full range of erotic fantasies is too extravagant to be presented here with a certain cheerfulness. According to the courtesan's motto, "punishable enjoyments do not exist." Even the so-called "contrary love," homosexuality, is in no way "against nature," for it is one of the forms in which we follow our taste and hence the passionate movements of the imagination.

A new phase in Thérèse's biography begins when she falls in love and discovers the "happy sympathy" that feels "as if one thinks with the organ of the other person upon whom this power is acting." The count with whom she falls in love and who takes her along to his estate as a mistress is also her final teacher, taking her from the friendship with Frau Bois-Laurier into the world of patriarchal wish fulfillment. Love, longing, happiness, and self-love are the objects of her "metaphysical conversations," in which the count develops the basic concepts of his sensualist materialism. According to this theory, we are entirely determined by our senses and by the passions they awaken. Our happiness consists in acting out of self-love and in satisfying the passions artfully and moderately. Spirit, the count explains, cannot be conceived independently of matter; indeed, it is actually to be viewed as the portion of matter in which passion finds its expression and proper moderation.

The truth of the thought determining this discourse, namely, "that we think in whatever way we do only by an extension of the organization of our bodies," is ultimately proven by a wager between the count and Thérèse — a wager that she knows full well is focused not just on this theory, but also on "the final thing" that she has denied him so far. He promises to provide her with "gallant" books and images, indeed, "the most striking" of such images, whereby she is obliged not to masturbate for fourteen days. If she fails to desist from masturbating, this virgin must place herself entirely at his disposal. "'My dear count," Thérèse answers, "you're trying to trap me, I know, but you will be the dupe yourself, I warn you now. I accept the wager. And what is more, I promise to do nothing every morning during the two weeks of the wager but read your books and look at your enchanting pictures!"

She relates to us as readers the *mise en abîme* of erotic readings that she performs in the same tone with which she also recollects the story for the count:

296

Everything was moved into my room as you ordered. For four days, I devoured the works of your library with my eyes, or to be more truthful, I ran from one to the next: works such as *L'histoire du portier des Chartreaux*, *L'histoire de la tourière des Carmélites*, *L'académie des dames*, *Les lauriers ecclésiastiques*, *Thémidores*, *Frétillon*, *La fille de joie*, *L'arétin*, and many, many others of the same kind. I paused in my reading only to look avidly at the paintings, where the most lascivious poses were rendered with a verve and expression that made the blood burn like fire in my veins. On the fifth day, after one hour of reading, I fell into a kind of ecstasy. Lying full length on my bed, the curtains wide open, two paintings — *The Feast of Priapus* and *The Loves of Mars and Venus* — were the center of my attention. My imagination became enflamed by the situations represented in them. I tore away all my robes and coverings, and without even considering whether or not the door to my room was open or closed, I began to imitate the positions displayed in the paintings. Each figure succeeded in making me feel what the painter was trying to express. Two athletes in the left-hand corner of *The Feast of Priapus* first enchanted me, transported me, because the tastes in pleasure on the part of the woman in the picture conformed exactly to my own.

Mechanically, my right hand moved to the spot where the hand of the man in the picture was so actively engaged, and I was just about to insert my finger there when suddenly I remembered where I was. I saw that it was only an illusion, that I was not the lady of the painting, and the memory of our wager obliged me to remove my hand. How far I was from believing you a spectator of my little weakness, if such a sweet penchant of nature may be called a weakness! And how stupid I was, lord! how foolish, to resist the pleasures of a real enjoyment! Those are the effects of prejudice — it blinds us, it tyrannizes us. Other parts of this first painting excited by turns both my admiration and my compassion.

Finally I turned to the second painting. What lasciviousness in the attitude of Venus! Like her, I stretched out indolently, my legs turned out slightly, my arms voluptuously opened, while I admired the passionate attitude of the Mars of the painting. The fire in his eyes and above all the noble bearing of his lance seemed alive to me, and passed into my heart. I sank into the softness of my bed, my hips grinding voluptuously, as if to carry before me the crown destined to be my conqueror.

"What!" I cried out to myself. "The gods give themselves the happiness I refuse! Ah, dear lover, I can resist you no longer! Appear, count! I no longer fear your dart. Come pierce your love. You may take me when, where, how you will — it's all the same to me. I'll suffer any pain from you, gladly, without a murmur. And, just to assure your triumph, here is my finger again where it will lose the wager!

What a surprise then! What a happy moment! You appeared suddenly, nobler, more masculine even than Mars in the painting. The light dressing gown you were wearing fell to the floor.

In this way, the act of penetration brings a happy ending to what we might call an erotic education, which begins with an arousal of fantasy and which is presented here as a kind of variation on the biography of a saint. What is analogously conceived is not only the stimulation that aims at the unity of soul and body in desire and lust, but also the depiction of the experience of unity that we encounter at the end of the passage. In both cases, the goal is intensity of experience, even if it is understood in an entirely different way in the light of reason than in religious experience. In the lives of both Teresa of Avila and Thérèse, the narratives also have a comparable relation to the reader. Both cases offer a model that does not simply represent some interesting model to be followed. They seek to become actualized through the fact that the images sink into the soul and arouse the passion that leads to apotheosis, divine freedom, or erotic rapture.

In this sense, what is most characteristic of the sort of libertine behavior that *Thérèse philosophe* embodies and brings to view is a stimulation of fantasy and of the passions through images and words — not, as is often believed, a "rational materialism." The power of expressed philosophical opinions pales in comparison with that of images, even if such opinions naturally remain important. What is more decisive, however, is the moment of theatricality that comes to the fore and explicitly affirms and employs the power of images. In this connection, the image of flagellation is grasped as a ritual of stimulation; like pornographic paintings and texts, it is employed quite consciously. In this connection, we find a genuine theatricalization of the ritual of flagellation, whose arousing power is also discussed by the protagonists. Libertine culture is distinguished from spiritual culture through at least this difference: its self-conscious use of theatrical elements.

It is this deliberate employment of ritual and image that was a thorn in the flesh of the philosophical Enlightenment figures. This was confirmed by the publication of a work under the name M. de T*** in 1750 bearing the title *L'anti-Thérèse ou Juliette philosophe, nouvelle messine véritable.* This book, which was translated into German shortly after publication, was authored by the Encyclopedist François-Vincent Toussaint. The critique presented in this work is directed less against the obscenity of the text or the form of the materialist and sensualist doctrine it contains than against the overpowering of the passions through the weight of images. In *Thérèse philosophe*, as Toussaint correctly sees, enlightened materialism and the absolute prevalence of reason is subverted by the fact that all thinking, knowing, and willing is always already undermined by a dynamics of the imagination that stimulates the passions. What ultimately motivates the discourse of the novel is not some mediation of spirit and matter or thought and body in accordance with reason, no "liberation of sexuality." Instead, it is an art of living that is meant to overcome the opposition between spirit and body in such a way that ultimately a state of happiness appears "without trouble, without children, without any uneasiness at all." This is the model of an *ars erotica* that might be designated (not without irony) as both free-thinking and clerical — the heir to a model of religious stimulation of fantasy and anarchic subversion, both of them opposed to the Enlightenment project.

Hence the text of the *Thérèse philosophe* not only plays on the biography of Saint Teresa of Avila, but is also the heir to a thought that was fundamental for sixteenth-century Spanish mysticism and even for Neoplatonism: the thought that the path to union

299

with God must lead "beyond images by means of images." The stimulation of the imagination through images and words, which the author of the *Thérèse philosophe* presents as an erotic and poetological explanation, is linked both in mysticism and in the novel to a concept of unity. It is a unity situated prior to (or perhaps subsequent to) the dichotomy of body and spirit — a unity that takes up desire with oneness with God. In fact, Thérèse, who at the outset swears an oath against marriage as a way to leave the convent, has done nothing that displeases God, but has instead chosen a path that culminates in the apotheosis of divine desire.

Admittedly, the concept of conversion has thereby been fundamentally changed. In this context, flagellation plays a role not only in the descriptions of the life of Teresa of Avila from the seventeenth century, but also from the very opening of *Thérèse philosophe*. Flagellation is already connected with a child's play that Thérèse recollects. Later, it becomes the essential technique for stimulating both the body and fantasy during her time in the convent. The sight of flagellation is repeatedly described as the cause of "reveries" in which recollection mixes with fantasy and is open to a possible ecstasy that for Thérèse — as later, in Proust, for the Baron de Charlus — is not actually an experience of God, but simply an absolute intensity of experience. A decisive change occurs here, even if God remains present in the text until the very end. The loss of the wager with the count, which proves the power of images over our reason, is paid for with orgasm — with a "dying from pleasure" that is "all the work of God." The soul, which in this moment is nothing but sheer experience, since it is entirely captivated by "external sensations," is represented in the text as a unity with God that "suffices in itself" and that knows neither good nor evil. Here, too, we are reminded of the mystical discourse of Teresa of Avila and the emancipation of the concept of experience in the context of late medieval and early modern mysticism. In all of these cases, we encounter moments of the intensity of experience, moments that postulate an "overcoming of nature."

Thérèse, however, does not become a mystic. In the end, her

art of living consists (as the text concludes pragmatically and somewhat frivolously) of being happy by admitting sensations in their wide variety, "observing" them with the aid of reason and "through the regularity of her morals." If one may put it in this way, the contemplative unity of experience that stands at the end of the imaginative increase of desire is integrated once more into the everydayness of active life without absolute priority being granted to reason. What is decisive, instead, is the dietetics of the passions that was already thematized at the outset: the state of the humors, which must be maintained in equilibrium, even as the soul feeds on all possible intensive sensations and representations.

The Flagellants of the Marquis de Sade

For Sade, there is no longer any talk of such moderate, dietetically regulated, materialistically conceived "regularity of morals." Perhaps we should read *Philosophy in the Boudoir*, and perhaps Sade's work as a whole, as a radical answer to the *Thérèse philosophe* and the art of living that it depicts. In *Thérèse*, this art perhaps provokes the enlightened equilibrium of reason, but still postulates a healthy moderation and a materialistic ethics that holds physical desire in check. Sade goes much further than this.

The celebration of flagellation that is encountered throughout Sade's writings in a number of great flagellation tableaux was already noted by Karl August Fetzer, who knew his way around the secret history of the Jesuits, but also around the history of pornographic literature as a whole. Fetzer also related Sade's interest in the whip to the Cadière case and to the literary tradition it inaugurated. Concerning the unknown author of *Thérèse philosophe*, he writes:

> A lover of lascivious matters acquired a folio with engravings that was variously attributed to the Marquis d'Argens, Count Caylus, and the famous Mirabeau — who, it is well known, often sent his beloved Sophie copper etchings and shameful vignettes for her pleasure and her consideration. It was this material that first gave rise to the idea for the abominable book *Justine, or the Misfortunes of Virtue*. This is

the most dreadfully diabolical work of blasphemy, voluptuousness, and cruelty that ever entered into a human brain. It is an eloquent and enduring monument to French frivolity and to the boundless damnation of morality of that period, and all the more dreadful insofar as the book was accessible to everyone for quite some time. Napoleon finally ordered ten thousand copies of the work to be pulped. Its central idea is the mania for flagellation.

This remark by Fetzer is presaged by Sade himself, who in his *Histoire de Juliette* describes *Thérèse philosophe* as the "simple form of an immoral book" that in his own writings he wishes to surpass — and succeeds in surpassing. The concluding healthy moral moderation of *Thérèse* no longer has any validity for Sade. It is in his claim to absoluteness, which makes the arousal of passion and the conservation of the state of arousal into the sole valid principle of life, one lying beyond all morality and all nature, that flagellation becomes the authentic and atheistic "means of salvation," freed from all theology. It is no longer merely a praxis that stimulates passion and fantasy both physiologically and psychologically, but the model of an ever-enduring and ever-renewable arousal. In the universalization of libertinage and the quasi-mechanical practice of sexual actions, the enthusiasm that marks the elementary moment of biography in the life of Teresa of Avila and in *Thérèse philosophe* now becomes an everyday practice. Seen from this standpoint, everything is geometry and a serial unfolding of passions, but perhaps no longer the "true passion" of which Thérèse speaks. The theater of physical desire becomes the theater of cruelty, where eros and thanatos join anew in every act without the sacrifice pointing beyond the ephemeral moment of aroused pleasure, except in the accompanying philosophical discourse.

The basis for this is found in the fact that the arousal of passion becomes a principle that no longer knows fulfillment — a fulfillment that in *Thérèse philosophe* is still possible and desirable in a kind of erotic apotheosis. Libertines find their niche in Sade's novels (as he writes in the *Idée sur les romans*) as a counterimage of the hero or heroine who strives for virtuous perfection. In this sense, it is unthinkable that Sade could follow a development like that of *Thérèse*, which provides a kind of variation on the life of a saint. What is central is neither virtue nor vice, and also not immoderate enthusiasm, but rather chaotic nature itself. This nature has its place in the human heart, since "the passions" arise there and lead to a Promethean gesture of liberation.[60] Sade renounces the ethically charged Enlightenment concept of nature and the representation of an originally good nature in favor of the monstrous, the deviant, and the capricious, which appear as genuine catalysts of passion and imagination. Enjoyment and excess become synonymous. Moderation (which characterizes even the conclusion of *Thérèse*) comes to look like stupidity — or at least like a strategy of the bourgeois lifestyle that restricts the most extreme possibilities of enjoyment and freedom.

Sade turned against the sexual morality of the Encyclopedists that Karl August Fetzer later found so compelling. Such morality includes, for instance, the view of Samuel Auguste David Tissot, who advises us "to perform coitus when nature impels us," but not "when our imagination demands it." Under the entry for "Passions" in the *Encyclopédie* of Denis Diderot and Jean d'Alembert, we read that "passions are the sickness of the soul." This means above all the passion of love, as considered under the entry "The Erotic," which is regarded as a "form of melancholy." The author of the article, d'Aumont, remarks further that every excess of erotic passion further destroys the ability of reason to control the passions. Hence, from the outset, reason must curb the overpowering force of the imagination, which goes hand in hand with the passions, with a view to the requirements of nature. With this model, the leaders of the Enlightenment sought to draw us away from the "unhealthy" sexual morality of the church, which for them meant a sexual morality corrupted by the dominance of fantasy. At the same time, they postulated a new and ideal moderation involving an equilibrium between nature and reason. This moderation (as in Rousseau's concept of a *morale sensitive*) aimed at nothing less than a control of the images that are arousing the senses and charged with affects. Hence, it aimed at a proper framing of the dynamics of passion and imagination that permanently threatens an eclipse of reason.[61]

This type of control is flatly opposed by Sade's scenarios, whose character as tableaux vivants are made evident by text and illustration alike (figures 5.14–5.16). These scenarios try to link up with the logic of the passions that we find in *Thérèse philosophe*. At the same time, Sade seeks to push that logic to the point where nothing can be grasped besides the circular self-affirmation of an affective dynamics in which rationality is dissolved. *Thérèse philosophe* imitates the spiritual arousal of a Teresa of Avila by developing it in erotic terms and pushing imagination to make its breakthrough; Sade does this with the erotic arousal found in *Thérèse*. It becomes the model of arousal as such, which ultimately dissolves the very bonds of nature. It thereby converges, at least in formal terms, with the ascetic aspiration to break loose from the fetters of fallen nature.

It should be remarked here that Georges Bataille's economy of expenditure stands closer to Sade than might seem to be the case. For Bataille, too, it is a question of a radical affirmation, inspired by his reading of Nietzsche. And for both Sade and Bataille, the figure of the cleric already plays the role of the initiator who sets sensualism and libertinage underway. This is shown by Juliette's fate, as well as by an entire series of other figures. In *Juliette* itself, it is the abbess who embodies philosophical education, a free-thinking attitude, a clerical antibourgeois attitude, and sensual voluptuousness:

> The nun I refer to was called Madame Delbène. For five years she had been the abbess of the house and was nearing her thirtieth year when I made her acquaintance. To be prettier than she were a thing impossible; a fit model to any artist, she had a sweet, celestial countenance, fair tresses, large blue eyes where shone something tender and inviting, a figure copied after one of the Graces. The victim of others' ambition, young Delbène had been shut up in a cloister at the age of twelve in order that an elder brother, whom she detested, might be rendered wealthier by the dowry their parents were thus

Figures 5.14 through 5.16. Flagellation scenes from the Dutch edition of Sade's *Justine* (*La Novelle Justine, ou Les malheurs de la vertu*, 1797).

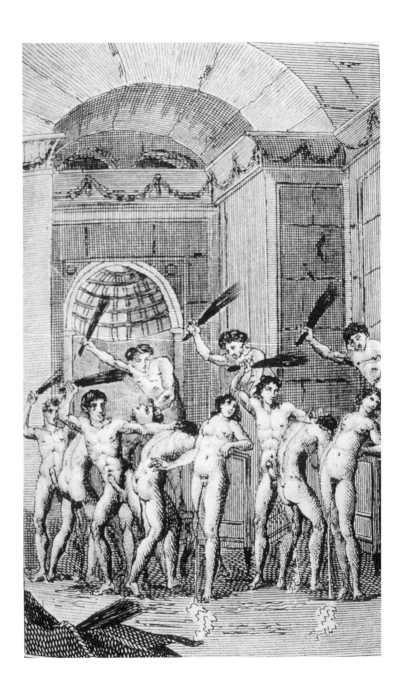

spared from having to set aside for her. Imprisoned at an age when
the passions begin to assert themselves clamorously, although none
of this had been of her choosing, for she'd then be fond of the world
and of men in general, it was only by mastering herself, by coming
triumphant through the severest tests, that she at last decided to give
over and obey. Very precocious, having conned all the philosophers,
having meditated prodigiously, Delbène, while accepting this condemnation to retirement, had all the same kept two or three friends
by her. They came to visit her, to console her; and as she was exceedingly rich, they continued to furnish her all the literature and all the
delights she could desire, even those that were to do the most to fire
her imagination, already very lively and little cooled by the effects of
seclusion.... I have no need to say that among recluse women the
thirst for the voluptuous is the sole motive for close friendship; they
are attached one to the other, not by virtue, but by fucking.[62]

Separation from the world of the family, which the monastery
produces in accord with the postulate of the Gospel, becomes
instead the condition of a voluptuous stimulation — obviously
against the intentions of the church, but involving from the outset
an apparently conspiratorial link between nuns and father confessors. Ultimately, this stimulation aims at nothing more than endless new situations of sensual arousal. The sensualism defended
by Sade forms a kind of diabolical bond with the tradition of the
stimulation of the imagination that he draws from the *Thérèse
philosophe* (among other places), a work that points back in turn
to spiritual traditions. In Sade's world, this signifies that happiness
is directly connected with the arousal of the senses and the passions and that every stimulation of the senses and the imagination
therefore strengthens the experience of happiness.

This is what the Abbess Delbène conveys to her student Juliette to enable her to "scorn public opinion" and overcome
"honor, law, religion." When it comes to enjoyment, it hardly
matters whether the source of the arousal is beautiful or ugly. All
that matters is the intensity of the experience: "A new cosmos
will arise before you. A consuming, blissful fire will stream

through your veins and will inflame that electrical fluid on which life depends. All creatures that surround you will then seem all the more to be destined victims of your perverse heart. There will no longer be fetters or chains for you. Everything will swiftly disappear in the embers of your desire." The pantheism of Spinoza, whom Sade praises in this connection as the "creator of the philosophy of nature," here becomes a perversely inverted atheism whose fury assumes the intensity of the mystical experience of God — but without there being any God.

In this connection, one must speak of a variation on spiritual models. After Juliette is initiated, a long speech follows from Delbène, who asserts to Juliette that religious belief and morality are erroneous. However, this speech does not simply lead to an alteration of Juliette's viewpoints, but "sets her afire" so that she throws herself "gratefully in the arms" of her friend. "Your caresses," Juliette reports, "thus become even more fiery, and hence our passions are kindled by the torch of philosophy." In this way, philosophy, which immediately transforms itself into an art of living, becomes a vividly figurative way of thinking and speaking of precisely the kind for which the Enlightenment figures reproached the clergy — especially the Jesuits. That is to say, it is a rhetoric of images that first unfetters the passions and (with La Mettrie's 1715 *Art de jouir*) makes the "whims of the imagination" into the germ of all physical desire. The spirit of philosophy is immediately translated into voluptuousness, and "the more spirit one possesses, the more one enjoys voluptuousness." The philosophical discussions between the nuns repeatedly serve not only to fill the space between the orgiastic scenes, but actually pass immediately into such scenes and indeed often accompany them. Their function consists of practicing enlightenment not as an empowerment of reason, but as the arousal of endlessly new possibilities of enjoyment that absorb one's reason completely.

From a variation on the mystical-ecstatic saint's life as practiced in *Thérèse philosophe*, a new sort of discourse has now arisen. It makes the liberation of the aimless physical desire for passionate enjoyment (also the goal of mystical ascesis) into the germ of a philosophical life project. Religion, which is thereby "annihilated" by a philosophy rooted in passion, also serves here as a useful foil, since it provides the image and model of the disfiguring descent that is the only way that voluptuousness can be attained. Or at least this is what is implied by the abbess's tone as she concludes her long discourse:

> "Frequently we hear the passions declaimed against by unthinking orators who forget that these passions supply the spark that sets alight the lantern of philosophy; who forget that 'tis to impassioned men we owe the overthrow of all those religious idiocies wherewith for so long the world was plagued. 'Twas nought but the fires of emotion cindered that odious scare, the Divinity, in whose name so many throats were cut for so many centuries; passion alone dared obliterate those foul altars. Ah, had the passions rendered man no other service, is this one not great enough to make us indulgent toward the passions' mischievous pranks? Oh, my dears, steel yourselves to brave the aspersions they'll always be ready to cast upon you, and so as to know how to scorn infamy as it must be scorned, familiarize yourselves with all that can attract the charge, multiply your little misdeeds; 'tis they that will gradually habituate you to braving come what may.... No, my friends, no, virtue shall never make for our happiness. He lies who pretends to have found happiness there.... For my part, this do I declare to you: that with all my soul I detest, I hate virtue.... Yes, I'd have it known, inscribed, permanently decided that I'm a whore; I'd like to forswear, rend this veil, break these disgraceful oaths that prevent me from prostituting myself publicly, from soiling myself like the lowest of the low. I confess to you that I'm capable of envying the fate of those heavenly creatures who ornament street corners and slake the filthy lust of whoever strolls by; they squat in vile degradation, in ordures and horror do they wallow; dishonor is their lot, they are insensible to it, to everything...what fortune! and why should we not labor thus to become, all of us? In the whole world, is not the happiest being he in whom there beats a heart rock-hardened by passions...who has by passion been brought to where he is immune to all save pleasure?

And what need has he to be susceptible of any other sensation? Ah, my friends, were we advanced to that degree of turpitude, we'd no longer have the look of vileness, and we'd make gods of our errors rather than denigrate ourselves! 'Tis thus Nature points out to us all the gate to happiness: let us go that way."

"Eh? Godsfuck! See, they're stiff erect," cried the tempestuous Delbène, "they're aloft, resurrected, these divine pricks I've been palpating while addressing you. Behold, they're hard as steel, and my ass covets them. Come, good friends, come fuck my ass, this insatiable, thirsty ass of mine; into the utmost depths of this libertine ass spill fresh jets of sperm which, if such a thing be possible, will cool the burning ardor consuming my entrails. Hither, Juliette, I want to cunt suck you while our wights embugger me; squatting over your visage, Volmar will present her charms to you, you'll lech them, you'll sup on them while with your right hand you pollute Flavie and with your left you give Laurette's buttocks a smart spanking."

There are numerous means used by Sade to produce intensity, often accompanied by an oppressive monotony. These means include not only the evocation of a philosophical system of dialogues leading to an orgy, but also the perverted ecclesiastical context and its emphasis on vivid images. The point here is not just the motifs of victims and blood, but rather the arousing force of images, which is only increased by blasphemous abuses.

Following the passage just cited, the father confessor and the abbot, who participate in the orgy described, arrange what seems to be a ritualistic rape before an altar on which the Abbess Delbène services herself. What is staged in this way is not only a blasphemous transgression, but a program that can be explained in theoretical terms. As a motif of descent, even descent into hell, this is found both in Georges Bataille's experience of the abject and in the writings of Mechthild of Magdeburg, who in her *Fließendes Licht des Gottheit* (Flowing light of the godhead) says that she must humble herself "under the devil's tail" before she is able to rise up to God. And as the philosophical discussion in Sade leads directly to an outbreak of passion in which the origin

311

of passion becomes clear, this also happens through the intense use of images — a use referring to the ecclesiastical background of the history of stimulation. Philosophy and theology are not only related to one another and traced to a common origin, but are presented as the horizon of a convertibility of word (philosophy) and image (theology) in which flesh and imagination fuse together in arousal.

In particular, there is one outstanding passage that employs flagellation in this way. Obviously, flagellation is one of the privileged means of arousal, even for Sade, since it links physiological arousal with a remembrance of exemplary images of ascetic ecstasy. Flagellation is a complement to writing and speaking. It is an effervescence that arouses and that also shows us that what guarantees truth is not the unity of nature and society, but rather a passion that surpasses the boundaries of both.

Juliette's friend Clairwil, to whom she delivers four women, informs Juliette about her cravings:

"Well, then. Send for your four women; and if you wish to see me discharge, find some switches." — "Switches?" — "Switches, rods, lashes, however you please to call them." — "Do you whip, my dear?" — "Until blood flows, my darling. And I endure like treatment. It's the most delicious passion I know of; none surer to inflame my entire being. Nobody doubts nowadays but that passive flagellation is of prime efficacy; it is a matchless restorative, supplying new vitality to the frame wearied by overindulgence. No wonder then that all those who have worn themselves to a frazzle in riot and sport have regular and avid recourse to the painful and invigorating operation of flagellation, supreme remedy for exhaustion from feebleness about the loins or total loss of strength, or for a cold, vicious, and oddly organized constitution. This operation necessarily implies a violent commotion in the lax or deficient parts; it procures a voluptuous irritation that heats them and causes the sperm to leap with infinitely increased force: the keen sensation of pain in the parts upon which the blows are applied subtilizes the blood and accelerates its circulation, quickens the spirits by furnishing excessive heat to the genitals; in short, it provides to the libidinous person in quest of pleasure, at such times as they are not naturally forthcoming, the means for consummating the libertine act and for multiplying his impudicious joys beyond the limits imposed by that unkind Nature.

As regards active flagellation, in all the world can there be a greater delight for hard-hearted, tough-minded individuals like us? Is there another that so clearly bears the stamp of ferocity, that, briefly, more fully satisfies our Nature-given penchant for cruelty? Oh, Juliette! To break in to this degradation some youthful object, appealing and mild and who when possible is somehow related to us, harshly to inflict upon her this form of torture, all the characteristics whereof are so emphatically voluptuous, to be amused by her tears, excited by her distress, irritated by her capers, inflamed by her writhings, by that voluptuous dancing performed to the music of pain, to make her blood flow, her sweat, tears, to feast upon them, upon her pretty face to mark and exult at contortions of sufferings and the twitching caused by despair, with one's tongue to lap up those floods incarnadine so nicely contrasting with the lily fairness of a soft white skin, to feign to relent for an instant only to inspire terror the next by threats, to carry them out, and in doing so, to use yet more outrageous and more atrocious means, to spare nothing in your rage, to have at the most delicate parts, those very ones Nature seems to have created to be venerated by fools, such as the breasts or the interior of the vagina, such as the face itself — Oh, Juliette! that is joy. Is it not, as it were, to encroach somewhat upon the public hangman's domain? Is it not to play his role, and by itself does not this idea suffice to provoke an ejaculation with people who, unspeakably jaded as are we, indifferent to everything simple and commonplace, must study deeply and seek far if we are to find again what our excesses have caused to lose? Nor ought you be surprised to discover this taste in a woman. That same Brantôme, from whom we borrowed a term a moment ago, with charming candor and naïveté offers us various examples in support of these theses."[63]

Yet unlike in Pierre de Brântome's *Vies des dames galantes* (Lives of fair and gallant ladies), from which Sade borrows numerous flagellation stories, the examples here should not be "offered casually as rough sketches," but rather should be depicted "with forceful strokes" so that the word should carry the same power of arousal as the whip. This is certainly the case in the monologue of Delbène just cited. In this manner, Sade's text, like the images of medieval ascetics, should arouse the reader in exemplary fashion. The explanation from Clairwil's mouth is followed by a scene in which she severely flogs the four women who stand at her disposal. In doing so, she reaches an erotic frenzy that in Sade's choice of words corresponds to what can be found in the relevant article of the *Encyclopédie*. Even the bodily symptoms agree, for "from her own eyes flames dart, her breathing quickens and becomes hoarse, her breasts heave in cadence with the beating of the heart." She becomes the "goddess of sensuality." In the process, she confesses that through flagellation and violence she is driven to an extreme in her sensual imagination. At this point, she continues, she is prepared to do almost anything and might gain the greatest joy from torturing a man so as to revenge "my sex for the horrors men subject us to when those brutes have the upper hand." Instead, they all sit down at table, after which all of them indulge themselves in numerous orgasms:

> Clairwil, quite as eccentric in her comportment at table as in bed, quite as intemperate, no less curious in the article of eating than in the other of fucking, fed only on fowl and game, and they had to be boned and then served up disguised in all sorts of forms; her usual drink was sweetened water, and it had to be iced regardless of the season, and to every pint of this liquid she added twenty drops of essence of lemon and two spoonfuls of orange flower extract; she never touched wine, but consumed large amounts of coffee and liqueurs; she ate in excessive quantity; furthermore, of the better than fifty dishes put before her she attacked every one.[64]

Not only in flagellation, but also in eating and drinking, it is a matter of transgressing the limits that nature and reason set for the enlightened spirit. Every increase produces new possibilities of arousal, every transcending of the customary produces a new freedom. In *À rebours* (Against the grain), the decadent writer Joris-Karl Huysmans later employed this same principle in the service of a radical critique of modernity as embodied in the heroic figure des Esseintes.

In this way, flagellation becomes the paradigm of a new kind of transcendence. In its passive form, it negates the forces of nature and thus the natural moderation of the libido. In its active form, it induces a form of arousal that repeatedly transgresses the limits of imagination and that cannot be held in check by reason. Clairwil begins by discussing both forms. She presents them in exemplary fashion and hence for Juliette produces the vividly arousing incentive to join her secret society of dissipation. In this society (just as was claimed about the Cryptoflagellants of Thuringia in the fifteenth century), all boundaries are dissolved between spouses, brothers, sisters, children, lovers, beloved, and friends in favor of a limitless circulation in which each and every person attains boundless satisfaction. The principle of this utopian antisociety is a permanent arousal in the form of the deterritorialization of natural determinacy. Its emblematic presentation are the whip and the rod, which embody the unity of physical and psychical arousal. The convertibility of word and image, narration and example, spirit and flesh, is made visible in the scenes or in the staging of flagellation.

What is thereby asserted is not something "outer" or "inner," not an "authentic nature" or a Romantic "integrity" and "authenticity," but the moment of arousal itself. This moment is embedded within natural determinacy and discursive positivity and constantly seeks to blow both of them apart. In this respect, Sade's texts are concerned not only with the "sadistic" pleasure of the one who does the whipping, but also with a "masochistic" desire that sometimes coincides with the sadism, as in Clairwil's case. Moreover, the two forms are often linked, as in the narrative of the robber chief Brisa-Testa, who is initially fettered, aroused, and flogged by Sophie and Emma, whereupon they exchange roles, and Sophie allows herself to be whipped by him. Passion and action here are complementary moments of a process that unfetters the passions and that in arousal also relieves the passions of any subjective determinacy. They unfold in a continuum of pleasure and desire that is determined neither by nature nor by morality or reason and that also completely unhinges the concepts of "sadism" and "masochism."

Given this entirely un-Romantic deterritorialization, Sade's work is repeatedly viewed as a radical form of enlightenment that anticipates the failure of the utopia of social equilibrium led by reason and that conceives of freedom as an absolute lack of measure, much as the mystics did. For this reason, Sade demands of literature (especially novels) that it pursue nothing but the study of the passions in their crudest and most objective forms of expression. At the same time, he emphasizes not only that his language is meant as a style of presentation (such as that of Brântome) but that it also wants to unleash the very fire of which it speaks. The principle that one grasps in *Thérèse philosophe* as a variation on spiritual ascent should also be known and felt as the basis of freedom and happiness. What characterizes Clairwil or Juliette, then, is not some melancholic introspection or moral pursuit of perfection. Instead, it is the mirroring of objective passions that are endlessly lived, reconstructed, and addressed by the libertines in their philosophical discussions, which become sites of arousal in their own right. These "depth studies" of the human heart, as Sade calls his texts, are simultaneously an exploration, evocation, and provocation of the passions.

It would be a misunderstanding if we were to speak of this procedure as a psychology of figures. Here it is a matter of overcoming the distance between depth and surface and hence of letting the depth become surface. The passions thereby become objective, losing entirely their individual and subjective conditions, even if they realize them once more in the moment of enjoyment. Just as the participants in the Sadean orgies endlessly pass from dialogue to deed and from deed to dialogue, a circle in which every word incites deeds and every deed evokes words, so, too, the writing of Sade should be seen as an art that arouses the senses and the passions — and that translates everything into objective terms, including the inclinations of individual figures. Writing is therefore analogous to the flagellation that unleashes in the Sadean protagonists the abysses of the passions. Both function as a form of staging in which arousal is produced and transmitted in a manifold of images of passion, images that whip up further fantasies in their own right.

Yet this is not the only analogy between whipping and writing. In view of the manic repetition that we encounter in the writing of Sade, we might also speak of a more general commensurability in which writing assumes the rhythm and ritual of whipping. The fact that the passions should be freed from their individual and subjective husks might initially be regarded as a provocative or even false thesis. Yet every mutation of physical desire in the look and actions of a person is less a subjective expression than an endlessly new possibility of desire, which is present independently of any subjective wish and transcends all natural and social boundaries. In Sade — and especially in Sade — the whip is an emblem of the deterritorialization that first occurs in the arousing text.

The Transfiguration of Nakedness

Fetzer's polemic against the Cryptoflagellants of Thuringia refers to an "Adamite" moment, one coupled with a radical idea of penance and an awaiting of the Apocalypse. According to contemporary reports, the Cryptoflagellants (or at least a portion of this late medieval sect) would meet in a cellar and perform secret ceremonies in which everyone undressed, with "fathers and daughters, mothers and sons, brothers and sisters," in short everyone, having sexual intercourse with one another. Here, too, we have an image of pure and objective passion, because the performance of the act in darkness dissolves all subjective determinations and hierarchical social differences. According to these (probably fictional) reports, everyone at such orgies had intercourse with whomever happened to be sitting nearby. This accusation arose not from actual observation of the sects of Thuringia, but from the stockpile of images connected with heresies

317

since early Christian times and employed throughout church history.

The origin of the Adamite movement of late antiquity remains quite uncertain, for even Epiphanios, who was the first to report of this heresy, declares that he had heard barely anything about them.[65] According to his report, which is followed by Augustine as well as John of Damascus, the adherents of this sect would come naked to church service together. In this way, their church became an imitation of paradise, and the community of Adamites became that of Adam and Eve. They were, reports Augustine, "naked, while they celebrated the liturgy, naked, while they listened to the Scriptures, naked, while they were praying, naked, while they received the sacraments, and they believed their church to be paradise." They rejected marriage, and according to the reports of early Christian writers, they had nightly meetings where the most shameless rituals and orgies took place. Theodoret already reports that after a communal meal, they would put out the lights, and each person would have intercourse with whomever was sitting closest. Moreover, they are said to have viewed this practice as a mystical initiation in which natural and social differentiations were extinguished and union with the divine was enacted. According to Theodoret (who following Clement of Alexandria equated the sect with the Gnostic Carpocratians), Prodicus was its founder; according to Epiphanius, it was a man named Adam; according to Augustine, the sect took its name from Adam himself.

From this we can conclude that while much about the movement remained vague to early Christian writers, we can perhaps surmise some sort of connection with a libertine-Gnostic movement with connections to the so-called Barbelognosis. We have reports on the Barbelognostics from Epiphanius and Hippolytus. They tell us that after banquets, men and women would devote themselves to outrageous behavior, with each guest requiring his wife to offer *agape* to his brothers. Following the communion of the *sperma*, the entire community prayed naked so as to demonstrate complete openness to God. According to an account by

Hippolytus, the Barbelognostics declared that everyone must mix together, for all earth is earth, and it does not matter where the seed is sown — simply *that* it be sown. Hippolytus states further that they should also be happy to have intercourse with unfamiliar women and that they should call this practice perfect divine love.[66] This libertine spirit of late antiquity is attacked by Paul in 1 Corinthians (6.12, 10.23), where he opposes those who believe they have power over everything since they possess the true gnosis. In this state, where libertinage and gnosis are bound together, nothing can touch the liberated Gnostics. "Ama, et fac quod vis" ("love, and do what you will") is another saying that medieval "Gnostic" freethinkers drew from the writings of Saint Augustine. They are said to have read it, against Augustine's own intentions, as granting legitimacy to the actualization of divine freedom on earth and in this life.[67] They thus became the (perhaps imaginary) forerunners of a tradition that also includes a great number of utopian projects of the nineteenth and twentieth centuries that linked social reform with sexual libertinage.

Nonetheless, we still have only a vague notion of the historical background of the present-day image of heretics and "free" spirits in late antiquity and the Middle Ages. Even what we do know is mediated through the typology of heresies created by the church and hence the image that it constructed of heresy as it unfolded over the course of history. Beginning in the Middle Ages, the ecclesiastical authorities disparaged all possible heretic sects, whether Cathars, Waldensians, "free spirits," or flagellants, by means of a series of typical stock images: nakedness, ritual copulation, assembly in the dark, subterranean chambers, renunciation of marriage, and the communal ownership of women. This may be a result of the particularly radical form of spirituality encountered in certain flagellants and mystics of the Middle Ages and early modernity. But occasionally some role is indeed played (even in the work of Peter Damian) by "Adamite nakedness" before the eyes of God. As we have seen, a central place also comes to be occupied by an antinomian and spiritualist motif in which flagellation is performed by the penitents themselves as the union of both penance and absolution. This lifts the penitent to a state of purity that no longer appears subordinate to the church's mediation of salvation. Such elements were seized upon by the Inquisition wherever they were even the least bit present and were connected with the stock images of heretics familiar since the patristic period. In the late Middle Ages, they were increasingly connected with elements familiar from the persecutions of witches. The term "Luciferians," for instance, which appears in this context as a somewhat arbitrary name for heretical groups, draws a suggestive relation between supposed Adamite rituals and notions of the alliance between witches and the devil. Here the subject of repeated critique and Inquistorial persecution is not found in magic, as in the case of witches. Instead, it is the shameless mixing of the sexes and the destruction of the forms of social connection and libidinal economy — family, kinship, and temporal and ecclesiastical hierarchy.

According to defamatory sources, nightly orgiastic festivals were organized by a sect of Taborites or Nicolaites (a subbranch of the Hussites) in 1421 on an island in the Luschnitz River near Neuhaus. Here, too, everyone was supposedly naked; here, too, people are said to have mixed at random and to have possessed both goods and women in common:

> They all went naked, both men and women. They formed groups, lay down together, and danced naked with one another. Among them were beautiful women and virgins. And they founded their law with what Scripture tells us about tax collectors: "Truly, I say to you, the tax collectors and the harlots go into the kingdom of God before you." (Matthew 21.31). Hence they admitted no one to their community who was not a tax collector (sinner) or a harlot, and even the smallest girl they admitted had to be deflowered and was required to pursue illicit acts with them.

According to the accusation, they drew no distinction between lord and serf, between priest and layman, or between blood relatives and others.

This movement, too, seems to have been determined in part by the expectation "of the imminent Last Judgment." According to contemporary sources, the members of the sect presumed that the church would rise in such innocence that humans would live on earth "like Adam and Eve in paradise,"

> and that no one would stand ashamed before anyone else. Hence a few of them already walked about naked, both men and women. They also said that everyone should be as if brothers, that there were no masters, and that no one should be subjected to anyone else. For this reason they called themselves brothers. Taxes and interest rates would cease, and there was no one who could force them to pay taxes. They said that women would have their children without affliction or pain.

They regarded the ritual actions of the church as superfluous. Books were burned, and plundering rampages were conducted by night in surrounding villages. Contemporary sources claim that people even invented their own rituals:

> All men and women undressed and danced around a fire while singing the Ten Commandments. Then they would suddenly stand, looking at one another. And if a man was wearing a loincloth, the women would tear it away, saying: "Leave your prison, give me your spirit and receive mine in turn," whereupon each man and each woman would sin with one another. They were absorbed by sodomite cravings, which they called divine love and divine will. Thereafter, they bathed in the river and were married by "Moses," their leader. They knew no shame, and all lay together in a hut. By night they would murder, and by day they would commit illicit acts. They feared neither cold nor heat and hoped to be able to wander naked over the entire earth like Adam and Eve in paradise.[68]

One of their guiding passages of Scripture was Genesis 9.7 "And you, be ye fruitful, and multiply; bring forth abundantly in the earth, and multiply therein."

In these reports, too, the descriptive fantasy of the chroniclers mixes with the received categories of the Inquisition — as well as with an indisputable grain of historical truth. This reflects the truly radical attitude that pushed the so-called Adamites in a rather different direction from the Hussites and similar pre-Reformation movements. What was central here was an inversion of all values and a series of excessive practices, fuelled by expectation of the Apocalypse, with the aim of restoring the lost life of paradise. As a result, the order of the world based on hierarchical differentiation and regulated exchange was abandoned in favor of a free-spirited libertinage, with property and marriage replaced by a free circulation of goods. This critique of hierarchy was also connected with a theory that the radical otherness of the community of free spirits was both an intimacy with the divine ground and an empowerment for the morally liberated consumption of the world "beyond good and evil." It thereby expressed an eschatology of radical presence that projected the struggle between good and evil onto the relations between the chosen ones and others. Simultaneously, it viewed the restoration of the originary state of nature and the resurrection of the flesh as actualized in every least deed performed by the chosen ones.

Despite considerable differences, we are not so far removed here from the fantastic scenes of the pornographer, such as those found in *Thérèse philosophe* and the works of Sade. Hence, the irony of historic fate is also an element in the genealogy of this fantasy. At first it was the ecclesiastical heresiologists and Inquisitors who believed that the "free spirits" and flagellants were those who went naked by night and devoted themselves without limit to their cravings; in the eyes of libertines and Enlightenment figures, the same role was ascribed to church Inquisitors and to priests in general — and especially to the Jesuits. It was they who were supposed to uncover souls in the darkness of the confessional, encourage the expression of desire, and seduce minds and ultimately bodies. For anticlerical Enlightenment critics, no less than for pornographers, priests had become the agents of physical desire pursued in the manner of a satyr — a desire in which word and image, spirit and flesh, became convertible in an unregulated circulation of fantasies and of the body. In this way, we could rightly designate clerics, monks, and nuns as the inventors of the thoroughly erotized soul and of the underground libertine lifestyle.

Pornography has far more in common with this priestly realm than with the crude or obscene medieval and early modern "popular" traditions of lewdness and bawdiness to which it is sometimes linked by literary scholarship. The pornographic literature of modern times has little to do with that vulgar tradition. What becomes evident here is not the "simultaneous unfettering of the figural potentiality of language and of a repressed discourse that was nothing other than a return to the repression of the claims of the senses conditioned by Christian dualism — and hence also of sensual languages," as has been asserted of the Renaissance and the "carnivalistic Middle Ages" in a sort of late-Romantic transfiguration at the hands of scholars.[69] Instead, it is a construction of erotic intensities and possibilities of experience that is due primarily to the discourse of priests in all its mutations. Hence, the erotic fantasies that find cultivated expression in Pietro Aretino's *Ragionamenti* (Dialogues) and his *Sonetti lussuriosi* (Lewd sonnets), which became determinative and paradigmatic for the ensuing centuries of pornographic literature (one need only think of the readings of Thérèse), did not rise up "from below," as the carnivalistic thesis holds. They are due instead to a subtle play of images at the other end of the scale of literary-poetic culture from the "people's" end. The patristic, medieval, and early modern reports of "Adamites" (also an elite movement, assuming it existed) mostly transmit slanderous or condemnatory statements. But here they form an imaginary foil that at certain points (such as in flagellation, nakedness, and in antinomian arguments) employed more or less genuine historical events to stimulate the fantasies of a poetically inclined elite. On the side of the Inquisition, as on the side of pornography, the transmission of these stories pursued a similar aim — the arousal of the passions for or against either libertine freedom or free-spirited heresy and shamelessness.

According to the *Encyclopédie* (which relies on earlier church historians and which belongs to the historical context of Sade and the author of *Thérèse philosophe*), the sect of Adamites arose in the twelfth century near Antwerp, led by a "Tandème" or "Tanchelin." In this case, as well, it is supposed that "the difference between laymen and priests was dissolved" and "sexual dissipation and adultery" were declared to be "holy and commendable acts." Ultimately, there was a reference to the "Turlupins," a sect that is supposed to have taught that once humans reach a certain state of perfection, they are freed from every law. In this way, they are "also freed from the law of reason, to which the wise must submit themselves." Instead, the perfected ones have to become liberated from the divine laws in the name of passion and of an immediate relationship to God. All of them, writes the author of the "Adamites" article, "ran naked through the streets and committed the most shameless misdeeds." Certain Anabaptist groups are also classified here among the Adamites, as well as small groups in Flanders, Bohemia, and Germany. What all of them had in common was the interest in renewing an original "state of nature," seeing themselves as "new Adams," going about naked and conducting shameless ceremonies. In closing, the author of the *Encyclopédie* article compares the Adamites with adherents of the Priapus cult in antiquity. Yet he also emphasizes the difference between them, for what the former shared with the latter was "the spirit of debauchery," not the honoring of Priapus and the tradition of the cult.

What is reflected in this *Encyclopédie* article is the anecdotal prehistory of the libertine fantasy as encountered in Sade and *Thérèse philosophe*. Yet the so-called "Turlupins," who had already been a target of the antiflagellation critic Jean Gerson,[70] were viewed in this article as *libertins*, not heretics. They were said to stand for "nature, nakedness, and public intercourse with women, as the ancient Cynics did." In this way, they opposed not only ecclesiastical authority, hierarchical means of salvation, and social differentiation, but also enlightened reason and its concept of an ideal equilibrium between "nature" and "reason."

The transfiguration of nakedness, as found in the fantastic history of these heresies, in some way makes up the common basis of a specific libertine spirit, providing it with a set of exemplary scenes. As a form of conspiratorial shamelessness, such transfiguration is also not foreign to the pornographic discourses that build on tales such as those of Cathérine Cadière. The first lesson that Sade's protagonist learns from the abbess Delbène concerns nakedness. Her mistress teaches that nakedness is the most natural thing in the world and therefore cannot be associated with any sort of shame. Yet this reappropriation of the state of nature as a shameless nakedness also sets in motion the radical *overcoming* of nature that Sade advocates, since nakedness (as we have seen above) attempts to recuperate a more originary nature *beyond* nature.

Peter Damian argued in similar fashion, though with a different aim, when he defended the flagellation of the naked body against critics of this practice. For Damian, too, it was a matter of restoring the Adamite state of humans in the eyes of God. Like Adam in paradise, humans should feel no shame before God (or before other people) when devoting themselves to naked flagellation. Just as the naked Christ felt no shame on the cross, the naked flagellant should feel no shame before others. "Nudus nudum Christum sequi": "nakedly follow the naked Christ." So goes the guiding phrase (strongly influenced by Saint Jerome) of Christian and especially monastic ascesis, a phrase deeply important to Peter Damian. According to theological doctrine, the restoration of Adam signifies not just the return to an original state prior to the Fall, but the restoration of Adam as Christ — that is to say, the recuperation of the Adamite immediacy with God, which in the temporal world can only occur in the reenactment of suffering. Only when this reenactment is completed, only in the carrying out of suffering, is the new Adam born and the new immediacy with God established. Nakedness thereby becomes a condition of possibility of true penance in the form of a laying bare that alone is able to lead humans in suffering into an immediate relation with God and in which the human assignment to the realm of the former nature is overcome. For this reason, Irish monks in the

Middle Ages, entirely in keeping with this theological paradigm, stripped themselves naked at night and threw themselves for the sake of penance into ice-cold water while reciting psalms and prayers, much like the *conformatio* through flagellation of their late medieval successors.

Stated more briefly, the overcoming of shame initially uncovers the state of nature that represents openness and readiness for penance and that through suffering is then overcome in favor of the realm of liberating grace. The trauma of the loss of the innocence of paradise, which finds its first expression in shame and which the monk makes explicitly visible in his retreat into the desert, will be ritually overcome in the staging of nakedness and of suffering. However, what the monk performs solely as a gestural action (which holds salvation in suspense, and which always stands under an eschatological reserve, even in meditation on the nakedness of the flagellated Christ),[71] becomes for the Adamite an ultimate reality in which the resurrection takes actual, bodily form through overcoming the captivity of the body. Thus, the Earth already appears to him once more as paradise — a place where he acts without a care, beyond good and evil, and where the convertibility of spirit and flesh becomes actuality through the overcoming of the law.

For Sade, as well, nakedness becomes an initiating moment of radical openness beyond good and evil. Nakedness permits the power of imagination to run free, as it does in Sade's writings. Wherever his discourse begins, this means primarily that shame over nakedness should be overcome. This is also the case in the education of Eugénie in *Philosophy in the Boudoir*. "Modesty," Dolmancé explains in that work, "is an antiquated virtue," while decency is "a Gothic notion with few champions today" that must be entirely overcome.[72] There is freedom only once this step into nakedness has taken place.

In the passages cited, we encounter a sort of metaphysics of nakedness that grasps it as the initiation of transgression of all natural and social norms by means of grace or physical desire. As an ideal of naturalness beyond civilized norms, this concept of naked-

ness is shared even in the twentieth century in a weakened, modi-
fied, and morally reterritorialized form by followers of nudist culture. Even now, as in the Adamite traits of the hippie movement,
one encounters a spiritualization of nakedness and of "sexuality,"
usually bound up with a new moralization and disciplining.

The ideal of nakedness, especially in connection with flagellation, is defended in a very specific way by Ernst Schertel, who
in 1929–1932 published a four-volume work with the title *Der Flagellantismus als literarisches Motiv* (Flagellantism as a literary
motif). It was reissued in 1957 with a new preface and in lavish
form; its twelve installments were circulated in numbered copies
restricted to subscribers alone. In order to avoid censorship, the
work was supposedly "available only to researchers and a limited
circle of those with scholarly interests" who "by ordering and receiving the volume [were] obliged to make use of it only through
private studies, and not to pass it on to any third party." Schertel,
who received his doctorate under Rudolph Eucken in Leipzig in
1911 with a dissertation on Schelling's *Metaphysics of Personality*,
also published some so-called "Akt-Kunst-Bücher" (nude art books)
with large numbers of illustrations (sometimes under the pseudonym Karl Stendal-Hohenscheid). These works bear such titles as
Weib, Wollust und Wahn (Woman, voluptuousness, and illusion),
Das Weib als Göttin (Woman as goddess), *Der Sturm auf das Weib*
(The storming of woman), *Der Teufel der Sittlichkeit* (The devil of
morality), and even *Nacktheit als Kultur* (Nakedness as culture).

His work on flagellation gives us a mass of observations and
analyses that lead to a rather comprehensive claim. Here, too,
nakedness forms the decisive moment of an overcoming "of the
ostracizing of everything sexual that has burned the West for two
thousand years, leading to the most fearful tensions." In his view,
this is now coming to an end, thanks not only to the "wide-rang-
ing and deep-delving sexual research of recent decades," but
above all due to the contributions of "sports and the culture of
nudity." What Schertel has in mind with this vision of humans
liberated in their nakedness is a restoration of "natural man," in
opposition to the "asexual . . . cultivated ideal human," to whom

327

the author in 1957 bids farewell once and for all. The order of the day is no longer the "cultivated man" and no longer "violation by authority," but rather "freely developed man" in his "self-unfolding." The liberation of humanity signifies an overcoming of the opposition between "chaste" and "unchaste" in the name of an attitude that is "free from superstition" and that "looks reality in the face." Against the background of this program of enlightenment, Schertel understands his work as a "document of humanity" that wishes to be "in the first instance a psychological work," and "not solely a history of flagellation, for instance."

What stands at the center of this psychology (as in other works by Schertel, which include *Der erotische Komplex* [The erotic complex], *Sitte und Sünde* [Morals and sin], *Magie in Geschichte* [Magic in history], *Theorie un Praxis* [Theory and practice], and his "Gnostic" novel *Die Sünde des Ewigen, oder Dies ist mein Leib* [The sin of the eternal, or, This is my body]) is the relation of "the phenomena of the sexual drive" to the "mythical thought of early man," which here forms the scientific equivalent of Adam. What Schertel has in mind is a "study of the primeval soul" that is developed in exemplary fashion in the first lines of his history of flagellantism. Flagellation is thereby not only a complementary element in the process of undressing and self-liberating, but also the essential moment of a pedophiliac ideal that is celebrated by Schertel's "scientific" Adamism. He writes:

> It is the infantile human of both sexes who forms the privileged object of the flagellomaniac. The infant type, who is still half caught up in dream life and not all that far removed from the essence of primeval man, does not yet represent that explicit "personalistic" form of existence that belongs to adults. He or she is more "thing" than "person": compared with that of the adult, his or her sphere of life is strange and distant, indeed almost animalistic. In physical force, he or she is inferior to the adult, materially lacking in independence, and dependent on authority. Hence, in the infant, all the necessary qualities seem to be present for serving the role of a fetishistic "victim."[73]

328

Schertel uses these sentences to introduce the first part of his study, which considers "the teenage girl" and like the rest of the work contains vivid pictorial material. The sentences above can very much be interpreted as the book's intellectual core, since they display the connection between an Adamite fantasy of primeval humans and a confusingly rich, diffuse, and perhaps only "paleopyschologically" intelligible vocabulary (to use Schertel's term). The rest of the work is of a similar cast. By means of a great mass of textual and pictorial material, it sketches a psychology of sexual liberation that can be described as altogether "Adamite" in which "early man" takes the place of Adam. Yet the texts and images that Schertel presents and analyzes in detail are not placed in the service of a deterritorialization of nature or of the imagination, as we find in the work of Sade. Instead, they are circumscribed by a "scientific" discourse that conceives the liberation of the "new Adam" and "new Eve" in its own psychological and naturalistic terms. In an analysis of a flagellation scene "drawn from the novel *Miss* by Sadie Blackeys" that deals with "the punishment of a teenage girl in a girl's school," we read as follows:

The text shows clearly how orgasmic ecstasis happens. The narrator tells us "how her sight gets blurred, how the blood pulsates in her temples and in her throat, how her heart seems to burst." She forgets everything and sees nothing else besides the fetish [i.e. the teenage girl's bottom] and the whip that "tears it open." Indeed one might say that the narrator feels herself to be the rod that performs the torturing "Gamos" with the fetish and glows in the inferno of fusion in which the identity of "ego" and "id," in which the orgasmic primal ground — "God" — achieves breakthrough and manifests itself in imageless rapture. The hearths of repression are opened, the soul "communicates" with its Luciferian-seraphic depth and bursts into nothingness. Then sober everyday life returns once more, the "pinched face of the teacher" exhorts the requirements of remaining awake, the fetish is again shut away in the tabernacle (in the "frail covering of the underpants"). And she who was only a short time previously elevated as a victim, as a "*Theophor*" — i.e., as the bearer of the divine-Satanic sorcery — is now once more a girl like the rest, who sits on her bench with a soft "Ah!" as if nothing had happened. At the conclusion of the report, the dark undertone is "Go, the mystery is gone!"[74]

This passage may be taken as a model for the entire book. It gives us information about the position assumed by flagellation in Schertel's Adamite vision. According to him, in flagellation, the everyday world collapses, and a sacred zone becomes visible in which an originary nature becomes manifest that is not covered up by civilization. This, if you will, is the new Adamite paradigm. What initially appears as punishment in the school is in Schertel's view (and without the least trace of irony) actually a holy ritual — a sacrifice in which the true archaic dynamic of drives succeeds in breaking through, fusing together with the divine ground of nature in a kind of *unio mystica*. In this way, flagellation for Schertel is also a necessary correlate of the delivering of naked man to his "true state of nature." It is grasped as a ceremony, one in which the exposed body becomes a "victim" within a quasi-sacramental system of actions that reproduces the so-called "mystical" or "organic" unity with the primal ground. All the concepts of the Christian theory of sacraments and of liturgy are thereby reformed and reinterpreted by means of Schertel's "paleopsychology."[75]

In Schertel's texts, we by no means find (as we do in those of Sade or Bataille) the aim of a blasphemous or frivolous misuse of theological concepts and religious language, but only an attempt at the aforementioned "paleopsychological" breakthrough. Although this presents itself as a scientific discourse that wants to replace the tradition of *spiritual* experience with a *psychological* vocabulary, there is actually a significant connection between the two. What we have established in other texts (whether they be lives of saints or pornographic texts) in which the stimulation of imagination stands in the foreground holds here, as well. After all, Schertel's collection of case histories, along with the medical and psychological terminology, no doubt aims primarily at the arousal of fantasy.

330

Worthy of note here is the historical tradition to which Schertel's text belongs, which is visible, for example, in the fact that the
orgiastic facial expression described by Schertel in the text is
identical even in its choice of words with that of Sade's Clairwil,
Fetzer's Father Girard, and the "erotomaniacs" of the *Encyclopédie*. In all of these cases, we encounter a citation from the
stock descriptions of ecstatic states. In some contexts, this takes
the form of spiritual ecstasy, in others, orgiastic enjoyment, and
in still others, an expression of "hysteria," respectively. Yet as
concerns the link between nakedness, flagellation, and the mysticism of orgasm (as construed by Schertel), we should speak neither of the return to a religious purification of ecstasis nor of a
return to erotic stimulation and deterritorialization. Rather, we
must speak of a psychologistic "scientific Adamism" that projects
the dream of transfigured and guiltless nakedness "beyond good
and evil" into a secular world and in this way resacralizes nakedness in the forms of erotic flagellation that lead humans as "victims" back to orgiastic *unio*.

The so-called paleopsychology sketched by Schertel (whose
vocabulary is sometimes reminiscent of the phantasmagorias of
Wilhelm Reich) is nothing but a modern Adamism in its own
right. Yet it is an Adamism that has nothing of the radicality and
antinaturalism of libertine lifestyles, but instead (as "scientifically
justified") breathes the rather conventional air of nudist vacation
camps and suburban swingers' clubs. As part of this neo-Adamite
setting, flagellation does not mean an unfettering of fantasy, but is
a gesture that is supposed to call up something sacred through
arousal. But in view of the scientific transfiguration that ultimately
forbids deterritorialization, this gesture is no longer able to
redeem the sacred from nature. For this reason, insofar as theatricality is evoked here at all, it is in no way comparable to the staged
world of the libertine, with all its salons and castles. In one sense,
its pathos is mostly grotesque or absurd; in another sense, in its
claim to be the liberation of "natural, repressed sexuality," it is all-
powerful. In this way, the ritual of flagellation presented by Schertel reiterates the absolute validity of the dispositif of sexuality and

biopolitics. It is a question of liberation in the name of the "natural" and thus ratifies the "sole dominion of sex" to which Foucault refers when speaking of the moderns. Thus, even the unfettering of the imagination and of the passions typical of the discourse of the libertine, in which every gesture is lustfully staged, is hereby renounced. In its place we find a "holy" truth that has its site in "sex" or in the "living out of sexuality." It thereby promises a freedom to humans that, at the beginning of the twenty-first century, mainly inspires the personal ads of periodicals.

CHAPTER SIX

The "English Vice"

The activities reported from England by historians of flagellation in the nineteenth century seem to aim neither at a pseudosacral depth nor an Adamite transfiguration (as Ernst Schertel saw it), but are concerned with the erotic pragmatics of obtaining an unusual yield of sheer physical pleasure. "In England," notes Karl August Fetzer, who takes his information from contemporary travel reports, "the classical land of freedom, whipping, scourging, and flailing were in vogue from an early date, and are still so, even though there are no Jesuits to be found."

English Predilections

Fetzer was not alone in this view. In the nineteenth century, England was regarded as the veritable homeland of erotic flagellation. Even the Italian scholar Mario Praz, in his 1932 work on Algernon Charles Swinburne, wrote that "sexual flagellation was practiced in England far more often than elsewhere." According to Praz, it was in France that the expression *le vice Anglais* or "the English vice" first emerged. We may suppose, as he does, that the phrase first appeared in written form in Aimé Peladan's *La vertu suprême*, in which two chapters dedicated to "the English vice" deal primarily with the sadistic inclinations of the English.[1] The sexual historian Iwan Bloch confirms this picture of a sexual culture marked by flagellomania. In his *Das Geschlechtsleben in*

England (Sexual life in England), which first appeared in three volumes from 1901 to 1903 (with a revised version in 1912 in Berlin), he writes as follows: "flagellomania, that is to say, the longing to scourge and whip and the fondness for the use of the rod, [can be described] as one of the peculiar vices of the English. One can also regard this passion, which is widespread among all ages and classes, as the most interesting chapter in the history of English sexual life." Even if the desire for beating can be found among all peoples, "the assertion that England has been and to some extent remains the classic nation of flagellomania can be maintained with perfect justice."[2] He is followed in this judgment by other sex researchers from the turn of the century, who speak of England as the "promised land" or "stronghold" of flagellantism (as Albert Eulenburg puts it). Moreover, a glance at French or German flagellation literature shows that a great part of the relevant pornographic publications are either actual or purported translations from the English. Only after the turn of the twentieth century did a comprehensive literature of flagellation arise there, above all in Germany. In these texts, as well, English names are especially preferred for the characters, since England was still regarded as the homeland of flagellant tendencies. Yet for the twentieth century as a whole, the weight of evidence from libraries leads us also to rank Germany and perhaps the United States along with England as nations that have produced a far richer flagellant literature than others, such as Spain, Italy, or France.

The Bibliography of Flagellation
The continental view of England in the nineteenth century is confirmed by a "Supplement" to Meibomius's *Utilité de la flagellation dans les plaisirs de l'amour et du marriage* (The utility of flagellation in the pleasures of love and marriage), which was appended to a new French edition (published in 1879 in Brussels) of the first, fundamental medical work on flagellation. Meibom's treatise, discussed in some detail below, had been perceived for some time as a source of erotic inspiration, rather than as a med-

334

ical text. In this connection, the Goncourt brothers report in their journal of April 7, 1862 on the visit of an English aristocrat (described as a "fool" and a "monster") who lived in Paris and ranked as an outstanding example of English perversion. This man "opened up a large piece of furniture . . . in which an interesting collection of attractively bound erotic books was stored" and "handed me a copy of Meibomius's *Utilité de la flagellation dans les plaisirs de l'amour et du marriage*. The volume was bound by one of the premier bookbinders in Paris and furnished with engravings depicting phalluses, skulls, and instruments of torture for which he himself had provided the drawings."

The Brussels edition of Meibom's work, with its attached supplement, was received in similar fashion. This confirms anew the Continental judgment about the erotic predilections of the English, since it contains an overview of English flagellation scenes and related literature. Indeed, in view of this ample material, we might speak of a true culture of flagellation that Continental observers thought they had uncovered in England. The anonymous author of the so-called *Supplément* writes as follows:

A highly educated English bibliophile, writing under the pseudonym Pisanus Fraxi, published two highly interesting works in 1877 and 1879: an *Index librorum prohibitorum* and a *Centuria librorum absconditorum*. Both works appeared in small luxury editions and were not intended for sale. They treat of flagellation in some detail. A vast number of English books are dedicated to this theme; flagellation is an element in all erotic works written in English and often enough is even illustrated in these works. Flagellation was a typical practice in girls' boarding schools, and letters on this topic were published in 1870 in a women's magazine (*The Englishwoman's Domestic Magazine*). The same letters later appeared separately under the title *Letter on the Whipping of Girls and the Corporal Punishment of Children*.

The two works by Fraxi seem to have been entirely unknown outside England; hence, it will be of interest to present a few excerpts here. The author mentions a large work entitled *Curiosities of Flagellation*, of which five octavo volumes were announced, printed in Brussels on behalf of a London publisher. The first volume was completed in 1875.

At the beginning of this century, London was home to a number of luxuriously furnished apartments dedicated entirely to the secrets of flagellation. Here, women best described as demimondes (or even quartermondes) took an active or passive part. The names of some of these artists have been preserved: Mistriss [sic] Collett, who had also visited kings since at least George IV; her niece Mistriss Mitchell who was very famous; Mistress James, who was initially the chambermaid of Lady Clanricarde and who finally retired with a great fortune; Mistriss Potter, who died in 1873; and above all, there was Mistriss Theresa Berkly, who earned herself an unparalleled reputation in such matters. The mass of torture instruments at her disposal was extraordinary. The rods were constantly soaked in water so that they might remain supple and flexible. She possessed whips that were furnished with needles and others with hard strips of dried leather. The enthusiasts of this extraordinary passion lacked for nothing in her presence.

The most excessive example is also the most horrifying: a London tailoress, Mistriss Browrigg, whipped her employee Marie Clifford so often and so severely that she died from it. In 1766, the tailoress was sentenced to death and hanged, for at the time it was not customary to take account of mitigating circumstances, and the reprieves granted so often today were exercised only rarely.

An English periodical, *The Bon Ton Magazine* of December 1792, describes with more or less fictional details a lady's club that gathered each Thursday in one of the wealthiest sections of London. Each time it was at least twelve people, six active and six passive. Fate determined the group to which one belonged. The Lady President would place herself at the right end of the row, passed the rod to the others, and possessed the privilege of being the first to strike. The ceremony would last a longer or shorter time, as the body parts that were struck turned a crimson color. Thereafter everyone would exchange roles, and those who had first wielded the rod would now submit to it.

In his *Centuria*, Pisanus Fraxi mentions a priest of the Anglican Church, the Reverend Zachary Crofton of the Saint Botolph congregation in London, author of a great number of theological works, who was cited before the court of Westminster in 1860 for whipping his maid.

An Englishman, John Davenport, wrote a book entitled *Aphrodisiacs and Anti-Aphrodisiacs*, in which he asserted that flagellation, if practiced on the buttocks and neighboring zones of the body, would have a strong effect on the reproductive organs due to numerous sympathetic relations of the nervous system at the end point of the spinal cord.

Returning once more to Mistriss Berkly, Pisanus Fraxi tells us a few racy details about the events in her home. If the enthusiast wanted to whip someone, he was offered one of the ladies of the establishment (Hannah Jones, Sally Taylor, One-Eyed Peg, or Black Bet Ebony). The price depended on the quantity and strength of the blows that one wished to administer. It was always more than a few guineas. In 1828, Mistriss Berkly also invented a machine that was described by Pisanus Fraxi. The "gentleman" who wished to be whipped would lie down on the machine and receive on his naked backside a shower of blows that bewitched him.

This "honorable lady" — as Brantôme would have called her — died in 1836. In the course of just eight years, she had earned more than ten thousand pounds sterling. Although she wrote her memoirs or autobiography, no one dared publish them.

The wealth amassed by Mistriss Berkly was bequeathed to her brother, a missionary in Australia, but he refused to accept money originating from such a shameful source. Even Dr. Vane, a physician whom the lady often visited, also spurned the inglorious inheritance. He also destroyed her correspondence, which filled numerous boxes and contained the names of many people of high social rank.

It is often remarked that women, especially those of high rank, take more pleasure in the rod than men.

Old men occasionally participated in the following ridiculous game: a woman would visit them in the morning when they still lay in bed. She would treat them as if they were small boys who did not wish to go to school. She ordered them to do so, and they refused, whereupon she flogged them briskly.

337

The aforementioned Mistriss Potter was cited by the police court in Westminster in 1863, accused of having whipped a young girl. But matters were settled favorably, and the accuser withdrew the complaint. Yet it was certain that Potter's house was an establishment where torments occurred. The price of a session ranged from five to fifteen pounds. That is to say, only wealthy people participated, since only they were able to afford such fantasies.

In a travel report by an Englishman about Holland from around 1750, we read that one of the most beloved shows was a woman blessed with a large behind. Harlequin and Paillasse enjoyed themselves by taking turns striking at it quite forcibly. Various positions were tried. For instance, one of the actors would take her on his shoulders, which made her especially suitable for blows doled out by his comrade. With the smacking of the blows, the spectators would double over with mirth and an uproarious laughter.

Various English poets have sung the praises of flagellation. Pisanus Fraxi speaks in the *Centuria* of a poem in three cantos entitled *The Rod*, by Henry Laïng, Oxford 1754. He also mentions *The Rodiade*, by George Coleman, London 1810.

As is usually the case in flagellant and pornographic literature of the period, the author's name and publication date of the text from which these reports are drawn are pure fabrications. The (also unknown) publisher of the Brussels edition of Meibom in 1879 and of the just-cited collection of anecdotes and bibliographical entries of English works emphasizes that the book could not have appeared any earlier than 1820. On the following pages, he reports additional titles that he found in Fraxi and makes special note of their illustrations and frontispieces, which obviously gave him special fascination. He cites *The Charm, The Night School,* and so on Brussels (London) 1874, a thirty-page booklet whose author is "an ardent devotee of the rod" — yet the "four poems in verse," as the bibliographer remarks with Fraxi, "are of no value." A work entitled *Exhibition of Female Flagellants* first appeared in London without a date and was afterward reprinted in 1830 with the fictitious publication date of 1793, then again reprinted in 1860 and 1872 with the fabricated date of 1777. A few of the editions singled out for special mention were richly illustrated. A work called *Fashionable Lectures Composed and Delivered with Birch Discipline* appeared without a publication date around 1750 and was reprinted on numerous occasions. Another work entitled *The Merry Order of Saint Bridget, Personal Recollections of the Use of the Rod* appeared in London in 1868 with the false date of 1857. Our text comments as follows: "This story of The Merry Order of Saint Bridget consists of twelve letters from a young woman to her friend. The order has been founded in a French castle by a few women who all had a taste for flagellation. The author emphasizes the importance that was to be granted in this procedure to grace, elegance, and dignity."

The portrait of English flagellation scenes and related literature provided in the appendix to the Brussels edition of Meibom is quite extensive and specific. The unknown author continues his enumeration of interesting texts:

Mysteries of the Flagellation: A History of the Secret Ceremonies of the Society of the Flagellants. London, undated (1863), 8 pages. Several anecdotes, including those of Saint Francis, who was whipped by the devil. The book also names several addresses where flagellation is secretly practiced (the "Elysée," the "White Horse," etc.).

Lady Bumtickler's Revels: A Comic Opera, in Two Acts, (undated). Octavo, 75 pages. 6 engravings. Reprinted around 1840. The work begins with a prose dialogue between Lady Belinda Flaybums and Lady Graveairs. The opera follows, partly in prose and partly in verse. Not that we hold an especially high opinion of this book, but it is one of the less stupid examples of this genre.

Madame Birchini's Dance: A Modern Tale. London, octavo, 47 pages (toward 1790). The edition is numbered as the ninth, which is dubious. It is more likely the first and only edition, published perhaps around 1840. This "modern narrative" contains a collection of anecdotes in prose, the *dance* is in prose. The name "Birchini" is derived from "birch," as in "birch rod." This lets us know what is going on in this work. A young nobleman, grown impotent through his excesses, is able to restore his powers thanks to the arts of Madame Birchini and in this way is able to give his young wife his long-awaited proofs of love.

The Romance of Chastisement, London, undated (1866), octavo, 112 pages, with eight low-quality lithographs. This contains a narrative by Miss Darcy concerning her stay in a castle where flagellation is practiced without interruption. In 1870 there appeared a sequel under the same title, with the addition of *Revelations from the School and the Cellar by an Initiate* (1870, octavo). The author discusses his topic with great enthusiasm. In his view, the victim should receive the blows with the greatest enjoyment.

Additional works are mentioned, such as the *Sublime of Flagellation*, *Venus School Mistriss, or Birchin Sports*, and finally James G. Bertram's 1870 work *Flagellation and the Flagellants: A History of the Rod in All Countries*. As concerns the work *Venus School Mistriss*, the text remarks:

In a foreword, the editor informs us that flagellation no longer seems ridiculous or painful once one has been initiated into its Elysian mysteries oneself. In London there are so many enthusiasts of this passion that more than twenty luxurious establishments owe their very existence to it. In this great city there is not a single temple to the goddess of Paphos in which the rod is not used at least occasionally. The editor adds that there are three types of enthusiast of flagellation: those who want to be whipped, those who want to whip women, and finally those who are content to watch. There is a great crowd of old generals, admirals, lawyers, lords, politicians, doctors, etc., who regularly enjoy the pleasures of active and passive flagellation. Even many young people, and many men who still possess their full power, do the same.

Bibliographical Imagination

Hence, the main sources that we learn of through Meibom's late-nineteenth-century editor are the bibliographical compilations of "Pisanus Fraxi." With this name, we are of course confronted once more with a pseudonym. It is that of Henry Spencer Ashbee, whom we have already encountered as a critic of the church and who published (on March 30, 1877) a work with the title *Index librorum prohibitorum: Being Notes Bio-Biblio-Icono-graphical and Critical, on Curious and Uncommon Books*. This work was published privately and was lavishly printed and beautifully designed. It contains a long introduction, a comprehensive bibliography of over four hundred pages, a directory of sources, and an index. Ashbee offers not just a list of inaccessible and hard-to-find works, but a kind of genealogical compilation of pornographic texts and erotic fantasies. In the ensuing years, he expanded this first bibliography with two additional volumes, the *Centuria librorum absconditorum* and the *Catena librorum tacendorum*. In this way, Ashbee not only produced the first comprehensive bibliography of pornographic literature, but also established a model of bibliographical-pornographic imagination to which even Guillaume Apollinaire and Pascal Pia were indebted in their directory of pornographic books from the so-called Enfer of the Bibliothèque Nationale in Paris. Other great bibliographies of pornographic literature might be ascribed to the same tradition, since in all such cases it is a matter of texts that disclose a literary and archival underworld, along with a forbidden imagination and reality presumed to lie behind them.

To read the assembled titles — which are meant to evoke an ever withdrawn, persecuted, and suppressed reality — excites the fantasy in a manner altogether comparable to that of reading the texts themselves. Indeed, the experience is perhaps even stronger, since it presents the unattainable texts as phantasma of an even less accessible world and thereby stimulates both desire and imagination simultaneously. The bibliography places itself in a relation to the pornographic and flagellant texts comparable to the relation between the text and the actuality. Here, too, what lies

concealed behind the text is an imaginary world of infinite freedom and arousal that stirs the spirit. The Meibom editor in Brussels also situates himself in this tradition of the arousal of the
imagination by means of a vast index, one that finds physical
desire and arousal even in the practice of bibliography. On this
basis he constructs his phantasmagoric picture of the English
flagellomaniacs.

Ashbee's work is not just a bibliography. With its excerpts
from various works and its extensive description of illustrations,
it is also a document of the wealthy man's erotic passion for
collection and an outright *sui generis* pornographic work. Its manner of presentation doubtless suggests that it springs from the
same social classes and the same passions that are usually placed in
flagellant clubs, even in the pornographic films and literature of
today. In these bibliographies, as is already true in Pietro Aretino's
sonnets and the corresponding illustrations by Giulio Romano, it
is a matter of erotic artifacts circulating amid an aristocratic, free-
thinking, intellectual elite.[3] The interest in more or less subtle
and ever-concealed eroticism and in libertine, theatrical, and
spectacular pornography parallels the experience of travel in general — a form of curiosity about the world that began to develop
in modern times, also in England.

Ashbee, who amassed a considerable fortune as a trader, invested it not only in travel, but also in a vast erotic library and
bibliography marked by a cosmopolitan orientation. The "sexual
researcher and historian of morals" Iwan Bloch described Ashbee
as the "greatest savant of human sexual life and its aberrations
throughout the entire world and among all peoples, someone
who earned his knowledge through far-ranging travels over many
years in all portions of the globe." Pornographic materials formed
only one part of Ashbee's collection, although an important one.
(Other highlights included his collection of significant editions of
Cervantes's works.) Later, following initial resistance, his collection entered the holdings of the British Library. These volumes
used to be kept in the so-called Private Case, comparable to the
special section of the Bibliothèque Nationale in Paris known as

the Enfer, abolished only under François Mitterrand. However, the Ashbee collection did become accessible to the public during the 1970s.[4]

A glimpse of Ashbee's collection allows us to see that the collecting of books and the writing of bibliographies is equivalent not just to travel, but also to an intellectual act that (much like the intensity of writing found in the works of Sade) complements the repetitive structure of the flagellant ritual itself. This is reflected not only in the correspondence between Ashbee and Swinburne, whose endless curiosity drives them to seek out a continual supply of new underground texts. The libraries of texts on the theme of flagellation, whether amassed by Ashbee or others, take shape in a similar form and rhythm of repetition, mirroring the acts of whipping in scenes of an arousing character. Unlike most other pornographic literature, which generally survives underground in the form of collections of forbidden novels, life stories, and pictures, the flagellant texts consist mostly of individual anecdotes that are passed down and reconfigured. For the most part they are held together in a makeshift narrative framework, and otherwise they scarcely have any dramatic connection with one another at all.

From this we conclude that when desire for the whip is uncovered, this desire can indeed be found in various configurations, yet it departs from all known forms of narrative drama. What counts, instead, is only the individual scenes, which speak in no terms other than those of gesture, rhythm, and analogous repetition. As is generally the case in pornographic literature, the coming-of-age novel often provides the basic model, yet the moment of flagellation itself leaves little room for development. Wherever such room is opened up, the texts always have recourse to the repertoire of typical pornographic narrative models. However, more strongly than in other pornography, and sometimes also more fatiguingly, what comes to the forefront in this way is the repetition that forms the true essence of flagellation literature. The literary form corresponding to it is not the novel, but the anecdote that reports a singular event without being able to fit it

343

into a dramatic plot. The archive of such anecdotes is the porno-graphic flagellant library. Its most genuine form is not the contin-uous narrative, but the bibliography of pornographic literature and relevant textual passages assembled by Ashbee. This bibliog-raphy, as part of a "universal bibliography" dreamed of by the author in the foreword to the *Catena librorum absconditorum* as a summa of all worldly experience, is also the archaeology of an unknown intellectual underground — an intellectual underground that emphasizes the sensual experience of rarity that excites both flagellant and bibliomaniac alike. Both of them live in a compara-ble state of never-ending rhythmic arousal. "To the bibliomaniac, the real lover of books for their own sake, these unknown and outcast volumes, these pariahs of literature, are infinitely more universally cherished fellows and acquire additional value for him in proportion to the persecution they have suffered, their scarcity, and the difficulty he experiences in acquiring them."[5]

Hence, according to Ashbee, the task of the bibliographer of erotica is not simply to compile a dull list, but rather to awaken to life "what the book contains." Since the framework of the bib-liography should not be blown apart by excessive detail, what is required is a "condensation" — one that both offers a good over-view and also makes possible an exact knowledge of individual books by means of excerpts. Ashbee's bibliography is thus less an erotic library (of which it wishes to form one fragment) than a stroll through the stacks and galleries of forgotten and forbidden books, which once again take form and unfold their seductive force. In this voyage through the stacks (even if it be merely stacks imagined on the basis of the bibliography), all the scattered erotic literature is first ordered into a corpus — one in which titles, tables of contents, anecdotes, the informal knowledge of biblio-philes, and editorial remarks are linked to a world of fantasy in which flagellation has its place. Even when flagellation stands at the concealed center of things as a genuine paradigm of arous-al, it belongs to the same taxonomic repertoire as sodomy, trib-adism, bestiality, necrophilia, and other eccentric practices. As a rule, these are not presented as pathological phenomena, but are

344

assigned "in a somewhat arbitrary manner" (as Ashbee concedes) to national passions. Within this geographical mapping of erotic inclinations, sodomy is said to have had its origin in Bulgaria, from where it spread especially to Turkey and Italy and then into France. Tribadism was practiced in Turkey and France, while bestiality was favored by the Romans, just as it still is by the Italians. As Ashbee points out, it was Italian soldiers besieging Lyon in 1562 who first introduced this custom into France, as well: the troops are said to have brought along goats, with whom they are said to have "satisfied their brutal desire." As for flagellation, although for a long time it was "used . . . in all Roman Catholic countries by priests," Ashbee agrees with Fetzer and Bloch that it now has the most adherents in England.[6]

The bibliography of forbidden books has an encyclopedic character, possessing archeological, ethnographic, and genealogical aspects that are merely sketched by Ashbee, and it displays a tone that is simultaneously frivolous and ironic. Thus, it presents its own peculiar experience of the world in the form of short and striking bibliographical anecdotes suggesting an analogy between the arousing force of flagellation and the arousal of the collector's mind.

Pornographic Scenarios

Henry Spencer Ashbee spent a good deal of time in Paris. There he was friendly with the English libertine Frederick Hankey, who styled himself in the city as a new Marquis de Sade. Ashbee was also falsely viewed as the author of an autobiography entitled *My Secret Life*. This privately printed work consisted of eleven volumes of around forty-two hundred pages. These volumes, most likely published around 1890, were marked "Amsterdam. Not for publication" and displayed no author's name. As Steven Marcus has tried to show, what they present is in some sense the concealed side of Victorian sexual culture — the silent dimension of the world portrayed in the novels of Dickens.[7] What was omitted and censored from the Victorian novel is here spoken aloud in all its clarity and all its raunchiness, though I would not follow Marcus in speaking of the "repressed." The question is not whether this autobiographical report is fiction or reality, even if one cannot help but note the realistic style or suggestion of reality in the work. More interesting is the text itself and the pornographic discourse that follows a tradition alive in England since the beginning of the seventeenth century. Here, too, a key role is played not only by "normal sexuality" (as Steven Marcus terms it) in its manifold forms and with the multiplication of sexual partners typical of this genre, but also by flagellation.

While flagellation does not rank among the individual passions of the author, it does seem to arouse his curiosity. It should be emphasized more generally that *My Secret Life* is a testament not so much of sexual escapades as of an insatiable curiosity open to all forms of arousal. This curiosity finds its true niche in modern times against all scientific and moral condemnation of vulgar curiosity. Sade's strategy, which consisted in incorporating "all topoi *contra vanam curiositam*" and "turning them against their original inclination," thereby making "the novel the sole site" where "the science of man can be conducted,"[8] is realized in this anonymously published novel or life history. But this does not mean that some "truth of sexuality" appears that (as Marcus holds) lay hidden behind closed Victorian doors. Instead, there is simply an endless play of masks and metamorphoses that first took shape in the notebooks of the unknown author. What we find in this text is not an "uncovering of repressed sexuality," but a collection of the greatest possible number of forms and figures that, in quasi-experimental fashion, unfold and multiply the dimensions of passion and imagination.

One day, the author entered a flagellant bordello with his mistress, Helen Marwood, who seems to have shared his curiosity and his predilections. The owner of this establishment was known as "the abbess." She had promised to admit them as spectators to a flagellation:

> Both H. and I strongly desired to see the operation and then heard that some men liked to be seen by other men when being flogged. If

346

we would come on a certain day, there would be then a gentleman who had a taste for being made a spectacle, and she would arrange for us to see it — for pay, of course. We went on the day, but the man did not appear. . . .

At our next visit, the flagellation came off. As H., who'd only her chemise on, and I, my shirt and wearing a mask, entered the room, there was a man kneeling on a large chair at the foot of the bed, over which he was bending. Over the seat and back of the chair was a large towel to receive his spendings. He had a woman's dress on tucked up to his waist, showing his naked rump and thighs, with his feet in male socks and boots. On his head was a woman's cap tied carefully round his face to hide whiskers — if he had any — and he wore a half mask which left his mouth free. At his back, standing, was one youngish girl holding a birch and dressed as a ballet dancer, with petticoats far above her knees, and showing naked thighs. Her breasts were naked, hanging over her stays and showing dark-haired armpits. Another tall, well-formed, though thinnish female, naked all but boots and stockings, with hair dyed a bright yellow, whilst her cunt and armpit fringes were dark brown, stood also at his back — a bold, insolent-looking bitch. . . .

What he had done with the women before we entered, we were told afterwards by Yellow Head, was very simple. He'd stripped both women naked and saw the one dress herself as a ballet girl, nothing more. Neither had touched his prick nor he their cunts. When the door was closed after we entered, he whispered to the abbess that he wanted to see my prick. Determined to go through the whole performance, I lifted my shirt and shewed it big, but not stiff. He wanted to feel it, but that I refused. "Be a good boy or Miss Yellow (as I shall call her) will whip you hard," said the abbess. "Oh — no — no — pray don't," he whispered in reply. He spoke always in whispers. . . . He never turned round during this but remained kneeling. Then after childish talk between him and the abbess (he always in whispers), "Now shall she whip you, you naughty boy," said the abbess — and "swish," the rod descended heavily upon his rump.

"Oho — Ho — Ho," he whispered as he felt the twinge. I moved round to the other side of him where I could see his prick more plainly. It was longish, pendant.... Swish, swish went the birch, and again he cried in whispers, "Ho, Ho." ... Yellow Head from behind him felt his prick. — The abbess winked at me. — Then he laid his head on the bedstead frame and grasped it with both hands, whilst very leisurely the birch fell on him and he cried, "Ho — Ho." His rump got red, and then he cried *aloud*, — "Oh, I can't," — then sunk his voice to a whisper in finishing his sentence. — Yellow Head again felt his prick, which was stiffer, and *he* sideways felt *her* cunt, but still not looking around.

There was a rest and a little talk, he still speaking in whispers. The abbess treated him like a child.... Yellow Head then took up the birch, and H. and I moved to the other side of the bed. Both of us were excited....

I moved round him again, looking curiously at his prick, which was not stiff. — "Let *him* feel it," he whispered more loudly than usual. I felt and frigged it for a second. Whilst I did so, swish swish, fell the rod on his rump, which writhed.... Yellow Head laid hold of his prick, gave it two or three gentle frigs, and out spurted a shower of semen. Then he was quiet...he was lifeless....

Neither of us had seen such a sight before; never had either of us even seen anyone flogged, and we talked about it till the abbess came up.... [Later on] we heard more about the rich victim...who was between fifty and sixty.[9]

In commenting on this passage, Marcus especially emphasizes "the ritualistic quality of such behavior," "the confusion of sexual identity," the "unmistakable pregenital character of this activity," and the "pronounced fear of the genitals and severe disturbances of potency." Against this, I would prefer a reading centered in the standpoint of theater over one defined by psychopathology and oriented toward the scientific paradigm of functionality and the psychological ideal of genital sexuality. Marcus tells us "how truly and literally childish such behavior is" and adds that the text displays "the pathos of perversity and its structural melancholy." But this foreshortens the dimensions of the scene, making it appear grotesque and almost surreal. We cannot agree with the following conclusion by Marcus: perversion "is more than a condemnation; it is — or was — an imprisonment for life." This observation, which has the air of a Freudian interpretation of the 1960s and a modern discourse on sexuality based on genital functionality, is contradicted by the manner in which flagellation is presented in its effect upon the author and by how we encounter it in the texts of pornographic literature that celebrate whipping.

What the passage from *My Secret Life* places before our eyes is really a staging of curiosity that moves the spectator and that serves as the correlate of the arousal of the actor and the observer. In no way does the staging reflect the inconsolable sadness referred to by Marcus as the prejudiced agent of an ostensibly enlightened sexual politics. Instead, it reflects the intensity with which the imaginary and the real cross into one another — a crossing mirrored above all in what it means for the author to write down his experience and to enjoy it. The passage takes pleasure in the most precise descriptions of what took place and in the (possibly unsuccessful) attempt to present to the reader something that has placed the author and his companion into a state of the highest arousal. As Marcus observes in turn, the unknown author by no means experiences the world of sexual obsessions as a prison (which according to modern critics he must do), nor does he seek in his "literary activity ... an exit from the dilemma."[10] What is actually fascinating here is that the act of writing down memories becomes a site where the sensations and the curiosity aroused by the scene are evoked once again — indeed, they are staged anew in their intensity. The drama of flagellation observed by the writer and his lady friend, so pitiful and ridiculous in our eyes, has no small effect on him, but instead becomes a stimulus through a staging of the correlation between curiosity and arousal.

The act of writing also stages his memory of the experience in an arousing way — a staging through which fantasy and sensation become more and more intoxicated. This does not lead to fulfillment in the genital sense, but only to repetitions that, without any of the Romantic mourning over the infinite lack of being or authenticity that typifies the voice of modern historians, are staged anew in writing, endlessly multiplied in their stimulating quality. The sensation evoked by the writing is a new sensation amplified further by this evocation, one that becomes the basis for new erotic encounters that enter into the writing in their own right. What is central is experience as such — not experience with a view to something determinate, such as the finality of genital performance, but the experience that is irreducible in its intensity and that produces a *mise en abîme* comparable to an erotic cabinet of mirrors.

Here, as usual with the kind of erotic experience reported by *My Secret Life*, the visual sphere plays a decisive role, along with the tactile. The flagellation scene reported by the author cannot simply be understood as infantile regression into childlike linguistic and tactile worlds, but is instead a staging and hence an amplification of the experience of the world in which spectators participate, including the one who is whipped. The author of *My Secret Life* and his companion are captivated by what they see. It is not merely the sight of the male and female genitals that form the central moment of the experience, apart from penetration and orgasm. It is the sight of the staging of the arousing incident, or perhaps more accurately, the sight of the erotic itself as the staging of the convergence of imagination and desire.

The flagellation literature of the eighteenth and nineteenth centuries is difficult to describe. It cannot be grasped as a homogeneous corpus, for it encompasses portions of novels as well as short stories, dialogue pieces, dramas, games, comic operas, and verses. There are also letters, reminiscences, and reportage that all claim to be authentic reports and may in fact be so. What is common to all these literary genres is that whenever they speak of flagellation, the narrative breaks apart into concise elements that do not hold together very cohesively. As with the passage just cited, such elements transmit an intensity that is ultimately actual only in the aroused imagination. In this way, the textual passages become exemplars of arousal, and thus the entire genre of flagellation literature (if we can speak of such a thing) is characterized by the anecdotal and the exemplary, which feed the imagination and let curiosity form as arousal. From the story of flagellation related by *My Secret Life*, we learn that what satisfies curiosity is not knowledge of the object, but rather arousal itself, which takes shape as an event induced by an object.

Swinburne's Rods

The most famous English flagellant, and the most infamous flagellant in the history of literature, is surely the writer Algernon Charles Swinburne. There is frequent talk among scholars of a "lifelong obsession" and of "Swinburne's problem," as biographers refer to it in tones of shame. For years, this aspect of his life was suppressed until granted its proper place by Mario Praz, Jean Fuller, Phillip Henderson, and Ian Gibson. As shown especially by Praz and Gibson, what is noteworthy in Swinburne's celebration of flagellantism is the voyeuristic moment, the specific emphasis on suffering, and the glorification of the most dreadfully imperious of beautiful women. Lucrezia Borgia, Maria Stuart, and Rosamond are the protagonists of his fantasy — he whose image of style was inspired by the Pre-Raphaelites. Melancholic, dreadful, bloodthirsty, and pitiless character traits stand in the foreground. Swinburne's conception of the Middle Ages and antiquity have the same general tone. For him both epochs were periods of a sensual immediacy expressed in orgiastic lust, bloody violence, and holy suffering. The sinful heroine, the dreadful and avaricious dominatrix, the suffering female martyr, the condemned beauty, and the courtesan standing beyond all values become figures in a pantheon of heroines where apotheosis is to be reached only through pain and through unbounded sensual arousal.

Already as a twelve-year-old, following an ecstatic experience during the Eucharist, Swinburne had composed a Christian drama that praised the desire for martyrdom (*The Unhappy Revenge*, 1849). In *Laugh and Lie Down* (1859), the young hero Frank experiences the most perfect sensual pleasure as the whipping boy of the courtesan Imperia. Despite his increasing distance from the church, Swinburne cultivated his interest in medieval matters to an especial degree during his student years in Oxford and sought

to exhaust the vivid imagery of passion and pain even in his radical atheism. He drew on legends of the saints and martyrs, which
excited him greatly. Along with Swinburne's deeply felt mysticism of the sea and of elemental forces, much of his work hinges
on the sort of hagiographic transfiguration in suffering familiar
since the Middle Ages. Such transfiguration became a means for
arousing poetic fantasy in exemplary fashion, even for Marcel
Proust and Joris-Karl Huysmans. Swinburne writes in the *Whippingham Papers* that a poet's work is born from the wish to arouse
a sensation of suffering and abandonment: "One of the great
charms of birching lies in the sentiment that the flogged is the
powerless victim of the furious rage of a beautiful woman."[11]
Inspiration, inspired writing, and poetic mania are simply the
expression of this submission: a translation of the blow that the
whip delivers to the body, thereby arousing fantasy.

Mario Praz has shown that Swinburne has much in common
with Théophile Gautier, Flaubert, and Baudelaire, and even with
his own disciple Oscar Wilde. Yet perhaps no other writer has
made flagellation such an important part of his life and writing.
IIis unpublished epic poem *The Flogging-Block* fills one hundred
and sixty-five manuscript pages, most of them covered on both
sides. Nor was this poem some sort of passing occasional piece:
Swinburne worked on it for many years and gives a vivid and
enthusiastic report of scenes remembered from Eton, which he
entered at the age of twelve on April 24, 1849. The majority were
pictures that he had seen in Eton or that he himself had painted.
He wrote similar things for anonymous publications on such
themes, as in *The Whippingham Papers* (1887) or *The Pearl* (1879–80).
Even now, much of this material has still not been published.[12]

No doubt Swinburne had felt the rod himself as a student in
Eton; no doubt he had often witnessed how other students were
whipped and perhaps later sought to gratify this desire himself in
the bordello. He supposedly told his friend George Powell that
"the river and the flogging block" are the only two things in Eton
that he would wish to see again. In his texts, the memory of the
pleasure of swimming in the river (from earliest childhood he

enjoyed nothing more than swimming in the sea) is often linked with the experience of blows on the block as an image of the rapture of the senses. What is always central for him, as can be seen in the poems, is the visual living and reliving of flagellation, usually as an actual ritual of stripping naked. The exposed backside, the rhythm of the blows, the increasing reddening during the blows corresponding to the shame of the one being punished, the trembling, and finally the tears — these are the elements of a fascination that determined Swinburne's entire life: "How each cut makes the blood come in thin little streaks / From that broad blushing round pair of naked red cheeks." In these lines we hear physical pleasure, irony, and the transfiguration of what he often witnessed and lived as a pupil. The pleasure in pain, especially in his own pain, first seems to retreat into the background, while in turn the theatricality (and hence the deliberately produced character of the event) plays a chief role. This is confirmed by the texts "Charlie's Flogging," "Reginald's Flogging," "Algernon's Flogging," and "Rupert's Flogging."

What is especially central here is flogging as a drama that unfolds before the eyes of his peers. Viewing and seeing are contrasted with movement, with the temporal course of punishment and the expression of pain. This is true to such an extent that we might easily agree with many commentators that Swinburne had an obsession with the buttocks. This may certainly have been the case, yet what the poems really stage is an interest in reflection and in the manner in which the gaze is captured by rhythm and image. The blows of the rod and the movements and discolorations of the buttocks are presented as a moment of erotic fascination and also as an exemplary scene of erotic fascination. That is to say, they are exemplars of the simultaneous arousal of the body through blows and of fantasy through the witnessing of the drama. The sole and primary goal of desire and lust is formed not by stripping naked, by movements, or by the reddening of the buttocks, but rather by the liberating absorption of gaze and imagination in the arousal that arises in this way. The desire to see, the enjoyment of the arousal of fantasy through the witnessing of spectacle, becomes the basis for flagellation to attain a meaning that surpasses mere punishment or the erotic stimulation of the buttocks.

When this doubling is overlooked, the interpreter misses that the relevant poems are not only evidence of a "pathology," of sexual obsession or "fetishism," but also amount to a poetic and poetological reflection that becomes clear in the example of flagellation. Swinburne's rhetorical strategy is more complicated than might be supposed from a first glance at the apparently simple texts, for it always emphasizes the moment of staging. What is described, what is narrated, is not merely punishment with the whip, not merely the sight of the rod that strikes the naked buttocks, but the staging of this action as a ritual on the "flogging block" in which the same arousal that lies at the basis of poetic creation takes shape and becomes visible.

What belongs to the intensification of the sense impressions in flagellation is obviously also not pain:

> Knowest thou not... that a nerve may quiver and be convulsed with actual pain while the blood is dancing and singing for joy like a nymph drunken? That to be pinched and torn by the lips and teeth and fingers of love is a delight enduring when one is past kisses and when caresses have no sting and savour left in them? That the ache and smart of the fleshly senses are things common alike to pleasure and pain?[13]

It is precisely here that fantasy outstrips the "sexual obsession with the buttocks" in a manner that does not permit us to make such a psychopathological reduction as to speak of "Swinburne's problem," thereby entirely cutting away the rhetoric that is in play. In the connection of the red of the backside with the red of shame in the face, in the presentation of injury and the metaphysics of pain, in the detailed presentation of the drama of flagellation, Swinburne expresses above all else that it is a matter of sensuality as evoked in similar and illuminating form by Pre-Raphaelite art. The image of impure purity, rejection in the shape of a mythical beautiful woman, the pain at the basis of all life and experience, are moments that find perhaps their most succinct form of staging in flagellation. This image is the perfect embodiment of how the trace of arousal engraves itself in the body and the spirit, thereby opposing an "inner experience" and living image to fleeting desire.

This mystical increase of experience and the intensity of experience, which we encounter in similar fashion in Georges Bataille's works and in certain places in the young Foucault, naturally cannot break free of its long history.[14] In a letter to his friend Richard Monckton Milnes, Swinburne reveals the specific context through which he interprets the punishment that he receives with the rod. Not surprisingly, it concerns Sade's *Justine*. He reports that this work disappointed him at first and actually amused him. He would break out in laughter, he told Milnes in a letter, as would his friends as he read to them from the text. He held Sade above all others as a bad writer and not at all the pagan philosopher he proclaimed himself to be. Swinburne speaks to a fictional Sade in the form of a direct address:

> You take yourself for a great pagan physiologist and philosopher — you are a Christian ascetic bent on earning the salvation of the soul through the mortification of the flesh. You are one of the family of Saint Simeon Stylites. You are a hermit of the Thebaid turned inside out. You, a Roman of the later empire? Nero knows nothing of you; Heliogabalus turns his back on you; Caracalla sniffs contemptuously at the sight of you, Cotytto veils her face ... Venus Cloacina dips down into her gutter, and Priapus turns to a mere fig tree stump. Paganism washes its hands of you.[15]

Despite this explicit distancing, which accuses Sade's work of being insufficiently radical and paradoxically (but insightfully) of being too close to Christian asceticism, we find hints of references to Sade throughout Swinburne's letters and his later literary work. In these passages, Sade is viewed above all as an apologist of disinhibition and pain. Yet we may also connect Sade with Swinburne's "unfettering of fantasy," which made an impression on his

355

contemporaries and was often received with its "aberration of ideas" as "unspeakably shocking."[16] In the relation between Swinburne and Sade, it is not a matter of pain as such, but of stimulation and the arousal of the senses. (Swinburne, following Sade, compares it to the effect of perfume or a dip in the ocean.) Pain is an example, perhaps the ideal poetic example, of the most sublime sensation — for it remains the image and figure of the intensification of sensual-imaginative perception. It is thereby linked with other moments that evoke a boundless intensity, such as the scent of firewood, which Swinburne associates with the fateful blows of punishment at Eton.

The poet celebrates the "flogging block" and summons its Muse. For him (in a striking parallel with the image of the recitation of the Psalms during flagellation, as in Peter Damian), the block becomes a harp, and the person being punished resembles its strings. The bench where the pupil kneels is the most important stimulus of the imagination, for Swinburne imagines the possibilities offered by fantasy when his friend Powell sends him a postcard with an image of the "Eton block." He writes: "if I were but a painter   ! I would do dozens of different fellows diversely suffering. There can be no subject fuller of incident, character, interest — realistic, modern, dramatic, intense, and vividly pictorial."[17]

Swinburne repeatedly staged such incidents in brothels, perhaps with some female friends, thereby reminding us of the medieval ritual origin of flagellation. Especially during 1868, but perhaps even earlier, he seems to have paid regular visits to a brothel at 7 Circus Road in London known as the Verbane Lodge, a place to which he was introduced by a friend. At a cost that pushed him to the brink of financial ruin, he would have himself whipped by two women, described by his acquaintance and biographer Edmund Gosse as "golden-haired and rouge-cheeked ladies." What we can gather from the various letters that speak vaguely of his brothel visits is that this "Sadian-Paphian spring" (Swinburne's words) bought him not only the enjoyment of flagellation, but other erotic pleasures, as well.[18]

On the basis of seventeen letters written by Swinburne be-

tween 1899 and 1902 to his cousin Mary Gordon (later Mary
Gordon Leith), which have been housed in the Huntington Library since 1972, we can see that she had shared his passion for
flagellation ever since their youthful days together. This is made
quite evident in the letters in which Mary Leith (in her role as
author she is also known as "Mrs. Disney Leith") resumed the
correspondence in 1891 after its interruption in 1865.[19] Her playful manner of doing so and the manner in which this woman
(who in the meantime had written ten novels of her own that are
rich in flagellation scenes) relates the blows of the rod to the act
of writing are indications that she, too, drew a close connection
between poetic creativity and the desire for the rod. For Mary
Disney Leith, as for Swinburne, pain and physical desire were not
some extrinsic aspect of writing, but elementary moments of
writing, no less than of the erotic sphere.

This is given vivid and detailed expression in Swinburne's
unfinished work *Lesbia Brandon*. Margaret, abandoned by her
beloved, speaks of the pain that is induced by the consoling song:

> It's odd that words should change so just by being put into rhyme.
> They get teeth and bite; they take fire and burn. I wonder who first
> thought of tying words up and twisting them back to make verses,
> and hurt and delight all people in the world for ever. For one can't
> do without it now: we like it far too much, I suspect, you and I. It
> was once an odd device: one can't see why this ringing and rhyming
> of words should make all the difference in them: one can't tell where
> the pain or the pleasure ends or begins.[20]

In one novel by Mary Disney Leith in particular, *From Over the
Water* (1884), critics believe they have found a counterpart to *Lesbia Brandon* as well as the document of a lost and allied passion.
Where this text resonates most clearly with Swinburne is perhaps
in the gesture that closely binds poetic writing with the memory
of punishment with the rod or verse with the rhythm of the whip.
The whip, which strikes the body and arouses it, is like verse,
which injures and arouses the spirit and which at the same time

evokes physical desire and pain in reader and writer alike. This convergence of rod and verse is the nucleus of a Swinburnean mystical poetics of arousal in which spirit and body fuse together.

James Joyce

It is not known whether James Joyce was ever whipped during a visit to a bordello. But reminiscences of theatrical scenes of punishment with the whip are not rare in his work.

> It can't be helped
> It must be done.
> So down with your breeches
> And out with your bum.

We find these words in *Portrait of the Artist as a Young Man*.[21] The lines are redolent of Swinburne's flagellation poetry, even if Joyce otherwise thoroughly excludes Swinburne's influence, except perhaps in a few scattered poems. Like the verses of Swinburne, these lines also emphasize the theatrical character of punishment with the rod, which is not merely a painful penance, but a staging of the body, a shaming and submission before the eyes of spectators who are captivated by the scene. The latter aspect is more strongly emphasized by Joyce, while the visual and descriptive moment that dominates in Swinburne recedes into the background. Moreover, the pain sensed by Stephen Dedalus when he is beaten is a sensual experience of its own kind and intensity, one whose qualities Joyce describes quite precisely. Hence, just as in Swinburne, the relationship between writing and blows is central. But here it is especially the sound, the "high whistling sound" of the rod, that seems to be associated not only with pain, but also with the "the slow scraping of the pens" to which Stephen listens. Even in the expectation of the blows, received as punishment for losing his glasses, his attention is focused on the sound that precedes the pain and suddenly fuses with it. Later, in two letters to Nora, Joyce expresses his own wish to be beaten, and perhaps to repeat what Stephen brings before his mind.

Corresponding to Joyce's own wish to be whipped, there is a passage in the Circe episode of *Ulysses* where Leopold Bloom (playing on the pornographic novels of the eighteenth century) is whipped as "James Lovebirch" by "several highly respectable Dublin ladies."[22] Bloom is theatrically accused of having sent them erotic letters under the pseudonym "James Lovebirch" that asked them to perform illicit acts. Bloom is finally punished by the three in a burlesque scene. It all follows the pattern of flagellant clubs or brothels as depicted in pornography, but with an ironic and grotesque twist. Moreover, the letter that Bloom is accused of having written uses the expression "Venus in furs" to play on Sacher-Masoch's novel of the same name. The same style characterizes the three aristocratic ladies as they dole out a ruthless beating to Bloom, who had really wished for nothing more than "the spanking idea. A warm tingling glow without effusion. Refined birching to stimulate the circulation." In this way, they unexpectedly turn him into Leopold von Sacher-Masoch.

But let us return to biography: to Nora and James Joyce. Many of the letters written by Joyce to Nora in December 1909 (from Dublin to Trieste, where she had remained) contain erotic fantasies. "You seem to turn me into a beast," he writes to her on December 3, and he writes as this "beast" that seems to know nothing other than the lustful desire for Nora and her desire for him. Here we also find the stock figure of degradation, of Joyce's own worthlessness and the glorification that stylizes Nora into an erotic goddess or "holy whore," as we have encountered in Swinburne's image of women. What also belongs here is the fantasy of flagellation, performed by the stylized dominatrix upon the man, whose gestures of submission end in the tone of a prayer:

> Tonight I have an idea madder than usual. I feel I would like to be flogged by you. I would like to see your eyes blazing with anger. I wonder is there some madness in me. Or is it love madness? One moment I see you like a virgin or madonna the next moment I see you shameless, insolent, half naked and obscene! What do you think of me at all? Are you disgusted with me?

I remember the first night in Pola when in the tumult of our embraces you used a certain word. It was a word of provocation, of invitation and I can see your face over me (you were *over* me that night) as you murmured it. There was madness in *your* eyes too and as for me if hell had been waiting for me the moment after I could not have held back from you.

Are you too, then, like me, one moment high as the stars, the next lower than the lowest wretches?

I have *enormous* belief in the power of a simple honourable soul. You are that, are you not, Nora?

I want you to say to yourself: Jim, the poor fellow I love, is coming back. He is a poor weak impulsive man and he prays to me to defend him and make him strong.

I gave others my pride and joy. To you I give my sin, my folly, my weakness, and sadness.[23]

On December 13, Joyce repeated himself, at times almost verbatim. Yet on this occasion, the fantasy of punishment is more strongly marked by a moment of arousal (which Joyce calls "my own mad fashion"), one that grows during the course of writing and is amplified through the depiction of flagellation.

Punish me as much as you like. I would be delighted to feel my flesh tingling under your hand. Do you know what I mean, Nora dear? I wish you would smack me or flog me even.... I would love to be whipped by you, Nora love! I would love to have done something to displease you, something trivial even, perhaps one of my rather dirty habits that make you laugh: and then to hear you call me into your room and then to find you sitting in an armchair with your fat thighs far apart and your face deep red with anger and a cane in your hand. To see you point to what I had done and then with a movement of rage pull me towards you and throw me face downwards across your lap. Then to feel your hands tearing down my trousers and inside clothes and turning up my shirt, to be struggling in your strong arms and in your lap, to feel you bending down (like an angry nurse whipping a child's bottom) until your big full bubbies almost touched me and to feel you flog, flog, flog me viciously on my naked quivering flesh!! Pardon me, dear, if this is silly. I began this letter so quietly and yet I *must* end it in my own mad fashion.[24]

The image sketched by Joyce in his letter, like the other pornographic fantasies in the letters from around this time, is an erotic stimulation in which Nora should also participate and have a role. It is a fantasy of endless reciprocal arousal, which increases from letter to letter in the possibility of writing even "dirtier" and in this way for both to outdo each other. Yet this is not a mere erotic squabble. Instead, just as with Swinburne, it is also an image of writing. It is the obscenity that reaches its peak in a flagellation fantasy, in this case the manic-poetic arousal, that makes the words permeable on the body and its many images. Language becomes full with the stimulation of the bodily, and the moment of erotic arousal is transferred to language and to poetic fantasy.

Hence, flagellation for Joyce is not only associated with "concealed homoerotic desire," as might first be assumed and as scholars in fact suggest. This may be present to some degree. It is illustrated in one of the stories in *Dubliners* through the figure of the old lecher who dreams of whipping young lads.[25] In *Portrait of the Artist as a Young Man*, the desire for the rod is also evoked. In Joyce, the theater of punishment is no doubt especially a moment of intensive experience, one achieved nowhere else than in the linguistic multiplication of gestures, in the shifting between punishments and caresses. What is hidden behind punishment with the rod and the fascinated view of its staging is not merely a homoerotic desire that transgresses the borders of the permissible or even a transgression of most pornography, where whipping is usually heterosexual or lesbian. Nor is there concealment of some wish to transform the ritual that conceals an inadmissible homoerotic inclination into a more admissible heterosexual game (albeit a "perverse" one).[26] Instead, the passages in which Joyce speaks of flagellation suggest the intensity of an erotic game whose seriousness and radical corporeality are woven through with numerous literary allusions, making literary experience the condition of an amplification of bodily experience.

The genre in which the rod is addressed most vividly is the personal letter. Here it is the gesture of writing itself, the gesture of writing as an act of address, that stands in close correlation with the whip. Poetic mania, the "holy madness" of the poet to which Joyce alludes at the close of the passage cited, is (here, as nowhere else) to be grasped through the example of flagellation. Like writing, whose tone Stephen hears before he himself receives the blows, the blows of the rod are initially a fetish or finite moment through which transcendence is expressed and projected into the finite realm. This transcendence (unlike for Swinburne, where the words harbor a mystical sense that the words, like blows of the whip, bring into motion) is now dissolved in the play of association, in seriality, in the productivity of language itself — all of them due to the arousal of fantasy.

Education and Staging

What is now needed is a brief excursus into the origin of the supposedly typical English flagellomania on the heels of our reading of Swinburne and Joyce. Even among the interpreters of these authors, we regularly encounter the commonplace that the proverbial predilection of the English for flagellation can be explained by the educational methods of English schools or by Victorian sexual morality, such as through an "inversion" of the Victorian ideal of manhood.[27] Naturally, no one will deny that the ideal of bourgeois existence marked by extreme self-control is contradicted in the flagellation fantasies that we encounter in many anonymous texts, especially in the Victorian epoch, with their "childishness" and "disconnectedness," their "lack of linguistic and narrative structure," their "confusion of sexual identity," and their "playing with the exchange of roles," as the usual characterizations go. Yet this cannot be the sole form of explanation, since it misappropriates the genuine productive moment in the history of flagellation, which from Sade to Joyce appears as the analogue of poetic writing.

362

Even Ian Gibson's explanations of Swinburne's flagellomania in *The English Vice* are ultimately no more than the desired proof of its connection with the custom of English educators of whipping their pupils extensively. This seems to have been especially the case at Eton, which may then also provide an explanation of why this obsession was so widespread in England — even though, as Fetzer remarked, there were no Jesuits to promote it. And true enough, we can hardly deny the decisive influence of "English educational methods," as the practices in question are termed in brothels even today.[28] According to contemporary reports, punishment with the whip was customary not merely at Eton and similar institutions, but in many schools, among parents in the household, and in the educational sphere more generally. This is shown by the numerous discussions in periodicals and newspapers of the nineteenth century, especially toward century's end.[29] They prove how contentious the widespread use of punishment with whips and rods was at the time — moreover, they allow us to acknowledge the degree to which the public was fascinated by the theme and how well the reading public was entertained by the relevant "experiential reports." The point is not to dispute the seriousness of these discussions, in which it is often impossible to separate fact from fiction. Nor is it to render harmless the problem of punishment with the whip. Yet even in the contemporary articles and letters to the editor of the *Saturday Review*, the *New Family Herald*, and the *Englishwoman's Domestic Magazine*, we find the same thing that was encountered in Swinburne in the form of fascination with the "Eton block." The vivid description and visual presentation, often quite comparable to that of pornographic novels, also dominates the discussions in newspapers and turns them into exemplary scenes of arousal.[30]

After reading Swinburne, it seems especially necessary that a theatrical moment should be identified at the heart of the spread of flagellation, before having recourse to other sorts of explanations. His poems that refer to punishment by the whip at Eton place special emphasis on the desire for theater and the arousal it unleashes. This coincides entirely with the arguments employed by pedagogues and politicians against punishment with the rod, since these arguments are mostly not concerned with pain and with the dubiousness of corporal punishment, but with the problem of arousal stemming from the theatricality of the event. Many of them seem to be embarrassed precisely by what most *fascinates* Swinburne: that the body is displayed and staged in such a way that it is placed before the eyes of one's fellow students. Disapproval of this practice led to the fact that girls in the nineteenth century were rarely punished in this way, but also led to viewing punishment with the rod on the naked buttocks of students with increasing distrust. What was unbearable in the eyes of society was thus precisely the moment of staging that so fascinated Swinburne and Joyce and that for Swinburne, in particular, became the authentic image of writing. After all, for Swinburne, there was nothing that aroused the spirit, fantasy, and affects like blows from a rod. The sort of arousal that is more discernible in the case of blows with the rod than elsewhere caused increasing outrage among more progressive spirits, who for humanistic and psychologistic reasons vehemently rejected corporal discipline. The central requirement was the development of a "healthy young man," and this was further reason to forbid the arousing drama of punishment with the rod.

On psychological grounds, we can agree with the connection drawn by Ian Gibson between the flagellomania of Swinburne and punishment with the rod during his youth. Yet this cannot be the explanation for his passion for and fascination with blows of the rod. This treats the moment of the arousal of fantasy through punishment with the rod only as the beginning of "perverse sexuality" and not, as for Swinburne, as an image of the creativity of fantasy and its power to arouse the passions. Gibson thereby misses the weight of the theatrical and the significance of flagellomania, which is connected primarily with the desire for drama and the arousal of the imagination. We should not be surprised in this connection by the resurfacing of the archetype of the seductive and despicable priest, especially the Jesuit. (Sade is also relevant for Swinburne here, despite his initial rejection of the French

pornographer.) It is the Jesuit who lends to the diabolical hero
(whom Swinburne views as a fusion of mystical evangelist and
materialist ironist) the traits of the seducer who unscrupulously
makes use of the power of images.[31] This type of the post-Jesuit
"diabolical hero" finds its apotheosis in the portrait sketched by
the Goncourts or Maupassant of the "sadistic Englishman." As a
"hybrid cross between Swinburne, Wilde, and Byron," he is
finally sketched by Aimé Péladan in *Le vice errant* (1902) in the
following words:

> He instinctively despised this lean, bald-headed Englishman with the
> cunning face of a bad priest. With his sharp chin, his hollow cheeks,
> his bitter smile, with his eyes (above all with his eyes, piercing and
> uneasy, which lie deeply embedded under the dome of a broad
> thinker's forehead) Filde [an allusion to Swinburne] was reminded
> very much of Dante — admittedly of a Dante who had gladly re-
> mained in the circles of an ambiguous hell. In this emaciated profile
> of the Florentine school there lay something filled with secrets, but
> even more a biting mockery. Under the noble forehead, the eyes
> glowed with an evil longing; under the irony of the mobile pupils
> was concealed a cruelty that worked even more penetratingly when
> the pupils did not move.[32]

PART THREE

Therapeutics

Chapter Seven

The "Healing Whip"

In his *Geschichte der Flagellantismus und der Jesuitenbeichte* (History of flagellantism and the Jesuit confession), Giovanni Frusta writes:

> It would be contrary to truth to assert that the system of flagellation, in its generally encompassing significance, was an invention of Christianity. We find traces of it among numerous ancient peoples: among Hebrews, Persians, Indians, and especially Greeks and Romans. From the latter two, along with the Hebrews, it passed into the Christian realm. But it did not do so immediately, during the first few centuries, in its fanatically and perniciously excessive use as an ascetic or penitential means of healing.[1]

Here Frusta is referring not only to the judicial or educational use of flagellation, but also to the ritual uses that were supposedly practiced by Syrians, Greeks, and Romans (figure 7.1). Naturally, these remain interesting both to flagellants and to the historian of their deeds.

Ritual Flagellation
Along with numerous anecdotes of a folkloric, ethnographic, and pseudoethnographic character,[2] the most frequent references are to "the institution known as the Lupercalia." This festival took

Figure 7.1. Ritual flagellation in antiquity (Pompeii, Villa dei misteri, first century BCE).

place every year in Rome on the fifteenth of February and was portrayed by Frusta according to the description given in Bayle's article on the topic in the *Encylopédie*. The Lupercalia were centered in the grotto on the northwestern slope of the Palatine Hill, where Remus and Romulus were supposedly suckled by the she-wolf. This was also the holy site of Faunus, the god of shepherds and fertility, to whom goats were sacrificed at the time of the new year. From the skins of these animals, celebrants cut the so-called *februa*, or purification strips, which were used to strike women and girls by the Luperci, who marched through the streets in sheep's clothing (figure 7.2). All of this was part of a ritual of fertility and purification that was a thorn in the side of the early church, especially due to the use of lascivious songs and gestures. The *lupercus* is a male wolf who symbolizes fertility and lewdness, which are also symbolized by the blows that have been meaningful in other ritual contexts from antiquity until today. Similar fertility rites can still be observed in certain processions at Advent, May Day, and New Year's Day in the Alpine regions, processions in which "savage" figures playfully beat girls and young women with rods or leather straps.

The moment of renewal and purification that is central here is ritually expressed and performed by the movement of figures who primarily evoke a "savagery" outside the bounds of all civilization, a savagery that they represent with their blows as the origin of an immediate arousal. The fertility to which this ritual is devoted is withdrawn from civilized rationality and given over to an immediacy understood in vitalistic terms — an immediacy expressed in the moment of arousal and propagated through such arousal. Hence, what we encounter here is both the staging of the diabolical realm and the ritual nakedness belonging to the state of nature.[3] Among other things, it refers to a return to the spontaneity of arousal that characterizes both faun and satyr. In the ritual staging of this return, the fertility that lies beyond human power is conquered ever anew.

Figure 7.2. Lupercalia in ancient Rome (studio of Annibale Carracci, sixteenth century, Bologna, Palazzo Magnani).

Healing through Blows

Along with this ritual significance of flagellation as cited by modern flagellation literature (and to which we refer only in passing), there exists a medical-dietetic tradition. It is not just Sade and early modern pornography that point to the physically salubrious and healing effects of flagellation. Rather, the entirety of modern flagellant literature appeals to the medical tradition, as we have seen in assorted authors running the gamut from Boileau to Sade and Joyce. We should now examine some of the texts of this medical tradition.

Flagellum salutis (The healing whip) is the title of a treatise published in 1698 by Kristian Frantz Paullini, who was the town doctor of Eisenach from 1689 until his death. The complete title has a rather baroque form:

FLAGELLUM SALUTIS
Or:
A Curious Narrative
Of How with
Blows
All Manner of Serious, Chronic, and Nearly Incurable Diseases
Often
Can Be Quickly and Thoroughly Cured,
Discussed and Demonstrated
Throughout with All Manner of Agreeable and
Amusing Histories,
Remarks by the Author Himself, and Other Subtle and Remarkable
Things
By Kristian Frantz Paullini
Published by the House of Friedrich Knochen, Franckfurt am Main.
MDCXCVIII.

Following a typical humanistic literary trope, Paullini tells us that he wrote this treatise at the urging of his friends. For him, the most important thing is to gaze upon "each and every thing with amused consternation" and to call out "delightedly," "Lord, how can your works be so great?" He continues as follows: "Indeed, the works of the Lord are great. Whoever takes heed of them takes pleasure in them. Accordingly, I have recently demonstrated and praised the incomprehensible goodness and wisdom of my God by considering feces — despised by all the world, yet so wonderful and mysterious — according to David's example: 'I will praise you, o Lord, with all my heart; I will tell of all your wonders.'" Shortly before this time, Paullini had devoted a detailed work to the subject of feces, entitled *Heilsame Dreck-Apotheke, wie nemlich mit Koth und Urin fast alle . . . Kranckheiten . . . curirt worden* (Salutary pharmacy of filth, how namely almost all . . . diseases . . . can be cured with feces and urine). Along with feces, the whip and the rod also belong among those mysteries that God bestowed on his creation and that allow us to know him. The author continues:

> On this occasion, we wish to speak of a number of mysteries and of the healthy effect of blows on various diseases. Do not be taken aback if you owe all your health and welfare to blows. It is certainly terrifying when the evangelists say: then Pilate took Jesus and had him flogged. Yet if this had not happened, you could not now cry out to him and say: "Lord, Thou art my refuge, my portion in the land of the living!" [Psalms 142.3–5][4]

From all the forms of flagellation as reported in the various anecdotes, we can gather the wonderful and secret effects of God and the usefulness both of recollecting the tradition and of flagellation itself. This physicotheology of the whip goes hand in hand with the lust for the many varieties of the phenomenon and for the historical and anecdotal material that testifies to this variety. Without a doubt, the publication of *Flagellum salutis* was motivated not only by theology and medicine, but also by the publication of the somewhat older works of the doctors Johann Heinrich Meibom and Thomas Bartholin, which serve as a thematic basis for Paullini's writings (and which I will describe shortly). In all of these cases, the impulse for the works came from interested and business-savvy publishers: as might be imagined, the piquant aspects of the theme promised to have a favorable effect on sales of the book. From the outset, the book trade was always driven by fascination for the curious, the new, and especially the erotic.

Paullini explains the title of his work as follows:

> Attila was called *Flagellum Dei*: the scourge of God. All diseases are scourges of this kind. It is therefore miraculous that one whip should be able to heal another. That is why I call this little work *Flagellum salutis* — a healing whip. But if the name displeases you, then name it whatever you wish. It is enough if every now and then there should be EX DURIS GLORIA: so that from what is hard, you can also expect happiness and honor.[5]

Paullini earned his doctorate in Leiden in 1673 and in the same year received a call to the University of Pisa. He chose instead to settle down in Hamburg as a practicing physician. Beginning in 1675, he served as personal physician and historiographer to the bishop of Münster. From 1681 to 1688, he worked as a physician and chronicler in the service of Rudolf-August of Braunschweig-Wolfenbüttel. Paullini was a member of the most important learned societies of his day: the Pegnesian Order of the Flower, The Fruit-Bearing Society, and the German Academy of Scientists Leopoldina. He had earlier written a work that was concerned at least peripherally with the practice of whipping and its usefulness. *Zeit-kuertzende erbauliche Lust* (Edifying lust and pass-time) was the title of this book, which appeared in 1693. It cited a whole series of examples of flagellant healing and other practices related to the whip. This doctor of Eisenach also refers in this context to his sources, which include both Meibom and Bartholin. He makes plain his intention to take up the theme of flagellation in a work of its own: "While it has already been described elsewhere how forceful blows have suddenly and thoroughly cured certain vexing illnesses, I will show this in more complete detail and more orderly fashion in a peculiarly curious little treatise, with all manner of strange histories."[6]

Meibom's Treatise

Paullini quickly turned his intention into deed. From a medical standpoint, his *Flagellum salutis* entirely follows the prescriptions of Meibom and Bartholin, although Paullini considerably extends the case histories, and permits himself countless digressions. However, the theory of flagellation and the medical justification that this book offers of it is drawn from a text (or rather, a whole corpus of texts) whose history is rather complex, texts that fundamentally shaped all of European flagellation literature.

The rise of this corpus dates back to 1639 in a meeting between the two friends Johann Heinrich Meibom (born in Helmstedt in 1590, the town doctor and personal physician to the bishop in Lübeck) and Christian Cassius (court counselor to the bishop and duke) as they drank wine at the home of their colleague Martin Gerdesius. In the French translation of the text from the end of the eighteenth century, this far from spectacular event somehow becomes an *orgie bachique*, or bacchanal orgy.[7] During the discussion, Meibom mentions that in the history of medicine, there is a tradition (and with good reason) of using blows with whips and rods as a means of healing. The two others react with disbelief: "I no longer recall how we reached the point where I was praising physical blows as sometimes having salubrious effect, but do remember that they viewed my claim merely as nothing more than deliberate paradox." We may suppose that their curiosity was especially provoked when Meibom contended further that flagellation plays a role in erotic stimulation, a role that can be explained in physiological terms. The disbelief of his friends impels the doctor to write a treatise on the subject. This takes the form of a letter that discusses the matter thoroughly.

The title of this epistle to his friend Cassius runs as follows: DE FLAGELLORUM USU *in re veneria, et lumborum renumque officio,* EPISTOLA. *Ad* V. C. CHRISTIANUM CASSIUM, *Episcopi Lubecensis et Holsatiae Ducis Consilarium* (On the use of whips in matters of love, and on the function of the loins and kidneys. Letter to Christian Cassius, counsel to the bishop of Lübeck and Holstein). A few later sources that cite this text refer to Cassius (who had the letter printed in Leiden in 1639 and 1643, perhaps without the knowledge of the author) as the bishop of Lübeck, which lends an additionally piquant note to the matter. This publisher's trick was one element in the reception history of this text, which pushed it ever further into the realm of erotic literature, where it finally came to be seen as the testament of an orgy.

Not surprisingly, the treatise immediately awakened the interest of readers and publishers alike. Printings of the *Epistola* are attested for 1639, 1643, 1765, and 1770 in Leiden and other places. Moreover, there were also pirated editions from an early date, such as the one published in Paris in 1757. Daniel Paullus, a Copenhagen publisher who wished to reissue the treatise around 1660, made the request a few years later to the Copenhagen doctor, natural scientist, and polymath Thomas Bartholin that he should take charge of an expanded new edition. Bartholin referred him to the author's son.

Heinrich Meibom, Johann's son, was also a respected physician and professor in Helmstedt. He still possessed the manuscript of the booklet, which contained his father's marginal notes. Given his fear of censorship, Heinrich Meibom asked the older and better-known Bartholin to prepare the new edition himself and to incorporate his father's notes. As a result, in Copenhagen and Frankfurt in 1669–70, a remarkable work on flagellation appeared, to the great joy of readers and publishers alike:

THOMAE BARTHOLINI
JOAN. HENRICI MEIBOMI, Father
HENRICI MEIBOMI, Son
ON THE USE OF WHIPS

In Medical Practice and in Matters of Love.
With Short Treatises on the Function of the Kidneys by Joachimi
Olhasii and Olai Wormii Frankfurt, by the Publisher Daniellus
Paullus. MDCLXIX.

In the following centuries, this volume appeared in countless new editions and numerous more or less competent reworkings and

377

translations. It is made up of the following parts: a motto supplied by the publisher ("Delicias pariunt Veneri crudelia Flagra; / Dum nocet, illa iuvat, ecce nocet": "Cruel flagellation prepares the pleasures of Venus. / As long as it hurts, it helps. Then let there be pain!"); the response written by Bartholin to the younger Meibom, along with his supplemental remarks (DE FLAGRORUM USU MEDICO, AD Virum Clarissimum HENRICUM MEIBOMIUM EPISTOLA); the original treatise of the elder Meibom, with the marginal notes of the manuscript owned by his son (JOAN. HENR. MEIBOMI DE FLAGRORUM USU IN RE VENERIA ...); the letter of the younger Meibom to Thomas Bartholin (VIRO SUMMO THOMAE BARTHOLINO HENRICIUS MEIBOMIUS, S.D.); and finally, an appendix on the function of the kidneys (JOACHIMI OLHAFI et OLAI WORMII DISSERTATIUNCULAE DE USU RENUM. Ex Musaeo TH. BARTHOLINI), which by way of introduction, contains a few additional glosses on the theme of flagellation that were perhaps added by the publisher.[8]

In this book we have a genuine compendium that constitutes an example both of the humanistic culture of science and discussion and of an early modern publisher's marketing savvy. While Meibom's original text is still guided primarily by medical interests (albeit interest in a far-flung and obscure subject), Paullini's book is already oriented toward the curiosity and lust of his readers for piquant details. This can be seen from the publisher's motto, but especially from the history of the book's reception. Reprints were arranged in Frankfurt in 1669 and 1670. As early as 1718, the text was anonymously translated into English "by a physician" (his name, suppressed on the title page, was George Sewell) under the title, *A Treatise on the Use of Flogging in Venereal Affairs*, published in London along with a *Treatise of Hermaphrodites* by E. Curll. Reprinted anew in 1761 and 1798, the treatise was finally adopted as volume 4 of the *Library Illustrative of Social Progress* and under this rubric was made accessible to a public that was interested in enlightened erotic literature. Hence, Meibom's text, which initially seemed to have no such aim, finally entered a tradition in which matters of social reform were linked with an interest in sexual freedom and erotic permissiveness. At the same time, as becomes apparent in the history of its reception in France, it became interesting for the enthusiasts of erotically piquant literature and has remained of interest into the twentieth century.

In 1792, a year of revolution, the text was translated into French and published in Paris. The translator was Claude-François-Xavier Mercier de Compiègne, and the book appeared under the following title: *De l'utilité de la flagellation dans les plaisirs du marriage et dans le médecine, et dans les fonctions des lombes et reins: Ouvrage curieux, traduit du latin de Meibomius, orné de gravurses en taille-douce, et enrichi de notes historiques et critiques, auxquelles on a joint le texte latin. Paris, chez Jac. Girouard, 1792* (On the usefulness of flagellation in marital pleasure and in medicine, and in the functioning of the loins and kidneys: A curious work, translated from the Latin by Meibomius, decorated with intaglio engravings, augmented with historical and critical notes, accompanied by the Latin text. Paris, chez Jac. Girouard, 1792). A second edition appeared in 1795. A third edition, corrected and completed by Barthélémy Mercier, the abbé de Saint-Léger, was published in revolutionary year VIII (1800). The following phrase was now added to the title: *Nouvelle édition, revue, corrigée et augmentée du joli poème de l'Amour fouetté* (New edition, revised, corrected, and augmented by a lovely poem "Cupid whipped.") The erotic poem was written by the playwright and librettist Louis Fuzelier. As we learn from a nineteenth-century bibliophile's notice, the editions of 1795 and 1800 also contained

> a very beautiful, unsigned frontispiece. It depicts Cupid being flogged by the nymphs. Venus hovers in the clouds, sitting in her wagon, drawn as usual by two doves. She gives one of the nymphs a whip with leather straps. Cupid, whose quiver has fallen to the ground, lies like a small child over the knee of a nymph, his behind pointed in the air. She strikes him with the stem of a rose, while a third nymph ties together a bundle of rods.[9]

A further, identical French edition, prepared in 1801 in Besançon (the title page says "London") and promoted with extensive publicity, seems to have been confiscated by the police immediately following publication. Joseph-Marie Quérard reports in *La France littéraire* in 1843, referring to Meibom's book, that the printer advertised the publication with placards that were affixed even to the church doors. Such advertising is said to have provoked a scandal and finally even provoked the intervention of the police and the confiscation of the books. Here we see the end of the Age of Revolution, in which Meibom's texts first appeared under the auspices of libertinage and sexual liberation. Bibliophiles and collectors of the early nineteenth century emphasized how difficult it was to obtain a copy of the volume. Moreover, the volumes intended for sale were as a rule stripped of their piquant title illustration. In 1824, the author of the article in the *Biographie nouvelle des contemporains* on Claude Mercier (who died in 1800 at age thirty-seven) notes that the work was "now less rare, since a considerable number of copies, which had obviously been forgotten, were rediscovered in an attic." Mercier, who like many of his contemporaries was an author of countless assorted writings and compilations, earned his living during the Revolution as a bookseller. Along with patriotic and revolutionary works, he also composed an *Éloge du sein des femmes, ouvrage curieux* (Eulogy on the breasts of women, a curious work), an *Éloge du pet, dissertation historique, anatomique, philosophique sur son origine, son antiquité, ses virtus* (Eulogy on the fart, a historical, anatomical, and philosophical dissertation on its origin, its antiquity, and its virtues), and in 1780 a pornographic work with the title *La foutromanie, poèm lubrique en six chants* (Fuckmania, a lubricious poem in six cantos). The *Biographie nouvelle* justified his "horrifying productions" by saying that he "had to support a large family with the earnings of his literary activity."

Barthélémy Mercier (who was probably not related to Claude), to whom we owe the completed and reworked 1800 French edition of the text, lost the financial support of his monastery due to the stress of Revolution. Thereafter, he supported himself as librarian and bibliophile. Beginning in 1792, he was a member of the Commission des Monuments. According to the *Biographie nouvelle*, he acted in this capacity until his death in 1799, rendering especially outstanding service in saving collections of books from destruction.

The history of French printings of Meibom's work has additional stages in which we can trace its reception through both the libertine and Enlightenment contexts, which were often linked. A Brussels edition of 1879 also contains, along with other well-known texts, a treatise *De la bastonnade et de la flagellation pénale* (On bastonade and penal flagellation), by Joseph D. Lanjuniais, and a few poems on the theme of flagellation. The British Library possesses a copy of this edition containing hand-colored drawings.[10]

Beginning in 1788, this treatise often circulated with a further text under the title *Aphrodisiaque externe, ou Traité du fouet et des effets sur le physique de l'amour: Ouvrage médico-philosophique, suivi d'une dissertation sur tous les moyens d'exciter aux plaisirs de l'amour, par D***, mèdecin* (External aphrodisiac, or Treatise on whipping and its effects on the physique of love: A medico-philosophical work, followed by a dissertation on all the means capable of exciting the pleasures of love, by D***, physician). Written by François Amédée Doppet and published anonymously, this volume was newly provided around 1880 with the publication site "London" and appeared on the market along with the Mercier translation. Doppet was a Savoyard general born in 1753 in Chambéry. Along with writings on technical military matters, he published works on numerous topics: a defense of Rousseau's *Confessions* against its critics, a volume entitled *Mémoires politiques et militaires... contenant des notices intéressantes et impartiales sur la Révolution française* (Political and military memoirs... containing interesting and impartial observations on the French Revolution), works on magnetism, and a volume entitled *Médecin philosophe* (Philosophical doctor). His book on whipping was first published in Geneva in 1788 and for the final time in Moutiers in 1904.

Like Claude and Barthélémy Mercier, Doppet had a turbulent

life. After joining the cavalry at age sixteen, he left the service two years later to study medicine in Turin. As a doctor, he was especially involved in discussions of magnetism and the theories of Franz Anton Mesmer. In September 1791, he traveled to Paris, fascinated by the ideas of the Revolution, and became a Jacobin and a member of the National Guard. He founded the Allobrogen Legion, took part in the storming of the Tuileries, and finally in 1793 commanded the army that besieged and captured Lyon. Quite apart from Napoleon's contemptuous assessment, Doppet's military talents were obviously limited. Yet his humanitarian engagement seems to have been considerable and can be detected even in his treatise on flagellation. Stripped of his offices due to illness, incapacity, and the loss of protection, he spent his last years as a deputy and finally as a privateer in Savoy. Doppet's treatise is also included in the German translation of Meibom's corpus in J. Scheible's 1847 work *Schatzgräber in den literarischen und bildlichen Sonderbarkeit etc., hauptsächlich des deutschen Mittelalters* (The treasure hunter of literary and pictorial oddities etc., chiefly in the German Middle Ages). In this way, the German edition follows a reception of Meibom that is both erotically enriched and also (especially in Doppet) aimed at enlightenment and social reform and against corporal punishment.[11]

The Medical Significance of Flagellation
Johann Heinrich Meibom's little work, which followed such an astonishing path through the writings of various Enlightenment figures, flagellants, and critics of flagellation, arose from a half-scholarly and half-frivolous dialogue among friends in Lübeck in the early seventeenth century, as we have noted. This brief treatise answers the question that is posed in the form of a scholarly letter to a friend. By means of a series of examples, it argues that certain medical troubles and illnesses can be cured by means of blows. Hence, Meibom initially follows ancient authorities, which are cited extensively, supplemented with examples from folk medicine. According to the testimony of these authorities, blows with whips and rods are successfully employed when "the raving

man regains his reason" or when "erotic melancholy," the reaction to unrequited love, is cured. And whipping and beating are helpful in many other cases, as well:

> In chapter five of his book on "creeping illnesses," Coelius Aurelianus says that those afflicted by erotic melancholy must be whipped if no other means prove adequate and that this operation restored to many individuals their lost reason.
>
> In chapter four of his first book on "abstinence," al-Razi prescribes, on the authority of a famous Jewish doctor, that persons afflicted with love sickness should be bound, and if other means prove unfruitful, then they should be dealt with by means of hearty blows with fists and rods. This local remedy should be repeated numerous times in case it fails — for as the proverb says, one swallow doesn't make a summer.
>
> Anton Gaignier thinks as al-Razi does, and Valescus of Tarent says as follows: "If the patient is still young, then strike him on the buttocks with rods. If he still does not have an erection, throw him into a deep hole, limit him to bread and water, and give him very strict treatment."[12]

Reference is also made to Seneca, who believes that the four-day fever (quartan fever) can be driven away by flagellation. He also cites a series of additional sources that recommend flagellation either to gain weight or (as Campanella holds) to deal with constipation. Galen writes that slave traders use the whip when they want to "give their slaves a fresher appearance and stouter figure" or even that "wet nurses" beat "the behinds of the children ... before they return them to their mothers." In both cases, a healthy appearance and well-formed flesh are only feigned through flagellation. Meibom concludes: "It is certain that a swelling up of the flesh can be achieved in this way. Everyone knows the success of flagellation of the genitals with fresh nettles, since they lead the blood and the warmth of the body into that region." It is also prescribed to small children "to accelerate the course of the pox."

It is here that the Lübeck doctor first speaks of the sexually stimulating effect of blows. In the dialogue with Cassius, he openly declares, to the astonishment of his tablemates, that erection would be achieved according to the speed and quantity of blows. In order to demonstrate his theory, he appeals once more to ancient sources:

> Certain people are unable to perform sexual intercourse until they are goaded into it by blows with a rod. This strange ceremony kindles the flames of voluptuousness in them to such a degree that they foam at the mouth, and the member that bears witness to manhood rises to reach the sky as it oscillates according to the number of the blows that are applied. One easily takes this to be a scarcely credible joke. But my dear Cassius, I wish to employ all the means I can muster in order to convince you of the truth of these sentences. The testimony of credible authorities should be sufficient to prove to you that this is not a new method and that whimsy plays no role here at all. I will then proceed by way of reasons and examples that lead various doctors to recognize the importance of the matter. Therefore, I will not need to speak at length about the necessity of the use of nettles for the stimulation of sexual intercourse.
>
> Menghus Faventius (*Practica*, part two, cap. de passionibus membrum genitalium) assures us that nettles possess the wondrous property of causing the extension, swelling, and erection of the male member even in cases where its limp nature entails a hopeless case.
>
> Petron will instruct you, if you look into his works, that impotence is often healed through the use of nettles as lovers regain their spent procreative forces. On this topic he has Eucolpus speak as follows: "This part of my body, which used to be comparable to Achilles, later became as cold as snow and almost dead. It seems to have withdrawn into my innermost entrails and showed thousands of wrinkles. My rod looked like leather soaked in water, etc." Here I am merely transcribing the words of the author, who continues in the same style: "Enothea, priestess of Priapus, made it stiff as a horn through the use of watercress, which I applied as an ointment to the testicles. At the same time, she tickled me gently with a bundle of nettles beneath the navel and on the groin and hindquarters."

384

We will now hear Pico della Mirandola's comments on the matter. In chapter 27 of the third book of his work *Disputationes adversus astrologiam divinatricem* (Against the astrology), he relates the story of a friend:

"I know a man of very amorous temperament who nonetheless is unable to caress any woman without first being flogged. To no avail does his reason tell him that such a refined form of sensuality is actually a punitive action; indeed, he even complains to the whipper for not striking hard enough, as when fatigue or pity causes him to restrain himself. No sooner does the patient reach a peak of voluptuous sensation than he sees blood trickling from his wound as a result of the flagellation. Just a few days ago, he had the rod soaked in vinegar, which he intends to give to the woman who will service his lust. On his knees, he will ask her for the favor of striking him to the point that he bleeds. The more violently she gashes him, all the greater claim does she earn to his caresses. Only when he is completely exhausted by pleasure does he feel entirely in a voluptuous state. Whoever is not entirely morally corrupt must feel shame at such cold-blooded excess and loathe it."

Meibom draws additional proof from Campanella, Johannes Nerisan, and an astonishingly wide range of classical authorities. Meibom completes Pico's tale from additional sources and by referring to anecdotal reports of contemporary events:

Credible people . . . claim to have known a man who had lived just a few years earlier who combined a temperament so cold as to make him entirely incapable in the service of Venus with an imagination so lively as to torment him constantly with erotic images. Since he was naturally lacking in the warmth and physical force needed for the exertions of love, he had to awaken it violently with blows from a rod. It is hard to tell whether he gained greater enjoyment from such manipulations or from sexual intercourse itself. He even made pleas to those whom he used to choose as his tormenters. He would let the rods soak in vinegar for a day ahead of time. When he was not struck violently enough, he responded with scolding and with the most vehement complaints. As long as no blood had appeared, he claimed that the business was not yet at an end. He was perhaps the only man who felt pain and lust simultaneously, to the point that without pain, he was not able to obtain any voluptuous feelings. The flow of blood was the symptom of his highest enjoyment.

The famous doctor Otto Braunsfeld tells the following anecdote in his *Onomasticon medicinae*: "In Munich in my day there lived a man who was unable to perform his marital duties unless he was heartily whipped with rods." A parallel to this is formed by something that happened before my very eyes in Lübeck quite recently. A cheese and butter merchant of this city who had his stall on the Mühlenplatz was accused of numerous crimes, including adultery, and legal proceedings had been initiated against him. A prostitute with whom he had long had dealings stated before the court that the accused was entirely incapable of intercourse if he was not whipped beforehand with rods and that when he wished to achieve this purpose, she herself had to repeat the operation multiple times and double the dosage. The defendant initially denied this, but while being sharply questioned was caught in contradictions and in the end admitted everything. The truth of these facts was guaranteed by the judges themselves, Thomas Storning and Adrian Moller, both of them my friends and both still living.

Here, the French translator adds the following note: "Tamerlaine, the celebrated Asian conqueror, who called himself 'the son of God' and fathered 100 children and conquered 100 nations, also had himself whipped in order to increase voluptuous feeling." He also mentions Peregrinus, the Roman Cynic, who according to Lucan had himself whipped in public, and a further case related by Seneca and obviously overlooked by Meibom, who continues:

Since the truth of these stories is undisputed, let us merely strive to learn the reasons for such an apparently incredible practice. If one asks the astrologers, they will seek the cause in the influence of the stars, in a particular arrangement of the sky. Or they will give as the cause (as Pico della Mirandola describes) the planet Venus, which is dominant over human conception if its rays are directly in opposition with another star, and other miraculous explanations through which all guilt is ascribed to the baleful influence of a star.... Pico rightly discards this assertion and seeks another immediately acting cause. He ascribes the corrupted taste of his friend to years of indulging in it and continues his story as follows: "When I asked him the cause of such an unheard-of passion, he answered 'My upbringing is to blame. I spent the early years of my youth in an institution with other boys where flagellation was a favorite pastime and where whoever did this service for another received a great reward.'"

Caelius [Caelius Rhodiginus, *Lectionum antiquarum libri triginta*, book 2, chapter 15] shares Pico's view on the cause of this strange taste. "What is most disconcerting," Caelius adds, "is that this man does not hide the shamefulness of his inclination and actually passes strong judgment against it, yet the power of custom is so strong that his reason loses the struggle, and in the same moment as he condemns this shameful action, he already pursues it. But this custom had such deep roots because already during childhood he became acquainted with voluptuous sensations through using flagellation with his playmates. This is an apt example of what effect a good or faulty upbringing has on the whole of human life." ... "I must confess," I retorted, "that custom exercises such power that it is a kind of second nature. Aristotle already said as much...."

Galen shows in his treatise *On Custom* (chapters 2 and 3) with what strength and tyranny it dominates all our actions.... Perhaps in the matters described by Caelius and Pico, the duration over which the habit has endured has lent additional force to it? But the man in Munich found himself in a completely different situation than the butter merchant of Lübeck. Campanella raises the question "why was Pico's friend the only one among all his childhood companions who retained the memory of flagellation and the punitive custom into ripe old age? The consequences and vices of a custom are the same; it is the individual who once pursued them who must keep them alive."

Meibom finishes the thought as follows:

387

It is improbable that those aforementioned persons afflicted with this vice should already have prostituted themselves as children; for they could have formed only a weak idea of vices that they did not yet know. How enviable is the moral purity of Germany, which is not yet acquainted with the shameful refinements of astute voluptuousness. The scandalous palpitations of children of the same sex are unheard of here, and if ever one of them were found guilty, certainly punishment would overtake him. Quintilian, in his address for the soldier Marius, who had chosen a tribune as his Ganymede, had the following to say about our ancestors: "The Germans do not even know the name of this vice. It is found only among the Mediterraneans."

But in Meibom's view, the early homoerotic experience and conditioning through erotic stimulation in childhood from which Meibom excludes Germany on principle are just as incapable as astrology of explaining the desire and preference for the whip. Therefore, when seeking the relation between the whip and voluptuous arousal, we must look for another cause. Meibom begins his explanation with the observation that as a rule, "blows of the rod are applied to the buttocks," for "the genital areas are known to have uncommon excitability and cannot possibly endure blows of the rod for as long as needed for blood to flow. Consequently, only the hindquarters can serve as the suffering part on which the operation is performed." In lengthy terminological and physiological explanations on the anatomy of the spinal cord, musculature, kidneys, and blood vessels, he concludes that all of these parts should be considered as part of the "loins" and that their common function consists in the generation of semen:

> The loins include the greater part of the backside. This part of the body has five vertebrae, which are located under those of the breast, and beginning there they are delimited by the sacric bone. They are covered externally with muscles and a thick, fat skin and on the inside with muscles that form the protuberance known by the Greeks as *psoas* and the Latins as *pulpa* (which derives from *palpare*).

388

They hold the kidneys together to the left and to the right. In their full scope, they occupy the space of four vertebrae and are connected to the major veins and the arteries. The kidneys also receive the great veins known as the evacuating veins or the seminal vessels. One is located on each side.... The branchings of the veins and arteries extend over all of these organs. To the right ... the right seminal vein originates; the latter ... descends into the right testicle. On the left, the seminal veins come out of the base of the great artery and from the left evacuating vein.... The vessels that connect these organs are also built up out of infinitely many nerves originating in the spinal cord, by means of which the humors contained in the vertebrae seep out into the kidneys, penetrating not only their outer layer, but their entire substance. From the kidneys, the urine ducts move toward the bladder connected to it. During the act of procreation, all these parts participate in the same function. We refer to them with the general term "loins." ... Scholars have devoted fundamental investigations to the functions of each of these parts: namely, the bones, muscles, nerves, and veins. Cagnatus says ... that they all work together according to an immutable law of nature in order to produce the semen and to perfect the business of procreation.

The claim that procreation and the production of semen are a function of the kidneys and the "loins" is proven by the writings of medical scholars, the Bible, theological writers, and ancient sources. When referring to chastity, biblical authors speak therefore of "girding up one's loins." The list of authorities cited by Meibom includes Origen, Jerome, Tertullian, and the evangelists, as well as Martial and Catullus. All of them testify to the importance of the hips and the loins for procreation and erotic stimulation. Augustine, for instance, uses the expression "'kidneys' metaphorically for the joys of love." Therefore, one also speaks of the movement of the hips as a gesture that awakens desire. This connection is proven by the dictionaries and etymologies to which Meibom refers so as to emphasize the functional unity of the loins and the significance of the kidneys, which already "were

regarded by the ancients as the seat of procreative power." Everything that Meibom assembles is drawn from the tradition; in particular, he gets his medical knowledge from the writings of the
doctors Andreas Tiraquellus and Daniel Sennert. Yet he offers an
entirely novel theoretical account of "why blows of the rod that
are applied to the hindquarters or the loins perplex the spirit and
make us capable of the enjoyment of love."

Let us follow Meibom's remarks, which in the 1669 printing
also include a detailed discussion of all the opposed medical
opinions.

> Marsilius Cognatus and Montuus ascribe all procreative effects to the
> loins, for they are assembled from all the individual parts mentioned
> earlier: namely, from muscles, kidneys, arteries, vertebrae, nerves,
> etc. But for this reason the authorities ascribe the most importance
> to the seminal arteries that yield the fluid that gradually becomes
> white and thick, and is already or will soon become semen, and from
> here passes over into the testicles. While this fluid is abundantly
> present in the veins, and for this reason swells up and seeks to
> expand outward, it causes a pleasurable tingling, the veneral *pruritus*,
> or need to be emptied. This gives rise to the nightly flows of semen,
> especially among those who lie on their backs, which causes much
> heat to concentrate in the genitals.

This thesis finds additional confirmation from a series of medical
scholars, even though:

> every scholar seeks to explain the matter differently.... Montagnana
> says while interpreting a passage in Avicenna ... why this doctor
> traces impotence to a weakness of the kidneys, and after he explains
> that the semen reaches its highest perfection in relation to the
> degree of warmth of the testicles and the forces that spread through
> them, he adds that this material must necessarily be prepared in
> upper reaches of the body, in the area where digestion occurs
> (namely, in the gall bladder and kidneys). As a consequence, it
> depends on the constitution of the individual whether he is more or

less passionate.... Nemesius holds that the kidneys only empty a kind of salty moisture into the testicles, one whose sole function in these parts is *pruritus* and the heat of voluptuous fever. This is its only role in the act of procreation. "The kidneys," he says, "purify the blood, and in coitus are simply arousing, and are thus merely a secondary cause. The veins that course their way toward the testicles (*didimes*) pour into the kidneys a sharpness that urges one toward sexual intercourse, just as the sharp humors located between the skin and the flesh generally cause itching. While the outer part of this glans or acorn-shaped body is more tender and excitable than the skin in other parts of the body, this acid tickles the voluptuous organs far more strongly, and this biting sharpness produces lascivious thoughts, kindles the glow of love, and causes the ejaculation of the semen.

In closing, Meibom also records the view of his own teacher:

> Sennert ... assumes that the purpose of the kidneys is not limited merely to the arousal of the voluptuous tickling in the procreative regions. Rather, the kidneys also refine the moisture of the semen and expand into the other vessels. From this there follows, first, that the kidneys have a special kind of flesh belonging to them alone, but not very different from the substance of the heart and gall bladder.... Galen ascribes to this flesh ... the ability to process the blood, a purpose that it has in common with the *parenchyma* of all other vessels.... While of all the vessels the evacuation vein is the most important, and injects more blood into the kidneys than these need for their alimentation; also, the artery is too large to be able to filter the watery fluid (*serositas*) effectively. Thus, it is probable that nature, which does nothing without a purpose, gave these vessels such a large extension only so that they would contribute through a special function to her purposes. From this he concludes that the purpose of this operation can be none other than to lead the blood out of the artery into the kidneys. This blood then mixes its substance with the blood of the veins, and, altering its nature, forms the basis of the components of the semen and glides down into the testicles.

Especial support for Sennert's opinion arises from the circumstance that it has pleased nature, in the construction of the nerves and nearby vessels, to show a surprising manifoldness, from which it can arise that not all humans are equally receptive to voluptuousness, precisely because their complexion is different. Salomo Albert and Johannes Riolan...supply proofs of this. During the dissection of an executed criminal, they found three evacuation veins and on each side seminal arteries that proceed from the evacuation veins. Salomo Albert thus concluded that this wasteful abundance of vessels and of semen must necessarily have caused the insatiable lewdness in the man, which repeatedly returned even a few minutes before the execution, according to the unfortunate man's complaint. Riolan writes that this dissected man had been hanged due to trigamy, since his excess of force produced in him the need to marry three women at once.

Further case studies prove the constitutive relationship between the size of the kidneys and the inclination to voluptuousness that, by way of the function and dimensions of the kidneys, is also determined in a purely physiological way, that is to say, through the moderation or immoderation of the humors:

During the dissection of two people who had died from syphilis, Philipp Salmuth discovered that their kidneys were almost four times larger than average. Sennert thereupon directed a question to those who disagreed with his opinion: Then where do the volatile salts come from that affect the sense of smell when we approach all kinds of noncastrated animals? These salts are perspired out of all parts of the body, but they seem to have their origin in the kidneys. This is clearly the case among adults and does not appear in individuals of a tender age or who are not yet paired off [i.e., not yet sexually active]. Sennert makes appeal to Oribasius (*Collectorum medicinalium libri XVII*, book VI, chapter 39) to establish that an excess of seminal moisture held too long in the vessels is bad for the kidneys and that the consequences of this are the inclination toward a dissipated life, voluptuous dream imagery, and nocturnal pollutions. The doctors assert further that the constitution of the semen is dependent on that of the kidneys. Frequent erections also show that the kidneys suffer from too much heat, while by contrast, an excessively long abstention from sexual intercourse indicates a frosty temperature in the kidneys.

Aristotle, al-Razi, and Avicenna also give evidence in their writings for this discovery about the function of the kidneys. The inclination to voluptuous experience is strengthened when people lie on their backs, thereby heating their kidneys, as the passage cited above notes. Since it is humans alone who sleep on their backs, they are thus the only animals who are dominated by such boundless lewdness. Meibom continues:

> Sennert's view gains additional weight through the fact that Pliny (*Historia naturalis*, book XXXIV, chapter 18) recommends placing leaden plates on the loins and kidneys in cases where one wishes to moderate voluptuous stimulations. To this end, he cites the example of the orator Licinus Calvus, who successfully dealt in this way with the problem of an involuntary flow of semen. Galen reports (*De sanitate tuenda*, final chapters of books V and VI, and *Methodi medendi*, book XIV, chapter 7) that athletes would place leaden platters on the kidneys in order to suppress the flames of voluptuousness and to guard against nocturnal emissions. He knows of no better aid against priapism than to cover the loins with a bandage of rose oil thickened with cold water.

The cooling and calming of the kidneys always signifies a control of the balance of bodily fluids (the four humors), a reduction of the flow of semen and hence of desire, which is here understood completely as a mechanically, physiologically conditioned drive. By contrast, warming is always accompanied by an increase of desire and a correspondingly aroused imagination, as Meibom demonstrates with references to the observations of medical authorities.

Moreover (and this was also regarded as proof of the functional significance of the kidneys), kidney meat was regarded as an aphrodisiac:

393

The kidneys of certain animals, especially of the goat, are regarded as well equipped to strengthen one for doing the service of Venus. Aetius (already cited earlier) recommends to weak people who wish to have sexual intercourse that they consume skink flesh, as long as it is cut from the region of the kidneys. It causes erections. Is it perhaps due to a kind of analogy, based on the similar structure of these parts with the same organs in human beings, that one ascribes to the kidneys of this animal the power to perform sexual intercourse? One also prescribes to people who feel themselves incapable of procreation (among other remedies) strong friction, the laying of warm bandages on the kidneys and private parts, and diuretic substances such as *cantharides* [Spanish fly]. It is also recommended that one lie on one's back in order to maintain the loins in the requisite degree of warmth for awakening one's slumbering forces and leading the semen into the testicles. Al-Razi says (*Liber continens artem medicinae* 9, 5) that each time one rubs the kidneys with hot substances, the male member increases in thickness and hardness, from which erection must follow.

From this we can conclude that:

the kidneys are the most important organs of procreation in terms of both their constitution and the activity that nature has assigned to them. According to Cagnati, the veins and arteries convey the material and spirit of the semen into the kidneys; according to him, the *parenchyma* is the most distinguished portion of the kidneys, for it is here that the production of seminal moisture begins, here that it becomes fertile and finally receives in the seminal vessels the requisite degree of perfection. This is not only Sennert's opinion, but also ours. Hence, we do not need to reject the opinions of Nemesius, Isidor, Matthäus, Laurenberg, etc., if these assert that a salty liquid is mixed in with this fluid, that a sharply corrosive moisture filtering down from the kidneys reaches the testicles, and that its effects are the venereal *pruritus* and erection.

394

According to Meibom, the ancient sources and more recent medical theories were largely in agreement as to the function of the kidneys and loins in the production of seminal fluid. Philological acquaintance with the sources meshed neatly with more recent observations and case studies. On this basis, he believed, the effect of flagellation could ultimately receive an exact clarification. Meibom now turns to address the reader:

> I now hope to have proven to your satisfaction that flagellation on the back and on the loins contributes greatly to the revivification of an exhausted sex drive. It should therefore not disconcert us that people who have sunk lower than cattle in their dissipation seek in this painful operation of whipping a means against the exhaustion and weakness of the kidneys and against the loss of all their powers. This is to say nothing of those who, less out of sinful inclination than in order to make themselves capable of fulfilling marital duties, are forced to take refuge in unnatural means, since their cold temperament needs help to be aroused. Most likely, flagellation causes violent arousal in the slumbering members as well as voluptuous stimulations that are communicated to the semen. There is also the tingling sensation of the hurting limbs when the blood, having been thinned, now flows more abundantly, arouses the vital spirits, and spreads an uncommon warmth into the genitals. In this way, the exhausted lecher will venture to wring out of nature, so to speak, what nature wants to deny to the wastrel. And so he is in a position to satisfy his excessive desires by exceeding the boundaries prescribed to him by nature.

In a far more liberal spirit than the *Epistola* printed in 1643, the text closes with a concluding discourse to the author's friend. This involves an explicit medical recommendation of flagellation:

> Here, my dear Cassius, you have my judgment on this subject. But, you will object, this humiliating practice is pursued only by jaded lechers who roll about in the mud of sensuality. I ask, on the contrary: Why is flagellation as a nonpunitive action not worth considering, if

it serves frosty-tempered people as a means of procreation. Here, the method is not merely something to be excused, since it is actually quite necessary. Without the use of flagellation, the reproductive organ would render the marriage of such a man pointless and would condemn his tenderly beloved wife to eternal widowhood. Yet the use of this very means ensures the fulfillment of the wishes of both husband and wife alike, and allows the purpose of the marriage to be achieved. Precisely this sort of marital cripple is depicted in Virgil's *Georgics* (book 3), although he seems to be speaking of an old farm horse weakened by age. Delille's masterful translation of this passage is esteemed well beyond France, and for this reason it might also be welcome to German readers. Without hesitation, I include his lines here instead of Voss's [German] translation. They go like this . . .

> Quand des ans ou des maux il sentira le poids,
> Des travaux de l'amour dispense sa foiblesse;
> Venus ainsi que Mars demande la jeunesse.
> Pour son corps devoré d'un impuissant desir,
> L'hymen est un tourment et non pas un plaisir.
> Vieux athléte, son feu dés l'abord se consume:
> Tel le chaume s'eteint au moment qui s'allume.

[When the horse senses the weight of years and of afflictions, then he is freed from the obligation of the services of love. Venus and Mars belong to the young. But for those who are consumed by a powerless desire, the hymen is a torment, not a pleasure. The horse is like an aged athlete, whose fire is immediately consumed — like a passing fancy, extinguished in the very moment it is lit.]

Such a husband feels himself incapable of paying off even half the debts owed to his impetuous lady creditor. I know full well, dear Cassius, that you will never take refuge in such measures. I am even prepared to swear an oath on your behalf, under penalty of abstaining from the joys of love for fifty days, if I have perjured myself in any way. I have known both you and your doctor for a long time and in no way deceive myself in believing that you might not be furnished with the best possible capacities for the service of a husband.

The infallible rules of my art, as well as my exact knowledge of your physical constitution, make my judgment on the matter a kind of duty. Moreover, I also have a reliable guarantee for the truth of my assertion in a creature that already begins to stir in the belly of your tender spouse, for whose fortunate entrance into the sublunary world I appeal to Lucina's assistance. As for what concerns other people, who need a whole load of blows on their hindquarters as a means of healing, so do I forbid you to make unlimited use of this type of cure. It is not only those who frolic with the Muses who must abstain from feelings of jealousy, but also, and for even better reasons, the disciples of Aesculapius.

Scribonius Largus, in an epistle to C. Julius Callistus, writes: "Envy is a dreadful vice, one that degrades man. It is a vice that generally should be abhorred, especially by doctors, for if the love of man is foreign to their souls, the love that ought to be the basis of their profession, then they deserve to be entirely abandoned by gods and men."

Only out of love for you, dear friend, in order to satisfy your longing for knowledge, did I resolve to give my judgment on such a delicate theme. Whatever fate might befall this treatise among specialists, you yourself should draw the best possible use from it and further preserve your friendship for me, which does me honor. And be lenient with the innocent jokes that are sprinkled here and there [in this treatise], for they lead us nonetheless to serious reflections. And take care of your health, which I value as highly as my own.

From Case Histories to Lascivious Anecdotes

Heinrich Meibom, the son of Johann Heinrich Meibom, reconsidered the subject a generation later on the basis of different conditions and more advanced physiological knowledge. When asked, he admitted that he was not really interested in the theme of flagellation proper. In a letter to Thomas Bartholin, he notes that his father was still beholden to the medical views that prevailed prior to Harvey's discovery of the circulation of the blood in 1628. Moreover, he is unable to follow his father's opinion concerning the responsibility of the kidneys for the production of semen. He

397

rejects this supposition entirely, though in some respects he does adapt the older theory to the new situation. For the younger Meibom, as for the elder, the unity of the vessels, back, and loins remains unproblematic. His mechanical-physiological explanation of flagellation continues to refer to them as a functional unity. The circulation of the blood, now interpreted as driven by the heart, is thus regarded as being heated by the blows of the whip and therefore as flowing more abundantly; the kidneys are no longer regarded as the source of sperm, but as the origin of the blood and warmth, and hence also play a role in the possible heating of the body. According to the modern explanation, the reason that flagellation leads to erection is because the blood in the region of the kidneys, when heated by the blows, flows more intensively into the testicles and stimulates the production of semen.

Thomas Bartholin had already written elsewhere about such topics as unicorns, the wound in Christ's side, and the use of snow in medicine. But the text that he contributed to the Meibom edition of 1669 adds nothing new. His purpose seems to be to express agreement with both the elder and younger Meibom. At the same time, he does not want to give up the biblical understanding of the function of the kidneys, which Heinrich Meibom had altogether abandoned. Apart from this, Bartholin's letter is little more than a brief presentation of his scholarly knowledge of passages from classical literature that speak of flagellation.

Johann Heinrich Meibom, Pico della Mirandola, and Caelius Rhodiginus were not libertines or freethinkers — indeed, when writing about flagellation, they refer repeatedly to "scandalous inclinations" and "shameful drives."[13] The same holds for the younger Meibom and for Bartholin. Meibom calls pederasty and homosexuality "perverse acts of shame" that are fortunately unknown in Germany and are worthy of severe punishment. With respect to passionate erotic flagellants, he calls them the victims of "refined voluptuousness."[14] His son and Bartholin write in these tones, as well. For all of these figures, despite their occasional ambiguous irony, when they speak of flagellation, it is above all a matter of medical commentary and of the therapeutic use of flagellation. Meibom explicitly states that in the case of "sinful love," flagellation as a means of arousal is morally reprehensible. Yet he regards the prescription of flagellation (as he suggests in closing, as he did earlier to his friend Cassius) as entirely reasonable if an incapable husband wishes to perform his marital duties. A genuine and explicit defense of the specifically erotic use of flagellation such as we later encounter in pornographic authors who make frequent appeal to Meibom is found neither in the work of the Meiboms nor in that of Bartholin, although all three allow for it in connection with the due performance of intercourse in marriage.

At the same time, it should also be emphasized that these medical men did not regard flagellation as a "sexual practice" or as a specific perversion, but as a stimulus that keeps the state of the humors in balance or arouses them in cases where the temperament is too cool or nature has lost its force. What is "sinful" and "reprehensible" is not flagellation, but merely the misuse of it — flagellation as an aid and stimulus to the impermissible and immoderate performance of sexual acts outside the legitimate framework of marriage. Hence, a correct handling of the scourge in accordance with what is natural and permissible is certainly allowed in cases where the blows of the whip restore natural balance and the husband attains renewed vigor.[15]

As has rightly been remarked,[16] there is no talk of "sexuality" in this text, unlike in the later work of Karl August Fetzer, *Der Flagellantismus und die Jesuitenbeichte* (Flagellantism and the Jesuit confession). For Meibom, there is not a specific form of sexual perversion or specific form of sexuality that can be defined as lust for the whip, such as "sadism" or "masochism." (As we will see later, it was quite different for Richard von Krafft-Ebing and for the epistemology of sexual psychopathology.) Yet it must be stressed that Meibom does speak of perversion. He is quite traditional in this respect and excludes from normality those who act "contrary to nature": those who practice homosexual acts. He also speaks in quite traditional terms of voluptuousness, of the stimulation of fantasy, and of the transgression of boundaries that are set for humans by nature — that is to say, by physiology and the mechanics of the economy of the humors. Yet flagellation does not belong to such voluptuous transgression merely by arousing the humors, the imagination, and the genitals. Rather, it becomes transgressive only when it fails to serve a legitimate purpose. In this period, there was in fact no category of flagellation as a "sexual deviance," although modern readers might judge that Pico della Mirandola's discussion comes fairly close. Nor is there any particular group of individuals characterized specifically by their desire for flagellation. This did not happen until the nineteenth century. For Meibom, flagellation was still a practice with medical and therapeutic justification that under certain circumstances can be useful to anyone when the powers of procreation and lust are weakened.

Let us return once more to the corpus of texts with which we began. In his letter to the younger Meibom, Thomas Bartholin points especially to the healthful effect of blows on malingerers:

> Blows have a special power to heal feigned illnesses. Not seldom do we see people quickly convalesce through the use of this method — people who had behaved as if they were afflicted with the epilepsy. Such people, who are healed even before they become ill, make doctors take notice of the prophylactic value of blows of the whip and strikes of the rod, and as a consequence they can no longer impose upon their fellows with invented illnesses. I also knew lazy workers, always faking some illness out of a reluctance to work, who preferred to return to their duties after being subjected to the whip. From this we can also see its usefulness for dispelling mental illnesses. Thus, during Lent in Italy, one sees enthusiastic penitents who pay for their sins by whipping so hard as to tear whole pieces of flesh out of their backs — a method already utilized in the cult of Cybele, as we read in Claudian (*In eutropium* 1).

Yet behind this rather martial outlook, a certain ambiguity also becomes apparent. Bartholin emphasizes that "the praiseworthy Meibom the elder [has] shown in many examples...the usefulness ... of strokes with a rod ... in the play of lovers.... We will spare the reader an account of this, so as not to offend chaste ears." Yet this declaration is merely a deceptive mask, for in the pages that follow we encounter a series of examples that betray Bartholin's lust for piquant anecdotes (at the very least) and for the genuine content of his treatise — flagellation in erotic matters. He also emphasizes more strongly than Meibom the significance of flagellation in the physiology of women. As he states when introducing this theme:

> As a consequence, it is not yet necessary to recall that Venetian who always, like Cupid in Anacreon's poems when he was ready for the labors of love, made use of a cane as his indispensable weapon. We should not fail to recollect here that the fertility of women is greatly promoted by this method. The women of Rome knew this quite well, and therefore they banished blows of the whip from the Lupercalia, a practice ridiculed by Juvenal in his second satire. The ancient commentator noted: infertile women placed themselves before the atoning Luperci and had themselves flogged either by a whip or by strips of goatskin. The fact that they aimed at the palm seems to be derived less from superstition than from the experience that blood inflamed by blows on the hand flows more quickly toward the heart, and from here it flows through the arteries into the uterus, which having been warmed in this way becomes more capable of voluptuous passion, so that conception is made easier.

Following brief historical explanations on the Roman Lupercalia ritual, Bartholin gives a few additional ethnographic observations on "Persian" and "Russian" women in order to round out the picture before quickly ceasing his list of examples and expressing agreement with Meibom's theory. What he thereby carries out is an epistemological displacement, one in which the medical theme that still stands at the forefront in Meibom's text is entirely removed in favor of a collection of anecdotes that arouse and satisfy curiosity. Among other tales, Bartholin also tells us the "following little history" that Barclay used "as evidence for the truth of his report" that among Russian women "the tenderness of the husband is measured according to the number of blows he dishes out." Bartholin tells the story as follows:

> A German emigrated to Russia. His name, if you wish to know it, was Jordan. In the place where he settled, he got married. He did not fail to give proofs of his affection, yet he did not succeed in driving away the melancholy of his wife. When he asked her the cause of her gloom, she replied: you only feign to love me, yet I know full well that you do not respect me at all. These words were accompanied by a deep sigh. When the husband wished to know how he had made her ill, so that he might know his error and cast it aside, she answered: "Why have I had to go for a long time without the blows with which you expressed your love for me? For in our country this is how one knows that a wife is not a matter of indifference to her husband." Jordan was so astonished that he could not laugh. When he was finally able to speak again, he promised to consider her wishes at the next opportunity that presented itself. This happened soon enough. His wife had silly notions, which the husband sought to drive off with the aid of his cane. The whip had its effect, for thereafter the woman loved her husband once again with her previous tenderness. The same anecdote is also told by Peter Peträus of Erlsund in his Muscovite chronicle, excerpt 5, which also adds that the newlywed husband in Russia is less likely to neglect the acquisition of rods than of any other part of his essential household equipment. The rods are certainly not used for punishment, and consequently they serve no other purpose than the one already mentioned.

We also find the same tale in Montesquieu's *Lettres persanes* (Persian letters), and from this source they enter the general literature concerned with flagellation, such as Dr. Castor's 1899 work *Der Flagellantismus in der Gegenwart* (Flagellantism in the present day).

Bartholin concludes his discussion as follows:

I hold with Meibom the elder that flagellation of the loins heats the kidneys, with the result that the semen is aroused or its flow is increased.... Nothing is easier to understand than the fact that through the accelerated circulation of the blood, which is caused by the local warmth at the places that are beaten, the fires of passion are kindled. The extent to which the warmth of individual parts of the body contributes to this is proven by lying on one's back, which always leads to emissions during sleep, and only the heat in the loins can be the cause of this. If this region is rubbed vigorously, there arises an amorous tickling, which is something they do in Paris in excessive ways, often leading to a shorter life.

For Johann Heinrich Meibom, at least in the early version of his treatise, the theme of flagellation seems to have given cause to write a treatise on the kidneys and loins (to which the greater part of the text is devoted) and to tackle this subject matter in a thoroughly baroque and rhetorical manner in conversation with his friends by means of an anecdotal example. Yet the glosses and marginal notes added by the elder Meibom to the work, which were incorporated into the expanded edition, give the impression that the interest of Meibom himself in the erotic elements of the theme had increased since the first edition. This standpoint is then expressed even more clearly by Bartholin.

The fact that the erotic aspect became increasingly important in the reception of the Meibom-Bartholin compilation is established by the success of the work and the surprising history of how it was presented to readers. In the 1847 edition, the title of the book now read: *Die Nützlichkeit der Geißelhiebe in den Vergnügungen der Ehe, sowie in der ärztlichen Praxis, und die Verrichtungen der Lenden und Nieren.* (The usefulness of blows of the whip in the pleasures of marriage, as well as in medical practice, and the functions of the loins and kidneys).[17] The German text adopts from the French editor the remark that it seeks "to make up for the dry style of Meibomius by means of the excerpts from Brantôme and the extended notes added to the work," for "our motive" is "none other than to help friends of literature, and at a fair price, to become acquainted with a work that becomes increasingly rare." In addition (and here once more the German edition follows the late eighteenth-century French edition), the editor has "brought together [in the introduction] everything of importance for the history of flagellation by adding for the reader's sake a brief and fundamentally relevant excerpt from the work on this subject by the abbé Boileau."[18]

In this way, the various manners of thematizing flagellation converge in a literary form aiming at both conversation and arousal. Allusions to "marital pleasure" now stand at the forefront, as expressed in new forms of justification for the publication of the text. This now happens, perhaps not surprisingly, in a manner congruent with Jacques Boileau's critique of religious flagellation practices. Boileau's enterprise is the paradigm that the editor and new translator of Meibom also upholds in his note "To the reader!": "We ask that you take note of the preliminary remarks and the introduction to this writing, whose appearance, in the eyes of strict moralists, needs some justification. The reasons offered by Abbé Boileau in his own defense may also in the same way absolve the translator of Meibomius of all accusations."

The "notes" and "excerpts" from Pierre de Brantôme's *Vies des dames galantes* (The lives of gallant ladies) incorporated by the French translator and adopted by the German editor turn the text into a kind of frivolous game that was foreign to the original text. To give just one example of the increasing accumulation of suggestive and dubious anecdotes, as well as the great displacement in how the work was being received, the translator remarks as follows:

We cannot deny ourselves the pleasure of enriching the reflections of Meibom with an anecdote that not only belongs directly to our subject, but also gains interest through the great esteem in which the hero of the anecdote is held. He is no one less than a friend of Augustus Caesar — the governor of Egypt, that charming poet who moved in an environment shaped by Horace, Virgil, Tibullus, and Catullus, who like the latter two poets sang the joys of love and ultimately (as

404

Pliny reports) died a sweet death while falling asleep on the bosom of the one who gave his life its happiness. Mr. de Lignac reports to us that this darling of the Graces was able to obtain the intoxicating expressions of favor of one young girl only when she had received blows with the rod on the behind from her father. She suffered this discipline from her father as punishment for her dissipations, but it was this very procedure that caused her to be even more persistent in her vice and thus served the purposes of the voluptuous poet. This trait of hers brings a similar one to mind, of which I myself was the eyewitness. A student of rhetoric, my fellow pupil, was once threatened by the rector of the school with a rod. He knew how to escape this threat with an answer that was as cheeky as it was indecent: "If you hit me with the rod, you would do me a service that I do not dare describe. You know only too well that at my age we no longer fear it."[19]

Medical "Enlightenment"

These sorts of supplements to the text gradually led Meibom's treatise in the direction of erotic literature, as happened especially in France and England in the eighteenth and nineteenth centuries. In this way, Meibom's medical work entered a field of texts, of adaptations and compilations, that enriched their subject with gratuitous erotic details. On the one hand, this turned it into the central node of an endless accumulation of anecdotes; on the other hand, it became a foundational gesture of enlightenment, sexual liberation, and libertinage. At the center of this field of texts, we find along with Meibom's, J. Scheible's 1788 work *Schatzgräber in den literarischen und bildlichen Seltenheiten* (Treasure hunter of literary and pictorial oddities), as well as a German translation of General François Amédée Doppet's *Histoire du fouet* (History of whipping). The German title runs as follows: *Das Geißeln und seine Einwirkung auf den Geschlechstrieb, oder das äußerliche Aphrodisiacum, eine medizinisch-philosophische Abhandlung. Nebst einem Anhang: über die Mittel, welche den Zeugungstrieb aufregen. Von D****, praktizierender Artz* (Flagellation and its effect on the sex drive, or The external aphrodisiacum, a medical-philosophical treatise. Along with an appendix: On the means that excite the drive to procreate. By D****, practicing physician).

Doppet begins with Meibom's treatment of the theme, although he finds that his predecessor "has not treated his subject exhaustively . . . since he is satisfied with showing what influence flagellation has on the awakening of the sex drive."[20] By contrast, the former general, Doppet, addresses the following themes: in chapter one, "the effect of flagellation on the genitals"; in chapter two, he analyzes "how this effect occurs"; in the third chapter, he sketches "aberrations . . . brought about by misuse of this type of punishment"; in chapter four, he gives pedagogical advice. What is central for Doppet (along with his anticlerical polemic and the notion of liberal school reform) is "health," along with an ideal of natural life inspired by Jean-Jacques Rousseau. Doppet justifies his treatment of the subject by pointing to the practice of confession, in which obscene subjects are also raised with a view to the health of the soul. For him, by contrast, it is a matter of the health of the body. Hence, his analysis is aimed at "the innate passion of man," which seeks the pleasures of "voluptuousness." "Whoever once becomes acquainted with them will strive to taste them anew and will devote himself to the enjoyment of the moment without worrying about the desires of the next day." Herein lies the genuine danger, for "although sexual stimulation is recognized to be necessary, one should yield to this drive only moderately, since overstimulation weakens the body."[21] It is necessary to find measure and equilibrium for the temperament, to set limits to the power of love, and to respect its mechanical and physiological limitations. It is "because many do not recognize these limits that we see on a daily basis so many thirty-year-olds and forty-year-olds who look like old men." It is not the case that "with the disappearance of one's force, the desire is also gone," but rather "it is precisely the exhausted sensualist who becomes ever more insatiable in his longings. Impotence goads him ever more violently toward enjoyment, and his longings exhaust his nature with ever new requirements." The same vicious circle also applies to prostitution, which stimulates desire, and the art of proper attire

and seduction, which lets no one rest and arouses us all. In order
to continue participating in this world of arousal, one has "sought
to awaken the pleasures of love by tormenting the body."

Doppet also refers to the case of Pico's friend, to whom he
mistakenly ascribes an entire series of similar cases that were
handed down from antiquity and that therefore have nothing to
do with the modern decay of morals. "Voluptuous frictions, summoned forth by means of strokes with the rod and similar means,
were already known to the priestesses of Venus in Babylon, Tyre,
Athens, and Rome. They were simply perhaps a bit less elegant
than the methods employed by their contemporary colleagues in
London, Paris, Naples, and Venice."

Through the power of association, Doppet now shifts to a case
from the Paris of his own day and links the case histories found in
Pico and the medical treatises with the games of prostitutes:

> For a moment, let us imagine ourselves in one of those places where
> voluptuousness is offered for sale. It is here, more than anywhere
> else, that we find the opportunity to convince ourselves of how often
> people take refuge in flagellation if they are preparing themselves to
> give a good battle to the god of love. As soon as we enter that temple
> of Venus, we notice similar devices of the most various kinds. The
> priestess of voluptuousness shows us a bundle of rods held together
> by a very elegant bow. Thereupon she leads us to a flail, which at the
> end of every cord has a point of gold or silver, the grip or handle is
> made of rosewood, and the trimming of some highly precious mate-
> rial. If you ask her, like a simple man from the provinces, what these
> weapons are used for, she will answer you in a childlike manner:
> "They serve to prepare you for pleasure." Nor does a prostitute scorn
> the actual use of such devices. Indeed, she accommodates you with
> them from the start, for she does not despair of their effectiveness,
> even when a seventy-year-old man stands before her. I myself once
> witnessed a strange scene that provided proof that wisdom is no
> defense against love. To be specific, during my stay in Paris, I was
> summoned to one of the many brothels in the Rue Saint-Honoré in
> order to provide emergency medical assistance to a priestess of Venus

who had fallen ill during the practice of her profession. As I entered her chamber, I heard from the neighboring room the abusive words of a quarreling woman. The woman awaiting my assistance did not even give me time to ask about the source of the commotion: in a soft voice, she bade me be silent, lifted the curtain cautiously, and let me look through a small opening, which displayed a drama of the most ridiculous kind. This scene, which I later learned was played regularly twice per week, went as follows: the chief figure, a lovely brunette, displayed her naked neck, calves, and hindquarters. Around her there stood four old men wearing splendid wigs. Their garb, their bearing, and their facial expressions all compelled me to bite my lip in order to suppress laughter, which I held back only with difficulty. These gray sensualists were playing "little schoolmaster," just as boys sometimes do among themselves. Keeping the bundle of rods in her hand, the harlot let each of them in turn receive the lower discipline; the one who received the most blows also happened to be the weakest among them. These sick men kissed the behind of their mistress while she exerted herself in disciplining their unchaste skin, and the comedy reached its end only when the limpening of nature made a mockery of all further exertions. My patient found my astonishment quite amusing and proceeded to tell me numerous and even more comical anecdotes of a kind that unfold daily in her own peculiar nunnery better than elsewhere. Whereupon she remarked: "We have perhaps the most important office in Paris, for we enjoy the distinction of being permitted to use the rod on the most respected members of the clergy, the civil service, and the business world." Is there any need of further examples to show that strokes with a rod are often used as a means of stimulus to sexual intercourse? One need only ask prostitutes to become convinced of this sad truth.

Like Pico della Mirandola and the early modern medical tradition, Doppet rejects astrology as an explanation of the passion for flagellation. Yet he also joins Meibom in refusing to blame habits acquired in childhood: "The remote cause of these dissipations is occasionally the result of a vice-ridden upbringing, but here it is only a question of seeking the proximate cause, and this is possible only if we bring physiology and anatomy to bear on the question." What must be recognized above all else is that flagellation warms a part of the body and "leads the blood to that place in great quantity"; in this way it is able to "accumulate the heat of life in a specific part of the body" and hence "promote the erection of the member." In his theory, Doppet follows the Meibomian tradition, which (like Bartholin in a few brief remarks) now explicitly relates to women. Since the blows of the whip must fall on the buttocks in order to make one "capable of intercourse," it is the "warmth" produced in this way, "insofar as" it "grips the loins" through its effect on kidneys and vessels, that places both male and female genitals in a state of arousal. In this way, "blows with the whip on the backside [cause] the erection of the member" and "[enable] an exhausted sensualist once more . . . to do battle with the god of love." Such blows also heat the female genitals and awaken the lust of women.

More clearly than in Meibom's physiological explanation of flagellation, for Doppet (the apologist of Rousseau), an interest in nature and diet comes to the forefront. This interest is expressed most decisively in the anticlerical Enlightenment critique of the lifestyle of monks and nuns, a lifestyle said to contradict all nature and all reason. "Love is a need of all creatures," Doppet writes, and it would therefore be "in vain . . . to wish to smother this fire at the onset of sexual maturity." For this reason, "the monastic vow goes hand in hand with perjury . . . and whoever wishes to remain loyal to his duty will at the very least always feel unhappy." Doppet concludes that as a minimal measure, all objects must be removed from the monasteries that stimulate desire and thereby increase unhappiness. It seems paradoxical that flagellation is practiced in monasteries, since it "arouses every fiber in us" and along with the flow of humors arouses the imagination to the utmost. He asks as follows:

> Should one not carefully remove everything from the monastery that necessarily injures decency — or that, to employ the terms of the casuists, awakens the tickling of the flesh? The use (or rather misuse)

of the discipline should therefore be abolished, since the consequences always have a pernicious effect. The only good thing is that the ceremony of flagellation is conducted in the dark, for if one were to illuminate this pious gathering with a torch held in the hand, one would become convinced that penance always ends with self-abuse or with the involuntary flow of semen.

Thus, what a contradiction we find in the performance of these heroes of chastity! Every morning they guzzle two or three glasses of a drink prepared from plants that is supposed to cool off the blood, and in the evening they flagellate themselves with cords or small chains in order to recall the very heat that they had counteracted earlier in the day.

At the very least, one should not speak of flagellation and the discipline in the presence of the nuns, for the female sex is more easily excitable and even more subject to emissions.

It seems that the custom of flagellating oneself or others is found mainly among monks. If they were at least restricted to whipping themselves, that would be a lesser evil. But there are some among them who are shameless enough to prescribe flagellation to beautiful female penitents and who even perform the flagellation themselves after the penitents leave the confessional. How many countless confessors have seduced young girls in this way! How many sensualists have abused a dignified office in order to practice the greatest vices with impunity! Often enough, the courtrooms echo with the justified complaints of those unlucky ones who fell victim to their own credulity. We have seen more than once that the law has punished criminals of this kind.

Everyone knows the stories of various adventures of a few Franciscans who, as soon as they were alone with their penitents, commanded them to kneel down and lift up their skirts and struck their hindquarters, or whipped them violently in proportion to the sins they had committed, ending this discipline by laying the beautiful sinners on their stomachs "and pulling one end of the rope [i.e. the rope the Franciscans wear as belts] from behind through them, which makes the pious one swoon and supplies her with an image of the paradise of Mahomet.

410

It is a striking phenomenon that in all ages and among all peoples, unchastity and the lowest sort of moral corruption were connected with the holiest customs. In the temples, they committed the "Netturalia"; all the Roman matrons were thereby gathered in worship. Over the course of many years, the Emperor Nero, his priests, and his lovers took advantage of the credulity of some people while sharing in the dissipation of others. Since this festival was celebrated only at night, one did not have to blush, since the sighs that were heard were interpreted as outbursts of holy enthusiasm. The pilgrimage to Mecca, which for the Persians and Turks was the very epitome of all that is holy, contributed to worsening morality among most people. In Spain and Italy, I myself have seen religious enthusiasts following a consecrated banner, circulating through the streets, and flagellating themselves in memory of the Passion of Christ under the windows of their beloved....

Yet I would digress too much from my purpose if I gave more space to such discussions.... I only repeat here how necessary it is to abolish flagellation in the monasteries, since it merely encourages the sex drive that is meant to be suppressed. I would even forbid, under penalty of the strictest punishment, that monks be able to see each other unclothed, for a young celibate needs only a small amount of stimulation to become warm. A nun of eighteen years of age who comes in the evening to wash the fleas from her body seldom ends her quest without making a sacrifice to love [i.e., by means of her own hand]. Perhaps she does not wish to succumb to it, but even the least contact serves to make the boiling juices overflow.

Following a harsh attack on the monastic system, Doppet continues his genealogy of the originally monastic forms of stimulation and arousal:

Those who believe that they do a service to God when they flagellate their bodies must truly have a strange concept of the Creator!... A wise man of the world has rightly asserted that a savage man living in the woods by gazing at the sky and at nature reaches a worthier concept of divinity and is much closer to the true religion than is the Carthusian in his cell, who deals only with the figures of his over-heated imagination.... The author [Sébastien Mercier] of the book *L'an deux mille quatre cent quarante* [The year 2440] gives a lively depiction of the folly of those young people who enthusiastically lock themselves up in the walls of monasteries and of whom we believe that they find some sort of holy transformation of life there. May the words of this wise man serve to deter others who might likewise wish to hurl themselves into living crypts. As he wails: "What fearful illusion enchains in a dungeon countless beauties who, concealing from themselves and others the glow that is granted to their sex, must feel eternal confinement as something all the more oppressive. In order to imagine this sensation, one would have to occupy her place; anxious, trusting, misled by a proud enthusiasm, this girl would believe for a long time that religion and God alone could fill her soul. In the excess of her enthusiasm, she suddenly feels in her heart the stirrings of that invincible longing that she previously never knew. The unchaste fire blazes in her heart all the more strongly in her withdrawal from the world. She fights an unconscious battle, she blushes, and her longing only grows. She looks about and notices how she is closed off alone under lock and bolt, while her entire nature feels itself drawn toward a fantastical object that is stimulated all the more by her overheated fantasy. From this moment onward, all peace disappears for her. Nature has summoned her to the happiness of offspring, but an eternal bond condemns her to remain unhappy and childless. Now she discovers that the law deceives her, and that the yoke that takes away her human freedom cannot be a divine yoke, and that religion, which makes her so miserable, is highly opposed to nature and to reason. But of what use are all complaints? The silence of the night covers her tears and buries her sighs. The burning poison that flows in her arteries destroys her stimulations, corrupts her blood, and acceler-ates her death. She herself opens the coffin in which her troubles will eternally slumber — the sole consolation left to her."

Since the founders of the monastery system separated the two sexes from each other, they must not have been thinking of the abuses that were a necessary consequence of this rule. Since the aroused senses are difficult to silence, the victims of illusion sealed up in the monastery walls must ponder over means either to satisfy their desire for love or else to deceive it. Driven by a quite excusable and inherently guiltless instinct, these vigorous prisoners seek the desire that they renounced among others of the same sex. Self-abuse and imbecility were the result of this. The vice of which the Jesuits are often accused springs directly from the incarceration of blossoming youth. The nuns, as well, sought to attain the satisfactions of voluptuousness with one other in a manner contrary to nature.

But these vices are no longer limited to the monastic hiding places. From here, they entered the world at large and raged to such a degree that the laws had to defend against them, and even so they could not entirely be eliminated. Since then, a number of rich men have seduced their male servants, and more than one duchess has sighed for her chambermaid. Oh, you monsters! Do you expect to appear chaste in the eyes of your fellow men? Are you afraid of becoming a victim of the other sex? You are ashamed to display human weakness and would rather throw yourselves into the arms of crime, which arouses general indignation against you.

In the monastery, then, the excerpt just cited tells us, the rod and the whip must be abolished, since they appear as a genuine emblem and instrument of a reprehensible overheating of fantasy — one that even threatens to undermine the bourgeois world. By the same token, Doppet believes that the rod and whip should also be eliminated from childhood upbringing.

Instead of leading our little ones with good examples, we seek to lead them with abusive words, threats, and corporal discipline! And in what does the latter consist? In the rod. Mothers have recourse to it every time their children break a glass. Tutors make use of it to beat an enthusiasm for Latin into their pupils, a language that often brings the young to despair, but that, it seems, will soon be removed from the curriculum.

What is the consequence of frequent use of the rod? Boys are so accustomed to it that in their games they use the rod themselves as a toy, as indicated in the passages cited earlier from Pico della Mirandola and Coelius Rhodiginus.

Certainly there are other methods of punishment for dealing with idleness and the other vices of the young. For Jean-Jacques [Rousseau] has written six volumes on the upbringing of children without even once showing the use of the rod on his pupils. But although his work has been met with general applause, the upbringing of youth is in as bad a state as ever.

I will concede that there are times when corporal punishment for children is essential; but must one, for this reason, direct the blows precisely against the buttocks? Even in the first six years of life, we already know that the private parts should be covered. But years later, our own educator forces us to unbutton our pants, lift up our shirt, and show him all of our secret places! Does one perhaps wish in this way to belittle this part of the body even more by exposing it to the gaze and the touch of a teacher?

Let us at least restrict such discipline to cases where it is actually needed! But how often do other motives guide those teachers who live in celibacy! In my school years, I have noticed often enough that thin or skinny boys were only seldom brought to the bench.

The pleasure that some pedants receive from the sound produced by the blows of the rod betrays that this ceremony, repeated so often, is undertaken for reasons other than discipline. Cruel and immoral creatures! Who gave you the right to maim the youth and bring them into the service of your lusts? I repeat that such abuses, however longstanding they may be, deserve the attention of the government, and require reform....

The evil custom of directing blows against the buttocks just as often presents the opportunity to be performed with the bare hand. This teaches children to provide such a service to each other, as well. This touching of the private parts leads to an arousal of sensuality that becomes their culture and custom for ever afterward.

Boys who are brought up together, if this type of punishment is used on them, become bawdy talkers together. They touch one another and turn quickly into pederasts, such as one often encounters in the Jesuit monasteries. It is justly cause for wonder that the clergy voluntarily assumes the burden of instructing the youth, since among us it is traditional always to have recourse to the rod. One would think that the decency displayed by the priestly class would prevent them from even looking at a naked bottom, let alone touching it. But in the previous chapter I already had the chance to remark that abbots and monks are especially fond of giving blows with the rod. The cries and tears of an innocent person do not move them, for the voluptuous sight of a beautiful behind suppresses all nobler feelings in them. It has been remarked that it was always monks who inspected penitentiaries, and even monks who founded them. For these voluptuous punishers, it was always only a matter of being able to gape at and touch a good number of backsides. And in so doing, they knew how to behave in such a way that dimwitted fathers were good-natured enough to reward them for such services with a good pension.

I regard such considerations as sufficient grounds for leading the government to make it a duty for pedagogues to devise another method of punishing the youth. If this subject seems too unimportant for the government, then I at least await consideration of my wishes from the parents, hoping especially that they will strive to keep anything far from the sight of their children that might lead them to evil.

What Doppet criticizes in the use of beating as a disciplinary method is not merely its brutality and even heartlessness, but especially its secret and deliberately concealed moment of arousal. For this reason, he returns at the close of his text to the function of the whip as an aphrodisiac, a theme prominently announced in his title. Like Meibom and the tradition stemming from him, he does not justify whipping in all cases. Here, too, just as in questions of upbringing, it is a question of seeking alternatives and finding the "natural balance." Instructions to this end are given by Doppet in an appendix on means of stimulating the sex drive and an index of aphrodisiacs. The treatise closes with a list of aids that are able to "cool off an excessively temperament" and that therefore are beneficial to the health of the "celibate who wishes to avoid dealings with professional harlots," as well as to the wife for whom the "caresses" of her husband "become threatening." According to Doppet, the use of aphrodisiacs and tempering methods should aim at establishing a healthy equilibrium that both takes into consideration the nature and temperament of the individual and is also able to satisfy it. For Doppet, flagellation does not belong to these means, for those people are "unfortunate, who need such means of stimulation . . . since they can forcibly arouse lust only through violent pains."

What is responsible for this (and here Doppet departs from Meibom's physiological-mechanical justification of flagellation) is a "peculiar taste" such as one finds in "sensualists." As a rule, these are "only jaded sinners who had already spent their force in youth" and therefore "seek out such unnatural means of assistance." Doppet compares those who need the whip for stimulation to "men in whom the sex drive arises only when they see two energetic creatures performing a sexual act." Even the "use of such a resource," he concludes, "betrays an extraordinary bodily weariness." Therefore, "of all means of arousing the sex drive . . . the rod is the most reprehensible and at the same time the most shameful and is thus often used by female prostitutes." And he adds the following remark: "Prostitutes form, so to speak, the limit between celibacy and marriage; they are the sacrifices with which the state purchases the virtue of other women. They have the profession to compensate anyone who seeks sanctuary with them for the strictness of all-too-chaste women."

Hence, flagellation and prostitution belong to a borderland that in Doppet's view should be tolerated, since doing so guarantees the stability of common life and of "natural sexuality" within marriage. Even if the practice of flagellation is "reprehensible," it still has its place, which is "medically-philosophically" disclosed. The enlightened discourse pointing out that "voluptuousness that obtains the union of the two sexes . . . is the strongest that humans can feel," also emphasizes its democratic-egalitarian character: "The despised shepherd feels no less blessed in the lap of his

Colette than a sovereign in the arms of his mistress." In this respect, the aids and aphrodisiacs that Doppet offers (thereby fulfilling his "professional medical duty") are meant to give adequate expression to a fundamental aspect of human nature. Criticizing the "strict silence" of his professional colleagues, he states openly here that "the act of procreation is no less a command of nature than are the needs of eating, drinking, urination, and excretion." Therefore, the doctor must provide a remedy in cases when the required forces of nature are not present or no longer present. This is done by Doppet's treatise, which at the same time denounces the reprehensible status of flagellation as practiced by clerics, monks, nuns, and bad parents and educators. What is common to all such figures is that all fail to respect the balance set by nature and arouse the imagination to a perverted degree. In this framework, flagellation arises as the answer to a life devoted all too intensely to voluptuousness and to the accompanying "exhaustion" and "emaciation" that require ever stronger stimuli and thereby threaten to become lost in a world of pure arousal. Since flagellation always remains bound up with this context, Doppet's progressive Enlightenment perspective causes him to turn against the medical prescription of blows:

> Indisputably, flagellations in specific cases are of decisive importance, but other methods of no mean effect have been preferred. Such methods have included embrocations and fomentations, cupping glasses, mustard bandages, mugwort, and *vesicatoria*. Flagellation was once widely used, and from this derives the custom of having fools be whipped. For since madness is explained as the consequence of too great a rush of blood into the brain, so it is regarded as the most appropriate means of healing it, if by means of blows the humors are again conveyed back to the lower portions of the body. For this reason, fools receive daily blows of the whip and no other nourishment except bread and water. This barbaric treatment was the consequence of an incorrect theory. Perhaps prisoners were whipped in certain correctional institutions for the same reason (I do not know if this custom has since been abolished by the

Lazarites), for it was believed that the reason of fools was not in the best condition, and one wished in this abusive way to bring about their cure.

Paullini's Collection of Curiosities
Let us return in closing to Kristian Paullini and to his way of playing with the ambiguity of flagellation, which Doppet and all of post-Enlightenment psychopathology rejected in favor of "natural" behavior. Paullini refers in his late seventeenth-century work to Meibom's "charming and curious little book,"[22] from which he had already drawn the tale of the cheese merchant of Lübeck for use in his own work, *Zeit-kuertzende Erbauliche Lust* (Edifying lust and pass-time).[23] Paullini's *Flagellum salutis* is a treatise of popular medicine that transmits a rich fund of anecdotes drawn from the entire literary and medical traditions, including the popular medical traditions. He especially likes to refer to *De medica historia mirabilis* by Marcellus Donatus and to the aforementioned volume of Meibom and Bartholin. Paullini is a compiler who shows off his scholarship, who permits himself every possible digression, and who in his language never shies away from the most extreme ribaldry. Enlightenment and sexual liberation in the name of an absolute "naturalness," as encountered one hundred years later in Doppet, is obviously not yet his topic. Rather, as he emphasizes, his topic is the praise of God, whose greatness can be discerned even in the most curious aspects of the earthly realm.

When it comes to actual theory, Paullini is dependent on his sources. For instance, his history of cures for quartan fever by blows, which Meibom already cited from ancient sources, comes from the commentary on Seneca by Justus Lipsius ("the black, sluggish moistures...are heated by whipping, made thinner and more fluid, and by the violent motion finally forced out through the expanded sweat pores"). Otherwise, Paullini follows Meibom, adopting the son's more modern position on the theme of stimulation via flagellation. He discusses the various opposing positions. Only seldom does he voice criticism or skepticism when retelling individual cases. What he loves best are not so much theoretical positions as stories and examples, including recapitulations of earlier attempts at explanation. Often he leaves it to the reader "to judge for himself." With respect to most of the cases described here, historians of medicine speak of a collection of accidental cures. Quite often, Paullini remarks ironically of individual therapeutic recommendations that "he who wishes may try it." When it comes to matters of love, we also sense the irony in Paullini's somewhat conventional remark about depression resulting from unrequited love: "If one becomes melancholic or even crazy-headed out of love and is unable to obtain other means for dealing with it, it is best to reach for the rod, and in this way many have learned their lesson well."

Behind the medical interests, what we encounter in Paullini's text is a comprehensive collection of all possible flagellation stories. They are introduced with a chapter on the voluntary flagellation of Christian monks and nuns in which Paullini speaks of "the noble Spaniard Ignatius of Loyola," as well as of "the spinster Teresa," the "Syrian flagellants," and the medieval flagellant processions. From this, the good doctor of Eisenach concludes that "whoever wants to join the list of the righteous children of God" must "suffer greatly." In his view, the Bible justifies use of the rod in raising children, which does not mean that "headless, brainless, conscienceless pedants, who have barely even examined the *Donat* properly" — the *Donat* is a manual of grammar, signifying that the teachers are barely educated themselves — "are permitted to beat everything into tender heads, only to leer at the pupils' backsides."

The most general justification of whipping rests essentially on the point that we are all fools and need discipline by God, and we need the rod from childhood onward in order to remain in control of our reason. This reasoning proceeds through a comprehensive form of casuistry. The first chapter of the book concerns "blows," the second deals with "melancholy," the third with "mania, or raving madness," the fourth with "paralysis," the fifth with "epilepsy," the sixth with "stupidity," the seventh with "hardness of hearing," the eighth with "toothache," the ninth with "dislocation of the jaw," and the tenth with "muteness." In this way, he is dealing primarily with diseases of the head that can be cured with blows. The section that follows is concerned with "diseases of the middle part of the body," the fourth section with those of the "lower body," the fifth with "the use of blows for all manner of fevers." Under these rubrics, all possible cases have been collected in which a punch, a blow, a stroke with a switch, or a smack from a scourge (whatever it may be) has led to the more or less spontaneous healing of a specific affliction. Hiccups and "stitches" in the side are discussed in immediate proximity to the theme of the "all-too-strong ticklings of Venus." Like other authors, Paullini remarks in a self-evident spirit of Pico's friend "that he was an insatiable chap, but so sluggish and incapable when it came to the Cyprian arts that he was incapable of the least bit of it before crudely lubricating himself." He also refers once more to Caelius Rhodiginus and Andreas Tiraquellus, to the man from Munich, to Braunsfeld, to the Venetian, to Bartholin, and to the Lübeck cheese merchant described by Meibom. He tops it all off with a story in the same vein about "a considerable man" from "the United Netherlands" and the report of a "credible friend," the "town doctor of a distinguished free city." This man

reported to me on July 14 of the preceding year that a slovenly old bitch had told her friend a short time earlier in the hospital that a certain man had summoned her (along with another woman of the same type) to the woods. After she arrived there, the chap had cut rods for them, and showed his bare backside, and asked them to strike it heartily — which they did. It is easy to conclude what he began to do with them next.

Unlike those of his forerunners who tell the tale, Paullini now adds as follows:

But it is not only men who are heated and encouraged to lewdness by blows, but also women, so that they might conceive more quickly and more often. This is why Roman women allowed themselves to be whipped and flogged by the Luperci. For as Juvenal sings,

Steriles moriunter, etillis
Turgida non prodest condita pyxido Lyde:
Nec prodest agili palmas praebere Luperco.

[They die infertile; for them, the curative methods of Lydia are of no use, nor does it help if they expose their palms to the blows of the nimble Lupercus.]

But why does he speak only of the palms, the flat part of the hand? The blood in the hand, heated by blows, courses through its circulation into the heart, and from there by way of the arteries to the mother [i.e., the uterus], which thereby becomes heated and leads to lewd behavior and thereby also enables the woman to conceive. As for the rod that is used in the Lupercalia, we hear from Festus Pompeius that the Romans gave it the name crepos from crepitum pellicularum [the bursting of the skins]. For when they struck one, it would burst. The widespread custom at this ugly festival was that they would root about naked, and if they encountered a female, they would strike her with hides, that is to say, with rods covered with dog skin or goatskin in such a way that they emitted a tone or a sound and burst and increased the sensation of pain. Plutarch calls this sort of fighting a purgation or purification.

Along with the Roman Lupercalia, Paullini is interested in the fact that "a few nations, especially the Persians and Russians, above all the women, regard blows as an especial sign of love and favor." He refers to the aforementioned anecdote of the German emigrant Jordan, who supposedly mistreated his Russian wife by not beating her, as well as to the corresponding dispute among contemporary travelers in Russia as to whether the anecdote was true. Afterward, he returns to the discussion of Pico's friend and to the question of what "the reason might be that sexual intercourse is stimulated by blows." The explanation that he gives follows Meibom entirely. Paullini discusses the functional unity of the loins and kidneys with respect to the act of procreation, which also emerges from Holy Scripture and was already known to "wise antiquity." He cites extensively from the sources and uses

421

the familiar arguments to explain that the heating of the loins and kidneys, such as when "one lies on his back" it will lead to his "having sexual dreams, and he will be stimulated to the emission of semen while sleeping and dreaming." Thus it happened with Pico's friend that "with blows and with the violent movements they occasioned, the loins" were heated. "The kidneys also boiled up, so that blood and spirits flowed more amply into them, the semen was inflamed, the appetite increased, and the will became more powerful."

Paullini, who in his analysis of the Lupercalia beatings also appeals to the circulation of the blood as an explanatory paradigm, is thoroughly familiar with the modern critique of Sennert's and Meibom's presentation of the function of the kidneys. He stresses as follows:

> It is obviously not the case that anything moves from the kidneys downward into the testicles. Nevertheless, we can be sure that the heat of the loins plays an important role in the play of Venus, and this is the reason why physicians apply warm or cold compresses in the region of the loins — that is, to arouse or to tranquilize the desires. In the region of the loins and kidneys we find major blood vessels. If these are heated, the blood starts to overflow, and it must flow into the spermatic arteries with all its power and heat, and so the spermatic matter, which is easily moved to begin with, becomes aroused.... Thus, the heat of the kidneys, the blood of the testicles, and the genital area are heated, as well. This is the reason why those who have heated kidneys tend to be more lecherous than others. And this is the reason, as well, why the blood of those who receive beatings in the area of the loins becomes heated and causes the blood in the seminal arteries (in the testicles and the genital area) to boil and overheat, especially when the beating goes hand in hand with dirty fantasies. *Flagellum* comes from *flagro*, that is to say from *flagrare*, because the body starts to burn and overheat when it is whipped. This is also confirmed by the *Questions* that are said to be written by Aristotle. One of these questions addresses the issue of why those who engage in horseback riding experience more intense desires of

422

love. The answer is clear: it comes from the heat and the movement. Here again, the movement heats up the blood in the loins and then the blood in the seminal arteries.[24]

Without a doubt, Paullini's greatest interest in his collection of the effects of flagellation lies in those things treated under the rubrics of "the ticklings of Venus" and "sexual intercourse." The following section, with which the book concludes, discusses how to cure fever in three chapters. Strangely enough, it is barely longer than another single chapter that covers "lethargic sexual intercourse." In this connection, it is noteworthy that Paullini (like Doppet later) also emphasizes the effect of flagellation on women and explains it through his presentation of the Lupercalia. In this way, he extends and modernizes Meibom's model in a very specific way, since following the younger Meibom, he underscores the importance of the circulation of the blood. It thus becomes clear how centrally and almost exclusively flagellation is bound up with the stimulation of sexual desire. It is such desire, even if all other possible purposes and therapeutic possibilities are mentioned, that is ultimately the secret meaning of flagellation. However, Paullini (unlike Doppet) by no means links flagellation with the category of the "unnatural." The stimulation of flagellation consists instead in the fact that it is part of the variety of the world in all its richness. And this variety speaks the praises of God, even in cases where it is a matter of erotic arousal.

CHAPTER EIGHT

Pico's Friend; or, The Basis
of Flagellomania

The most frequently cited anecdote in flagellation scholarship comes from a work on astrology by the Renaissance author Giovanni Pico della Mirandola. This little tale is beloved by both doctors and natural scientists, since it explicitly poses the question of why humans enjoy being whipped. In this 1492 polemic against astrology, Pico reports the case of an acquaintance who was unable to perform coitus without being whipped beforehand. The story is already known to us in the versions related by Meibom and Bartholin. When Pico asked his acquaintance about the origin of this peculiar connection of desire and pain, the answer was that he and his friends had mutually whipped and aroused one another in youth.

By telling this story, Pico does not mean to raise a question of sexual pathology. Rather, he wishes to demonstrate that the cause of his friend's behavior did not lie in the position of the stars. He wants to establish for posterity not so much the effects of flagellation as an aphrodisiac, but the power of custom or habit in our behavior — especially in the case of custom that reaches back to childhood. In this way, a model is established that explains the origins of desire for the whip, at least in certain cases. All of the texts concerned with flagellation discuss this case and Pico's account of it: Caelius Rhodinigus in 1542 (in his *Lectionum antiquarium libri triginta*, book 11, chapter 15), Andreas Tiraquellus in

1561 (in *De legibus connubialibus*, 15, n.5), and Marcellus Donatus in 1588 (in *De medica historia mirabili*; book 4, chapter 18). Tiraquellus adds a further anecdote taken from Otto Braunsfeld's 1534 work *Onomasticon medicale* found under the heading "Coitus," which thereby entered the stock material of flagellation literature. As seen in the preceding chapter, this anecdote also returns in Meibom and later authors, on up to the nineteenth-century studies of sexual psychology and psychopathology.

However, the texts just cited do not just transmit anecdotes from Pico and Braunsfeld. They also dispute Pico's basic thesis: that the passion of his friend sprang from the habits of his youth and that hence they should not be viewed astrologically or in a mechanical-physiological sense, but in the terms of developmental psychology as a customary behavioral pattern. In 1635, Tommaso Campanella is said to have raised the critical question of why other youths who played this game in childhood did not become flagellomaniacs. This objection (cited by Meibom) weakened Pico's explanation only in part, at least according to most observers. For Meibom and the tradition he initiated, this mania was primarily a result of mechanical-physiological stimulation. The attempt was made (as seen in the passages from Doppet cited earlier) to supplement the mechanical viewpoint with the psychological explanation provided by Pico's thesis on the formation of a habitus. Over time, it became the established opinion among doctors that childhood, long-standing habits, the temperament of the individual, and ultimately the play of fantasy form the remote causes motivating the desire for blows from the whip, which are then immediately able to stimulate the libido and bring about an erection. Even Richard von Krafft-Ebing, in his *Psychopathia sexualis*, retells Pico's narrative in identical fashion (in the version found in Paullini's *Flagellum saluti*), but from the new, modern standpoint of sexual pathology.[1]

From Astrology to Psychopathology

More famous than Pico's anecdote is a second reminiscence that is retold every bit as frequently and refers to a passage from

Rousseau's *Confessions*. This anecdote immediately entered the communal stockpile of flagellant stories. Karl August Fetzer reports it as follows: "While Voltaire adopted an attitude of amusement and ridicule whenever he spoke of flagellation, there was the contrasting case of Rousseau, who with the dangerous insight of one who knows the history of the soul and the development of the sexes, provides us with a more than racy tableau of the great danger of this dubious means of correction."[2]

Krafft-Ebing, who discusses flagellation in 1886 in his *Psychopathia sexualis*, turns Rousseau's narrative into an exemplary case history, one that completes the work of his oft-cited authority Meibom. Moreover, Krafft-Ebing also refers in later editions to Doppet and Boileau, as well as to W. M. Cooper's *Der Flagellantismus und die Flagellanten*. Thus, his "psychopathological study" moves in the atmosphere of a predominantly anecdotal tradition that relies to a large extent on literary examples. For him, too, it is a question of explaining how "sexual libido may ... be induced by stimulation of the gluteal region (castigation, whipping)." This is confirmed by case studies drawn from the literature and from Paullini's *Flagellum salutis*. Once more we encounter Pico's friend, Otto Braunsfeld, and Meibom's Lübeck cheese merchant, all of whom had to be whipped before they were capable of sexual penetration. We also find the famous passage from Rousseau's *Confessions* where he reports on the sensual experiences he enjoyed through the blows of a governess, Mademoiselle Lambercier. Krafft-Ebing's account of the scene runs as follows:

> Rousseau ... tells in his *Confessions* (part 1, book 1) how Miss Lambercier, aged thirty, greatly impressed him when he was eight years old and lived with her brother as his pupil. Her solicitude when he could not immediately answer a question and her threats to punish him if he did not learn well made the deepest impression on him. When one day he received blows at her hands, along with the feeling of pain and shame, he also experienced a sensuous pleasure that incited a great desire to be whipped by her again. It was only for fear of disturbing the lady that Rousseau failed to find other

opportunities to experience this lustful, sensual feeling. One day, however, he unintentionally gave cause for a whipping at Miss Lambercier's hands. This was the last time; for Miss Lambercier must have noticed something of the peculiar effect of the punishment, and she did not allow the eight-year-old boy to sleep in her room anymore. From this time, Rousseau felt a desire to have himself punished by ladies who pleased him, à la Lambercier, but he asserts that until he became a youth, he knew nothing of the relation of the sexes to each other. As is known, Rousseau was first introduced to the real mysteries of love in his thirteenth [actually thirtieth] year and lost his innocence with Madame de Warrens. Till then, he had only feelings and impulses attracting him to women in the nature of passive flagellation and other masochistic ideas. Rousseau describes extensively how he suffered, with his great sexual desires, by reason of his peculiar sensuousness, which had undoubtedly been awakened by his whippings, for he reveled in desire and could not disclose his longings. It would be erroneous, however, to suppose that Rousseau was concerned merely with flagellation. Flagellation only awakened ideas of a masochistic nature. At least in these ideas lies the psychological nucleus of his interesting study of self. The essential element with Rousseau was the feeling of subjection to the woman. This is clearly shown by the *Confessions*, in which he expressly emphasizes that "To be at the knee of an imperious mistress, to obey her orders, to have to ask her pardon, this for me was a very tender pleasure."

This passage proves that the consciousness of subjection to and humiliation by the woman was the most important element. To be sure, Rousseau was himself in error in supposing that this impulse to be humiliated by a woman had arisen by association of ideas from the idea of flagellation: "Never daring to declare my tastes, I amused myself at least by relationships which reminded me thereof."[3]

What Rousseau calls "goût," which he portrays entirely as a peculiarity and as a specific constellation of desire, by no means takes only the form of a "perversion" in Krafft-Ebing's presentation. Rather, it becomes a characteristic of a psychical configuration of which the exemplary form is later provided by Leopold von

Sacher-Masoch and his relation to the "cruel woman" (see figures 8.1–8.3). This principally literary image is now mediated through the "self-observation" of Rousseau and becomes the blueprint for his interpretation of flagellation scenes. The woman with the whip, "Venus in furs," who is not only the protagonist of Sacher-Masoch's novels and a fashionable figure of contemporary culture, but was also actualized in Sacher-Masoch's wife "Wanda,"[4] thus becomes the symptom of a "sexual deviation" called "masochism." Through the lens of this concept, Rousseau's voluptuous scene turns into a document of "deviance." At the same time, it also becomes the key to the explanation that can be applied to Pico's friend and the entire tradition of flagellation. In this way, by means of an objective psychological understanding of the "libido sexualis," the aphrodisiac moment of flagellation (which Meibom and the early modern tradition of the medicinal theory of the humors regarded as fundamental) recedes into the background. What emerges in its place is a paradigm that isolates and views as a pathology the fantasies of the "masochist."

Flagellation and arousal here are no longer connected with physiology; rather, they break with physiology and form an authority of their own. Passive, voluntary flagellation comes to be seen "as an expression of the desired situation of subjection to the woman," and this aspect is now more significant than triggering "erection reflexively by irritation of the nerves of the buttocks" through flagellation. Krafft-Ebing completely distinguishes "those dissipated individuals who are not psychically perverse, but physically weakened" who have recourse to flagellation as a form of aphrodisiac from those perverse individuals for whom "the principal thing is subjection to the woman" and for whom "the punishment is only the expression of this relation."

The particular interpretation of the case histories that Krafft-Ebing uses to prove this distinction is especially clear in the example of the "perversions of the Vita Sexualis," which he views as an unfettering of fantasies and strong affects. Above all else, perversion means boundless arousal. Hence, the modern feeling of shame experienced by many of the subjects in Krafft-Ebing's case

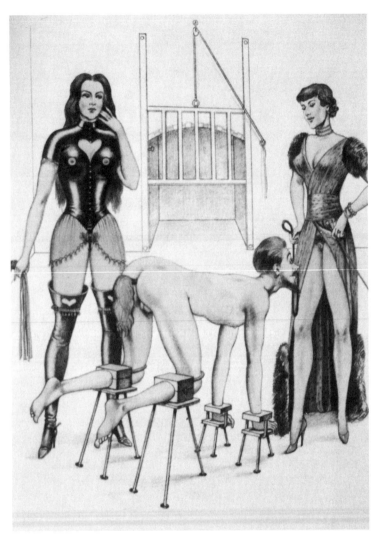

Figures 8.1 and 8.2. Illustrations from Bernard Montorgeuil, *Dressage,* c. 1930
(Paris, Bibliothèque nationale).

Figure 8.3. Book jacket from 1930 (Juana Lapaz, *L'inquisiteur moderne*, Paris, c. 1930).

histories is traced especially to the fact that the arousal of fantasy and its images do not admit of scenes corresponding to "normality" at all. The rituals constructed in this way by the "perverse flagellant" thereby displace fulfillment via coitus (the supposed normal case of "natural," heteronormative, and genital sexuality) and become "a means to the end of mental satisfaction of his peculiar desire."[5]

As Krafft-Ebing occasionally remarks, it is a question here of "comedies," of "prearranged programs" or dramas, in which actions with a strong affective charge are repeatedly restaged and made the basis of an intensive experience. Flagellation (which has a specific role within such fantasy scenarios of voluptuousness without coitus) is thus a moment that arouses the imagination and finds genuine enjoyment in such arousal. As we follow Krafft-Ebing's (one-sided and rudimentary) explanations of masochism and flagellation, this is also the place where we can speak of "perversion." Perversion, whether it be "inherited" as Krafft-Ebing believed, or stems from childhood, as psychoanalysis teaches us,[6] should be seen in the case of flagellation as the privileging of a ritual centered on arousal, as well as the unfettering of fantasy itself. One example of this sort of theatrical arousal, which tends to explode the boundaries of everydayness, is now called "masochism." By contrast, normalcy in Krafft-Ebing's terminology means that the development of fantasy remains subordinate to a "natural sexuality" focused on coitus — on heterosexual, genital performance.

J. Sadger, a "nerve doctor in Vienna," expressed his agreement with the views of "Giovanni Frusta" (i.e., Fetzer) in a study published in 1913 in the *Jahrbuch für psychoanalytische und psychopathologische Forschungen*. Sadger attests that "the flagellated one [is fulfilled by] . . . a mystical feeling composed of sensuality and fantasy. It is a feeling of humiliation under the power of someone stronger, of having his personality transposed back into childhood." Sadger gives a detailed critique of Krafft-Ebing's explanation of the "sado-masochistic complex" and an especially detailed commentary on the physiological aspects of flagellation. He has no doubt that the concept of the "sexual" refers not primarily to a psychophysiological constellation, but to the dynamics of the affects and of imagination. For him, this is obviously no longer directly linked to the condition and equilibrial state of the humors (as was still the case for Meibom), but is actually liberated from the humors and is therefore in need of a special control. "Normal" sexuality (meaning the connection of physiological functionality with an imagination that never transgresses the boundaries of this functionality) thus always implies that the arousing images do not explode the framework of this naturalized normality.

Only in the case of heterosexual married couples did Martin Luther grant legitimacy to "lust and desire," which were already conceded by the medieval handbooks to be necessary for procreation. As seen from the texts of Krafft-Ebing and above all of Sadger, lust and desire were regarded as justified by the sexual psychopathology of the turn of the century only when they are subordinated to the functional and teleological unity of heteronormative genital sexuality and hence to the aim of marriage. Medicine and psychopathology thus became the agent of a Protestant and Enlightenment iconoclasm with respect to the link between imagination and sexuality. Unlike the Catholic approach, such iconoclasm did not simultaneously turn "lust and desire" into taboos while also exploring and transforming them. Instead, it bound them to a sole legitimate institution: marriage, which is meant to dissolve all ambiguity of arousal. In this way, marriage (which in the Middle Ages was viewed in the Pauline manner as a "means of salvation against fornication and unchastity" and of preventing distance from God in self-generated pleasure) became a privileged site where "natural" desire unfolds its productivity within the framework of "nature." At the same time, all other lust was banished and all arousal disciplined.

For the Protestant-bourgeois household, the marital bed becomes the "altar" that no unfettering of the imagination should be permitted to endanger.[7] The imagination is now entirely subordinate to the divine institution of marriage and no longer knows

434

the freedom of ascetic-imaginative arousal, which Luther already had described as a danger and as a gateway to fornication. Given the "natural" way that lust belongs to married life, it is stripped of any power of arousal that could endanger the bourgeois household. For Sadger, who is very much an agent of this tradition, it is this sort of binding of the imagination that is at stake in connection with natural sexuality.

In this history of sexual discourse, this manner of dealing with fantasy by controlling its power of arousal is extracted and isolated as the very core of *Psychopathia sexualis*. This is clearly visible in a book with this title by Heinrich Kaan, published in 1844 in Leipzig. The imagination is obviously no longer linked to the equilibrium and flow of the humors in the body, as was still true for Meibom and for the early moderns more generally. Instead, it is separated from the doctrine of humors and subordinated to a concept of "normal sexuality" that is viewed as a conditioning factor or highest authority. Kaan distinguishes between a sexual life in conformity with "nature" or with the "nisus sexualis" or "instinctus sexualis," before which fantasy must bow, and deviations from this norm ("aberrationes"). "There are," he continues, "countless forms of such deviation, of which the most loathsome are: onanism or masturbation, pedophilia, lesbian love, sex with cadavers, and sexual intercourse with animals or with statues."

Flagellation does not appear in this catalog of aberrations. And in the truly psychopathological portion of the study, the only example discussed in detail is onanism, the favorite topic of sexual pathologists since the eighteenth century. Nonetheless, Kaan's text makes clear how a field defined in medical terms as pathological comes to be constituted — a field including voluntary flagellation, as well. There had always been talk of actions "contra naturam" (such as bestiality, sodomy, and homosexuality), but this was primarily an ethical category referring to sinful transgressions. By contrast, Kaan now postulates a scientifically defined unity of nature and morality, one to which the imagination should be subordinated. "Unnatural" acts are mentioned by Plato, who in fact used the expression "against nature" ("para physin") for the first time. But the reason he considers them reprehensible is not because they are pathological, but rather (especially in the context of the *Laws*) because they express a lack of self-control. The apostle Paul, who develops the same concept in Romans 1. 26–27, sees acts of this kind (such as homosexuality) as a form of behavior that is deeply pagan and out of keeping with God's law. Hence, for Plato and Paul, acts "against nature" are not a symptom of illness in the medical-pathological sense, but are characterized instead in social, ethical, and religious terms.[8] What dominates here is a concept of nature that supposes the constitutive activity of the man and passivity of the woman and also (in Paul's case) restricts these two aspects exclusively to the fields of natural procreation and marriage. From this standpoint, especially in the Middle Ages, the natural aim of the libido fuses together with marital procreation. "Sex" in its "God-given natural form" means nothing other than marriage, heterosexuality, and genitality.[9] Given this sort of stipulation of deviant acts, all the aforementioned deeds can be termed "contrary to nature." But in the earlier period, this referred only to morally reprehensible acts, never to illness.

As was clear from Meibom and other early modern authors, flagellation was at first not clearly distinguished in scientific terms from normal phenomena as a pathological phenomenon — not even when it was a matter of erotic stimulation. Instead, flagellation was regarded as a specific praxis, one that under certain conditions displayed specific intended or unintended effects, indulged in by specific people for specific reasons. Meibom lets us know that the most legitimate form is the kind that helps a man fulfill his "marital duties" so as to satisfy "nature." It is reprehensible only if an underlying "exhaustion" comes about through immoral behavior.

It is Kaan and his contemporaries who first define "sexuality" as a medical object for the doctor and the scientist — an object to which flagellation is subordinated. This confirms Foucault's thesis that the unifying object of human knowledge and social praxis is usually conceived as "sexuality." Also typical of Kaan's perspective is that fantasy is subordinated entirely to the modern concept of libidinal economy: in other words, to "normal sexuality" as a regulated, natural satisfaction of drives. A "healthy fantasy" follows a "healthy nature." By contrast, an overextravagant fantasy reflects not only a moral transgression of the norm and hence a morally dubious commerce with the libido, but an actual sickening or malformation of the psychical and physical constitution — of the underlying normality that determines "healthy sexuality."

Kaan's explanations are informative even when he does not speak explicitly of flagellation, since they show us how the object of "psychopathia sexualis" is constituted. "What," Kaan asks, "is 'psychopathia sexualis'?" He answers as follows:

> How is it possible that a well-educated and well-cultivated man should become dominated by shameful vices unknown even to savage peoples, forbidden by reason, and forbidden and strictly punished by law? The grounds for this cannot lie outside the circumstances of which we are asking, for among all peoples, in all regions, at the most various times... we repeatedly encounter vice [Kaan is speaking here primarily of onanism], and few are immune to it. The reason for this does not lie outside us, but within us: namely, in the sickly power of fantasy that produces rash desire and finds various tricks and paths for satisfying the sex drive. Namely, as soon as the sex drive is satisfied in ways besides the natural one, it becomes accustomed to doing so, and when the stimulation of the lascivious fantasy is repeated, it will immediately react to this fantasy. This agreeable reaction has an incredible power over humans, and neither a strong will nor reason is able to free men from it. In all deviations and aberrations of the sex drive, it is fantasy that paves the way for its satisfaction to deviate from the laws of nature. All deviations are hence nothing other than various forms of one and the same thing, and they interweave with one another. Boys inclined to masturbation fall prey most easily to other vices of the sex drive, even if they no longer masturbate at a later age, and in shameful people, both masturbation and other vices appear in unison. Thus, in all aberrations of the sex dive it is the aroused and sickly power of fantasy that

437

confuses the spirit. Hence, it seems correct to me to consider all these phenomena as a sickness of fantasy that arises from the sexual system and also enlivens it. In a word, I combine them together under the concept "pysychopathia sexualis." In the strict sense, "psychopathia sexualis" refers to adults with a normal sex drive — that is to say, to the voluntary act of the arousal of fantasy and of the sexual system. And in fact, there are countless things that (in accordance with the specific idiosyncracy of any individual soul) kindle the fantasy, arouse the sex drive, and cause a longing for coitus. With this disease it is a matter of the phenomenon that others falsely describe as "psychic onanism." . . . I have considered onanism in [the following] little work, insofar as it is the most widespread and frequent case of sexual aberration [psychopathiae sexualis]. But what is said here about onanism is equally true of the other aberrations.

The author adds in a footnote that one person may be aroused by "a beautiful foot, another by hands, a third by the bosom, and a fourth by teeth." For this reason, the games of arousal are entirely "miraculosa," as Kaan puts it.[10] Yet it is no longer a question of the "wondrous variety" that Kristian Paullini describes with such astonishment and that he interprets as marks of the divine presence, but of symptoms of an aroused and sickly imagination.

What is decisive for the overextravagant power of fantasy within the "sexual system," a power that Kaan makes responsible for all "sexual aberrations," is a premature corruption of the craving for love in children and youths that Kaan regards as originally pure. This happens when arousal is produced for its own sake and without any sense of measure. What arises from this is a man "devoted to the voluptuousness of the body and whose entire life is dominated by the sex drive."[11] Hence, it is the arousal of fantasy, forming the kernel of an "aberration" that begins in childhood and shapes the entire life, that should be regarded as an illness. The "healthy drive" (whose economy can be described as a "law of nature") is corrupted by fantasy when it begins to "run wild." Medicine needs to act in the name of "nature and reason" to ensure that this does not happen.

In closing, we should note that Kaan's arguments, for all their terminological differences and psychopathological procedures, are not so far removed from those of Abbé Boileau. In 1700, in his critique of ascetic flagellation, Boileau reflected on the medical literature known to him: "From this it now follows clearly that the animal spirits of man, when they are struck by nettles or by blows of the whip, are pushed forward toward the genitals and produce violent movements toward unchastity. These impressions quickly enter the brain, where they paint lively images of forbidden joys, bewitch the understanding through their deceptive stimulations, and put chastity on its last legs." Yet there is something that distinguishes Kaan from Boileau and earlier critics of flagellation, something that is so typical of Kaan. I refer to the concepts of "sexual system" and "natural sexuality," which offer a unitary framework for the "natural" integration of the arousal and control of fantasy and for the description of deviance. These themes, along with the underlying concept of normality, form an important polemical background to the censorship of the so-called "Talmudic-Jesuitical" overstimulation of the imagination.

Sexual Science, Ascesis, Performance

Anyone who consults a contemporary twentieth-century handbook of sexual psychology will come across an explanation of flagellation combining the mechanical-physiological and psychopathological explanations. In flagellation ("the most frequent of all sexual idiosyncracies"), we must distinguish between the active and passive forms.

> Passive flagellation summons up reflexive arousal of the spinal and sympathetic ejaculation centers of the man and leads in both sexes through strong blood influx to an arousal of the genitals (penis, clitoris). Active flagellation, through the rhythmic movement of arms and upper body, summons up strong muscular stimuli. The spasms of the body as it is struck mimic those of coitus and thereby summon up psychic stimuli. Also, the colorful stimulation of the reddened parts of the skin (and sometimes of actual blood), in opposition to

439

the white or pink skin of the body that is not struck, are often mentioned by active flagellants as a special attraction of flagellation.[12]

A distinction is drawn here between whipping, being whipped, and self-whipping, but the author presupposes that flagellation, as a "sadomasochistic" ritual, is kindled "by childhood memories of being beaten by a beloved person (father, mother)."[13] In clinical terms, and hence from the standpoint of psychology and medicine, this may sometimes be the case, even if it is somewhat dubious in view of the modern culture of sadomasochistic experience. Yet the psychological explanation reduces the complexity of the flagellation rituals, subordinating them entirely to the functional context of the modern dispositif of sexuality. In this way, flagellation not only loses its possible spiritual significance (the specific theatrical function of imaginative and arousing bodily staging within a ritual context), but also loses the erotic-libertine dimension of liberated arousal. Flagellation becomes a mere "idiosyncracy." It loses all claim to be practicing a ritual aimed at arousal itself and transcending "sexuality." From the standpoint of psychopathology, it is no more than an "incomplete" form of sexual performance, or in the best case a reprehensible form of foreplay. This can be seen even in Steven Marcus's presentation of the flagellation scenes in *My Secret Life*: in his view, every gesture related to "sexuality" is really only legitimate and entirely healthy when it aims at genital performance or gains its meaning from this performance. The same holds for the handbook of Ernest Bornemann, which reflects the ideology of the "sexual revolution" and from which the passage just cited is drawn.

Although these works do not openly equate a fabricated "naturalness" with normality and moral integrity (a disastrous trait of Kaan's sexual psychopathology), they nonetheless imply a concept of normality that relates "healthy sexuality" and hence "healthy arousal" to successful genital performance. Hence, one notes with astonishment that despite the occurrence of the "sexual revolution," there has been no basic paradigm shift for modern sexuality with respect to what is permitted and what is forbidden.

440

Admittedly, "sexuality" has become the focal point of a model of liberation. Yet it finds justification not in the enjoyment of numerous possible stimulations (i.e., in the enjoyment of arousal itself), but in the enjoyment of arousal insofar as it aims at genital unification and the naturalized image of finality that it implies.

At the beginning of the twenty-first century, it should be obvious that this need not be procreation. As Marcus and Bornemann emphasize, it can be instead the reality of a "ripe and authentic relation" to which all imagination must be subordinate.

In this respect, modern sexuality's new understanding of "sexuality" as a key productive power has not done away with the medieval, early modern, or Protestant image of marriage as a salvatory institution where sex has a "natural" place. Instead, it has merely turned this image into something positive, making it the core of self-perception and the disciplining of affective-imaginative arousal. In our own time, this has long since expanded into a ubiquitous brand of pornography that to some extent replaces real presence. What this reflects is not so much a *liberation*. Instead, it reveals the possibility of freeing up the imagination for the unfolding of erotic arousal, now positively determined (and disciplined) as "healthy sexuality." Such an unfolding is presupposed by any "liberation" in the name of nature. But it has lost all the ambiguity that it still possessed in ascetic praxis and radical libertinage, in which the arts of arousal turned against nature time and time again.

Let us return once more to the beginning of this study: to spiritual flagellation, established in the eleventh century as an ecclesiastical practice. Against all expectations, it is still a subject of church handbooks, even in the twenty-first century. As a rule, such books warn of physical danger to the body more than anything else. From the standpoint of pastoral medicine, this means that flagellation can cause harm

> through creating actual wounds, and if frequent flagellation occurs before they are fully healed, they can become chronic sores. Violent blows with a heavy scourge on soft parts of the body can also cause

441

injuries to internal organs or superficial blood vessels. Therefore, a scourge should have no sharp edges, and flagellation should only touch the back (excluding the soft parts of the loins) and such areas as the shoulders and the arms (the "upper discipline"). What is especially to be avoided in flagellation are the genitals, the entire stomach, and, for women, the breasts. The so-called "lower discipline" of the buttocks and upper thighs is not recommended. — Persons inclined toward sexual perversion must be forbidden to practice flagellation. Among sadistically inclined people, it provides the cause of aphrodisiac stimulation and results in the danger that they might inflict the discipline on others; in the masochistically inclined, such stimuli would be summoned forth by the idea of the discipline being applied to them.[14]

The reference to sexual perversion is entirely missing in the first editions of the book. It was perhaps unthinkable apart from the discourse of "sexuality." But ultimately, as the preceding passage testifies, the discourse of sexuality dominant for the moderns was also asserted as primary even in the modern ecclesiastical language of asceticism. And this discourse ultimately undermines the culture of affective-imaginative arousal at the heart of flagellation rituals in favor of a "natural" sexuality oriented toward functional normality and institutional legitimacy.

In this way, remnants of the ascetic and erotic-imaginative traditions, which are mostly absent in the life of the modern church, can scarcely be found any longer in the realm of ecclesiastical piety, aside from certain rituals during Holy Week. If they are still found at all, it is only in artistic performance. Biopolitics and psychopolitics (Foucault's modern "dispositif of sexuality") have thereby triumphed over the seductive power of images unleashed in flagellation. (Yet such triumph may be merely preliminary, given the multiplication in the media of new cultures of imagination at the turn of the twenty-first century.) This politics has also achieved preliminary victory over an arousal that does not grant final authority to "the sexual," which dominates the markets and powers the expansion of the media in our own time, but views it as merely one of the preliminary sites of its staging.

Despite the often apocalyptic spiritual claims connected with flagellation in the Middle Ages, what this praxis displays is fragmentation, splintering, and disintegration. This in turn unleashes affective-imaginative arousal from the teleologically binding status to which it was exiled by the discourse of "sexuality." This sort of unleashing was the goal of the libertines, who were focused on nothing but the endless repetition of arousal, and also was the goal of the ascetic practices of nuns and monks, who were focused on the repetition of exemplary scenes from the life of Christ.

Performances by artists such as Marina Abramovic (figure 8.4), Bob Flanagan, and above all Ron Athey (who stage similar rituals today) aim at a new evocation not so much of the religious-ascetic context, but at the fragmentation, alienation, and singular exemplarity that make the ritual's impact visible. In this way, as with monks, nuns, and libertines, the framework of play and spectator is transgressed, since the spectator is compelled to witness genuine pain and actual torture. The expression used by Athey for his deeds is "bearing witness," a phrase that plays on religious traditions. He thereby refers not to a representation or reification of the authentic, but to the rhythmic performance itself, in which the Christian-ascetic ritual becomes an "alchemy," a transformation of performer and spectator at the same time. That is to say, it becomes a permanent transformation of the body in pain through the desperate and perhaps all too artificial search for a recuperation of the always already lost "real" in the victim.[15] What is aimed at is not the sympathy of the spectator with the sufferer. Rather, it is the unfulfillable promise of an affective catharsis in which the human being himself affirms the tragically "violent and contradictory forces that drive him about,"[16] a catharsis that he himself (in a state of arousal) evokes and produces time and again. As Bataille thus describes it, such recourse to ascetic rituals does not explode the discursive order of the world. Rather, discursive control is exhausted by a spiritual and erotic arousal of fantasy that the modern economy of "natural sexuality" attempts to subordinate.

443

Figure 8.4. Marina Abramovic, *Spirit House*, 1997, video stills.

Epilogue

The last two chapters again shifted the context of our narrative, which was initially oriented toward Christian ascetic techniques, then toward erotic practices. In the eyes of contemporary scholarship, voluntary flagellation is not a phenomenon to be interpreted in religious, spiritual, and erotic terms — or even merely in erotic terms. Rather, it is viewed as a practice whose meaning can be understood only in its relation to "sexuality." It was Foucault who described the discursive and normative naturalization of sexuality in the modern period, the constitution of the object now called "sexuality" that became one of the stock figures of psychology and anthropology in the twentieth century. His historical research, which partly contradicts the traditional hypothesis of repression, is to some extent confirmed by the materials presented in this book. But this book has also placed the theme in a different light. Foucault already showed that the formation of a discourse about sex, the establishment of a universal knowledge about it (as found especially in the eighteenth and nineteenth centuries), turns out not to be primarily a repression or control of "sexual activity." Rather, it turns out to be a deliberate liberation within the framework of a biopolitics oriented toward marriage, one that nonetheless aims at a control of the imagination in the name of "natural sexuality." On the one hand, then, discursive knowledge aims at a normalization and a territorial enclosure of the libido with a view to specific practices. On the other hand, it entails in particular a disciplining of the imagination and a radical elimination of all ambiguity. That is to say, it seeks to eliminate the conspiratorial connection between imagination, affect, and libido that is always found in confessional praxis, religious rituals, and erotic flagellation. Ambiguity became unbearable, since it always already suspends the univocal status of the privileged natural form of arousal. As a consequence, the only place imagination is now allowed to occupy is the arts.

The Paradigm of "Sexuality"

In Sade's writings, flagellation was able to found the rhetoric of pornographic literature only because it suspends the representation of "determinative nature." The ambiguity of the arousing image appeared to the defenders of ascetic flagellation such as Gretser and Thiers as tolerable and even necessary insofar as it made up the foundation of spiritual transformation in the turn toward God since the high Middle Ages. Yet in the eyes of Enlightenment critics, it became unbearable, for it circumvents the relation of reason to the absolute. For them, it was no longer a matter of turning affective imaginative arousal into the basis for a transformation of the soul — a process leading to the complementary freedom of humanity and God. Instead, it was a question of submitting arousal to rigorous control so as to ensure that reason would ground freedom in its own terms. The psychopathology of sexuality as established in the nineteenth century stands at the end of this path, where imagination is subordinated to a "natural sexuality" ratified by reason, a "natural sexuality" that possesses its finality in the heteronormative performance of the "sexual act." The spiritual and erotic transgression of the borders of such nature can only seem to be pathological in the eyes of reason.

However, such control does not altogether succeed. The arousing play of images pursued by religious and libertine flagellants remains, through the possibility of transgression and the image of endangerment, the exemplary case of a stimulation that cannot be traced entirely to sexuality, since it challenges the finality implied by this very concept. As a contrast to the biopolitics that the mod-

446

erns transformed into a general age of universal sexualization (that is, of a "normal," "genital," and "productive" sexuality), we have here a bodily practice that seems "perverse." Instead of satisfaction, it evokes the boundless character of fantasy and the endless multiplication of arousal. This praxis does not gain its subversive character (if we can speak of such a thing) by emerging as a specific sexual practice or "truer sexuality" through appeal to "nature." Rather, its subversive force stems from its ultimate rejection of the dominance of the "sexual" or "sexuality" over the body (including the imaginary body) and indeed its rejection of the dominance of "nature" in general.

Hence, it should be self-evident that we are not speaking of some Romantic turn toward any authenticity or transfiguration of the body. What flagellation unleashes is of course of a bodily character and obviously amounts to a kind of erotic and spiritual desire. Yet what emerges in this way is not the "truth" of the body, desire, or imagination. What is actually unleashed is the imagination as the space of an installation of inner possibilities of experience. In this space, along with the images that are designed to arouse, what is staged is the possibility of arousal as an authority able to transcend "nature" in its religious or secular form. What is evoked in this way is the link of the imagination to the theatrical, the visual, and the life of images — a link that stages flagellation in exemplary fashion. For the flagellants, we might conclude, the free space of imagination as unfettered in either spiritual or erotic flagellation rituals precedes a sexuality grasped as "nature" and forms a realm of freedom through sheer repetition. Unlike "sexuality," this realm is not a substantial determination, but a space of possibility for unrestricted arousal. In the eyes of the ascetic, who in his passage through the imagination and affect ultimately aims at his purification from them, this space should be overcome through unity with the divine.

Control of the Imagination

The present book naturally wishes to make no historical claims as to whether a "more liberal" attitude of "the people" toward

447

"sexuality" in the Middle Ages and early modern times was increasingly repressed in modernity (as is often asserted by historians of sexuality and of mentalities). On the one hand, it seems unsuitable to construct a dichotomy of "people" versus "elite" for the material presented here. On the other hand, "sexuality," as we have seen, cannot be hypostatized as some sort of transhistorical reality. There is no denying that a religious elite sought to exercise controls that, following the Reformation and Counter-Reformation, were eliminated by an Enlightenment elite with its own ambitions of control. It is perhaps equally indisputable that a "civilizing" repression occurred that, alongside the controls of everyday violence, also aimed at the satisfaction of drives and an economy of affects. Yet this does not mean (as Foucault has noted) that "sexuality was repressed," as if an apparently liberal attitude toward sexual desire (one that has perhaps never existed) was submitted to rigid control. Rather, "sexuality" first developed as a form of the encoding of desire in the "discursive formation" of sex. Ultimately, in the magazines and talk shows of the late twentieth century, it became the center of the self-perception of the subject.

The rise of the word "sexuality," in which Foucault shows a process of discursive formation, marks both the beginning of a new epistemological structure and the endpoint of an unfolding dichotomy. This began (initially with the Protestants, but eventually also in the Enlightenment discourse of sexual ethics as rooted in a new naturalism) when a critique of the dynamics and significance of the affective-imaginative complex gained the upper hand in spiritual life. At the end of this path stands the discursive formation of sexuality in modern sexual research and sexual psychopathology, which grasps sexuality in positive fashion, but in so doing ascribes a specific site to the erotic imagination. Freedom or autonomy are no longer grasped as an unleashing of the imagination, but rather as a commerce with nature led by reason, a commerce to which affective-imaginative arousal is also subordinated. Only when this productive control succeeds does the imagination ultimately see itself mobilized anew and unleashed into the world of the modern media.

Thanks to all of this, actions that in the Middle Ages served ascetic practice and in the seventeenth and eighteenth centuries survived as a libertine remnant of the ascetic-ecstatic culture of arousal are initially excluded and declared to be pathological. Nonetheless, they have remained alive well into late modernity in literary and artistic form. Even for Georges Bataille and the young Foucault, this culture of arousal belongs to the movements of disintegration that unfold in the Middle Ages and in modernity. Yet what is subversive here (if we wished to view these movements as a Romantic rebellion against the dominant discourse of science and enlightened consciousness) is not that they speak in the name of a "repressed sexuality." Instead, what is subversive is that they postulate and establish a discursively undisciplined and undisciplinable arousal, even when we initially seem to be dealing with sexuality. It is undisciplinable since it possesses no frame of reference and therefore does not refer to a hypostatized concept of nature, freedom, or God. Instead, it merely constitutes a differential space in which imaginative arousal appears as the "other" of a reason that is both controlling and controlled. Hence, imaginative arousal by no means withdraws from the insignia of power, but reflects power in its very images and its gestures of staging. Nonetheless, it undermines the primacy of rational discourse in its performative appeal to its affective and imaginative poverty.

The arousal of the flagellant is exemplary precisely because it always performs and thematizes this constitutive relation of dominance and submission, power and powerlessness. To have called our attention to this fact is one of the chief characteristics of a whole tradition of erotic variations on the lives of the saints, one that reaches its high point in the work of Sade and its attack on Rousseau's enlightened pedagogy. Sade's utopian scenarios of desire and lust become genuine allegories of an arousal of the imagination that rejects the control of reason (even when their perfect choreography makes them seem like the very epitome of reason) and ultimately abolishes the body itself. In this way, as Pier Paolo Pasolini has portrayed in *Salò*, they are altogether comparable to the fascist rituals for arousing the individual and the masses.

In view of present-day discussions of the performative, it should also be remarked that they are not merely rituals of arousal. Instead, they are ritual stagings of the performative itself and of the performative force of writing (as becomes especially clear in Swinburne, Proust, and Joyce). Ritual flagellation does not claim to constitute yet another discourse, one opposed to the discursive-rational control and regulation of word and gesture. Instead, it tries to constitute what is never able to be expressed in representation. Hence, it is a question of bottomless imaginary spaces and events. For Sade, it is "the abyss of desire and passion"; for Teresa of Avila, it is "the divine abyss" in the "dark night" of her existence; for Damian, it is "the space of the tribunal and of the struggle" that the flagellation opens up; for Swinburne and Joyce, it is the gesture of writing itself.

Admittedly, these spaces, too, are images that are evoked and whose meaning is arousal. What is present (even if never actually present) is what withdraws from representation, which happens here only where imagination fuses with this abyss of withdrawal through arousal. Visual art depicts such abysses (indeed, *is* such an abyss) when it presents itself as what can never be recuperated by representation, word, or concept. This happens in those moments when the claim of discursive reason always sees itself decomposed by an event that it is never able to reach. Thus, we might conclude in only apparently paradoxical fashion, the spirit of libertinage is a permanent deconstruction of the promise of the modern world — the promise that truth, happiness, and self-experience could be regarded as the actualization of a "natural and liberated" sexuality ordered by the provisions of reason, medicine, and psychology.

Proust's Flagellation Fantasy

Flagellation, which we have come to see as emblematic of the arousal of fantasy, is a symbol belonging to both the libertine and the ascetic. As such, flagellation does not refer to some autonomy of the body or the soul, of sex or of physical pleasure. Rather, the heart of its emblematic importance lies in its ritual of decomposition — one that attempts to dissolve all utterable meaning into a kind of pictorial arousal. In the intensity of experience, it does not gain its pleasure through any possible fulfillment. From the standpoint of the dominant, principally genital sexuality, the flagellant is perverse indeed. Yet we can still conclude with Roland Barthes that the flagellant is "perverse, and therefore happy," since he or she turns the moment of experience into a genuine fetish. In this sense, the praise of the whip stands in contrast to all taming of erotic and spiritual passion and with the sheer enjoyment of arousal. It is an enjoyment that, in its ascetic gesture of apotheosis, refuses both the Platonic and Stoic moderation of passionate devotion as well as the functional integration of fantasy in the modern dispositif of sexuality.

We will close this with a passage from Marcel Proust. At the end of *Le temps retrouvé* (Finding time again), Proust tells us how Monsieur de Charlus has himself whipped by a sailor in a male bordello. This scene is no mere anecdote informing us about Charlus and his sexual predilections. As early as 1927, Edmond Jaloux's review of Proust's work (which was regarded as morally reprehensible by numerous contemporaries) observed that this flagellation scene is a moment of towering significance. It is not only the staging of a specific inclination of the Baron de Charlus. More than this, it bridges the gap to the discussion a few pages later of the narrator's knowledge of why the taste of the madeleine at the beginning of the novel gives him an unexpected feeling of happiness and liberates him from any fear of death. The moment of recollection, the intensity and complexity of visualization that characterizes Proust's great work, is reflected in a very peculiar way in the flagellation of Monsieur de Charlus. This cannot be interpreted symbolically, but only as a theatrical model that reveals the aims of the novel, among other things.

The flagellation scene, which is followed in Proust's text by descriptions of bombardment and fire, has been described as a "descent into hell." The individual motifs can be related to apocalyptic imagery in which desire shows its true face and appears on the dramatic stage.[1] In this context, the scene where Charlus is whipped forms the culminating point of an experience of the

451

Parisian night entirely comparable to the mystical descent into darkness and to the motif from Mechthild of Magdeburg of being cast "under the devil's tail." The narrator first tells us of an encounter with Monsieur Charlus and of his "intensity of contact and of gaze exceeding the bounds of propriety." After Charlus's departure, his path leads "deeper into the maze of these dark streets" of Paris, through squares robbed of life by war and its economic restrictions, until the narrator (to his surprise) discovers a lively house with soldiers going in and out. Driven by curiosity, he enters and takes a room: number forty-three. He tells us that

> soon I was taken up to Room 43, but the room was so unpleasantly airless and my curiosity was so great that, once I'd drunk my cassis, I went downstairs again, then, a new idea having struck me, I went back up, past the floor that Room 43 was on, as far as the top floor. Suddenly, from a room set apart from the others at the end of the corridor, I thought I heard stifled moans. I walked quickly in their direction and placed my ear to the door. "I beg you, mercy, mercy, have pity, untie me, don't hit me so hard," said a voice. "I'll crawl, I'll kiss your feet, I shan't do it again. Have pity." — "No, you piece of filth," replied another voice, "and if you scream and drag yourself about on your knees like that, you'll be tied to the bed, and there'll be no mercy," and I heard the sound of a whip, probably one with nails to give it extra sharpness, for it was followed by cries of pain. Then I noticed the room had a small round side-window and that somebody had forgotten to draw the curtain behind it; advancing stealthily through the darkness, I slid up to the window and there, chained to a bed like Prometheus to his rock, receiving the blows which Maurice was delivering with a whip which was indeed studded with nails, I saw, already running with blood, and covered in bruises which proved that the flogging was not happening for the first time, there, right in front of me, I saw M. de Charlus.

Charlus is fettered, not like Christ, but rather like a "consenting Prometheus [who] had himself nailed by Force to the rock of pure matter." He is fully conscious of the "illusion" produced here

452

— of the fact that this scene is entirely staged. The man who whips him seems not to be genuine enough in his words and gestures actually to make present the unattainable beloved Morel, whom the narrator evokes while interpreting the scene. Nonetheless, the staging gives an opportunity for reminiscence, for the attempt at a construction of "authentic" life, even if, as constructed, it is an impossible one — as we can see from the dialogue between Charlus and the bordello manager and the callboys. The classification of similar "types" that lies at the basis of the staging, and hence of Charlus's experience of stimulation, is the actual core of the ritual that Charlus allows to be conducted on him. In this ritual, and only in this ritual, does the possibility lie concealed of bringing to light the unconscious and hidden intensity of things and the circumstances of life. The widely desired "authenticity" (if we may permit ourselves to use this term) does not refer to a representable truth, but rather to the truth of the moment of experience in which time unfolds simultaneously as past and as present. The abandonment of Christ, and that of Prometheus as evoked in this scene, refers to a moment of total absorption in arousal. Perhaps — at least for Charlus — there is nothing else to be grasped in the staging of such abandonment and in its replacement (adequate for a modern dandy) by a "medieval fantasy." The flagellation scene concludes as follows:

> Anyway, aberrations are like love affairs in which pathological defects have spread everywhere, have completely taken over. The presence of love can still be recognized, even in the maddest of them. The insistence of M. de Charlus on having his hands and feet fastened by shackles of proven strength, on begging for the rod of justice, and, so Jupien told me, for other ferocious props which, even from sailors, were extremely difficult to obtain — they having been used for the infliction of punishments which have been abolished everywhere, even where discipline is at its most rigorous, on board ship — had its roots in M. de Charlus's whole dream of virility, attested if necessary by brutal acts, and in all that inner illumination, invisible to us, but glimpses of which he projected through these

acts, of penal crosses and feudal tortures, which adorned his medieval imagination. It was the same sentiment that made him, each time he arrived, say to Jupien: "I hope there will not be an alert this evening, for I can just see myself consumed by this fire from heaven like the inhabitants of Sodom." And he would pretend to be afraid of the Goths, not because he actually felt the least shadow of fear, but in order to have the pretext, as soon as the sirens started up, of rushing off into the shelters of the Métro, where he hoped for pleasure from the casual contacts in the darkness, with vague dreams of medieval dungeons and oubliettes. In short, his desire to be chained and beaten betrayed, in its ugliness, a dream just as poetic as other men's desire to go to Venice or to keep a mistress. And M. de Charlus clung so tenaciously to the illusion of reality created by his dream that Jupien had to sell the wooden bed that used to be in Room 43 and replace it with an iron bed that was better suited to the chains.[2]

All of this confirms the remark by Ernst Robert Curtius that Proust wanted to depict "the whole of our experience, the totality of the real."[3] Yet depiction does not mean representation in images — it is a mimesis of arousal that summons forth a *frémissement de bonheur* or "trembling of happiness," one that leads the depiction through the experiential sensation of similarity into the heart of things and the heart of enjoyment. A sound, a smell, a stumble, or a touch evoke this relation to the things and situations that are crossroads of present and past, memory and living experience. In this experience, things show their "true face" precisely through the fact that their arousing force unfolds in recollective perception. It is a force that unites present and past in the feeling of happiness.

This is shown in exemplary fashion by the flagellation scene, which depicts both the staging of similarity (that of the sailor with the unattainable beloved, that of the scene itself with the seductive fantasy images of Charlus) and its inevitable failure. In this connection, Edmond Jaloux speaks of the "painting of this night," observing that "the pleasure for Charlus consists in the systematic elaboration of a world of images, which (in itself incomprehensible, unreal, dreamlike, and often terrifying) expresses nothing other than the dominance of fantasy — as in the search for happiness of a young man or young woman who express their desire in images which they believe to be pure."[4] It is surely true that fantasy predominates in this remark. Yet the exemplary case of flagellation shows that it is not a question of fantasy itself, of its ascent into ever new layers of images. Instead, it is a question of an arousal in which past and present, memory and perception, senses and soul, coincide. In this way, flagellation, which is always and primarily rhythm, does not negate time, as could easily be believed in some cases. Instead, the soul (as was already the case among medieval flagellants, with their gestures of eschatological mimesis) no longer lives in time — rather, time lives in it. The same can be said of erotic flagellation.

As an arousal that aims at such an opening onto time and the experience of time, the ritual of flagellation points beyond the horizon of understanding that initially ascribes it to the history of sexuality or spirituality, a spirituality of the type that masks its underlying sexuality only with difficulty. The exemplary character of the scene in which Monsieur de Charlus is whipped immediately makes clear that such ascription is impossible. It is an example of the play of images — one in which the imagination, fed by desire, strides forward. And at the same time (unlike the ascetics, who believed they found unity with God beyond the imagination) the imagination, moved by desire, finds in arousal an uncircumventible principle of its own — a principle in which time itself unfolds.

455

Notes

A note on biblical references: The translator has consulted the Revised Standard edition. However, nearly all (if not all) biblical quotes are embedded in larger quotes from older sources. These older texts did not use a standard vernacular version of the Bible, but instead were translated from the Latin. Thus, each text shapes the text toward the argument that the author is trying to make. Consequently, it does not make sense to insert the text from a modern standard version, and we have simply translated the entirety of quotes that contain biblical quotations.

CHAPTER ONE: SUFFERING, TRANSFIGURATION, AND THE SCOURGE

1. Ancelet-Hustache, "Les *Vitae sororum*," pp. 340–41.

2. *Die Offenbarungen der Adelheid Langmann*, p. 37.

3. *Leben und Gesichte der Christina Ebnerin*, p. 11.

4. See Greith, *Die deutsche Mystik*, pp. 382–85; Muschg, *Die Mystik in der Schweiz*, pp. 205–10.

5. Pfister, "Hysterie und Mystik."

6. *Heiligen-Lexikon*, vol. 1, pp. 783ff. Peter Damian's story of the life of Dominicus Loricatus can be found in *Letter 44*, ed. Reindel, vol. 2, pp. 21–25; ed. Blum, vol. 2, pp. 231–35, his *vita* in *Letter 109*, ed. Reindel, vol. 3, pp. 200–23; ed. Blum, vol. 3, pp. 207–26. For the practice of commutation, see Vogel, "Composition légale et commutations."

7. See *Letter 109*, ed. Reindel, vol. 3, pp. 200–23; ed. Blum, vol. 3, pp. 207–26. Compare also *Letter 44*, ed. Reindel, vol. 2, pp. 7–33; ed. Blum, vol. 2, pp. 231–35.

8. Paullini, *Flagellum salutis*, p. 15.

9. Thomas of Celano, *Legenda sanctae Clarae*, p. 16.

10. The examples are taken from Bertaud, *Discipline*, p. 1307, and from Gougaud, *Dévotions*, pp. 175–99.

11. Francis de Sales, *Oeuvres*, vol. 12, p. 357.

12. See Walter, *Unkeuschheit*, pp. 320ff., who provides a bibliography of research literature.

13. Francis de Sales, *Introduction to the Devout Life*, ed. Ross, 4, 12, p. 263.

14. See Strauch, *Margaretha Ebner*, pp. 20ff.

15. Ignatius of Loyola, *Spiritual Exercises*, ed. Ganss, 85–89, pp. 144–45.

16. Bertaud, *Discipline*, p. 1310.

17. Gougaud, *Dévotions*, p. 176.

18. Stöhr, *Handbuch der Pastoralmedicin*, pp. 419–21.

19. *Vita Pardulfi abbatis Waractensis*, pp. 28–29.

20. Regino of Prüm, *De ecclesiasticis disciplinis* 2, 442–44, pp. 369–70.

21. See Brown, *The Body and Society*.

22. *Vita S. Antonii* 47, *Patrologia Graeca*, vol. 26, p. 912.

23. Hadot, *Philosophy as a Way of Life*; Rabbow, *Seelenführung*.

24. Suso, *Deutsche Schriften*, ed. Bihlmeyer, p. 205; ed. Tobin, p. 214.

25. *Ibid.*, ed. Bihlmeyer, p. 34; ed. Tobin, p. 81.

26. *Leben und Gesichte der Christina Ebnerin*, p. 11; Suso, *Deutsche Schriften*, ed. Bihlmeyer, p. 16; ed. Tobin, pp. 70–71.

27. Angenendt, *Heilige und Reliquien*, p. 67.

28. *Ibid.*, pp. 66–68.

29. Angenendt, "Sühne durch Blut."

30. See Largier, "Der Körper der Schrift."

31. Scarry, "On Vivacity," pp. 4–5.

32. See Scarry, *Ibid.*, pp. 14–15.

33. See Keating, *Open Mind, Open Heart*.

34. For an overview, compare Schuppisser, "Schauen mit den Augen des Herzens" (with literature); Seegets, *Passionstheologie*.

35. See, e.g., *Spiegel van den Leven ons heren*, fol. 39r (illustration and prayer); Schuppisser, "Schauen mit den Augen des Herzens," p. 192 (illustration and prayer). See also the illustrations in *Le Jardin clos de l'âme*.

36. See Largier, "Figurata locutio."

37. *Aretino's Dialogues*, pp. 52–53.

CHAPTER TWO: IN PRAISE OF THE WHIP

1. Peter Damian, *Brief* 45, ed. Reindel, vol. 2, p. 36; ed. Blum, vol. 2, p. 245.

2. See "Geißelsäule und Geißelung Christi."

3. Mansi, *Sacrorum conciliorum collectio*, vol. 17, p. 293; Hefele, *Histoire des conciles*, vol. IV, 2, pp. 638–39.

4. Peter the Venerable, *De miraculis* 2, 9; *Patrologia Latina*, vol. 189, p. 919b.

5. See Bértaud, *Discipline*, p. 1304. Note also the punishment depicted in the *Liber ordinarius* of the monastery of Saint Jacques at Liège, pp. 113–14. The ritual follows the same pattern. See Thiers, *Critique*, pp. 184–96.

6. See Peter the Venerable, *Statuta* 53, *Patrologia Latina* 189, p. 1040a.

7. Descriptions of the rules of eremitic life can be found in Peter Damian's *Letters 18* and *50*, ed. Riedel, vol. 1–2; ed. Blum, vol. 1–2.

8. The *Vita Romualdi* of Peter Damian is edited in *Patralogia Latina* 144. A new Italian edition was provided by Giovanni Tabacco in 1957.

9. Mechthild of Magdeburg, *The Flowing Light of the Godhead*.

10. Peter Damian, *Sermo* 74, pp. 919ff.

11. Compare especially Peter Damian's *Letter 50*, ed. Reindel, vol. 2, pp. 77–131; ed. Blum, vol. 2, pp. 289–334.

12. Peter Damian, *Letter 56*, ed. Reindel, vol. 2, p. 158; ed. Blum, vol. 2, p. 365.

13. Peter Damian, *Letter 50*, ed. Reindel, vol. 2, p. 109; ed. Blum, vol. 2, p. 313.

14. Peter Damian, *Letter 161*, ed. Reindel, vol. 4, p. 136. Blum's English edition of Damian's letters is not yet finished.

15. Peter Damian, *Letter* 45, ed. Reindel, vol. 2, p. 36; ed. Blum, vol. 2, p. 245.

16. Peter Damian, *Letter* 45, ed. Reindel, vol. 2, pp. 36–37; ed. Blum, vol. 2, pp. 245–46.

17. *The Letters of St. Jerome*, vol. 1, pp. 165–66.

18. Peter Damian, *Letter* 56, ed. Reindel, vol. 2, pp. 155–158; ed. Blum, vol. 2, pp. 362–66.

19. Peter Damian, *Letter 161*, ed. Reindel, p. 144. Blum's English edition of Damian's letters is not yet finished.

20. See Durkheim, *The Elementary Forms of Religious Life*, pp. 458ff.

21. Peter Damian, *Letter* 45, ed. Reindel, vol. 2, p. 37; ed. Blum, vol. 2, p. 247.

22. Holstenius, *Codex*, vol. 1, p. 329.

23. *Ibid.*, vol. 6, p. 161. Other references can easily be found in the index of Holstenius's monumental work.

24. For sources see Bertaud, *Discipline*, pp. 1308–1309, and Gougaud, *Dévotions.*

25. *Liber ordinarius S. Jacobi*, pp. 113–14.

26. See Jungmann, *Die lateinischen Bußriten*, pp. 169–237.

27. Holstenius, *Codex*, vol. 6, p. 340.

28. *Ibid.*, p. 258.

29. *Ibid.*, p. 97.

Chapter Three: The Theater of the Flagellants

1. Hugh of Reutlingen, *Chronicon ad annum MCCCXLIX*, pp. 24–29. This is a free translation of Hugh's verse chronicle.

2. *Annales Ianuenses*, p. 241. See Segl, *Geißler*; Bailly, *Flagellants*; Bulst and Pásztor, *Flagellanten.*

3. Quoted from Hübner, *Die deutschen Geißlerlieder*, p. 57.

4. Helmold, *Chronica Slavorum*, p. 465.

5. *Annales Sanctae Justiniae Patavini*, p. 179.

6. *Ibid.*, pp. 179ff.

7. *Ibid.*

8. *Annales Mellicenses*, p. 509.

9. Aegidius li Muisit, *Chronica Aegidii li Muisis*, in *Corpus chronicarum Flandriae*, vol. 2, p. 352. See, pp. 346–61, the report of the flagellant movement from its first appearance in 1349 until its prohibition. The German translation from Schneegans, pp. 111–13 (in Hugh of Reutlingen, *Chronicon ad annum MCCCXLIX*) is emended.

10. Hübner, *Die deutschen Geißlerlieder*, p. 40.

11. *Gesta archiepiscoporum Magdeburgensium*, p. 437.

12. Achéry, *Spicilegium*, vol. 3, p. 111.

13. Martène, *Veterum scriptorum et monumentorum collectio*, vol. 5, p. 293.

14. *Annales Mechovienses*, p. 670.

15. Quoted from Bailly, *Flagellants*, p. 397.

16. Closener, *Straßburgische Chronik*, pp. 94–95. Also in *Chroniken der deutschen Städte*, vol. 8, pp. 116–17.

17. Closener, *Straßburgische Chronik*, p. 96; also in: *Chroniken der deutschen Städte*, vol. 8, p. 117.

18. Pfannenschmid reads the date as September 10, 1262. See Hübner, *Geisslerlieder*, p. 54.

19. Closener, *Straßburgische Chronik*, pp. 89–95. Also in *Chroniken der deutschen Städte*, vol. 8, pp. 111–17.

20. Henry of Herford, *Liber de rebus memorabilibus*, p. 281.

21. Mathias of Neuenburg, *Chronik*, p. 271.

22. Hübner, *Geisslerlieder*, p. 163.

23. All quotes are from the *Chronicon* of Hugh of Reutlingen.

24. See Graus, *Pest*, pp. 50–53.

25. Salimbene da Parma, *The Chronicle of Salimbene de Adam*, ed. Doren, vol. 2, pp. 127ff.; ed. Egger, p. 466; ed. Baird, p. 293.

26. Frederiq, *Corpus documentorum*, p. 197.

27. Edition of the texts in: Stumpf, *Historia flagellantium*. A partial edition has been published by A. Reifferscheid. The following quotes are from the editions of Stumpf and Reifferscheid.

28. *Articuli, quos tenuerunt et crediderunt heretici Zangerhusene.* Also in Stumpf, *Historia flagellantium*, pp. 26–32. For the "Cryptoflagellants," see Hoyer, "Die thüringische Kryptoflagellantenbewegung"; Erbstösser, *Sozialreligiöse Strömungen*; Kieckhefer, "Radical Tendencies."

29. Compare the *Instrumentum* printed in Förstemann, *Die christlichen Geißlergesellschaften*, pp. 174–77 and pp. 278–91. I have made slight corrections to Förstemann's text based on the Latin version.

30. *Gesta archiepiscoporum Magdeburgensium*, p. 481.

31. *Articuli ostenuerunt et crediderunt heretici capti in Sundirshausen et combusti.* Also in Stumpf, *Historia flagellantium*, pp. 32–35.

32. Haupt, "Zur Geschichte der Geißler."

33. Compare the report by Aegidius li Muisit for 1349: *Chronica Aegidii li Muisis*, in *Corpus chronicarum Flandriae*, vol. 2, pp. 346–61.

34. *Ibid.*, p. 361 and passim.

35. *Chronicon rhythmicum Austriacum*, p. 363.

36. Quoted in Hübner, *Die deutschen Geisslerlieder*, pp. 24 and 47.

37. Mansi, *Sacrorum conciliorum collectio*, vol. 25, pp. 1153–55. Compare also the *Chronica Aegidii li Muisis*.

38. Gerson, *Oeuvres*, vol. 2, p. 201.

39. *Ibid.*, vol. 10, pp. 46–51.

40. Hardt, *Concilium Constantiense*, vol. 1, pp. 86 and 126; vol. 3, pp. 98–105.

41. For a history of these brotherhoods, see *Il movimento dei disciplinati*. Compare also Meersseman, *Ordo fraternitatis*.

42. Edition of the statutes in Meersseman, *Ordo fraternitatis*, vol. 2, pp. 476–97.

43. See Vigo, *Statuto dei disciplinati*, pp. 19ff.

44. Ferlaino, *Vattienti*, pp. 41–48.

45. See *Il laudario* "Frondini."

46. *Gli Atti della visita apostolica di santo Carlo Borromeo*, vol. 1, part 2, pp. 189ff.

CHAPTER FOUR: AROUSING IMAGES

1. Chevallier, *Henri III*, p. 554. See Minois, *Le confesseur du roi*, pp. 284–89.

2. Amtmann, *Die Bußbruderschaften*, pp. 52–53.

3. *Ibid.*, pp. 380–82.

4. Eck, *De non tollendis Christi et sanctorum Imaginibus*. English edition contained in *A Reformation Debate*.

5. Gretser, *Virgidemia Volciana*, pp. 82ff.

6. *Ibid.*, p. 77.

7. Compare the edition of the document in Jedin, "Entstehung und Tragweite des Trienter Dekrets," pp. 181–86.

8. Richeome, *Trois discours*, p. 529. See Mühlen, *Imaginibus honos*.

9. Mühlen, *Imaginibus honos*, p. 164; Suso, *Deutsche Schriften*, ed. Bihlmeyer, p. 103; ed. Tobin, pp. 137–38. See Largier, "Der Körper der Schrift."

10. See Wadell, *Evangelicae historiae imagines*.

11. Gretser, *De cruce Christi*.

12. Gretser and Vetter, *Procession Buch*, pp. 229, 231, 264–65.

13. *Ibid.*, pp. 204–205.

14. *Ibid.*, pp. 211–14

15. Thiers, *Critique de l'histoire des flagellans*, introduction.

16. *Ibid.*, p. 49.

17. *Ibid.*, p. 107.

18. *Ibid.*, p. 72.

19. *Ibid.*, pp. 146–63.

20. *Ibid.*, pp. 172ff.

21. *Ibid.*, p. 180.

22. *Ibid.*, pp. 221ff. Thiers takes his information from Surius, *Historiae seu vitae sanctorum*, April, L.2, *Vita Sancti Vincentii Ferreri*, c.7.

NOTES

23. *Ibid.*, pp. 225ff. and 236ff.

24. *Ibid.*, p. 286.

25. *Ibid.*, chapters 16,17,18, pp. 301–67.

26. *Ibid.*, pp. 368ff.

27. *Ibid.*, pp. 407–408.

28. *Ibid.*, p. 418.

29. Boileau, *A Just and Seasonable Reprehension of Naked Breasts and Shoulders*, ed. 1678, pp. 16ff., 83ff., 91–94. A similar critique can already be found in Aegidius li Muisit, *Chronica*, p. 347.

30. Boileau, *Histoire des Flagellans*, ed. 1701, p. 3. An English version of this text was published anonymously by Jean-Louis Lolme in 1777 under the title *The History of the Flagellants, or The Advantages of discipline; Being a paraphrase and commentary on the Historia Flagellantium of the Abbé Boileau, Doctor of the Sorbonne . . . By somebody who is not Doctor of the Sorbonne*. The title of the second edition in 1783 was slightly different: *The History of the Flagellants: Otherwise, Of Religious Flagellations among different Nations, and especially among Christians.* My quotations are translated from the French text that followed the original Latin edition.

31. *Ibid.*, pp. 7ff.

32. *Ibid.*, p. 110.

33. *Ibid.*, pp. 167 and 176.

34. *Ibid.*, pp. 210–11.

35. *Ibid.*, p. 248.

36. Gretser, *De disciplinis* II 9, p. 149.

37. Boileau, *Histoire des Flagellans*, ed. 1701, p. 319.

38. "Aux mêmes Révérends Pères sur le livre des Flagellans composé par mon frère le docteur de Sorbonne." In Boileau-Despréaux, *Oeuvres*, vol. 2, p. 161.

CHAPTER FIVE: THE PRIEST, THE WOMAN, AND THE DIVINE MARQUIS

1. See Walter, *Unkeuschheit*, pp. 172–85.

2. Bloch, *Der Marquis de Sade und seine Zeit*, p. 289. See Bloch, *Marquis de Sade: The Man and His Age*, p. 156 and passim.

3. Fraxi, *Centuria*, pp. xix–xlix.

4. *Ibid.*, p. xx. Fraxi refers to Bartolocci, *Bibliotheca Rabbinica*, vol. 1, p. 77.

5. *Ibid.*, p. xxix.

6. Literature in Walter, *Unkeuschheit*, p. 493, fn. 11.

7. See, among many similar publications: Kaiser, *Josephsbrüder: Jesuitengeist und Judengeist* and Engels, *Der Jesuitismus*.

8. Bloch, *Marquis de Sade: The Man and His Age*, p. 39. Bloch takes his examples mainly from Wolf, *Allgemeine Geschichte der Jesuiten*.

9. Frusta, *Der Flagellantismus*, p. 17.

10. See Zimmermann, *Über die Einsamkeit*, vol. 2, pp. 223–30.

11. *Ibid.*, vol. 2, pp. 223–32.

12. *Ibid.*, vol. 2, p. 93.

13. Frusta, *Der Flagellantismus*, p. 61.

14. Henry of Kettenbach, *Ein new Apologia*, p. 576. Quoted in Walter, *Unkeuschheit*, p. 101.

15. Frusta, *Der Flagellantismus*, p. 105

16. *Ibid.*, p. 100.

17. *Ibid.*, p. 111.

18. See the materials, including the texts by Kurtzel and Schlichtegroll, in Marquis d'Argens, *Thérèse philosophe*, ed. Michael Farin and Hans-Ulrich Seifert.

19. Darnton, *Edition et sédition*, pp. 220–23.

20. Molinism was a system that was first developed by Luis de Molina and was largely adopted by the Jesuits to counter the Reformation's emphasis on predestination. It held that freedom of will was not destroyed by original sin and that free will remains unimpaired, even under the influence of divine grace.

21. Frusta, *Der Flagellantismus*, pp. 127–45. For the reception of this story see Fraxi, *Centuria*, p. 293, and *Catena*, pp. 449ff.

22. Frusta, *Der Flagellantismus*, pp. 224ff.

23. Chiniqui, *The Priest, the Woman, and the Confessional*, pp. 13–14.

24. *Ibid.*, pp. 61–62.

25. *Ibid.*, pp. 14–17.

26. Frusta, *Der Flagellantismus*, p. 150.

27. Philalethes, *Liguori, der Geburtshelfer des Unfehlbarkeitsdogmas, ein Totengräber der Sittlichkeit*.

28. See Vogel, *Le pécheur et la pénitence au Moyen Age* and Vogel, "Composition légale et commutations." For an overview of the practices of penance and confession, see Angenendt, *Geschichte der Religiosität*, pp. 626–58.

29. See Lutterbach, *Sexualität im Mittelalter*.

30. Meens, *Het tripartite boeteboek*, pp. 345ff.

31. Payer, *Sex and the Penitentials*, p. 14.

32. See Bériou, "La confession"; Gy, "Les définitions de la confession."

33. Angenendt, *Geschichte der Religiosität*, p. 651.

34. Suso, *Deutsche Schriften*, ed. Bihlmeyer, pp. 99–100; ed. Tobin, pp. 134–35.

35. Alain of Lille, *Liber poenitantialis* I 3 and 4, vol. 2, pp. 26ff.

36. See *The Irish Penitentials*; Finsterwalder, *Die Canones Theodori Cantuarensis*; Asbach, *Das Poenitentiale Remense*.

37. Alain of Lille, *Liber poenitentialis* I 26, vol. 2, p. 33.

38. Burchard of Worms, *Decretum* XIX 2, *Patrologia Latina*, vol. 140, p. 951. Compare XIX 5, *Patrologia Latina*, vol. 140, pp. 957–60 and pp. 966–68.

39. Petrus Damiani, *Liber Gomorrhianus* X–XIV, *Patrologia Latina*, vol. 145, pp. 172–75 and 186ff. Translation in Peter Damian, *Letters*, ed. Blum, vol. 2, pp. 3–53.

40. Compare the discussion of research literature in Payer, *Sex and the Penitentials*, pp. 13 and 119ff.

41. Alva, *A Guide to Confession*, pp. 135–36.

42. Payer, *Sex and the Penitentials*, p. 121. See also Lutterbach, *Sexualität im Mittelalter*, pp. 247ff.

43. Foucault, *The History of Sexuality, Volume 1: An Introduction*, p. 19.

44. Lutterbach, *Sexualität im Mittelalter*, pp. 256–67.

45. See Tamburini, *Methodus expeditae confessionis,* pp. 133–79; Liguori, *Istruzione e pratica*, vol. 1, pp. 439–63; Liguori, *Homo apostolicus*, vol. 1, pp. 351–68.

46. Liguori, *Institutio catechistica*, pp. 115–19.

47. Tamburini, *Methodus expeditae confessionis*; Liguori, *Institutio catechistica*, and Liguori, *Praxis confessarii*, pp. 50ff. The passages concerning the Sixth Commandment, pp. 13ff. and pp. 180–87, are nowhere to be found in the German translation (Liguori, *Der Beichtvater*).

48. See Liguori, *Institutio catechistica*, pp. 119–23.

49. *Ibid.*, chs. 1–2.

50. Schreckenbach, *Römische Moraltheologie und das 6. Gebot, 1. Teil: Graßmann und der Prinz von Sachsen*, p. 33.

51. *Ibid.*, *Römische Moraltheologie und das 6. Gebot, 2. Teil: Römische Moralentscheidungen*, pp. 37ff.

52. Liguori, *Istruzione e pratica*, vol. 1, pp. 443ff.

53. Philalethes, *Liguori*, pp. 16ff.

54. *Ibid.*, p. 24.

55. Walter, *Unkeuschheit*, pp. 109–20.

56. *Ibid.*, pp. 126ff.

57. The quotes on the following pages are from *Thérèse the Philosopher*, by Jean-Baptiste de Boyer, Marquis d'Argens.

58. Compare the life of Teresa in *Vollständiges Heiligen-Lexikon*, vol. 5, pp. 504ff.

59. See Walter, *Unkeuschheit*, pp. 333–37; for information about the historical background compare pp. 338ff.

60. Sade, *Idée sur les romans*, in *Oeuvres complètes*, vol. 10, pp. 61–80, especially pp. 74–80.

61. See Vila, *Enlightenment and Pathology*, pp. 182–224.

62. Sade, *Juliette*, trans. Wainhouse, pp. 3–4.

63. *Ibid.*, pp. 286–87.

64. *Ibid.*, p. 295.

65. Augustine, *De haeresibus* 31, *Patrologia Latina*, vol. 42, p. 31; Epiphanius, *Adversus octoginta haereses* 52, *Patrologia Graeca*, vol. 41, pp. 953–60; Theodoret, *Haereticorum fabularum compendium* I 6, *Patrologia Graeca*, vol. 83, p. 352; Clement of Alexandria, *Stromata* III 2, *Patrologia Graeca*, vol. 8, pp. 1112–13.

66. Epiphanius, *Adversus octoginta haereses* 26.4, *Patrologia Graeca*, vol. 338; Hippolytus, *Refutatio omnium haeresium*, ed. Duncker, VI 19.5, p. 255.

67. See Lerner, *The Heresy of the Free Spirit*; Vaneigem, *The Movement of the Free Spirit*.

68. A German translation of the texts is in Büttner and Werner, *Circumcellionen und Adamiten*, pp. 79–83.

69. Dubost, *Eros und Vernunft*, p. 35.

70. Gerson, *Oeuvres*, vol. 5, p. 163.

71. See Schuppisser, "Schauen mit den Augen des Herzens," p. 184.

72. Sade, *Philosophy in the Boudoir*, trans. Jones, p. 22.

73. Schertel, *Der Flagellantismus*, vol. 1, p. 1.

74. *Ibid.*, pp. 86ff.

75. *Ibid.*, vol. 2, pp. 115–21.

CHAPTER SIX: THE "ENGLISH VICE"

1. Praz, *The Romantic Agony*, pp. 225ff. and pp. 437–57 (appendix: "Swinburne and 'Le vice Anglais'").

2. Dühren [Iwan Bloch], *Englische Sittengeschichte*, p. 334.

3. See Findlen, "Humanism, Politics, and Pornography."

4. For the history of the Private Case and the Enfer, compare Hunt, "Obscenity and the Origins of Modernity."

5. Fraxi, *Index Librorum Prohibitorum*, p. xxvi.

6. *Ibid.*, p. xl.

7. Marcus, *The Other Victorians*.

8. Vinken, *Unentrinnbare Neugierde*, pp. 24ff.

9. Marcus, *The Other Victorians*, pp. 125–26.

10. *Ibid.*, pp. 126–27.

11. See Lafourcade, *La Jeunesse de Swinburne*, vol. 2, p. 132; Praz, *The Romantic Agony*, p. 227.

12. See Rooksby, *A. C. Swinburne*, pp. 34–41.

13. Swinburne, *The Chronicle of Tebaldeo Tebaldei*, 1861. Quoted in Praz, *The Romantic Agony*, p. 226.

14. Bataille, *Œuvres*, vol. 5, pp. 18ff.

15. Text quoted in Rooksby, *A. C. Swinburne*, p. 76.

16. See *Ibid.*, p. 151.

17. *Ibid.*, p. 154.

18. *Ibid.*, pp. 164–65.

19. *Ibid.*, pp. 265–66.

20. Swinburne, *Lesbia Brandon*, p. 333.

21. Joyce, *Portrait*, p. 44.

22. See Joyce, *Ulysses*, chapter 15, vol. 2, pp. 1007–15.

23. Joyce, letter dated September 2, 1909, in *Selected Letters*, pp. 166–67.

24. Joyce, fragment of a letter dated December 13, 1909, in *Selected Letters*, pp. 188–89.

25. Joyce, *Dubliners*, ed. Scholes, pp. 27ff.

26. See Lamos, "James Joyce and the English Vice."

27. See Marcus, *The Other Victorians*, pp. 104–105 and pp. 252–65.

28. See Cooper, *A History of the Rod*, pp. 398–461.

29. See *Ibid.*, pp. 462–77. Compare the discussion in *The Times*, June 13–14, 1904.

30. *Ibid.*, pp. 464ff.

31. Swinburne, *William Blake*, p. 158. Quoted in Praz, *The Romantic Agony*, p. 234.

32. Quoting from Praz, *The Romantic Agony*, p. 449.

CHAPTER SEVEN: THE "HEALING WHIP"

1. Frusta, *Der Flagellantismus.*

2. See Schwarz, *Die medizinische Flagellation*, pp. 13ff. and 27–32. All the histories of flagellation published since the nineteenth century contain a good number of such anecdotes.

3. See Heckenbach, *De nuditate sacra*, pp. 17–19.

4. Paullini, *Flagellum salutis*, introduction, p. 4. The volume contains two other treatises: *Wunderbare Kuren durch Musik*, by F. G. Nieten, and *Lebensverlängerung bis auf 115 Jahre durch den Hauch junger Mädchen*, by J. H. Cohausen, M.D.

5. *Ibid.*, p. 3.

6. Paullini, *Zeit-kuertzende erbauliche Lust*, introduction.

7. Meibom, *Utilité de la flagellation*, p. 37.

8. The following passages are translated from the German version of this text in *Der Schatzgräber in den literarischen und bildlichen Seltenheiten, Sonderbarkeiten etc. hauptsächlich des deutschen Mittelalters. IV. Theil: I. K. F. Paullini's heilsame Dreck-Apotheke, wie nemlich mit Koth und Urin die meisten Krankheiten und Schäden glücklich geheilet worden. II. Von dem Nutzen des Geißelns in medizinischer und physischer Beziehung, von J. H. Meibomius und Anderen*, ed. J. Scheible (Stuttgart: Kloster, 1847). This volume contains the letter written by Bartholin on October 24, 1669, pp. 248–60; the original treatise by Meibomius from 1639, pp. 260–84; a letter by Henry Meibom to Bartholin from "September 1669," pp. 285–91; a version of the treatise with additional materials (and with the new title *Die Nützlichkeit der Geißelhiebe in den Vergnügungen der Ehe, so wie in der ärztlichen Praxis, und die Verrichtungen der Lenden und Nieren*), pp. 293–351; *Bemerkungen des Thomas Bartholin (Auszug eines Schreibens desselben an Heinr. Meibomius)*, a paraphrase of the letter "vom 24. Okt. 1669"), pp. 351–59; an *Auszug aus dem Antwortschreiben von Meibomius Sohn an T. H. Bartholin* (a paraphrase of the letter from "September 1669"), pp. 359–63; as well as some additional *Zusätze*. The volume also contains another text on flagellation, *Das Geißeln und seine Einwirkung auf den Geschlechtstrieb, oder das äußerliche Aphrodisiacum, eine medizinisch-philosophische Abhandlung. Nebst einem Anhang: über die Mittel, welche den Zeugungstrieb aufregen. Von D****, praktizierender Arzt. Aus dem Franz. 1788*, pp. 367–424. The texts of this edition depend on the French translation published by Mercier in 1792. There is no question that the German publisher's motives

were primarily financial. He published also Frusta, *Der Flagellantismus und die Jesuitenbeichte.*

9. The French text: "un très-joli frontispice non signé, représentant Cupidon flagellée par les Nymphes; Vénus dans les nuages, assise sur son char, traîné par les deux colombes traditionelles, offre un fouet à lanières à l'une d'elles; l'Amour, don't le carquois est tombé par terre, est placée comme un bambino, le derrière en l'air, sur les genoux d'une Nymphe, qui le fustige avec une branche de rosier, tandis qu'une troisième est en train de lier une poignée de verges."

10. Call number: P.C.13.h.13.

11. Vital Puissant published under the pseudonym "Viest' Lainopts, Bibliophile," in "London and Paris 1875" the *Essais bibliographiques sur deux ouvrages intitulés: De l'utilité de la Flagellation, par J. H. Meibomius, et Traité du Fouet de F. A. Doppet, etc.*

12. Quotes and translations are based on *Der Schatzgräber*, pp. 307ff.

13. *Ibid.*, p. 318.

14. *Ibid.*, p. 319.

15. See Jacob, "The Materialist World," pp. 175ff.

16. Davidson, "The Emergence of Sexuality," p. 44.

17. *Der Schatzgräber*, p. 293.

18. *Ibid.*, pp. 296ff.

19. *Ibid.*, p. 348.

20. *Ibid.*, p. 370.

21. *Ibid.*, p. 372.

22. I quote the following passages from Paullini, *Flagellum salutis.*

23. *Ibid.*, p. 101, where we find this passage again.

24. "Von trägem Beischlaff," in Paullini, *Flagellum salutis*, pp. 73–83.

CHAPTER EIGHT: PICO'S FRIEND; OR, THE BASIS OF FLAGELLOMANIA

1. Krafft-Ebing, *Psychopathia sexualis*, p. 22.

2. Frusta, *Der Flagellantismus*, pp. 249f.

3. Krafft-Ebing, *Psychopathia sexualis*, pp. 110–11. Compare Rousseau, *Confessions*, p. 15.

4. See Wanda von Sacher-Masoch, *The Confessions of Wanda von Sacher-Masoch*, pp. 32–33.

5. Krafft-Ebing, *Psychopathia Sexualis*, pp. 93–114, 130–43.

6. For a critique of Krafft-Ebing see Sadger, "Über den sado-masochistischen Komplex."

7. Fischart, *Geschichtsklitterung*, p. 103. I am quoting from Walter, *Unkeuschheit*, p. 119.

8. See Lutterbach, *Sexualität*, pp. 41ff.; Walter, *Unkeuschheit*, pp. 75ff.

9. Walter, *Unkeuschheit*, p. 78.

10. Kaan, *Psychopathia Sexualis*, pp. 47ff.

11. *Ibid.*, p. 39.

12. Bornemann, *Lexikon der Liebe*, p. 395.

13. *Ibid.*, p. 112.

14. Capellmann, *Pastoralmedizin*.

15. Compare, for example, the video *On Edge: Ron Athey's Artful Crown of Thorns*, by C. Carr. See also Mennighaus, *Ekel*, pp. 492ff., 549–67.

16. Bataille, *Œuvres*, vol. 2, p. 351.

EPILOGUE

1. Robin, *L'imaginaire*, pp. 28ff.

2. Proust, *Finding Time Again*, pp. 117–48.

3. Curtius, "Proust," p. 81.

4. Jaloux, review of *Le temps retrouvé*.

Bibliography

The Bibliography includes sources and studies cited in the text and notes, as well as further literature of importance for the genesis of the book.

Primary Sources

L'Académie des dames, ou La philosophie dans le boudoir du Grand Siècle: Dialogues érotiques présentés par Jean-Pierre Dubost (Arles: Picquier, 1999).

Achéry, Luc d', *Spicilegium seu collectio veterum aliquot scriptorum qui in Galliae bibliothecis delituerunt*, 3 vols. (Paris: Montalant, 1723).

Aegidius li Muisit, *Chronica Aegidii li Muisis*, in *Corpus chronicorum Flandriae*, ed. Joseph-Jean de Smet, vol. 2 (Brussels: M. Hayez, 1841), pp. 111–448.

Ahle, Michael, *Die Moral der Jesuiten, eine Gefahr für Recht und Sitte* (Leipzig: Nationale Verlagsgesellschaft, 1937).

Alanus ab Insulis, *Liber poenitentialis*, ed. Jean Longère, 2 vols., Analecta mediaevalia Namurcensia 17–18 (Louvain: Editions Nauwelaerts, 1965).

Alva, Don Bartolomé de, *A Guide to Confession, Large and Small, in the Mexican Language*, ed. Barry D. Sell and John Frederick Schwaller, with Lu Ann Homza (1634; Norman: University of Oklahoma Press, 1999).

Ambrose, *De Iacob et vita beata*, Corpus scriptorum ecclesiasticorum latinorum 32, 2 (Vienna: F. Tempsky, 1897).

Ancelet-Hustache, Jeanne, "Les 'Vitae sororum' d'Unterlinden," *Edition critique du manuscrit 508 de la bibliothèque de Colmar, Archives d'histoire doctrinale et littéraire du Moyen Age* 5 (1930), pp. 317–509.

Annales Ianuenses annorum 1249–1264, ed. Gregorius H. Pertz, Monumenta Germaniae Historica: Scriptores 18 (Hannover: Hahniani, 1866; reprint, Stuttgart: Koch, Neff & Oetinger, 1990), pp. 226–48.

Annales Mechovienses, ed. Richard Röpell and Wilhelm F. Arndt, Monumenta Germaniae Historica: Scriptores 19 (Hannover: Hahniani, 1866; reprint, Stuttgart: Koch, Neff & Oetinger, 1989), pp. 666–77.

Annales Mellicenses, ed. Wilhelm Wattenbach, Monumenta Germaniae Historica: Scriptores 9 (Hannover: Hahniani, 1851; reprint, Stuttgart: Koch, Neff & Oetinger, 1989), pp. 480–535.

Annales Sanctae Justinae Patavini, ed. Philipp Jaffé, Monumenta Germaniae Historica: Scriptores 19 (Hannover: Hahniani, 1866; reprint, Stuttgart: Koch, Neff & Oetinger, 1989), pp. 148–93.

Anonymous, *Bottoms Up! A Spanking Proves to Be an Effective Stimulus* (ca. 1931).

———, *Experiences of Flagellation: A Series of Remarkable Instances of Whipping Inflicted on Both Sexes; With Curious Anecdotes of Ladies Fond of Administering Birch Discipline, Compiled by an Amateur Flagellant* (London: private printing, 1885).

———, *History of Flagellation Among Different Nations: A Narrative of the Strange Customs and Cruelties of the Romans, Greeks, Egyptians, etc. with an Account of its Practice Among the Early Christians as a Religious Stimulant and Corrector of Morals; Also Anecdotes of Remarkable Cases of Flogging, and of Celebrated Flagellants, with Numerous Illustrations* (New York: Medical Publishing Co., 1903).

———, *Jesuiten-Liebschaften, oder Die Väter der Gesellschaft Jesu in gutem Humor* (Rome and Paris: no publisher 1869).

———, *Ladies of the Whip* (no place, publisher, or date).

———, *Manon la fouetteuse, or the Quintessence of Birch Discipline, Translated from the French by Rebecca Birch, Late Teacher at Mrs. Busby's Young Ladies Boarding School* (London: Printed for the Society of Vice, ca. 1860).

———, *Mémoirs d'une danseuse russe: La flagellation en Russie* (Paris: no publisher, 1905).

———, *Venus School-Mistress, or Birchen Sports; Reprinted from the Edition of 1788* (New York: Blue Moon Books, 1987).

———, *Wahrhaffte und curieuse Liebes-Geschichte des Jesuiten Sainfroids und der scheinheiligen Eulaliae, aus dem Frantzösischen ins Teutsche übersetzet* (no place and publisher, 1729).

Anthony, see *Vita Antonii* and Athanasius of Alexandria.

Apollinaire, Guillaume, *L'Enfer de la Bibliothèque Nationale: Icono-bio-bibliographie descriptive, critique et raisonnée, complète à ce jour, de tous les ouvrages composant cette célèbre collection, avec un index alphabétique et une table des auteurs* (Paris: Mercure de France, 1913).

————, *Les onze mille verges* (Paris: L'Or du Temps, 1970).

Aretino, Pietro, *Aretino's Dialogues*, trans. Raymond Rosenthal (New York: Stein and Day, 1971).

————, *Kurtisanen-Gespräche*, trans. Heinrich Conrad (Munich: Heyne, 1991).

————, *La cortigiana*, ed. Giuliano Innamorati (Turin: Einaudi, 1970).

————, *Ragionamenti*, ed. Paul Larivaille and Giovanni Aquilecchia, 2 vols. (Paris: Les Belles Lettres, 1998–99).

————, *Ragionamento: Dialogo*, ed. Nino Borsellino (Milan: Garzanti, 1984).

————, *Sonetti lussuriosi (i Modi) e dubbi amorosi: Nuova edizione integrale*, ed. Riccardo Reim (Rome: Newton Compton, 1993).

Argens, Jean Baptiste de Boyer, Marquis d', *Thérèse philosophe*, ed. Jacques Duprilot (Geneva: Slatkine, 1980).

————, *Thérèse philosophe: Eine erotische Beichte; Aus dem Französischen von Heinrich Conrad. Mit 38 Illustrationen, einem Aufsatz von August Kurtzel, einer Erzählung von Carl Felix von Schlichtegroll, sowie Auszügen aus den Prozeßakten und Notaten der Herausgeber*, ed. Michael Farin and Hans-Ulrich Seifert (Munich: Schneekluth, 1990).

————, *Thérèse the Philosopher*, trans. H. F. Smith (New York: Grove Press, 1970).

[Argens, Marquis d'], *Thérèse philosophe, ou Mémoires pour servir à l'histoire du P. Dirrag, & de Mademoiselle Eradice* (Paris: La Haye, 1748).

Ars erotica, ed. Ludwig von Brunn, 3 vols. (Schwerte: Harenberg, 1983–89).

Artaud, Antonin, *Œuvres completes* (Paris: Gallimard, 1976).

Articuli, quos tenuerunt et crediderunt heretici capti in Sundirshausen et combusti, ed. Alexander Reifferscheid, in *Neun Texte zur Geschichte der religiösen Aufklärung in Deutschland während des 14. und 15. Jahrhunderts: Festschrift der Universität Greifswald 1905* (Greifswald: Abel, 1905), pp. 37–40.

Articuli, quos tenuerunt et crediderunt heretici Zangerhusene, ed. Alexander Reifferscheid, in *Neun Texte zur Geschichte der religiösen Aufklärung in Deutschland während des 14. und 15. Jahrhunderts. Festschrift der Universität Greifswald 1905* (Greifswald: Abel, 1905), pp. 32–36.

L'ascéticisme dans l'ordre de St. Dominique, ed. Matthieu-Joseph Rousset, 2 vols. (Paris, 1899).

Ashbee, Henry Spencer, *Bibliography of Prohibited Books*, 3 vols. (London 1877–85; facsimile New York: Jack Brossel, 1962).

———, [Pisanus Fraxi], *Catena librorum tacendorum: Being Notes Bio-, Biblio-, Icono-graphical and Critical, on Curious and Uncommon Books* (London: private printing, 1885).

———, *Centuria librorum absconditorum: Being Notes Bio-, Biblio-, Icono-graphical and Critical, on Curious and Uncommon Books* (London: private printing, 1879).

———, *Index librorum prohibitorum: Being Notes Bio-, Biblio-, Icono-graphical and Critical, on Curious and Uncommon Books* (London: private printing, 1877).

Athanasius of Alexandria, "Life of Antony," in *Select Writings of Athanasius*, Library of Nicene and Post Nicene Fathers 2, 4 (New York: Christian Literature Publishing Company, 1924; reprint 1957).

———, see also *Vita Antonii*.

Gli Atti della visita apostolica di santo Carlo Borromeo a Bergamo, ed. Angelo Giuseppe Roncalli, vol. 1, pt. 2 (Florence: L. S. Olschki, 1937).

Augustinus, Aurelius, *De haeresibus ad Quodvultdeum liber unus, Patrologia Latina*, ed. Jacques-Paul Migne, vol. 42 (Paris: Migne, 1841), pp. 21–50.

———, *De fide rerum invisibilium: Enchiridion ad Laurentium de fide et spe et caritate. De catechizandis rudibus. Sermo ad catechumenos de symbolo. Sermo de disciplina christiana. Sermo de utilitate ieiunii. Sermo de excidio urbis Romae. De haeresibus*, Corpus christianorum. Series Latina 46 (Turnhout: Brepols, 1969).

Ball, Hugo, *Die Flucht aus der Zeit* (Lucerne: Stocker, 1946).

Bartolocci, Giulio, *Bibliotheca magna rabbinica de scriptoribus, & scriptis rabbinicis, ordine alphabetico Hebraice, & Latine digestis . . .* , 5 vols. (Rome: Sacrae Congregationis de Propaganda Fide, 1675–94; reprint, Farnborough: Gregg, 1965–68).

Bataille, Georges, *Œuvres complètes*, ed. Michel Foucault, 12 vols. (Paris: Gallimard, 1971–88).

Bergmann, Ernst, *Katechismus der Jesuitenmoral*, 2nd ed. (Leipzig: Breitkopf and Härtel, 1936).

Bertram, James G., *The Merry Order of St. Bridget: Personal Recollections of the Use of the Rod* (York, 1857). New ed. "by Margaret Anson" (North Hollywood, CA: Brandon House, 1966).

————, *Une société de flagellantes: Réminiscences et révélations d'une soubrette de grande maison, par Marguerite Anson, adapté de l'anglais par Jean de Villiot, illustrations d'Adolphe Lambrecht* (Paris: C. Carrington, 1901).

————, see also Cooper, William M.

Beta, Ottomar H., *Darwin, Deutschland und die Juden, oder, Der Juda-Jesuitismus: Dreiunddreissig Thesen nebst einer Nachschrift über einen vergessenen Factor der Volkswirthschaft*, 2nd ed. (Berlin, 1876).

Bishop, George, *Flagellation: The Rod and the Whip* (Hollywood, CA: Genell, 1963).

Bizarre classix, vol. 1– (New York: Belier Press, 1970–).

Bloch, Iwan [Eugen Dühren], *Englische Sittengeschichte*, 2nd rev. ed. (Berlin: Marcus, 1912). First ed.: *Das Geschlechtsleben in England, mit besonderer Beziehung auf London*, 3 vols. (Charlottenburg: Lilienthal, 1901–1903).

Bloch, Iwan, *Der Marquis de Sade und seine Zeit: Ein Beitrag zur Kultur- und Sittengeschichte des 18. Jahrhunderts* (Hanau: Heyne, 1970).

————, *Marquis de Sade: The Man and His Age*, trans. James Bruce (New York: AMS Press, 1974).

Boileau, Jacques, *Histoire des Flagellans, ou l'on fait voir le bon et le mauvais usage des flagellations parmi les chrétiens . . . traduit du Latin de Mr. l'Abbé Boileau* (Amsterdam: François vander Plaats, 1701).

————, *Historia flagellantium: De recto et perverso flagrorum usu apud christianos, ex antiquis Scripturae, Patrum, Pontificum, Conciliorum, & Scriptorum Profanorum monumentis cum cura et fide expressa* (Paris: Apud Joannem Anisson Typographiae Regiae Praefectum, 1700).

————, *A Just and Seasonable Reprehension of Naked Breasts and Shoulders, Written by a Grave and Learned Papist, Translated by Edward Cooke, esq., with a Preface by Mr. Richard Baxter* (London: J. Edwin, 1678).

————, *De l'abus des nuditez de gorge*, 2nd ed. (Paris: Laize de Bresche, 1677).

Boileau-Despréaux, Nicolas, *Œuvres* (Paris, 1969).

Bornemann, Ernest, *Lexikon der Liebe: Materialien zur Sexualwissenschaft* (1978; Vienna: Ullstein, 1984).

Brantôme, Pierre de, *Vies des dames galantes*, ed. Maurice Rat (Paris: Club Bibliophile de France, 1953).

Buckle, Henry Thomas, see *Library Illustrative of Social Progress*.

Burchard von Worms, *Decretum*, in *Patrologia Latina*, ed. Jacques-Paul Migne, vol. 140 (Paris: Migne, 1853), pp. 537–1090.

Cabanès, Augustin, *Les indiscretions de l'histoire*, 6 vols. (Paris: Michel, 1903–1909).

Capellmann, Karl, *Pastoralmedizin*, 18th rev. and augmented ed., ed. Wilhelm Bergmann (Paderborn: Bonifacius, 1920).

Carrington, Charles, *Flagellation in France from a Medical and Historical Standpoint* (Paris: Charles Carrington, 1898).

Castiglione, Baldassare, *Der Hofmann: Lebensart in der Renaissance* (Berlin: Wagenbach, 1996).

Castiglione, Giovanni A., *Gli honori de gli antichi disciplinati* (Milan: G. B. Bidelli, 1613).

Castor, Dr., *Das sexuelle Moment im Flagellantismus* (Berlin: Wrede, 1899).

Cheffontaine, Christophe de, *Apologie de la confrérie des pénitents érigée et instituée en la ville de Paris par le très chrestien roy de France et Pollogne Henri III de son nom* (Paris, 1583).

Chiniqui, [Charles], *The Priest, the Woman, and the Confessional.* (New York: Christ's Mission, no date).

Choderlos de Laclos, Pierre A., *Les liaisons dangereuses* (Paris: Editions Rencontre, 1969).

Chronicon rhythmicum Austriacum, ed. Wilhelm Wattenbach, Monumenta Germaniae Historica: Scriptores 25 (Hannover: Hahnsche, 1880), pp. 349–68.

Chronik von Heiligenkreuz, see *Continuatio Sancrucensis*.

Die Chroniken der deutschen Städte vom 14. bis ins 16. Jahrhundert, hg. durch die Historische Kommission bei der Bayerischen Akademie der Wissenschaften (vol. 7, Magdeburg, vol. 1, Leipzig: Hirzel, 1869; reprint, Göttingen: Vandenhoeck and Ruprecht, 1962; vol. 8, Strassburg, vol. 1, Leipzig: Hirzel, 1870; reprint, Göttingen: Vandenhoeck und Ruprecht, 1961).

Closener, Fritsche, *Straßburgische Chronik*, Bibliothek des Literarischen Vereins in Stuttgart 1 (Stuttgart: Litterarischer Verein, 1843).

Coleman, George, *The Rodiad* (London: Cadell and Murray, 1810).

Le compagnie de' battuti in Roma nell'anno MCCCLXXXXVIIII (Bologna: Rist. Bologna, 1862).

Continuatio Sancrucensis secunda, ed. Wilhelm Wattenbach, Monumenta Germaniae Historica: Scriptores 9 (Hannover: Hahnsche, 1851), pp. 637–46.

Cooper, William M. [James G. Bertram], *A History of the Rod in All Countries: From the Earliest Period to the Present Time,* rev. ed. (London: Reeves, 1896).

———, *Der Flagellantismus und die Flagellanten: Die Geschichte der Rute in allen*

Ländern, ins Deutsche übertragen von H. Dohrn, mit Illustrationen, 2nd ed. (Dresden: Dohrn, 1903).

Corpus chronicorum Flandriae, ed. Joseph-Jean de Smet, vol. 2 (Brussels: Hayez, 1841).

Corpus documentorum inquisitionis haereticae pravitatis Neerlandicae, ed. Paul Fredericq, 5 vols. (Ghent: Vuylsteke, 1889–1906).

Corvin, Otto von, *Die Geißler: Historische Denkmale des Fanatismus in der römisch-katholischen Kirche; Ergänzungswerk zum Pfaffenspiegel, 330. Tausend* (Berlin: A. Bock, no date).

Cudgel, Th., *La Flagellation dans l'histoire et les tortures au moyen âge* (Paris: Librairie artistique, 1922).

D*** [François Amédé Doppet], *Aphrodisiaque externe, ou traité du fouet et de ses effets sur le physique de l'amour: Ouvrage medico-philosophique, suivi d'une dissertation sur tous les moyens capables d'exciter aux plaisirs de l'amour, par D***, médecin* (1788, no location or publisher; reprint, Lyon: À rebours, 2004).

———, *Das Geißeln und seine Einwirkung auf den Geschlechtstrieb, oder das äußerliche Aphrodisiacum, eine medizinisch-philosophische Abhandlung: Nebst einem Anhang über die Mittel, welche den Zeugungstrieb aufregen, von D***, praktizierender Arzt* (translated from the French in 1788), in *Der Schatzgräber in den literarischen und bildlichen Seltenheiten*, pt. 4, ed. Joseph Scheible (Stuttgart: Kloster, 1847), pp. 367–424.

Davenport, John, *Aphrodisiacs and Love Stimulants: With Other Chapters on The Secrets of Venus*, ed. Alan Hull Walton (New York: L. Stuart, 1966).

De Gregori, Giacomo, *Capitoli della prima compagnia di disciplina di San Niccolò di Palermo* (Palermo: no publisher, 1891).

Deutsch, Gustav A., *Die Jesuiten und ihre schändliche Moral, ihre "geheimen Instruktionen," ihre Unterdrückung durch den Papst selbst, ihre scheußlichen Grundsätze...* (Würzburg: Woerl, 1891).

Diez, Philippus, *Der Evangelische Lauttenschlager. Das ist: Zwo schoene unnd ueber alle Lautten liebliche Betrachtungen, bey dem Himmel Raeyen und Evangelischen Tantz, deren so in der Charfreytags Procession sich selbsten Discipliniren, erstlich in Spanischer Sprach beschrieben durch... Philippum Diez... hernach in die Lateinische, jetzo aber... in die Deutsche Sprach versetzt, durch Conradum Vetter* ... (Ingolstadt: Andreas Angermaier, 1610).

Donner, Johann, see Zeaemann, Georg.

Doppet, François Amédé, see D***.

Dühren, Eugen, see Bloch, Iwan.

Dumarchey, Pierre [Pierre MacOrlan], *Les Grandes Flagellées de l'Histoire: Etude sur la flagellation disciplinaire des femmes en Europe; 20 illustrations hors-texte par Jean MacOrlan* (Paris, no date).

Duriès, Vanessa, *Le lien* (Paris: J'ai lu, 1993).

Ebner, Christina, see *Leben und Gesichte der Christina Ebnerin*.

Ebner, Margareta, see Strauch, Philipp.

Eck, Johannes, *De non tollendis Christi et sanctorum Imaginibus...* (Ingolstadt: Lutz, 1522).

Ellmann, Richard, *James Joyce*, rev. and completed ed. (Frankfurt: Suhrkamp, 1994).

Encyclopédie, ou dictionnaire raisonné des sciences, des arts et des métiers, ed. Denis Diderot and Jean LeRond d'Alembert (Paris: Briasson, 1751–80; reprint, Stuttgart: Frommann-Holzboog, 1966–67).

Engel, Ludwig, *Der Jesuitismus, eine Staatsgefahr* (Munich: Ludendorffs, 1935).

Epiphanius, *Adversus octoginta haereses*, in *Patrologia Graeca*, ed. Jacques-Paul Migne, vols. 41 and 42 (Paris: Migne, 1858).

———, *Werke*, ed. Karl Holl, 3 vols. (Leipzig 1915–33); 2nd rev. ed., ed. Jürgen Dummer Griechische christliche Schriftsteller der ersten drei Jahrhunderte 25, 31, 37 (Berlin: Akademie-Verlag 1980 85).

Eulenburg, Albert, *Der Marquis de Sade: Vortrag gehalten im Psychologischen Verein* (Berlin and Dresden, no publisher, 1901).

———, *Sadismus und Masochismus* (Wiesbaden: Bergmann, 1902; 2nd ed., Wiesbaden: Bergmann, 1911).

———, *Sexuale Neuropathie: Genitale Neurosen und Neuropsychosen der Männer und Frauen* (Leipzig: Vogel, 1895).

Evagrios, Pontikos, *Über die acht Gedanken*, ed. Gabriel Bunge (Würzburg: Echter, 1992).

Farin, Michael, see *Lust am Schmerz* and Argens, Marquis d'.

Fetzer, Karl A. [Giovanni Frusta], *Der Flagellantismus und die Jesuitenbeichte: His-torisch-psychologische Geschichte der Geisselungsinstitute, Klosterzüchtigungen und Beichtstuhlverirrungen aller Zeiten* (Leipzig and Stuttgart, no publisher, 1834).

Fischart, Johann, *Geschichtsklitterung*, ed. A. Alsleben, Neudrucke deutscher Lit-eraturwerke des XVI. und XVII. Jahrhunderts 65, 71 (Halle: Niemeyer, 1891).

Förstemann, Ernst G., *Die christlichen Geißlergesellschaften* (Halle: Renger, 1828).

Foucault, Michel, *Dits et Ecrits*, 4 vols. (Paris: Gallimard, 1994).

————, *Histoire de la sexualité*, 3 vols., vol. 1, *La volonté de savoir*; vol. 2, *L'usage des plasirs*; vol. 3, *Le souci de soi* (Paris: Gallimard, 1976–84).

————, *The History of Sexuality, Volume 1: An Introduction*, trans Robert Hurley (New York: Vintage, 1978).

————, *Sexualität und Wahrheit*, vol. 1, *Der Wille zum Wissen* (Frankfurt: Suhrkamp, 1983).

François de Sales, *Introduction à la vie dévote*, ed. Etienne-Marie Lajeunie (Paris: Seuil, 1962).

————, *Introduction to the Devout Life*, trans. and ed. Allan Ross (London: Burns, Oates, and Washbourne, 1937).

————, *Œuvres*, 27 vols. (Annecy: Niérat, 1892–1932).

Fraxi, Pisanus, see Ashbee, Henry Spencer.

Fredericq, Paul, *De Secten der Geeselaars en der dansers in de Nederlanden Tijden de 14 de eeuw* (Brussels, no date or publisher given).

————, *Inquisitio haereticae pravitatis neerlandica: Geschiedenis der inquisitie in de Nederlanden tot aan hare herinrichting onder Keizer Karel V (1025–1520)*, 2 vols. (Ghent: Vuylsteke, 1892–97).

————, see also *Corpus documentorum inquisitionis*.

Frusta, Giovanni, see Fetzer, Karl A.

Fülöp-Miller, René, *Macht und Geheimnis der Jesuiten* (Leipzig: Grethlem, 1930).

Fürstauer, Johanna, . . . *mit Rohrstock und Peitsche: Eine Sittengeschichte der Flagellomanie, verbesserte Neuausgabe* (Konstanz: Exakt-Verlag, 1969).

Gay, Jules, *Bibliographie des ouvrages relatifs à l'amour, aux femmes, au mariage, contenant les titres détaillés de ces ouvrages, les noms des auteurs, un aperçu de leur sujet, leur valeur et leur prix dans les ventes, l'indication de ceux qui ont été poursuivis ou qui ont subi des condamnations, etc., par M. le c. d'I****, 2. édition, revue, corrigée et considérablement augmentée (Paris: J. Gay, 1864).

Gemälde aus dem Nonnenleben, see Lipowsky, Felix J.

Gerson, Jean, *Contra sectam flagellantium*, in Gerson, *Œuvres*, vol. 10, pp. 46–51.

————, *Gerson à Vincent Ferrier, Constance, 9 et 21 juin 1417*, in Gerson, *Œuvres*, vol. 2, pp. 200–202.

————, *Œuvres complètes*, ed. Palémon Glorieux, vol. 2, (Paris: Desclée, 1960), vol. 5 (Paris: Desclée, 1963), vol. 10 (Paris: Desclée, 1973).

Gesta archiepiscoporum Magdeburgensium, ed. Wilhelm Schum, in Monumenta Germaniae historica: Scriptores 14 (Hannover: Hahniani 1883), pp. 361–484.

Gibson, Ian, *The English Vice: Beating, Sex and Shame in Victorian England and After* (London: Duckworth, 1978).

Gide, André, *Journal, vol. 1: 1887–1925*, ed. Eric Marty (Paris: Gallimard, 1996).

———, *Journal, vol. 2: 1926–1950*, ed. Martine Sagaert (Paris: Gallimard, 1997).

Giovanni de Galeriis, *Il laudario dei battuti di Modena*, ed. Giulio Bertoni, *Zeitschrift für romanische Philologie*, Beiheft 20 (Halle: Niemeyer, 1909).

Goodland, Roger, *A Bibliography of Sex Rites and Customs: An Annotated Record of Books, Articles, and Illustrations in all Languages* (1931; reprint, London: Longwood, 1977).

Grassmann, Robert, *Auszüge aus der von den Päpsten Gregor XVI., Pius IX. und Leo XIII. als Norm für die römische Kirche sanktionierten Moraltheologie des Heiligen Dr. Alphonsus Maria de Liguori und die furchtbare Gefahr dieser Moraltheologie für die Sittlichkeit der Völker* (Stettin: R. Grassmann, 1909).

Greith, Carl, *Die deutsche Mystik im Prediger-Orden (von 1250–1350): Nach ihren Grundlehren, Liedern und Lebensbildern aus handschriftlichen Quellen* (1861; reprint, Amsterdam: Rodopi, 1965).

Gretser, Jacob, *De cruce Christi rebusque ad eam pertinentibus libri quatuor* (Ingolstadt: Andreas Angermaier, 1598).

———, *Disciplinbuch. Das ist: Von der Leibscasteyung und Mortification, welche nach altem und der Catholischen Kirchen wolbekanntem Brauch durch Geißlen oder Disciplinen geschicht und ueblich gehalten wirdt, erstlich Lateinisch ... beschrieben durch P. Jacobum Gretserum ... Jetzo aber ... verteutscht durch P. Conradum Vetterum ...* (Ingolstadt: Andreas Angermaier, 1609).

———, *De disciplinis*, see Gretser, *Disciplinbuch* and *Opera omnia*.

———, *De sacris et religiosis peregrinationibus libri quatuor: Eiusdem de Catholicae ecclesiae processionibus seu supplicationibus libri duo; Quibus adiuncti: De voluntaria flagellorum cruce, seu de disciplinarum usu libri tres* (Ingolstadt: Adam Sartorius, 1606).

———, *De spontanea disciplinarum seu flagellorum cruce libri tres* (Cologne: Hermann Mylius, 1606).

———, *Opera omnia*, 17 vols. (Regensburg: Peez & Bader, 1743–41). Volume 4 contains the following relevant titles: *Defensio rituum ecclesiae, pars I, De disciplinis: 1. De voluntaria flagellorum seu disciplinarum cruce libri III; 2. Spici-*

legium de usu voluntariae per flagra castigationis pro III libellis de disciplinis; 3.
Praedicans vapulans et disciplinatus ob III libellos de disciplinis; 4. *Virgidemia*
Volciana; 5. *Agonisticum spirituale in gratiam duorum Praedicantium*; 6. *Athlet-*
icae spiritualis geminae, legitimae et illegitimae, libri II; 7. *Praedicans Heauton-*
timerumenos.

————, *I. Virgidemia Volciana. II. Antistrena Polycarpica . . .* (Ingolstadt: Adam
Sartorius, 1608). The volume also includes: Jacobi Gretseri, . . . *De spontanea*
disciplinarum seu flagellorum cruce libri tres.

Gretser, Jacob and Conrad Vetter, *Procession Buch. Das ist: Catholischer Grundt*
vnd außführliche Erklärung Von den heiligen Bettfahrten, Creutzgängen vnd
Processionen, so nach vhraltem Gebrauch in der gantzen allgemeinen Christenheit
gehalten werden . . . erstlich Lateinisch, jetzo aber auch Teutsch . . . in offentlichen
Truck befördert. . . . (Ingolstadt: Andreas Angermaier, 1612).

Haas, Karl M., *Das Theater der Jesuiten in Ingolstadt: Ein Beitrag zur Geschichte des*
geistlichen Theaters in Süddeutschland, Die Schaubühne 51 (Emsdetten in
Westphalia: Lechte, 1958).

Hardt, Hermann von der, *Magnum oecumenicum Constantiense concilium de uni-*
versali ecclesiæ reformatione, unione, et fide . . . , 6 vols. (Frankfurt and Leipzig:
C. Genschius, 1697–1700).

Hayn, Hugo, *Bibliotheca erotica et curiosa Monacensis: Verzeichniss französischer,*
italienischer, spanischer, englischer, holländischer und neulateinischer Erotica
und Curiosa, von welchen keine deutschen Übersetzungen bekannt sind (Berlin:
Harrwitz, 1889).

————, *Bibliotheca Germanorum erotica: Verzeichniss der gesammten deutschen ero-*
tischen Literatur mit den Übersetzungen und Angabe der Original- und Markt-
preise, 2. stark vermehrte Auflage (Leipzig: Unflad, 1885).

————, *Vier neue Curiositäten-Bibliographien: Bayrischer Hiesel, Amazonen-Lit-*
teratur, Halsbandprozeß und Cagliostro, Bibliotheca selecta erotico-curiosa Dres-
denis (1905; reprint, Berlin: Zentral Antiquariat der DDR, 1967).

Hefele, Carl J., *Histoire des conciles d'après les documents originaux*, ed. Henri
Leclercq, 12 vols. (1907–52; reprint, Hildesheim: Olms, 1973).

Heilbrunner, Jacob, *Flagellatio Jesuitica: Jesuiterische Lehr vom genannten frey-*
willigen Creutz der Disciplinen oder Geisel, auch von desselben Frucht und Ver-
dienst; Sampt deroselben, wie auch aller praetendirten Behelff und Einreden,
außführlicher gegründter Ableinung, Dem für uns gegeiselten und gecreutzigten
Son Gottes zu Ehren, auch allen frommen Christen trewhertziger erinnerung vnnd

warnung gestelt, durch Jacob Heilbrunner . . . (Lauingen: Jakob Winter, 1607).

————, see also Zeaemann, Georg.

Heinrich von Herford, *Liber de rebus et temporibus memorabilibus sive chronicon*, ed. August Potthast (Göttingen: Dieterich, 1859).

Heldwein, Johannes, *Die Jesuiten und das deutsche Volk* (Munich: P. Müller, 1913).

Helmold von Bosau, *Helmoldi presbyteri Chronica Slavorum*, ed. I. M. Lappenbergius and Georgius Heinricus Pertz, Monumenta Germaniae Historica: Scriptores rerum germanicarum in usum scholarum 32 (Hannover: Hahnsche, 1868).

Helyot, Pierre, *Dictionnaire des ordres religieux, ou Histoire des ordres monastiques, religieux et militaires et des congrégations séculières de l'un et de l'autre sexe qui ont été établies jusqu'à présent: Mise par ordre alphabétique, corrigée et augmentée d'une introduction, d'une notice sur l'auteur, etc., et l'histoire des sociétés religieuses établies depuis que cet auteur a publié son ouvrage, par Marie Léandre Badiche*, ed. Jacques-Paul Migne (Paris: Migne, 1860).

Hieronymus, Sophronius Eusebius, see Jerome and *Vitae patrum*.

Hippolytus of Rome, *Hippolyti refutationis omnium haeresium librorum decem quae supersunt*, ed. Ludwig Decker and Friedrich G. Schneidewin (Göttingen: Dieterich, 1859).

Histoire de la table ronde . . . : *Histoire contenant les grandes prouesses vaillances, et héroïques. Faits d'armes de Lancelot du Lac, chevalier de la table ronde, divisée en trois livres, et mise en beau langage françois* (Lyon: Benoît Rigaud, 1591).

Hoë von Hoënegg, Matthias, *Procession unnd eigentliche Litaney, die im Römischen Bapsthumb von den Mönchen, Esawiten und andern Pfaffen mit grosser Andacht gehalten und gesungen wird: Entgegen gesetzt der Litaney M. Conradi Andreae, Jesuitischen Ordens, so er intituliret Geißlungs Procession, welche am Ende mit hinangesetzt in offnen Druck zur Nachrichtung mitgetheilet* . . . (Leipzig, no publisher, 1608).

Holstenius, Lucas, *Codex regularum monasticarum et canonicarum*, 6 vols. (1759; reprint, Graz: Akademische Druck- U. Verlagsanstalt, 1958).

Horn, Karl, *Die talmudischen Züge der Theologia Moralis des hl. Alphons von Liguori* (1942, no place or publisher).

Hugo von Reutlingen, *Chronicon ad annum MCCCXLIX*, in *Die Lieder und Melodien der Geißler des Jahres 1349 nach der Aufzeichung Hugo's von Reutlingen: Nebst einer Abhandlung über die italienischen Geißlerlieder von Dr. phil. Heinrich*

Schneegans, und einem Beitrage Zur Geschichte der deutschen und niederländis-chen Geißler von Dr. phil. Heino Pfannenschmid, ed. Paul Runge (1900; reprint, Hildesheim: G. Olms, 1969, and Leipzig: Breitkopf and Härtel, 1969).

Huysmans, Joris-Karl, *À rebours*, ed. Marc Fumaroli (Paris: Seuil, 1977).

Iacopone da Todi, *Laudi*, ed. Liliana Scrittore (Rome: Laterza, 1991).

Ignatius of Loyola, *Exercices spirituels: Texte définitif (1548)*, trans. Jean-Claude Guy, with commentary (Paris: Seuil, 1982).

————, *Spiritual Exercises and Selected Works*, ed. George E. Ganss (New York: Paulist Press, 1991).

The Irish Penitentials, ed. Ludwig Bieler, Scriptores latini Hiberniae 5 (Dublin: Dublin Institute for Advanced Studies, 1963).

Isabel de Villena, *Vita Christi*, ed. Albert-Guillem Hauf i Valls (Barcelona: Ed. 62, 1995).

Jerome, *The Letters of St. Jerome*, trans. Charles Christopher Mierow, intro. and notes by Thomas Comerford Lawler, vol. 1 (London: Longmans, Green, and Co., 1963).

————, *Lettres*, ed. Jérôme Labourt, vol. 1 (Paris: Belles Lettres, 1982).

Johannes von Erfurt, *Summa confessorum*, ed. Norbert Brieskorn (Frankfurt: Lang, 1981).

Joyce, James, *Dubliners* (London: Viking, 1982).

————, *Portrait of the Artist as a Young Man* (New York: Viking, 1964).

————, *Selected Letters*, ed. Richard Ellmann (London: Faber, 1975),

————, *Ulysses*, 3 vols. (New York: Garland, 1986).

Kaan, Henricus, *Psychopathia sexualis* (Leipzig, no publisher, 1844).

Kaiser, Anton, *Josephsbrüder: Jesuitengeist gleich Judengeist* (Leipzig: Klein, 1937).

Karlstadt, Andreas Bodenstein von, *Von abtuhung der Bylder, und das keyn Betdler unther den Christen seyn soll* (1522; reprint, Nuremberg: Verlag Medien und Kultur, 1979).

Keusch, Karl, *Die Aszetik des Hl. Alfons Maria von Liguori im Lichte der Lehre vom geistlichen Leben in alter und neuer Zeit* (Paderborn: Bonifacius-Druckerei, 1924).

Krafft-Ebing, Richard von, *Psychopathia sexualis*, trans. Franklin S. Klaf (New York: Stein and Day, 1978).

Kurtzel, August, *Der Jesuit Girard und seine Heilige: Ein Beitrag zur geistlichen Geschichte des vorigen Jahrhunderts* (1843, no place or publisher). Also in Marquis d' Argens, *Thérèse philosophe*, ed. M. Farin.

La Mettrie, Julien Offray de, *L'art de jouir* (Nantes: Le Passeur 1995).

————, *De la volupté: Anti-Senèque ou le souverain bien. L'Ecole de la volupté. Système d'Epicure*, ed. Ann Thompson (Paris: Desjonquères, 1998).

Lactantius, *Divinae institutiones*, Corpus scriptorum ecclesiasticorum latinorum 19 (Vienna: Tempsky, 1890).

Lainopts, Viest' [Vital Puissant], *Essais bibliographiques sur deux ouvrages intitulés De l'utilité de la Flagellation, par J. H. Meibomius, et Traité du Fouet, de F. A. Doppet, etc.* (London and Paris: Joh. Alex. Hoogs, 1875).

Lang, Karl Heinrich von, *Zur Homosexualität der Jesuiten*, 2nd ed. (Leipzig, no publisher, 1908).

Langmann, Adelheid, see *Offenbarungen der Adelheid Langmann*.

Lanjuinais, Joseph D., *La bastonnade et la flagellation pénales, considérées chez les peuples anciens et chez les modernes* (Brussels: Gay et Doucé, 1875).

Il laudario "Frondini" dei disciplinati di Assisi, ed. Franco Mancini (Pisa: Olschki, 1990).

Lea, Henry Charles, *A History of Auricular Confession and Indulgences in the Latin Church*, 3 vols. (1896; reprint, New York: Greenwood Press, 1968).

————, *A History of the Inquisition of the Middle Ages*, 3 vols. (New York: Macmillan, 1922).

Leben und Gesichte der Christina Ebnerin, ed. G. W. Karl Lochner (Nuremberg. Recknagel, 1872).

Leca, Victor, *La Discipline à l'école, au confessional et dans le boudoir: Correspondance anonyme publié par un journal anglais . . .* (Paris: J. Fort, 1910).

Liber ordinarius der Stiftskirche St. Aposteln in Cologne, see Odenthal, Andreas.

Der Liber ordinarius des Lütticher St. Jakobs-Klosters, ed. Paulus Volk, Beiträge zur Geschichte des alten Mönchtums und des Benediktinerordens 10 (Münster in Westphalia: Aschendorff, 1923).

Library Illustrative of Social Progress, ed. Henry Thomas Buckle, 7 vols. (London, no publisher, 1872). Vols. 1 and 2, *Exhibition of Female Flagellants in the Modest and Incontinent World*; vol. 3, *Lady Bumtickler's Revels: A Comic Opera in Two Acts*; vol. 4, *A Treatise of the Use of Flogging in Venereal Affairs*, by John Henry Meibomius; vol. 5, *Madame Birchini's Dance: A Modern Tale*; vol. 6, *Sublime of Flagellation: In Letters From Lady Tarmagant Flaybum*; vol. 7, *Fashionable Lectures, Composed and Delivered with Birch Discipline*.

Liguori, Alfons M. di, *Der Beichtvater, oder Gründliche Anleitung zur rechten Verwaltung des Bußsakraments* (Aachen: Hensen, 1842).

484

————, *Homo apostolicus*, 4 vols., *Opere* 60–63 (Monza: Corbetta, 1838).

————, *Institutio catechistica ad populum in praecepta decalogi et sacramenta*, *Opere* 64 (Monza: Corbetta, 1832).

————, *Istruzione e pratica pei confessori*, 5 vols., *Opere* 40–44 (Monza: Corbetta, 1830).

————, *Praxis confessarii ad bene excipiendas confessiones: Ad instructionem tyronum confessariorum* (Paris: Rusand, 1832).

————, *Theologia moralis secundum doctrinam s. Alfonsi de Ligorio doctoris Ecclesiae*, ed. Joseph Aertnys, Cornelio A. Damen and Ioannes Visser, 4 vols. (Turin: Marietti, 1967–69).

Die Limburger Chronik des Tileman Elhen von Wolfhagen, ed. Arthur Wyss, Monumenta Germaniae Historica: Scriptores qui vernaculi lingua usi sunt 4, 1 (Hannover: Hahn, 1883).

[Lipowsky, Felix J.], *Gemälde aus dem Nonnenleben, oder Enthüllte Geheimnisse aus den Papieren der aufgehobenen bayerischen Klöster, von einem Archivbeamten* (Munich, no publisher, 1808).

Lolme, Jean Louis de, *Memorials of Human Superstition* (London: G. Robinson, 1784).

[Lolme, John Louis de], *Beiträge zur Geschichte des menschlichen Aberglaubens, als Paraphrase und Commentar zur Geschichte der Flagellanten des Abt Boileau etc., von Einem, der nicht Doctor der Sorbonne ist, nach der zweiten englischen Ausgabe übersetzt* (Leipzig: Schwickert, 1785).

————, *The History of the Flagellants: Otherwise, of Religious Flagellations, among Different Nations, and Especially among Christians; Being a Paraphrase and Commentary on the Historia flagellantium of the Abbé Boileau, Doctor of the Sorbonne, Canon of the Holy Chapel, etc., By One Who Is Not Doctor of the Sorbonne*, 2nd ed. (London: G. Robinson, 1783).

Lucian of Samosata, *Werke in drei Bänden* (Berlin: Aufbau-Verlag, 1981).

Ludolf von Sachsen, *Vita Jesu Christi*, ed. Ludwig Maria Rigollot, 4 vols. (Paris and Rome: Palme, 1870).

Lust am Schmerz: Texte und Bilder zur Flagellomanie, ed. Michael Farin (Munich: Schneekluth, 1991).

Macarius Aegyptius, see Pseudo-Macarius.

MacOrlan, Pierre, see Dumarchey, Pierre.

Magdeburger Schöppenchronik, see *Die Chroniken der deutschen Städte*, vol. 7.

Mansi, Dominicus, *Sacrorum conciliorum nova et amplissima collectio, in qua praeter ea quae Phil. Labbeus et Gabr. Cossartius et novissime Nicolaus Coleti in lucem edidere ea omnia insuper suis in locis optime disposita exhibentur quae Joannes Dominicus Mansi lucensis, congregationis matris dei evulgavit*, 54 vols. (1901–27; reprint, Arnhem: H. Welter, 1960–62).

Martène, Edmundus, *Veterum scriptorum et monumentorum . . . amplissima collectio*, vol. 5 (Paris: Montalant, 1927).

Mathias von Neuenburg, *Die Chronik des Mathias von Neuenburg*, ed. Adolf Hofmeister, 2nd ed., Monumenta Germaniae Historica: Nova Series 4 (Berlin: Weidmann, 1955).

Mechthild von Magdeburg, *Das fließende Licht der Gottheit, nach der Einsiedler Handschrift in kritischem Vergleich mit der gesamten Überlieferung*, ed. Hans Neumann, Municher Texte und Untersuchungen zur deutschen Literatur des Mittelalters 100 (Munich: Artemis, 1990).

———, *The Flowing Light of the Godhead*, trans. Frank Tobin (New York: Paulist Press, 1998).

Medieval Handbooks of Penance: A Translation of the Principal Libri Poenitentiales, ed. John T. McNeill and Helena M. Gamer (New York: Columbia University Press, 1990).

Meibom, Johann Heinrich, *De flagrorum usu in re veneria, et lumborum renumque officio, epistola ad V. C. Christianum Cassium, Episcopi Lubecensis & Holsatiae Ducis Consiliarium* (Lugduni Batavorum: Ex Officina Elseviriana, 1643).

———, *Die Nützlichkeit der Geißelhiebe in den Vergnügungen der Ehe, so wie in der ärztlichen Praxis, und die Verrichtungen der Lenden und Nieren*, in *Der Schatzgräber in den literarischen und bildlichen Seltenheiten*, pt. 4, ed. Joseph Scheible (Stuttgart: Kloster, 1847), pp. 292–365. Expanded edition of the treatise with the writings of Bartholin and Meibom Junior.

———, *De l'utilité de la flagellation dans la médecine et dans les plaisirs du mariage, et des fonctions des lombes et des reins, ouvrage singulier traduit du latin de J. H. Meibomius, et enrichi de notes historiques, critiques et littéraires, d'une introduction et d'un index* (1795; reprint, Paris: Le Bibliophile Montmartrois, 1909).

———, *Utilité de la flagellation dans les plaisirs de l'amour et du mariage, traduit du latin de J.-H. Meibomius, suivie de la Bastonnade et la flagellation penale, par J.-D. Lanjuinais, et autres pièces en vers, nouvelle édition augmentée de notes historiques, critiques et bibliographiques* (Brussels: Gay et Doucé, 1879).

———, *Von dem Nutzen des Geißelns in medizinischer und physischer Beziehung, und von den Verrichtungen der Lenden und Nieren*, in *Der Schatzgräber in den literarischen und bildlichen Seltenheiten*, pt. 4, ed. Joseph Scheible (Stuttgart: Kloster, 1847), pp. 245–92. First edition of the treatise with the writings of Bartholin and Meibom Junior.

Meibom, Johann Heinrich, Thomas Bartholin, Heinrich Meibom, Ole Worm, and Joachim Olhafius, *De usu flagrorum in re medica & veneria, lumborumque & renum officio* (Frankfurt: Ex Bibliopolio Hafniensi Danielis Paulli, 1670).

Meusal, Walter J., *Invitation to the Dance. A Miscellany of Stories, Experiences, Letters, Articles on Corporal Punishment* (New York: Gargoyle Press, 1935).

Mirabeau, Honoré-Gabriel de Riquetti de, *Erotika biblion, avec annotations du Chevalier de Pierrugues: La conversion, ou Le libertin de qualité. Hic et Hec, ou L'art de varier les plaisirs de l'amour. Le rideau levé, ou L'éducation de Laure. Le chien après les moines. Le degré des âges du plaisir, introduction, essai bibliographique et notes par Guillaume Apollinaire* (Paris: Bibliothèque des curieux, 1921).

———, *Hic et Hec, ou L'élève des RR. PP. Jésuites d'Avignon* (Saint-Pierre-les-Nemours: EUREDIF, 1984). First publication listed as "Berlin 1798" and "Londres 1795." (Often appears in French under the title *Hic et Hec, ou L'art de varier les plaisirs de l'amour et de la volupté, enseigné par les R. P. Jésuites, et leurs élèves*. In German, the title is generally *Hic et Hec, oder Die Stufenleiter der Wollust*).

Mirbeau, Octave, *Der Garten der Qualen: Aus dem Französischen von Susanne Farin, mit acht Illustrationen und einem Dossier von Michel Delon, einer Lebenstafel und einer Bibliographie*, ed. Michael Farin (Stuttgart: Parkland, 1992).

———, *Le jardin des supplices, préface de Michel Delon, édition présentée et annotée par Michel Delon* (Paris: Gallimard, 1988).

Molinier, Etienne, *Des confrairies pénitentes, où il est traicté de leur institution, reigles et exercices* (Toulouse: R. Colomiez, 1625).

Montagnes, Bernard, *Les origines historiques des compagnies de pénitents de Provence*, in *Pénitents et confrèries du Sud-Est: Table ronde du 18 mai 1983, EHESS Marseille, Provence Historique* 34, 136 (Aix-en-Provence, 1984), pp. 125–46.

Morinus, Joannes, *Commentarius historicus de disciplina in administratione sacramenti poenitentiae* (Paris: Gasparus Meturas, 1651).

Mülmann, Johann, *Flagellum Antimelancholicum. Das ist: Christliche Geissel wider den Melancholischen Trawrgeist und Hertzfresser, aus Gottes Wort geflochten und auff allerley Fälle der Anfechtungen und Melancholischen Grillen gerichtet . . .*

487

erstlich von ... Johann Mülmann ... durch M. Christianum Mülman (Leipzig: Johann Glück, 1618).

[Musset, Alfred de], *Gamiani, oder, Zwei Nächte der Ausschweifung: Aus dem Französischen von Heinrich Conrad, mit zwölf Illustrationen, einem Essay von Iwan Bloch, einer Bibliographie und einem Nachwort von Albrecht Koschorke*, ed. Michael Farin (Munich: Schneekluth, 1990).

Nadal, Jerónimo, *Adnotationes et meditationes in evangelia quae in sacrosancto missae sacrificio toto anno leguntur...* (Antwerp: Nutius, 1594).

———, *Evangelicae historicae imagines ex ordine euangliorum, quae toto anno in missae sacrificio recitantur, in ordinem temporis vitae Christi digestae* (Antwerp: Nutius, 1593).

———, *Immagini di storia evangelica: Riproduzione integrale in facsimile dell'originale, Anversa MDXCIII, didascalie di A. Vivaldi, Roma MDXCIX*, ed. Nino Benti, Monumenta Bergomensia 43 (Bergamo: Edizioni Monumenta Bergomensia, 1976).

Nates, Gilbert, *Das System der Madame Duhoux* (no location, publisher, or date).

Nicolai, Friedrich, *Nachricht von der wahren Beschaffenheit des Instituts der Jesuiten* (1785; reprint, Rotterdam: Cagliostro, 1984).

Nider, Johannes, *Manuale confessorum* (Cologne: Conrad Winters, 1479).

Obereit, Jakob H., *Die Einsamkeit der Weltüberwinder nach innern Gründen erwogen* (Leipzig: Böhme, 1781).

———, *Vertheidigung der Mystik und des Einsiedlerlebens gegen Herrn Leibarzt Zimmermann* (Frankfurt: Eichenberg, 1775).

Die Offenbarungen der Adelheid Langmann, Klosterfrau zu Engelthal, ed. Philipp Strauch, Quellen und Forschungen zur Sprach- und Culturgeschichte der germanischen Völker 26 (Strassburg: Trübner, 1878).

Osuna, Joaquin, *Peregrinacion christiana por el camino real de la celeste Jerusalem, divida en nueve jornadas, quatro hospicios, que son unas estaciones devotas al modo del via-crucis...* (Mexico City: Bibliotheca mexicana, 1756).

P...., Gabriel, *Recherches historiques sur l'origine et l'usage de l'instrument de pénitence appelé discipline* (Dijon: V. Lagier, 1841).

Paenitentiale Sangallese, see Meens, Rob.

Palladios of Helenopolis, *Historia lausiaca: Die frühen Heiligen in der Wüste*, trans. and ed. Jacques Laager (Zurich: Manesse-Verlag, 1987).

Pardulf, see *Vita Pardulfi*.

Paullini, Kristian Franz, *Flagellum salutis. Das ist: Curieuse Erzählung, wie mit Schlägen allerhand schwere, langweilige, und fast unheylbare Kranckheiten offt, bald und wohl curiret worden, durch und durch mit allerley annehmlichen und lustigen Historien . . . bewährt und erläutert von Kristian Franz Paullini* (Frankfurt: Knochen, 1698).

———, *Flagellum salutis, oder Heilung durch Schläge in allerhand schweren Krankheiten*, in *Der Schatzgräber in den literarischen und bildlichen Seltenheiten*, pt. 2, ed. Joseph Scheible (Stuttgart: Kloster, 1847), pp. 1–107.

———, *Heilsame Dreck-Apotheke, wie nemlich mit Koth und Urin fast alle . . . Kranckheiten . . . curirt worden* (Frankfurt: Knochen, 1696).

———, *Philosophische Lust-Stunden oder Allerhand schöne anmutige . . . Curiositäten* (Frankfurt and Leipzig: Stoessel, 1709).

———, *Zeit-kuertzende Erbauliche Lust, oder, Allerhand ausserlesene, rar- und curiose, so nuetz- als ergetzliche, geist- und weltliche, Merckwuerdigkeiten: Zum vortheilhafftigen Abbruch verdrieszlicher Lang-Weil, und mehrerm Nachsinnen* (Frankfurt am Main: Knochen, 1693).

———, see also *Der Schatzgräber in den literarischen und bildlichen Seltenheiten*.

Peladan, Aimé Josephin, *La vertu supreme* (Paris: Flammarion, 1900).

———, *Le vice suprême* (Paris: Librairie des auteurs modernes, 1884).

Peter Damian, *Book of Gomorrah: An 11th-century Treatise against Clerical Homosexual Practices*, trans. Pierre J. Payer (Waterloo, Canada: Wilfrid Laurier University Press, 1982).

———, *Briefe*, ed. Kurt Reindel, 4 vols., Monumenta Germaniae Historica: Epistolae 2, 4 (Munich: Monumenta Germaniae Historica, 1983–93).

———, *De Laude flagellorum et, ut loquuntur, disciplinae*, in *Patrologia Latina*, ed. Jacques-Paul Migne, vol. 145, (Paris: Migne, 1853), pp. 679–86.

———, *The Letters of Peter Damian*, trans. Owen J. Blum, The Fathers of the Church: Medieval Continuation, vols. 1–4, 6 (Washington, D.C.: Catholic University of America Press, 1989).

———, *Liber Gomorrhianus*, in *Patrologia Latina*, ed. Jacques-Paul Migne, vol. 145 (Paris: Migne, 1853), p. 161–90.

———, *Petri Damiani vita Beati Romualdi*, ed. Giovanni Tabacco, Fonti per la storia d'Italia 94 (Rome: Istituto storico Italiano per il Medio Evo, 1957).

———, *Sermo 74*, in *Patrologia Latina*, ed. Jacques-Paul Migne, vol. 144 (Paris: Migne, 1853).

———, see also *Vita Romualdi*.

Peter the Venerable, *De miraculis,* in *Patrologia Latina,* ed. Jacques-Paul Migne, vol. 189 (Paris: Migne, 1854), pp. 851–952.

———, *Statuta Cluniacensia,* in *Patrologia Latina,* ed. Jacques-Paul Migne, vol. 189 (Paris: Migne, 1854), pp. 1023–46.

Pfister, Oskar, *Hysterie und Mystik bei Margaretha Ebner (1291–1351), Zentralblatt für Psychoanalyse* 1 (1911), pp. 468–85.

Philalethes, Petrus, *Liguori, der Geburtshelfer des Unfehlbarkeitsdogmas, ein Totengräber der Sittlichkeit,* Freundschaftliche Streitschriften 74 (Barmen: D. B. Wiemann, 1902).

Pia, Pascal, *Les livres de l'enfer: Bibliographie critique des ouvrages érotiques dans leurs différentes éditions du XVIe siècle à nos jours* (Paris: Fayard, 1998).

Praz, Mario, *The Romantic Agony* (Oxford: Oxford University Press, 1970).

Proust, Marcel, *Finding Time Again,* trans. Ian Patterson (London: Allen Lane, 2002).

Pseudo-Macarius, *Reden und Briefe,* trans. Klaus Fitschen (Stuttgart: Hiersemann, 2000).

Querero, Docteur, *La flagellation dans l'amour et dans la médecine* (Joinville-le-Pont: H. Pauwels, 1908).

Reade, Rolf S. [Alfred Rose], *Registrum Librorum Eroticorum* (London, privately printed, 1936).

Rebell, Hugues, *Femmes chatiées* (Paris: Mercure de France, 1994).

———, *The Memoirs of Dolly Morton* (Philadelphia: Society of Private Bibliophiles, 1904).

Reed, Jeremy, *When the Whip Comes Down: A Novel about de Sade* (London: Peter Owen, 1992).

A Reformation Debate: Karlstadt, Emser and Eck on Sacred Images. Three Treatises in Translation, trans. Bryan D. Mangrum and Giuseppe Scavizzi (Toronto: Centre for Reformation and Renaissance Studies, 1998).

Regino von Prüm, *De ecclesiasticis disciplinis,* in *Patrologia Latina,* ed. Jacques-Paul Migne, vol. 132 (Paris: Migne, 1853), pp. 175–399.

Richeome, Louis, *Trois discours pour la religion catholique: Les miracles, les saints, les images…* (Rouen: Theodore Reinsart, 1608).

Rogge, Heinrich, *Millionenfache Verhinderung gesunden deutschen Nachwuchses im christlichen Staat* (Magdeburg: Nordland-Verlag, no date).

Romuald, see Peter Damian and *Vita Romualdi.*

Rosenberg, Alfred, *Das Verbrechen der Freimaurerei. Judentum, Jesuitismus, Deutsches Christentum,* 2nd ed. (Munich: Lehmanns, 1922).

Rousseau, Jean-Jacques, *Confessions*, ed. Bernard Gagnebin, *Œuvres complètes*, vol. 1 (Paris: Gallimard 1959).

Runge, Paul, see Hugo von Reutlingen.

Sacher-Masoch, Aurora von [Wanda von], *Die Dame im Pelz* (Berlin: Schreiter, 1933).

————, *Damen mit Pelz und Peitsche* (Frankfurt: Ullstein, 1995).

————, *Echter Hermelin: Geschichten aus der vornehmen Welt* (Leipzig and Bern: G. Frobeen, 1879).

————, *Masochismus und Masochisten: Nachtrag zur Lebensbeichte* (Berlin: Seemann, 1908).

————, *Meine Lebensbeichte* (Berlin: Borngräber, 1906).

Sacher-Masoch, Leopold von, *Amor mit dem Korporalstock, und Eine Frau auf Vorposten: Zwei russische Hofgeschichten*, 6th ed. (Berlin: Jacobsthal, 1885).

————, *Die Ästhetik des Hässlichen* (Leipzig: Eckstein, 1880).

————, *Grausame Frauen: Erzählungen* (Munich: Heyne, 1980).

————, *Katharina II., Zarin der Lust: Biographischer Roman* (Munich: Heyne, 1982).

————, *Im Venusberg und andere Geschichten von den Messalinnen Viennas*, 6th ed. (Berlin: Frobeen, 1895).

————, *Venus im Pelz: Mit einer Studie über den Masochismus von Gilles Deleuze* (Frankfurt: Suhrkamp, 1980).

Sacher-Masoch, Leopold von and Wanda von Sacher-Masoch, *Szenen einer Ehe* (Vienna: Wiener Frauenverlag, 1996).

Sade, Donatien-Alphonse-François Marquis de, *Juliette*, trans. Austryn Wainhouse (New York: Grove Press, 1968).

————, *Juliette, oder Die Wonnen des Lasters, Werke in fünf Bänden*, vols. 3 and 4 (Cologne: Könemann, 1995).

————, *Œuvres complètes*, ed. Annie Le Brun and Jean-Jacques Pauvert, 15 vols. (Paris: Pauvert, 1986–91).

————, *Die Philosophie im Boudoir, oder Die lasterhafte Lehrmeisterin, Werke in fünf Bänden*, vol. 5 (Cologne: Könemann, 1995).

————, *Philosophy in the Boudoir*, trans. Julian Jones (New York: Creation Books, 1997.)

Sadger, J. [Isidor], *Über den sado-masochistischen Komplex, Jahrbuch für psychoanalytische und psychopathologische Forschungen* 5 (1913), pp. 157–232.

Salimbene von Parma, *Chronica fratris Salimbene de Adam Ordinis minorum*, ed. Oswaldus H. Egger, Monumenta Germaniae Historica: Scriptores 32 (Hannover and Leipzig: Hahnsche, 1905–13).

————, *Die Chronik des Salimbene von Parma, nach der Ausgabe der Monumenta Germaniae bearbeitet von Alfred Doren*, 2 vols. (Leipzig: Dyk, 1914).

————, *The Chronicle of Salimbene de Adam*, ed. Joseph L. Baird, Giuseppe Baglivi, and John Robert Kane (Binghamton, N.Y.: Medieval & Renaissance Texts & Studies, 1986).

Samuel, Docteur, *La flagellation dans les maisons de tolérance* (Paris, no date or publisher).

Sánchez, Tomás, *Aphorismi R. P. Thomae Sanchez totam decem eius librorum De Matrimonio Doctrinam compendio continents* (Graecii: Haupt, 1641).

————, *Disputationum de sancto matrimonii sacramento tomi tres* (Antwerp: Heredes Mart. Nuti et Joan. Meursium, 1614). Microfiche edition, The Catholic Reformation. Theology 34 (Leiden, 1987).

Der Schatzgräber in den literarischen und bildlichen Seltenheiten, Sonderbarkeiten etc., hauptsächlich des deutschen Mittelalters, IV. Theil: I. K. F. Paullini's heilsame Dreck-Apotheke, wie nemlich mit Koth und Urin die meisten Krankheiten und Schäden glücklich geheilet worden; II. Von dem Nutzen des Geißelns in medizinischer und physischer Beziehung, von J. H. Meibomius und Anderen, ed. Johann Scheible (Stuttgart: Kloster, 1847).

Scheible, Johann, see *Der Schatzgräber.*

Schertel, Ernst, *Der Flagellantismus in Literatur und Bildnerei*, 12 vols. (Schmiden bei Stuttgart: Decker, 1957). First edition in 4 vols. under the title *Der Flagellantismus als literarisches Motiv* (Leipzig: Parthenon, 1929–32).

————, *Scham und Laster* (Leipzig: Parthenon, 1930).

————, *Schellings Metaphysik der Persönlichkeit* (Leipzig: Quelle & Meyer, 1911).

————, *Der Sturm auf das Weib* (Leipzig: Parthenon, 1931).

————, *Die Sünde des Ewigen, oder Dies ist mein Leib* (Berlin: Die Wende, 1918).

————, *Das Weib als Göttin* (Leipzig: Parthenon, 1928).

————, *Weib, Wollust und Wahn* (Leipzig: Parthenon, 1931).

Schertel, Ernst [K. Stendal-Hohenscheid], *Nacktheit als Kultur* (Leipzig: Parthenon, 1927).

Schlichtegroll, Carl Felix [Georg Friedrich Collas], *Geschichte des Flagellantismus unter besonderer Berücksichtigung der Religionsgebräuche, des Erziehungswesens, der Sklaverei, der Strafrechtspflege... Vol. 1: Der Flagellantismus im Altertum* (Leipzig: Wigand, 1913). Also published later under the independent title *Der Flagellantismus im Altertum* (Leipzig: Wigand, 1932).

Schoettgen, Christian, *Christiani Schoettgenii de secta flagellantium commentatio* (Leipzig: Johann Christian Martinus, 1711).

Schreckenbach, Paul, *Römische Moraltheologie und das 6. Gebot: Unter besonderer Berücksichtigung der Liguori-Broschüre des Prinzen Max von Sachsen gegen R. Graßmann, 1. Teil: Graßmann und der Prinz von Sachsen*, Freundschaftliche Streitschriften 72 (Barmen: D. B. Wiemann, 1901).

——, *Römische Moraltheologie und das 6. Gebot: Unter besonderer Berücksichtigung der Liguori-Broschüre des Prinzen Max von Sachsen gegen R. Graßmann, 2. Teil: Römische Moralentscheidungen*, Freundschaftliche Streitschriften 73 (Barmen: D. B. Wiemann, 1901).

Schwesternbuch Katharinental, see Meyer, Ruth.

Schwesternbuch Oetenbach, see *Die Stiftung des Klosters Oetenbach*.

Schwesternbuch Töß, see Stagel, Elsbeth.

Schwesternbuch Unterlinden, see Ancelet-Hustache, Jeanne.

Scott, George Ryley, *The History of Corporal Punishment: A Survey of Flagellation in Its Historical and Sociological Aspects* (London: Torchstream, 1948).

Serarius, Nikolaus, *Sacri peripatetici zive de sacris ecclesiae catholicae processionibus libri duo* (Cologne: Gualtherus, 1607).

Suso, Henry, *The Exemplar, with Two German Sermons*, ed. Frank Tobin (New York: Paulist Press, 1989).

——, [Seuse, Heinrich], *Deutsche Schriften*, ed. Karl Bihlmeyer (1907; reprint, Frankfurt: Minerva, 1961).

Seyppelius, Johannes Jacobus, *Ritum flagellandi apud Judaeos*, 2nd ed. (Wittenberg: Meyer, 1670).

Spiegel van den Leven ons heren (Mirror of the Life of Our Lord): Diplomatic Edition of the Text and Facsimile of the 42 Miniatures of a 15th Century Typological Life of Christ in the Pierpont Morgan Library, New York, ed. W. H. Beuken and James H. Marrow (Doornspijk: Ed. Davaco, 1979).

Stagel, Elsbeth, *Das Leben der Schwestern zu Töss*, ed. Ferdinand Vetter, Deutsche Texte des Mittelalters 6 (Berlin: Weidmann, 1906).

Stalen, Johann, *Peregrinus ad loca sancta orthodoxus et pius demonstratus: Sive vindiciae sacrarum peregrinationum, processionum, invocationis sanctorum, cultus imaginum et miraculorum ecclesiae . . .* (Cologne: Jost Kalckhoven, 1649).

Statuto dei disciplinati, see Vigo, Pietro.

Steitz, Georg Eduard, *Wie beweisen die Jesuiten die Nothwendigkeit der Ohrenbeichte? Zusammenstellung der von H. Pater Roh am 23. November in der St.*

Bartholomaeuskirche zu Frankfurt entwickelten Beweisgründe und Widerlegung derselben, 5th ed. (Frankfurt: Völker, 1853).

Stern-Szana, Bernhard, *Bibliotheca curiosa et erotica: Beschreibung meiner Sammlung von Seltenheiten erotischer und kurioser Bücher* (Vienna: Halm & Goldmann, 1921).

Die Stiftung des Klosters Oetenbach und das Leben der seligen Schwestern daselbst, aus der Nürnberger Handschrift, ed. Heinrich Zeller-Werdmüller and Jakob Bächtold, in *Zürcher Taschenbuch, Neue Folge* 12 (1889), pp. 213–76.

Stock, St. George Henry, *The Romance of Chastisement, or Revelations of the School and the Bedroom, by an Expert* (Boston: Tremont, 1876).

Stöhr, August, *Handbuch der Pastoralmedicin mit besonderer Berücksichtigung der Hygiene* (Freiburg: Herder, 1887).

Strauch, Philipp, see *Die Offenbarungen der Adelheid Langmann*.

———, *Margaretha Ebner und Heinrich von Nördlingen: Ein Beitrag zur Geschichte der deutschen Mystik* (1882; reprint, Amsterdam: Schippers, 1966).

Stumpf, Augustinus, *Historia flagellantium, praecipue in Thuringia*, ed. Heinrich A. Erhard, *Neue Mittheilungen aus dem Gebiet historisch-antiquarischer Forschungen* 2 (1835), pp. 1–37.

Surius, Laurentius, *Historiae seu vitae sanctorum juxta optimam coloniensem editionem: Nuncvero ex recentioribus et probatissimis monumentis numero auctae mendis expurgatae et notis extornatae quibus accedit Romanum martyrologium breviter illustratum*, 13 vols. (Turin: Marietti, 1875–80).

Swinburne, Algernon Charles, *The Complete Works*, ed. Edmund Gosse and Thomas James Wise, 20 vols. (London: Heinemann, 1925–27).

———, *Lesbia Brandon*, ed. Randolph Hughes (London: Falcon, 1952).

———, *The Novels of A. C. Swinburne: Love's Cross-Currents, Lesbia Brandon* (New York: Farrar, Straus, and Cudahy, 1962).

———, *William Blake: A Critical Essay* (London: J. C. Hotten, 1868).

Tamburini, Tommaso, *Methodus expeditae confessionis, tum pro confessariis, tum pro poenitentibus, complectens libros quinque* (Cologne: Busaeus, 1657).

———, *Opera omnia* (Paris: Anisson & Posuel, 1679). Contains the following works: *Explicatio Decalogi, De sacramentis, De confessione, De Communione, De irregularitate, De sacrificiis missae*, and *De bulla crucuitae*.

Teresa de Avila, *Obras completas*, ed. Tomás de la Cruz, 3rd ed. (Madrid: Aguilar, 1982).

———, see also Villefore, Joseph.

Thelen, Friedrich, *Das Verhalten der Flagellanten in Realität und Phantasie* (Hamburg: Lassen, 1963).

———, *Die Welt der Flagellanten* (Hamburg: Lassen, 1960).

Theodoret, *Haereticarum fabularum compendium*, in *Patrologia Graeca*, ed. Jacques-Paul Migne, vol. 83 (Paris: Migne, 1859), pp. 335–556.

Thiers, Jean-Baptiste, *Critique de l'histoire des flagellans et justification de l'usage des disciplines volontaires* (Paris: Jean de Nully, 1703).

Thomas de Chobham, *Summa de commendatione virtutum et extirpatione vitiorum*, ed. Franco Morenzoni, Corpus christianorum: Continuatio mediaevalis 82B (Turnhout: Brepols, 1997).

Thomas of Celano, *Legenda sanctae Clarae virginis, tratta dal ms. 338 della Bibl. comunale di Assisi*, ed. Francesco Pennacchi (Assisi: Metastasio, 1910).

———, *Thesaurus Celanensis: Vita prima; Legenda ad usum chori; Vita secunda; Tractatus de miraculis; Legenda sanctae Clarae virginis; Concordance, Index, Listes de fréquences, Tables comparatives* (Louvain: CETEDOC, 1974).

[Toussaint, François-Vincent], *L'Anti-Thérèse ou Juliette philosophe, nouvelle messine véritable, par Mr. de T**** (La Haye: E. L. Saurel, 1750).

Het tripartite boeteboek, see Meens, Rob.

Venus Unmasked, or An Inquiry into the Nature and Origin of the Passion of Love, ed. Leonard de Vries and Peter Fryer (New York: Stein and Day, 1976).

Verges, Henry des, *Madam Birch & Company* (no location, publisher, or date).

Vetter, Konrad [Conrad], *Geißlung Procession welche im Lutherthumb nicht allein am Charfreytag, sonder das gantz Jar hinumb gehalten wirdt: Mit sampt einer andechtigen Letaney, Durch M. Conradum Andreae* (Ingolstadt: Andreas Angermaier, 1608).

———, *Lutherisch Disciplin Büchel. Zur Bekrefftigung unnd Handhabung deß treffelichen Buchs D. Jacobi Heilbronners wider das Papistische Geißlen und Durch Conradum Andreae* ... (Ingolstadt: Andreas Angermaier, 1607).

Vetter, Konrad, M. Conradi Andreae, etc., *Volcius Flagellifer. Das ist: Beschützung und Handhabung fürtrefflicher und herlicher zweyer Predigten von der unleydenlichen und Abschewlichen Geysel Proceßion, erstlich gehalten, hernach auch in Truck gegeben durch den Kehrwürdigen unnd Wolgekerten Herrn M. Melchior Voltz Lutherischen Predicanten zu Augspurg bey Sant Anna* (Ingolstadt: Andreas Angermaier, 1608).

———, see also Diez, Philippus.

Vigo, Pietro, *Statuto dei disciplinati di Pomerance nel Volterrano* (1889; reprint, Bologna: Comm. Per it Testi di Lingua, 1969).

Villefore, Joseph François Bourgoin de, *La vie de sainte Thérèse...,* 2 vols., (Paris: Estienne, 1756).

Villiot, Jean de, *La flagellation amoureuse dans l'histoire des moeurs et dans la litterature, suivie de la flagellation des femmes en France sous la Revolution et la terreur blanche* (Paris: C. Carrington, 1904).

Virmaître, Charles, *Les flagellants et les flagellés de Paris* (1902; reprint, Paris: Editions de Paris, 1985).

Vita Antonii, in *Patrologia Graeca,* ed. Jacques-Paul Migne, vol. 26 (Paris: Migne, 1857), pp. 835–976.

Vita Pardulfi abbatis Waractensis, ed. Wilhelm Levison, Monumenta Germaniae Historica: Scriptores rerum Merovingicarum 7 (Hannover and Leipzig: Hahnsche, 1920), pp. 19–40.

Vitae patrum sive historiae eremitae libri decem, ed. Heribert Rosweyde (Antwerp: Plantin, 1615). Reprinted in *Patrologia Latina,* ed. Jacques-Paul Migne, vol. 21 (Paris: Migne, 1849), and vols. 73–74, (Paris: Migne, 1849).

Vita Romualdi, in *Patrologia Latina,* ed. Jacques-Paul Migne, vol. 144 (Paris: Migne, 1853), pp. 953–1008.

Vollständiges Heiligen-Lexikon, ed. Johann Stadler et al. (Augsburg: Schmid, 1858)

Volz, Melchior, see Zeaemann, Georg.

woerenkamp, heinrich, und gertrude perkauf: erziehungs-flagellantismus (Vienna: Verlag für Kulturforschung, 1932).

Wollschoendorff, Nicolaus, *Disquisitio historico-theologica de secta flagellantium* (Leipzig: Gregorius Ritzsch, 1636).

Zeaemann, Georg, *Carnificina esauitica: Quatuor libri spontaneae flagellationi oppositi... Melchioris Volcii ... Authore Jacobo Heilbrunnero... Authore Georgio Zeaemanno...* (Wittenberg: Martin Henckel, 1613).

————, *Jesuvita revapulans: Apologetici tripartiti, quem flagellationi Jesuiticae A R. Et Cl. DD. Jacobo Heilbrunnero etc. superiore anno editae, Jac. Gretserus opposuit, refutatio theologico-scholastica... A Georgio Zeaemanno... Cum luculenta Jacobi Heilbrunneri praefatione...* (Lauingen: Jakob Winter, 1608).

Zimmermann, Johann G., *Über die Einsamkeit,* 4 vols. (Leipzig: Weidmann & Reich, 1784–85).

Secondary Literature

Alatri, Mariano d', *Aetas poenitentialis: L'antico ordine francescano della penitenza* (Rome: Istituto storica dei Cappucini, 1993).

Alberigo, Giuseppe, s.v. "Flagellants," *Dictionnaire d'histoire et de géographie ecclésiastique*, vol. 17 (Paris: Letouzey et Ané, 1971).

Amtmann, Radegunde, *Die Bußbruderschaften in Frankreich*, Arbeiten aus dem Seminar für Völkerkunde der Johann Wolfgang Goethe-Universität Frankfurt 7 (Wiesbaden: Steiner, 1977).

Ancona, Alessandro d', *Origini del teatro italiano: Libri tre con due appendici sulla rappresentazione drammatica del contado toscano e sul teatro mantovano nel sec. XVI*, 2 vols. (Rome: Bardi, 1971).

Angenendt, Arnold, *Geschichte der Religiosität im Mittelalter*, 2nd rev. ed. (Darmstadt: Wissenschaftliche Buchgesellschaft, 2000).

———, *Heilige und Reliquien: Die Geschichte ihres Kultes vom frühen Christentum bis zur Gegenwart*, 2nd rev. ed. (Munich: C. H. Beck, 1997).

———, *Sühne durch Blut*, Frühmittelalterliche Studien 18 (1984), pp. 437–67.

Aron, Jean-Paul, and Roger Kempf, *Der sittliche Verfall: Bourgeoisie und Sexualität in Frankreich* (Frankfurt: Suhrkamp, 1982).

Asbach, Franz B., "Das Poenitentiale Remense und der sogenannte Excarpsus Cummeani: Überlieferung, Quellen und Entwicklung zweier kontinentaler Bußbücher aus der ersten Hälfte des 8. Jahrhunderts," Ph.D. thesis, Regensburg, 1979.

Augustyn, Wolfgang, "Passio Christi est meditanda tibi: Zwei Bildzeugnisse spätmittelalterlicher Passionsbetrachtung," in Walter Haug and Burghart Wachinger (eds.), *Die Passion Christi in Literatur und Kunst des Spätmittelalters*, Fortuna vitrea 12 (Tübingen: Niemeyer, 1993), pp. 211–40.

Backman, E. Louis, *Religious Dances in Christian Church and in Popular Medicine* (London: Allen & Unwin, 1952).

Bailly, Paul, s.v. "Flagellants," in *Dictionnaire de spiritualité ascétique et mystique*, vol. 5 (Paris: Beauchesne, 1964).

Barnes, Andrew E., "Religious Anxiety and Devotional Change in Sixteenth Century French Penitential Confraternities," in *The Sixteenth Century Journal* 19 (1988), pp. 389–405.

Belting, Hans, *Bild und Kult: Eine Geschichte des Bildes vor dem Zeitalter der Kunst* (Munich: C. H. Beck, 1990).

497

————, *Das Bild und sein Publikum im Mittelalter: Form und Funktion früher Bildtafeln der Passion* (Berlin: Mann, 1981).

Benthien, Claudia, *Haut: Literaturgeschichte, Körperbilder, Grenzdiskurse* (Reinbek bei Hamburg: Rowohlt, 1999).

Bériou, Nicole, "La confession dans les écrits théologiques et pastoraux du XIIIe siècle: Médication de l'âme ou démarche judiciaire?," in *L'aveu, antiquité et moyen-âge: Actes de la table ronde organisée par l'Ecole française de Rome avec le concours du CNRS et de l'Université de Trieste, Rome 28–30 mars 1984*, Collection de l'Ecole française de Rome 88 (Rome: Ecole française de Rome, 1986), pp. 260–82.

Bertaud, Emile, s.v. "Discipline," *Dictionnaire de spiritualité ascétique et mystique*, vol. 3 (Paris: Beauchesne, 1957).

Bodenstedt, Mary, *The Vita Christi of Ludolphus the Carthusian*, The Catholic University of America Studies in Medieval and Renaissance Latin Language and Literature 16 (Washington, D.C.: The Catholic University of America Press, 1944).

Bois, Yves-Alain, and Rosalind Krauss, *Formless: A User's Guide* (New York: Zone Books, 1997).

Boskovits, Miklós, s.v. "Flagellanten," *Lexikon der christlichen Ikonographie*, vol. 2 (Freiburg: Herder, 1970).

Boucher, Jacqueline, *Société et mentalités autour de Henri III*, 4 vols. (Paris: Champion, 1981).

Boyle, Leonard E., "The Summa for Confessors as a Genre, and Its Religious Intent," in Charles Trinkaus and Heiko A. Oberman (eds.), *The Pursuit of Holiness in Late Medieval and Renaissance Religion: Papers from the University of Michigan Conference*, Studies in Medieval and Reformation Thought 10 (Leiden: Brill, 1974), pp. 126–30.

Braun, Walter, *Sadismus, Masochismus, Flagellantismus* (Flensburg: Orion, 1978).

Bremond, Henri, *Histoire littéraire du sentiment religieux en France: Depuis la fin des guerres de religion jusqu'à nos jours*, 11 vols., new ed. (Paris: Colin, 1967).

Brooks, Peter, *Troubling Confessions: Speaking Guilt in Law and Literature* (Chicago: University of Chicago Press, 2000).

Brown, Carolyn E., "Erotic Religious Flagellation and Shakespeare's *Measure for Measure*," *English Literary Renaissance* 16 (1986), pp. 139–65.

Brown, Peter: *The Body and Society: Men, Women, and Sexual Renunciation in Early Christianity* (New York: Columbia University Press, 1988).

Bullough, Vern L., and James A. Brundage (eds.), *Handbook of Medieval Sexuality* (New York: Garland, 1996).

Bürkle, Susanne, *Literatur im Kloster: Historische Funktion und rhetorische Legitimation frauenmystischer Texte des 14. Jahrhunderts*, Bibliotheca Germanica 38 (Tübingen: Francke, 1999).

Büttner, Frank O., *Imitatio pietatis: Motive der christlichen Ikonographie als Modelle zur Verähnlichung* (Berlin: Mann, 1983).

Büttner, Theodora, and Ernst Werner, *Circumcellionen und Adamiten: Zwei Formen mittelalterlicher Häresie*, Forschungen zur mittelalterlichen Geschichte 2 (Berlin: Akademie, 1959).

Bulst, Neithard, and Edith Pásztor, s.v. "Flagellanten," *Lexikon des Mittelalters*, vol. 4 (Munich and Zurich: Artemis, 1989).

Burt, Eugene C., *Erotic Art: An Annotated Bibliography with Essays* (Boston: Hall, 1989).

Bynum, Caroline Walker., "Docere verbo et exemplo. An Aspect of 12th Century Spirituality," Harvard Theological Studies 31 (Missoula: Scholar's Press, 1979).

———, *Fragmentation and Redemption: Essays on Gender and the Human Body in Medieval Religion* (New York: Zone Books, 1991).

———, *Holy Feast and Holy Fast: The Religious Significance of Food to Medieval Women* (Berkeley: University of California Press, 1987).

———, *Jesus as Mother: Studies in the Spirituality of the High Middle Ages* (Berkeley: University of California Press, 1982).

———, *The Resurrection of the Body in Western Christianity, 200–1336* (New York: Columbia University Press, 1995).

Cadden, Joan: "'Nothing Natural Is Shameful.' Vestiges of a Debate about Sex and Science in a Group of Late-Medieval Manuscripts," *Speculum* 76 (2001), pp. 66–89.

Caduff, Corina, and Joanna Pfaff-Czarnecka (eds.), *Rituale heute: Theorien, Kontroversen, Entwürfe* (Berlin: Reimer, 1999).

Caillois, Roger, *L'homme et le sacré* (Paris: Gallimard, 1950).

Camilla, Piero, *L'Ospedale di Cuneo nei secoli XIV–XVI: Contributo alla ricerca sul movimento dei disciplinati* (Cuneo: Biblioteca della Società per gli studi storici, archeologici e artistici della Provincia di Cuneo, 1972).

Campe, Rüdiger, *Affekt und Ausdruck: Zur Umwandlung der literarischen Rede im 17. und 18. Jahrhundert* (Tübingen: Niemeyer, 1990).

Castelli, Elizabeth, *Visions and Voyeurism: Holy Women and the Politics of Sight in Early Christianity* (Berkeley: Center for Hermeneutical Studies, 1995).

Chevallier, Pierre, *Henri III, roi shakespearien* (Paris: Fayard, 1985).

Chiffoleau, Jacques, "Analyse d'un rituel flamboyant. Paris, mai–août 1412," in Jacques Chiffoleau, Laura Martines, and Agostino Paravicini Bagliani (eds.), *Riti e rituali nelle società medievali*, 2 vols. (Spoleto: Centro italiano di studi sull'alto Medioevo, 1994), pp. 221–45.

Le Compagnie de' Battuti in Roma, Scelta di curiosità letterarie inedite o rare 20 (Bologna: Romagnoli, 1862).

Cusset, Catherine (ed.), *Libertinage and Modernity*, Yale French Studies 94 (New Haven: Yale University Press, 1998).

Czerwinski, Peter, *Gegenwärtigkeit: Simultane Räume und zyklische Zeiten, Formen von Regeneration und Genealogie im Mittelalter*, Exempel einer Geschichte der Wahrnehmung 2 (Munich: Fink, 1993).

Darnton, Robert, *Edition et sédition: L'Univers de la littérature clandestine au XVIIe siècle* (Paris: Gallimard, 1991).

Daub, Georg Heinrich, *Die große Leidens-Prozession in Heiligenstadt* (Heiligenstadt: Cordier, 1926).

Davidson, Arnold I., "Sex and the Emergence of Sexuality," *Critical Inquiry* 14 (1987), pp. 16–48.

Deakin, Terence J., *Catalogi librorum eroticorum: A Critical Bibliography of Erotic Bibliographies and Book-Catalogues* (London: Woolf, 1964).

De Clerck, Paul, and Eric Palazzo (eds.), *Rituels: Mélanges offerts à Pierre-Marie Gy, o.p.* (Paris: Cerf, 1990).

Delon, Michel, "De Thérèse philosophe à *La Philosophie dans le boudoir*: La place de la philosophie," *Romanistische Zeitschrift für Literaturgeschichte* 7 (1983), pp. 76–88.

Delumeau, Jean, *L'aveu et le pardon: Les difficultés de la confession, XIIIe–XVIIIe siècle* (Paris: Fayard, 1990).

Didi-Huberman, Georges, *Erfindung der Hysterie: Die photographische Klinik von Jean Martin-Charcot* (Munich: Fink, 1997).

———, *La ressemblance informe, ou Le gai savoir visuel selon Georges Bataille* (Paris: Macula, 1995).

Dinzelbacher, Peter, *Angst im Mittelalter: Teufels-, Todes- und Gotteserfahrung, Mentalitätsgeschichte und Ikonographie* (Paderborn: Schöningh, 1996).

———, *Handbuch der Religionsgeschichte im deutschsprachigen Raum, vol. 2:*

Hoch- und Spätmittelalter; Mit einem Beitrag von Daniel Krochmalnik (Paderborn: Schöningh, 2000).

Dubost, Jean-Pierre, *Eros und Vernunft: Literatur und Libertinage* (Frankfurt: Suhrkamp, 1988).

Dünninger, Hans, *Wallfahrt und Bilderkult*, ed. Wolfgang Brückner (Würzburg: Echter, 1995).

Durkheim, Emile, *The Elementary Forms of Religious Life*, trans. Joseph W. Swain (New York: Free Press, 1965).

Eisenbichler, Konrad (ed.), *Crossing the Boundaries: Christian Piety and the Arts in Italian Medieval and Renaissance Confraternities*, Early Drama, Art, and Music Monograph Series 15 (Kalamazoo: Medieval Institute Publications, 1991).

Elbaum, Jacob, *Repentance and Self-Flagellation in the Writings of the Sages of Germany and Poland 1348–1648* (Jerusalem: Magnes, 1992).

Elias, Norbert, *Über den Prozess der Zivilisation: Soziogenetische und psychogenetische Untersuchungen*, 2 vols. (Frankfurt: Suhrkamp, 1976).

Erbstösser, Martin, *Sozialreligiöse Strömungen im späten Mittelalter: Geißler, Freigeister und Waldenser im 14. Jahrhundert*, Forschungen zur mittelalterlichen Geschichte 16 (Berlin: Akademie, 1970).

Ferlaino, Franco, *Vattienti: Osservazione e riplasmazione di una ritualità tradizionale* (Milan: Jaca Book, 1991).

Fichte, Joerg O., *Die Darstellung von Jesus Christus im Passionsgeschehen der englischen Fronleichnamszyklen und der spätmittelalterlichen deutschen Passionsspiele*, in Walter Haug and Burghart Wachinger (eds.), *Die Passion Christi in Literatur und Kunst des Spätmittelalters*, Fortuna vitrea 12 (Tübingen: Niemeyer, 1993), pp. 277–96.

Findlen, Paula, "Humanism, Politics, and Pornography in Renaissance Italy," in Lynn Hunt (ed.), *The Invention of Pornography: Obscenity and the Origins of Modernity, 1500–1800* (New York: Zone Books, 1993), pp. 49–108.

Finsterwalder, Paul W., *Die Canones Theodori Cantuarensis und ihre Überlieferungsformen*, Untersuchungen zu den Bußbüchern des 7., 8. und 9. Jahrhunderts 1 (Weimar: Böhlau, 1929).

Fischer, Caroline, *Gärten der Lust: Eine Geschichte erregender Lektüren* (Stuttgart: Metzler, 1997).

Flandrin, Jean-Louis, *Le sexe et l'Occident: Evolution des attitudes et des comportements* (Paris: Seuil, 1981).

Felbecker, Sabine, *Die Prozession: Historische und Systematische Untersuchungen zu einer liturgischen Ausdruckshandlung,* Münsteraner theologische Abhandlungen 39 (Altenberge: Oros, 1995).

Forbes, Jill, "Two Flagellation Poems by Swinburne," *Notes and Queries* 22 (1975), pp. 443–45.

Frank, Karl Suso (ed.), *Askese und Mönchtum* (Darmstadt: Wissenschaftliche Buchgesellschaft, 1975).

Freedberg, David, *The Power of Images: Studies in the History and Theory of Response* (Chicago: University of Chicago Press, 1989).

Fryer, Peter, *Forbidden Books of the Victorians: Henry Spencer Ashbee's Bibliographies of Erotica* (London: Odyssey, 1970).

———, *Private Case — Public Scandal* (London: Secker & Warburg, 1966).

Fuller, Jean Overton, *Swinburne: A Critical Biography* (London: Chatto & Windus, 1968).

Fumaroli, Marc, *L'école du silence: Le sentiment des images au XVIIe siècle* (Paris: Flammarion, 1994).

Galli, Giuseppe, *Laudi inedite dei disciplinati umbri, scelte di sui codici più antichi,* Biblioteca storica della letteratura italiana 10 (Bergamo: Istituto italiano d'arti grafiche, 1910).

Gallop, Jane, *Intersections: A Reading of Sade with Bataille, Blanchot, and Klossowski* (Lincoln: University of Nebraska Press, 1981).

Gendolla, Peter, *Phantasien der Askese: Über die Entstehung innerer Bilder am Beispiel der "Versuchung des heiligen Antonius,"* Reihe Siegen: Beiträge zur Literatur-, Sprach- und Medienwissenschaft 99 (Heidelberg: Winter, 1991).

Gersmann, Gudrun, "Das Geschäft mit der Lust des Lesers: *Thérèse philosophe* — Zur Druckgeschichte eines erotischen Bestsellers," *Das Achtzehnte Jahrhundert* 18 (1994), pp. 72–84.

Gibson, Gail McMurray, *The Theater of Devotion: East Anglian Drama and Society in the Late Middle Ages* (Chicago: University of Chicago Press, 1989).

Girard, René, *La violence et le sacré* (Paris: Gallimard, 1972).

Gosse, Edmund, *The Life of Algernon Charles Swinburne* (London: Macmillan, 1917).

Gougaud, Louis, *Dévotions et pratiques ascétiques du moyen âge* (Paris: Desclée de Brouwer, 1925).

———, *Ermites et reclus: Etudes sur d'anciennes formes de vie religieuse* (Vienne: Abbaye Saint-Martin de Ligué, 1928).

———, s.v. "Flagellation," *Dictionnaire d'archéologie chrétienne et de liturgie,* vol. 5 (Paris 1923).

Graus, Frantisek, *Pest — Geissler — Judenmorde: Das 14. Jahrhundert als Krisenzeit*, Veröffentlichungen des Max-Planck-Instituts für Geschichte 86 (Göttingen: Vandenhoeck und Ruprecht, 1987).

Guillebaud, Jean-Claude, *La tyrannie du plaisir* (Paris: Seuil, 1998).

Gy, Pierre-Marie, "Les définitions de la confession après le quatrième concile du Latran," in *L'aveu, antiquité et moyen-âge: Actes de la table ronde organisée par l'Ecole française de Rome avec le concours du CNRS et de l'Université de Trieste, Rome 28–30 mars 1984*, Collection de l'Ecole française de Rome 88 (Rome: Ecole française de Rome, 1986) pp. 283–96.

————, *La liturgie dans l'histoire* (Paris: Ed. Saint-Paul, 1990).

Haas, Alois M., *Gottleiden — Gottlieben: Zur volkssprachlichen Mystik im Mittelalter* (Frankfurt: Insel, 1989).

————, *Mystik als Aussage: Erfahrungs-, Denk- und Redeformen christlicher Mystik* (Frankfurt: Suhrkamp, 1996).

————, "Sinn und Tragweite von Heinrich Seuses Passionsmystik," in Walter Haug and Burghart Wachinger (eds.), *Die Passion Christi in Literatur und Kunst des Spätmittelalters*, Fortuna vitrea 12 (Tübingen: Niemeyer, 1993), pp. 94–112.

Hadot, Pierre, *Philosophy as a Way of Life: Spiritual Exercises from Socrates to Foucault*, trans. Michael Chase, ed. Arnold Davidson (Oxford: Blackwell, 1995).

Hahn, Gerhard, "Die Passion Christi im geistlichen Lied," in Walter Haug and Burghart Wachinger (eds.), *Die Passion Christi in Literatur und Kunst des Spätmittelalters*, Fortuna vitrea 12 (Tübingen: Niemeyer, 1993), pp. 297–319.

Haimerl, Xaver, *Das Prozessionswesen des Bistums Bamberg im Mittelalter*, Münchener Studien zur historischen Theologie 14 (1937; reprint, Hildesheim: Olms, 1973).

Halperin, David M., "Forgetting Foucault: Acts, Identities, and the History of Sexuality," *Representations* 63 (1998), pp. 93–120.

Halperin, David M., John. J. Winkler, and Froma I. Zeitlin (eds.), *Before Sexuality: The Construction of Erotic Experience in the Ancient Greek World* (Princeton: Princeton University Press, 1990).

Hamburger, Jeffrey, *The Visual and the Visionary: Art and Female Spirituality in Late Medieval Germany* (New York: Zone Books, 1998).

Hammill, Graham L., *Sexuality and Form: Caravaggio, Marlowe, and Bacon* (Chicago: Chicago University Press, 2000).

Hanawalt, Barbara A., and David Wallace (eds.), *Bodies and Disciplines: Intersections of Literature and History in Fifteenth-Century England*, Medieval Cultures 9 (Minneapolis: University of Minnesota Press, 1996).

Haug, Walter, "Johannes Taulers Via negationis," in Walter Haug and Burghart Wachinger (eds.), *Die Passion Christi in Literatur und Kunst des Spätmittelalters*, Fortuna vitrea 12 (Tübingen: Niemeyer, 1993), pp. 76–93.

Haupt, Herman, "Geißelung, kirchliche, und Geißlerbruderschaften," in *Realencyklopädie für protestantische Theologie und Kirche*, vol. 6 (Leipzig 1899), pp. 432–44.

———, "Zur Geschichte der Geißler," *Zeitschrift für Kirchengeschichte* 9 (1888), pp. 114–19.

Heckenbach, Josephus, *De nuditate sacra sacrisque vinculis*, Religionsgeschichtliche Versuche und Vorarbeiten 9 (Gießen: Töpelmann, 1911).

Heitmüller, Elke, *Zur Genese sexueller Lust: Von Sade zu SM* (Tübingen: Konkursbuch, 1994).

Henderson, Philip, *Swinburne: Portrait of a Poet* (London: Routledge, 1974).

Hoyer, Siegfried, "Die thüringische Kryptoflagellantenbewegung im 15. Jahrhundert," *Jahrbuch für Regionalgeschichte* 2 (1967), pp. 148–74.

Hübner, Arthur, *Die deutschen Geißlerlieder: Studien zum geistlichen Volksliede des Mittelalters* (Berlin: de Gruyter, 1931).

Huizinga, Johan, *Herbst des Mittelalters: Studien über Lebens- und Geistesformen des 14. und 15. Jahrhunderts in Frankreich und in den Niederlanden* (Munich: Drei Masken, 1924).

Hunt, Lynn, (ed.), *Eroticism and the Body Politic* (Baltimore: Johns Hopkins University Press, 1991).

———, "Introduction: Obscenity and the Origins of Modernity, 1500–1800," in *The Invention of Pornography: Obscenity and the Origins of Modernity, 1500–1800* (New York: Zone Books, 1993), pp. 9–45.

———, *The Invention of Pornography: Obscenity and the Origins of Modernity, 1500–1800* (New York: Zone Books, 1993).

Ivanceau, Vintila, and Johannes Hoflehner, *Prozessionstheater: Spuren und Elemente von der Antike bis zur Gegenwart* (Cologne: Böhlau, 1995).

Jacob, Margaret C., "The Materialist World of Pornography," in Lynn Hunt (ed.), *The Invention of Pornography: Obscenity and the Origins of Modernity, 1500–1800* (New York: Zone Books, 1993), pp. 157–202.

Jaloux, Edmond, "Rezension zu *Le Temps retrouvé*," *Les nouvelles littéraires*, Paris, December 3 and 10, 1927.

Jauch, Ursula P., *Damenphilosophie und Männermoral: Von Abbé de Gérard bis Marquis de Sade; Ein Versuch über die lächelnde Vernunft* (Vienna: Passagen, 1990).

Jedin, Hubert, "Entstehung und Tragweite des Trienter Dekrets über die Bilderverehrung," *Theologische Quartalschrift* 116 (1935), pp. 143–88 and 404–29.

Jordan, Mark, *The Invention of Sodomy in Christian Theology* (Chicago: University of Chicago Press, 1997).

Jungmann, Josef A., *Die lateinischen Bußriten in ihrer geschichtlichen Entwicklung,* Forschungen zur Geschichte des innerkirchlichen Lebens 3–4 (Innsbruck: Rauch, 1932).

————, *Missarum sollemnia: Eine genetische Erklärung der römischen Messe,* 2 vols., 5th ed. (Vienna: Herder, 1962).

Kamper, Dietmar, and Christoph Wulf (eds.), *Die Wiederkehr des Körpers* (Frankfurt: Suhrkamp, 1982).

Kearney, Patrick J., *The Private Case: An Annotated Bibliography of the Private Case Collection in the British (Museum) Library* (London: Landesman, 1981).

Keating, Thomas, *Open Mind, Open Heart: The Contemplative Dimension of the Gospel* (New York: Continuum, 1995).

Kieckhefer, Richard, "Radical Tendencies in the Flagellant Movement of the Mid-Fourteenth Century," *The Journal of Medieval and Renaissance Studies* 4 (1974), pp. 157–76.

Klär, Karl-Josef, *Das kirchliche Bußinstitut von den Anfängen bis zum Konzil von Trient,* Hochschulschriften 23, 413 (Frankfurt: Lang, 1991).

Knipping, John B., *Iconography of the Counter Reformation in the Netherlands: Heaven on Earth,* 2 vols. (Nieuwkoop: de Graaf, 1974).

Köpf, Ulrich, "Die Passion Christi in der lateinischen religiösen und theologischen Literatur des Spätmittelalters," in Walter Haug and Burghart Wachinger (eds.), *Die Passion Christi in Literatur und Kunst des Spätmittelalters,* Fortuna vitrea 12 (Tübingen: Niemeyer, 1993), pp. 21–41.

Kottje, Raymund, *Die Bußbücher Halitgars von Cambrai und des Hrabanus Maurus: Ihre Überlieferung und ihre Quellen,* Beiträge zur Geschichte und Quellenkunde des Mittelalters 8 (Berlin: de Gruyter, 1980).

Krebs, Jean-Daniel (ed.), *Die Affekte und ihre Repräsentation in der deutschen Literatur der Frühen Neuzeit, Jahrbuch für Internationale Germanistik* A, 42 (Bern: Lang, 1996).

Kurzel-Runtscheiner, Monica, *Töchter der Venus: Die Kurtisanen Roms im 16. Jahrhundert* (Munich: C. H. Beck, 1995).

Ladisch-Gruber, Dagmar, s.v. "Geißlerpredigt," in *Verfasserlexikon*, 2nd ed., ed. Kurt Ruh et al., vol. 2 (Berlin: de Gruyter, 1980).

Lafourcade, Georges, *La Jeunesse de Swinburne (1837–1867)*, 2 vols. (Paris: Les Belles Lettres, 1928).

Lamos, Colleen, "James Joyce and the English Vice," *Novel* 29 (1995), pp. 19–31.

Laporte, Antoine, *Bibliographie clerico-galante: Ouvrages galants ou singuliers sur l'amour, les femmes, le mariage, le théatre etc. ecrits par les abbés, prêtres, chanoines, religieux, religieuses, évêques, cardinaux et papes* (1879; reprint, Genf: Slatkine, 1968).

Largier, Niklaus, *Diogenes der Kyniker: Exemplum, Erzählung, Geschichte im Mittelalter und in der Frühen Neuzeit; Mit einem Essay zur Figur des Diogenes zwischen Kynismus, Narrentum und postmoderner Kritik*, Frühe Neuzeit 36 (Tübingen: Niemeyer, 1997).

———, *"Figurata locutio:* Hermeneutik und Philosophie bei Eckhart von Hochheim und Heinrich Seuse," in Klaus Jacobi (ed.), *Meister Eckhart: Lebensstationen — Redesituationen*, (Berlin: Akademie, 1997), pp. 228–53.

———, "Jenseits des Begehrens — Diesseits der Schrift. Zur Topologie mystischer Erfahrung," in *Paragrana* 7 (1998), *Sonderheft zum Thema Jenseits*, pp. 107–21.

———, "Der Körper der Schrift: Bild und Text am Beispiel einer Seuse-Handschrift des 15. Jahrhunderts," in Jan-Dirk Müller and Horst Wenzel (eds.) *Mittelalter: Neue Wege durch einen alten Kontinent* (Stuttgart: Hirzel, 1999), pp. 241–71.

———, "Spiegelungen. Fragmente einer Geschichte der Spekulation," *Zeitschrift für Germanistik, Neue Folge* 3 (1999), *Sonderheft zum Thema Visualität*, pp. 616–36.

Leclercq, Henri, s.v. "Flagellation (Supplice de la)," *Dictionnaire d'archéologie chrétienne et de liturgie*, vol. 5 (Paris: Letouzey & Ané, 1923).

———, "La flagellazione volontaria nella tradizione spirituale dell' Occidente," in *L'Ospedale di Cuneo nei secoli XIV–XVI: Contributo alla ricerca sul movimento dei disciplinati* (Cuneo: Biblioteca della Società per gli studi storici, archeologici e artistici della Provincia di Cuneo, 1972), pp. 73–83.

Leigh, Michael, *The Velvet Underground* (London: The Annihilation Press, 1991).

Lerner, Robert E., *The Heresy of the Free Spirit in the Later Middle Ages* (Berkeley: University of California Press, 1972).

Lexikon der christlichen Ikonographie, s.v. "Geißelsäule," vol. 2 (Freiburg: Herder, 1970).

Lippe, Rudolf zur, *Sinnenbewußtsein: Grundlegung einer anthropologischen Ästhetik* (Reinbek bei Hamburg: Rowohlt, 1987).

———, Vom *Leib zum Körper: Naturbeherrschung am Menschen in der Renaissance* (Reinbek bei Hamburg: Rowohlt, 1988).

Lutterbach, Hubertus, *Sexualität im Mittelalter: Eine Kulturstudie anhand von Bußbüchern des 6. bis 12. Jahrhunderts* (Cologne: Böhlau, 1999).

Maggioni, Maria L., *Un manuale per confessori del Quattrocento inglese*, manuscript at Saint. John's College, Cambridge, Contributi del Centro studi sulla letteratura medio-francese e medio-inglese 11 (Milano: Vita e Pensiero, 1993), p. 35.

Marcus, Steven, *The Other Victorians: A Study of Sexuality and Pornography in Mid-Nineteenth-Century England* (New York: Basic Books, 1964).

Margerie, Bertrand de, *Du confessionnal en littérature: Huit écrivains français devant le Sacrement de Pénitence, Chateaubriand, Lamartine, Vigny, Verlaine, Huysmans, Claudel, François de Sales, Bossuet* (Paris: Ed. Saint-Paul, 1989).

Meens, Rob, *Het tripartite boeteboek: Overlevering en betekenis van vroegmiddeleeuwse biechtvoorschriften (met editie en vertaling van vier tripartita)*, Contributi del Centro studi sulla letteratura medio-francese e medio-inglese 11 (Hilversum: Verloren, 1994).

Meersseman, Gilles G., *Dossier de l'ordre de la pénitence au XIIIe siècle* (Fribourg: Editions Universitaires, 1961).

———, *Ordo fraternitatis: Confraternite e pietà dei laici nel medioevo*, 3 vols., Italia sacra 24–26 (Rome: Herder, 1977).

Menninghaus, Winfried, *Ekel: Theorie und Geschichte einer starken Empfindung* (Frankfurt: Suhrkamp, 1999).

Meyer, Ruth, *Das "St. Katharinentaler Schwesternbuch": Untersuchung, Edition, Kommentar*, MTU 104 (Tübingen: Niemeyer, 1995).

Michaud-Quantin, Pierre: *Sommes de casuistique et manuels de confession au moyen âge*, Analecta mediaevalia Namurcensia 13 (Louvain: Nauelaerts, 1962).

Minois, Georges, *Le confesseur du roi: Les directeurs de conscience sous la monarchie française* (Paris: Fayard, 1988).

Molin, Jean-Baptiste, and Annik Aussedat-Minvielle, *Repertoire des rituels et processionnaux imprimés conservés en France* (Paris: Fayard, 1984).

Monaci, Ernesto, *Appunti per la storia del teatro italiano, vol. 1: Uffizi drammatici de' disciplinati dell' Umbria* (Imola: Galeati, 1874).

Morgan, David, *Visual Piety: A History and Theory of Popular Religious Images* (Berkeley: University of California Press, 1998).

Morgan, Te, "A Whip of One's Own: Dominatrix Pornography and the Construction of a Post-Modern (Female) Subjectivity," *American Journal of Semiotics* 6 (1989), pp. 109–36.

Mosco, Marilena (ed.), *La Maddalena tra sacro e profano*, (Florence: Mondadori, 1986).

Il movimento dei disciplinati nel settimo centenario dal suo inizio (Perugia 1260), Appendici al Bolletino della Deputazione di Storia Patria per l'Umbria 9 (1962; reprint, Perugia: Centro di Ricerca e di Studio sul Movimento dei Disciplinati, 1986).

Mühlen, Ilse von zur, "*Imaginibus honos* — Ehre sei dem Bild. Die Jesuiten und die Bilderfrage," in Reinhold Baumstark (ed.), *Rom in Bayern: Kunst und Spiritualität der ersten Jesuiten; Katalog zur Ausstellung des Bayerischen Nationalmuseums Munich, 30. April bis 20. Juli 1997* (Munich: Hirmer, 1997), pp. 161–70.

Muir, Edward, *Ritual in Early Modern Europe* (Cambridge: Cambridge University Press, 1997).

Müller, Jan-Dirk (ed.), *"Aufführung" und "Schrift" in Mittelalter und Früher Neuzeit*, Germanistische Symposien, Berichtsbände 17 (Stuttgart: Metzler, 1996).

Murray, Jacqueline, and Konrad Eisenbichler (eds.), *Desire and Discipline: Sex and Sexuality in the Premodern West* (Toronto: University of Toronto Press, 1996).

Muschg, Walter, *Die Mystik in der Schweiz* (Frauenfeld: Huber, 1935).

Myers, W. David, *"Poor, Sinning Folk": Confession and Conscience in Counter-Reformation Germany* (Ithaca: Cornell University Press, 1996).

Ober, William B., *Bottoms Up! The Fine Arts and Flagellation* (Carbondale: Southern Illinois University Press, 1987).

Odenthal, Andreas, *Der älteste Liber ordinarius der Stiftskirche St. Aposteln in Cologne: Untersuchungen zur Liturgie eines mittelalterlichen Cologneischen Stifts*, Studien zur Cologneer Kirchengeschichte 28 (Siegburg: Schmitt, 1994).

Ohst, Martin, *Pflichtbeichte: Untersuchungen zum Bußwesen im Hohen und Späten Mittelalter*, Beiträge zur historischen Theologie 89 (Tübingen: Mohr, 1995).

Otis-Cour, Leah, *Lust und Liebe: Geschichte der Paarbeziehungen im Mittelalter* (Frankfurt: Fischer, 2000).

Palazzo, Eric, *A History of Liturgical Books: From the Beginning to the Thirteenth Century* (Collegeville, MN: Pueblo, 1998).

————, *Liturgie et société au Moyen Age* (Paris: Aubier, 2000).

Pásztor, Edith, and Neithard Bulst, s.v. "Flagellanten (Geißler, Flegler)," *Lexikon des Mittelalters*, vol. 4 (Munich: Artemis, 1989).

Payer, Pierre J., *Sex and the Penitentials: The Development of a Sexual Code, 550–1150* (Toronto: University of Toronto Press, 1984).

Paz, Octavio, *An Erotic Beyond: Sade* (Orlando: Harcourt Brace & Company, 1993).

Peiss, Kathy, and Christina Simmons (eds.), *Passion and Power: Sexuality in History* (Philadelphia: Temple University Press, 1989).

Rael, Juan Bautista, *The New Mexican Alabado* (Stanford: Stanford University Press, 1951).

Reichler, Claude, *L'age libertin* (Paris: Editions de Minuit, 1987).

Riemeck, Renate, "Die spätmittelalterlichen Flagellanten Thüringens und die deutschen Geißlerbewegungen," Ph.D. diss., Jena, 1943.

Robin, Chantal, *L'imaginaire du* Temps retrouvé: *Hermétisme et écriture chez Proust* (Paris: Lettres modernes, 1977).

Rocca, Giancarlo, s.v. "Disciplina," *Dizionario degli Istituti di Perfezione*, vol. 3 (Rome: Ed. Paoline, 1976).

Rooksby, Rikky, *A. C. Swinburne: A Poet's Life* (Aldershot: Scolar Press, 1997).

Rousseau, George S., and Roy Porter (eds.), *Sexual Underworlds of the Enlightenment* (Chapel Hill: University of North Carolina Press, 1988).

Rusconi, Roberto, "*Ordinate confiteri*: La confessione dei peccati nelle "Summae de casibus" e nei manuali per I confessori (metà XII–inizi XIV secolo)," in *L'aveu, antiquité et moyen-âge: Actes de la table ronde organisée par l'Ecole française de Rome avec le concours du CNRS et de l'Université de Trieste, Rome 28–30 mars 1984*, Collection de l'Ecole française de Rome 88 (Rome: Ecole française de Rome, 1986), pp. 297–313.

Russell, Kenneth. C., "Peter Damian's Whip," *American Benedictine Review* 41 (1990), pp. 20–35.

Russo, Marialba, *Gli eretici dell'Assunta* (Rome: De Luca, 1978).

Salisbury, Joyce E., *Medieval Sexuality: A Research Guide* (New York: Garland, 1990).

Salisbury, Joyce E. (ed.), *Sex in the Middle Ages: A Book of Essays* (New York: Garland, 1991).

Satzinger, Georg, and Hans-Joachim Ziegeler, "Marienklagen und Pietà" in Walter Haug and Burghart Wachinger (eds.), *Die Passion Christi in Literatur und*

Kunst des Spätmittelalters, Fortuna vitrea 12 (Tübingen: Niemeyer, 1993), pp. 241–76.

Scarry, Elaine, "On Vivacity: The Difference between Daydreaming and Imagining-Under-Authorial-Instruction," *Representations* 52 (1995), pp. 1–26.

Schlombs, Wilhelm, *Die Entwicklung des Beichtstuhls in der katholischen Kirche: Grundlagen und Besonderheiten im alten Erzbistum Cologne*, Studien zur Cologneer Kirchengeschichte 8 (Düsseldorf: Schwann, 1965).

Schmitt, Jean-Claude, *La raison des gestes dans l'occident medieval* (Paris: Gallimard, 1990).

———, "Rituels de l'image et récits de vision," in *Testo e immagine nell'alto medioevo*, Settimane di studio del centro italiano di studi sull'alto medioevo 41 (Spoleto: Centro Italiano di Studi sull'Alto Medioevo, 1994), pp. 419–62.

Schneider, Robert A., "Mortification on Parade: Penitential Processions in Sixteenth- and Seventeenth-Century France," *Renaissance and Reformation* 10 (1986), pp. 123–46.

Schuppisser, Fritz Oskar, "Schauen mit den Augen des Herzens: Zur Methodik der spätmittelalterlichen Passionsmeditation, besonders der Devotio Moderna und bei den Augustinern," in Walter Haug and Burghart Wachinger (eds.), *Die Passion Christi in Literatur und Kunst des Spätmittelalters*, Fortuna vitrea 12 (Tübingen: Niemeyer, 1993), pp. 169–210.

Schwarz, Hans Rudolf, "Die medizinische Flagellation, unter besonderer Berücksichtigung von Meibom, Bartholin und Paullini," Ph.D. diss, Zurich, 1963.

Schweicher, Curt, s.v. "Geißelung Christi," *Lexikon der christlichen Ikonographie*, vol. 2 (Freiburg: Herder, 1970).

Seegets, Petra, *Passionstheologie und Passionsfrömmigkeit im ausgehenden Mittelalter: Der Nürnberger Franziskaner Stephan Fridolin (gest. 1498) zwischen Kloster und Stadt*, Spätmittelalter und Reformation, Neue Reihe 10 (Tübingen: Mohr, 1998).

Segl, Peter, s.v. "Geißler," *Theologische Realenzyklopädie*, vol. 12 (Berlin: de Gruyter, 1984).

Seifert, Hans-Ulrich, *Sade: Leser und Autor*, Studien und Dokumente zur Geschichte der Romanischen Literaturen 11 (Frankfurt: Lang, 1983).

Sengpiel, Oskar, *Die Bedeutung der Prozessionen für das geistliche Spiel des Mittelalters in Deutschland*, Germanistische Abhandlungen 66 (Breslau: Marcus, 1932).

Senior, Matthew, *In the Grip of Minos: Confessional Discourse in Dante, Corneille, and Racine* (Columbus: Ohio State University Press, 1994).

Steer, Georg, s.v. "Geißlerlieder," *Verfasserlexikon*, 2nd ed., ed. Kurt Ruh et al., vol. 2 (Berlin: de Gruyter 1980).

————, "Die Passion Christi bei den deutschen Bettelorden im 13. Jahrhundert: David von Augsburg, 'Baumgarten geistlicher herzen,' Hugo Ripelin von Straßburg, Meister Eckharts 'Reden der Unterweisung,'" in Walter Haug and Burghart Wachinger (eds.), *Die Passion Christi in Literatur und Kunst des Spätmittelalters*, Fortuna vitrea 12 (Tübingen: Niemeyer, 1993), pp. 52–75.

Stewart, Pamela D. (ed.), *Testo, lingua, spettacolo nel teatro italiano del Rinascimento*, Yearbook of Italian Studies 6 (Montreal: Italian Cultural Institute, 1987).

Stone, Lawrence, "Libertine Sexuality in Post-Reformation England: Group Sex and Flagellation among the Middling Sort in Norwich in 1706–07," *Journal of the History of Sexuality* 2 (1992), pp. 511–26.

Székelÿ, György, "Le mouvement des flagellants au XIVe siècle: Son caractère et ses causes," in *Hérésies et sociétés dans l'Europe pré-industrielle, XIe–XVIIIe siècles; Communications et débats du Colloque de Royaumont*, ed. Jacques Le Goff, Civilisations et sociétés 1 (Paris: Mouton, 1968), pp. 229–41.

Taft, Robert, *The Liturgy of the Hours in East and West*, rev. ed. (Collegeville, MN: Liturgical Press, 1993).

Talvacchia, Bette, *Taking Positions: On the Erotic in Renaissance Culture* (Princeton: Princeton University Press, 1999).

Tentler, Thomas N., *Sin and Confession on the Eve of the Reformation* (Princeton: Princeton University Press, 1977).

————, "The Summa for Confessors as an Instrument of Social Control," in Charles Trinkaus and Heiko A. Oberman (eds.), *The Pursuit of Holiness in Late Medieval and Renaissance Religion: Papers from the University of Michigan Conference*, Studies in Medieval and Reformation Thought 10 (Leiden: Brill, 1974), pp. 103–25.

Thompson, Roger, *Unfit for Modest Ears: A Study of Pornographic, Obscene, and Bawdy Works Written or Published in England in the Second Half of the Seventeenth Century* (London: Macmillan, 1979).

Toschi, Paolo, *Dal dramma liturgico alla rappresentazione sacra* (Florence: Sansoni, 1940).

Toussaert, Jacques, *Le sentiment religieux, la vie et la pratique religieuse des laïcs en Flandre maritime et au "West-Hoek" de langue flamande aux XIVe, XVe et début du XVIe siècles* (Paris: Plon, 1963).

Traeger, Jörg, *Renaissance und Religion: Die Kunst des Glaubens im Zeitalter Raphaels* (Munich: C. H. Beck, 1997).

Treut, Monika, *Die grausame Frau: Zum Frauenbild bei de Sade und Sacher-Masoch* (Basel: Stroemfeld / Roter Stern, 1984).

Vandenbroucke, Paul (ed.), *Le Jardin clos de l'âme: L'imaginaire des religieuses dans les Pays-Bas du Sud depuis le XIIIe siècle* (Brussels: Martial et Snoeck, 1994). With contributions by Luce Irigaray, Julia Kristeva, Birgit Pelzer et al.

Vaneigem, Raoul, *The Movement of the Free Spirit* (New York: Zone Books, 1994).

Vila, Anne C., *Enlightenment and Pathology: Sensibility in the Literature and Medicine of Eighteenth-Century France* (Baltimore: Johns Hopkins University Press, 1998).

Vincent, John, "Flogging is Fundamental: Applications of Birch in Swinburne's *Lesbia Brandon*," in Eve Kosofsky Sedgwick (ed.), *Novel Gazing: Queer Readings in Fiction* (Durham: Duke University Press, 1997), pp. 269–95.

Vinken, Barbara, *Unentrinnbare Neugierde — Die Weltverfallenheit des Romans: Richardsons Clarissa, Laclos' Liaisons dangereuses* (Freiburg: Rombach, 1991).

Vogel, Cyrille, "Composition légale et commutations dans le système de la pénitence tarifée," *Revue de droit canonique* 8 (1958), pp. 289–318; 9 (1959), pp. 1–38 and 341–59.

————, *La discipline pénitentielle en Gaule des origines a la fin du VIIe siècle* (Paris: Letouzey et Ané, 1952).

————, *Les "Libri paenitentiales"* (Turnhout: Brepols, 1978).

————, *Le pécheur et la pénitence au Moyen Age* (Paris: Cerf, 1969).

Wachinger, Burghart, "Die Passion Christi und die Literatur," in Walter Haug and Burghart Wachinger (eds.), *Die Passion Christi in Literatur und Kunst des Spätmittelalters*, Fortuna vitrea 12 (Tübingen: Niemeyer, 1993), pp. 1–20.

Wadell, Maj-Brit, *Evangelicae Historiae Imagines: Entstehungsgeschichte und Vorlagen*, Gothenburg Studies in Art and Architecture 3 (Gothenburg: Acta Universitatis Gothoburgensis, 1985).

Waldstein, Wolfgang, s.v. "Geißelung," *Reallexikon für Antike und Christentum*, ed. Theodor Klauser, vol. 9 (Stuttgart: Hiersemann, 1976).

Walter, Tilmann, *Unkeuschheit und Werk der Liebe: Diskurse über Sexualität am*

Beginn der Neuzeit in Deutschland, Studia linguistica Germanica 48 (Berlin: de Gruyter, 1998).

Weiske, Brigitte, "Bilder und Gebete vom Leben und Leiden Christi: Zu einem Zyklus im Gebetbuch des Johannes von Indersdorf für Frau Elisabeth Ebran," in Walter Haug and Burghart Wachinger (eds.), *Die Passion Christi in Literatur und Kunst des Spätmittelalters*, Fortuna vitrea 12 (Tübingen: Niemeyer, 1993), pp. 113–68.

Wenzel, Horst, *Hören und Sehen, Schrift und Bild: Kultur und Gedächtnis im Mittelalter* (Munich: C. H. Beck, 1995).

Wimbush, Vincent L. (ed.), *Ascetic Behavior in Greco-Roman Antiquity* (Minneapolis: Fortress, 1990).

Wisch, Barbara, "The Passion of Christ in the Art, Theater, and Penitential Rituals of the Roman Confraternity of the Gonfalone," in Konrad Eisenbichler (ed.), *Crossing the Boundaries: Christian Piety and the Arts in Italian Medieval and Renaissance Confraternities*, Early Drama, Art, and Music Monograph Series 15 (Kalamazoo: Medieval Institute Publications, 1991), pp. 237–62.

Wollesen-Wisch, Barbara L., "The Archiconfraternità del Gonfalone and Its Oratory in Rome: Art and Counter-Reformation Spiritual Values," Ph.D. diss., University of California, Berkeley, 1989.

Zoepf, Ludwig, *Die Mystikerin Margaretha Ebner (c. 1291–1351)*, Beiträge zur Kulturgeschichte des Mittelalters 16 (1914; reprint, Hildesheim: Gerstenberg, 1974).

Index

Zone Books series design by Bruce Mau
Typesetting by Archetype
Image placement and production by Julie Fry
Printed and bound by Maple-Vail